RUINED EDEN *OF THE PRESENT*

Darrel Abel

RUINED EDEN
of the Present
HAWTHORNE, MELVILLE, AND POE

*Critical Essays
in Honor of
Darrel Abel*

Edited by G. R. Thompson and Virgil L. Lokke

Purdue University Press
West Lafayette, Indiana
1981

Second printing, April 1982

Book designed by James McCammack

Library of Congress Catalog Card Number 80-80816

International Standard Book Number 0-911198-60-1

Printed in the United States of America

Contents

III

Preface

For thirty years Darrel Abel
taught courses in American literature at Purdue
University. He has been a key figure in making the
humanities eminent at a major scientific and technological
institution. His work in the Department of English and
his efforts within the university community consistently
sought to elevate the standards of performance and the
quality of Purdue's undergraduate and graduate
programs. In the broader community of scholars, Abel
set standards of achievement that command high respect.
He is editor of *Critical Theory in the American Renaissance*
and author of some fifty articles on Hawthorne, Melville,
Poe, and other figures in American literature from
Thomas Paine to Eliot, Faulkner, and Frost. Always
concerned to integrate scholarship and teaching, he is
author of five volumes of introductory studies of Henry
James, Mark Twain, Walt Whitman, and Herman
Melville. One of his two Melville volumes has been
singled out by *Eight American Authors* as perhaps "the
most trustworthy introduction" to Melville. He is also
author of the widely known three-volume critical history
American Literature, which surveys major and minor texts
from the colonial period through the rise of American
realism.

The multiplicity of voices in this collection of essays in honor of Darrel Abel echoes the many voices that speak within Abel's own work. Criticism for Abel is the dialectic of positive and negative, with the positive relying on a fragile recognition that the ideal exists but in a series of tentative visions, caught in the language of the artist and restructured by reader or critic. We have taken our title, *Ruined Eden of the Present,* from an amalgam of Hawthorne and Abel in an effort to catch a theme central to Abel and to the writers to which he devoted his incisive criticism.

In "Giving Lustre to Gray Shadows: Hawthorne's Potent Art," Abel observes that "the Now of eternity is experienced in a state of feeling when a person's deepest springs of life have been opened, as in the first season of love. During the early years of his marriage, in the Old Manse, Hawthorne felt that happiness had 'opened the gates of Heaven' and given him 'glimpses inward.' In his fiction, however, his gates of vision opened more often into the ruined 'Eden of the present world'. . . ." By bringing to light some versions of gloom, by illuminating basic contradictions without losing them totally to paradox, Abel offers, through the act of reading and the act of criticism, the only affirmation possible to those of such Hawthorne-like temperament. Eternal verities are refracted in the act of criticism, which is an attempt to recognize an ideal Eden of individual and collective potential in the ruined Eden of the present.

The plan of the volume is straightforward. A memoir of Darrel Abel during his time at Purdue is followed by essays on criticism and textuality, in which Abel himself is the starting point for discussion. The themes of time, the ruined but not utterly lost Eden, the tension between eternal verities and temporal illusion, and between hope and despair, are elaborated in Virgil L. Lokke's "The Critic in the Context of His Time." This essay examines the assumptions and patterns of Abel's criticism not only in an effort to comprehend a single critic, but also to illuminate the position of the academic critic of the second half of the twentieth century.

From the end of the forties to the present, the academic critic has had to face elaborate shifts in taste, assumptions, and methodology, from moral and historical criticism, to New Criticism, to newer linguistic and semiotic criticism. In many ways, Abel is deeply representative of his time, re-examining his methodology, criticizing new methodologies (such as the New Criticism), and accommodating what he finds of value in these methodologies to his own criticism. He is more concerned with specific texts and their demands—their patterns of language and their moral, philosophical, and theological contexts—than with a theory of literature or criticism. Yet he has always been concerned with the variety of approaches available, and he is aware of the theoretical multiplicity of "texts." The first essay is followed by a discussion of the legacy of problems left by mid-century New Criticism. It is a polemic for a concept of a scientifically authoritative text; and while Abel might not fully accept its assumptions, he is sure to understand the impulse behind the quest for such stability in "scholarly" textuality. Brian Higgins and Hershel Parker in "The Chaotic Legacy of the New Criticism and the Fair Augury of the New Scholarship" view the influence of New Criticism as bearing a major portion of the blame for the decay of responsibly edited texts and for the endless reproduction of irresponsible critical interpretation. While the tone is combative and aggressive—and perhaps the possibility of producing "accurate" texts is too optimistically accepted—nevertheless one finds in the essay a plea for the restoration of the presence of the humanized voice of the author unfettered from the arbitrarily imposed abstraction of an internal unity, presumed by the canons of the New Criticism. This dehumanization of the author behind the text was a concern of Abel's early criticism.

Problems of the nature and status of texts, of referential and nonreferential language, of the literal and metaphorical, of self-evident values and truths, of the fictions of fictions, of the fictions of literary studies, of certitude and doubt—all find their speaking voices in the

other essays of this festschrift, which deal with the three
authors of the American renaissance about whom Abel
has written so authoritatively: primarily Hawthorne,
secondarily Melville and Poe. Other than restricting the
volume to Hawthorne, Melville, and Poe, we have not
sought to impose a pattern. Moreover, since most of the
contributors to the volume are eminent scholars of the
American romantic period, we have not insisted on
uniformity in documentation, leaving to contributors the
choice of whether to footnote and to what extent. The
volume thus represents, as it should, a medley of
approaches: comparative study of authors, essays on
figures, plot structures, and subtextual structures, essays
in literary history, biography, and bibliography, theme
studies, and essays in the history of ideas. In this variety
of critical strategies, the present volume complements
Abel's own practice. Moreover, in several of the essays,
Abel's work is specifically mentioned, to be extended *or
challenged.* We are confident that he will find in them the
"intelligent and considerate disagreement" that he once
said constituted "the life of critical discussion."

For example, Nina Baym, from a perspective
different from that of Higgins and Parker, also finds in
New Criticism a source of mistaken readings, especially
of *The Scarlet Letter.* Granting the significance of Abel's
contribution to Hawthorne criticism, Baym in "The
Significance of Plot in Hawthorne's Romances," takes as
her point of departure the limitations of the New Critical
approach. She finds that several of Abel's readings of
Hawthorne after his criticism of New Criticism yet reflect
a New Critical bias that essentially ignores the plot
because of the constraints of its implicit male-oriented
ideology and its explicit anti-romanticism. She contends
that both the romantic and the "radical" aspects of
Hawthorne's moral vision are insufficiently attended to.
Emphasizing language over plot, on the other hand, Roy
R. Male sees in Abel's essay, "Black Gloves and Pink
Ribbons: Hawthorne's Metonymic Symbols," an initial
recognition of the intricate theory of language that

pervades Hawthorne's work. In "Hawthorne's Literal Language," Male surveys recent theories of language as related to literature and literary criticism and makes a revealing application to Hawthorne's work. Male makes clear that Hawthorne's awareness of the paradox of language itself as both referential and self-reflexive is quite contemporary with the views of later twentieth-century theorists.

Even the most traditional approaches represented in this volume carry an implicit concern with critical strategies and the artifice of art. A different approach to Hawthorne's literary language is taken by Donald A. Ringe in "Romantic Iconology in *The Scarlet Letter* and *The Blithedale Romance.*" Ringe attempts to deal with recurring symbols that act not only as icons of each work in itself, but also as icons of the then current idea complexes, in order to suggest a taxonomy of Hawthorne's romanticism. Although Richard Harter Fogle's "Art and Illusion: Coleridgean Assumptions in Hawthorne's Tales and Sketches," initially seems to be an influence study, it is actually in a tradition highly compatible with certain of Abel's assumptions about the man of letters, for it is a broadly retrospective essay concerned not so much with Hawthorne's indebtedness to Coleridge as with the nature of Hawthorne's aesthetic imagination, in part derived from, in part parallel with that of Coleridge. The least "aesthetic" of the essays in this group, Seymour L. Gross's contribution, " 'Rappaccini's Daughter' and the Nineteenth-Century Physician," is an example of a traditional type of critical strategy, frequently employed by Abel, a history of ideas approach, in which the critic seeks evidence in the text for attitudes and ideas prevalent in the author's era. Gross focuses not on a literary icon, as does Ringe, but on a contextual social figure and finds in the tale a strong reflection of the characteristic criticism of the medical profession in Hawthorne's time.

Three essays employ various strategies of broadly biographical criticism. William H. Shurr's "Eve's Bower:

Hawthorne's Transition from Public Doctrine to Private Truths" combines history of ideas, close New Critical readings, and biography. It is a theological study framed by a non-Freudian psychology, with many Freudian undercurrents, in which the writer seeks a critical moment in Hawthorne's life. This was that transitional moment in which Hawthorne gained insight into his divided loyalties to two ruling ideological structures. As he examines Puritan and more specifically Calvinist theology, he finds them to be repressive models; he places them over against transcendental and antinomian philosophies and finds these to be more liberating, but they too were inadequate for Hawthorne. He contends that Hawthorne sought a private ethic, a personal redemption that would ultimately free him from overconcern with metaphysics. This moment of liberation is specifically located in the discovery of sexual and human warmth in a woman's love. This contention approaches Abel's view of Hawthorne, quoted earlier with reference to the title of this volume. The ruined Eden inherited from the Puritan past is in part regenerated in a rediscovery of Eve, and the Garden in Eve's bower. It is that rediscovery which freed Hawthorne for his great achievements of *Mosses, The Scarlet Letter,* and the other major works that followed.

Buford Jones's "Some 'Mosses' from the *Literary World:* A Critical and Bibliographical Survey of the Hawthorne-Melville Relationship" takes another kind of critical moment in an author's life as its subject: a great writer's intense encounter with a great writer. His essay moves from the biographical to the bibliographical. It is a careful, thoroughly documented description of the interdependent relationship between Hawthorne and Melville that corrects earlier inaccurate or insensitive treatments, showing how Melville found thematic and verbal structures he could deploy in his own writings. Jones demonstrates the range of contrasting attitudes that Hawthorne and Melville evoked from their contemporaries, especially as represented in the influential *Literary World,* and shows how it was that Hawthorne's reputation continued to grow more rapidly than that of Melville. Robert Milder's *"Nemo Contra Deum. . .* : Melville and Goethe's 'Demonic,'" is a complex essay that employs a wide range of interpretive strategies and seeks to fulfill a series of purposes. One function of the essay is to assess the possible influence of Goethe's concept of "Demonic" upon the writing of *Moby-Dick.* For Milder, however, the degree to which such influence can be demonstrated is not the most basic concern. What the essay more centrally seeks to accomplish is a tracing of the mind of Melville as it struggles toward a vehicle adequate to the presentation of his own vision of the metaphysical battle that proceeds in sensitive, perceptive, and intense minds. The essay is a psycho-biographical, speculative exploration of the mind of Melville and how it processed the texts and experiences that confronted him from *Mardi* to *Moby-Dick.* The result is simultaneously a reading of the presumed Melville behind the text and an interpretation of the more puzzling aspects of *Moby-Dick.*

In a different vein, Richard B. Hauck also calls attention to the "author" behind the text. In "Nine Good Jokes: The Redemptive Humor of the Confidence-Man and *The Confidence-Man,*" Hauck engages a Melville text from the perspective of theme, structure, and language. He takes certain assumptions from New Criticism and by focusing upon one of its fundamental values— irony—writes an essay demonstrating that the reader's impulse to uncover and fix meanings embedded in the text constitutes the supreme irony. There is, in short, no fixed meaning, and all who claim to have found such have been duped; they are the victims of the confidence-man behind the book, *The Confidence-Man.* Hauck's essay suggests that Melville's concern with the fiction of fiction and the problematic author-text-reader relationship results in the ironic perception that the ironic perception of the ambiguities of this relationship provides perhaps the only "redemptive" response available in an inscrutable, ruined world.

The critical approach of the first of the Poe essays, Barton Levi St. Armand's "Poe's Unnecessary Angel: 'Israfel' Reconsidered," represents a direct challenge to the history of ideas as formulated within Western thought and asks the question of "What is the text?" from a radical perspective. In an attempt to recover an esoteric mythos behind Poe's puzzling metaphysics, St. Armand posits that Poe's poetry and practice are actually anti-Western, occult, and hermetic. He assumes that "Israfel" is a sealed and secret text whose meaning may be revealed by the proper hermeneutic critic. He reads "Israfel" closely to discover a secret allegory, the meaning of which draws upon the Gnostic tradition. He contends that although Emerson attacks the conventional didacticism of the Unitarians in "Uriel," this revolt takes place primarily in the domain of Western thought; Emerson is therefore, for Poe, a "timid" philosopher-poet. Poe wants a revolt greater than Uriel's, an apocalyptic transcendentalism; the Mohammedan angel, Israfel, is the appropriate icon for this ideal, for, as the blower of the last trumpet, he will himself be destroyed in the final cataclysm. But he is also merely a mechanical singer in the prison-house universe of the ancient Archons. Any true Eden or Mohammedan paradise exists only in the apocalyptic poetry of an earthly redeemer-poet who knows there is no fixity to the cosmos, nor to any utterance.

Just as the early essays take as a point of departure Abel's Hawthorne work, the concluding essays of the volume have been generated by his most famous article, "A Key to the House of Usher." The contributors debate both Abel and each other. Patrick F. Quinn takes issue with G. R. Thompson's contention that he was himself, in an earlier critical study of Poe, extending the logical implications of Abel's essay. In "A Misreading of Poe's 'The Fall of the House of Usher,'" Quinn undertakes a careful literal reading of the text and finds evidence to question Thompson's central contention that the narrator is essentially unreliable. Thompson responds in "Poe and the Paradox of Terror: Structures of Heightened Consciousness in 'The Fall of the House of Usher'" with a more detailed development of his original reading, emphasizing the stages of the progressive deteriorization of the reliability of the narrator. He contends that Poe carefully balances the supernatural and the natural, creating an inherent ambiguity. In his rejoinder to Thompson's response, "'Usher' Again: Trust the Teller!" Quinn rebuts Thompson's analysis and observes that in imaginative/symbolist writing, diverse readings can be expected; but to read an interpretative essay differently is much less understandable. Finally, then, he finds Thompson's reading of Abel as incompatible with his own as Thompson's reading of Poe.

The last essay of the volume continues the debate from another perspective, though without reference to Thompson and Quinn. In "Playful 'Germanism' in 'The Fall of the House of Usher': The Storyteller's Art," Benjamin Franklin Fisher IV begins by assuming the importance of Abel's identification of the key terms, "life-death" and "reason-madness" as well as Abel's emphasis on the importance of the narrator. Fisher also asks the question that echoes throughout this festschrift: what constitutes the complete text? He observes that in recent critical theory questions of "textuality" are also matters of "contextuality." The context Fisher addresses is that of the Gothic, but he sees in the text "Usher" a playful and even parodic treatment of Gothic conventions by the author behind the text. By surveying closely aligned Gothic texts, he concludes that "Usher" may be regarded as a conscious travesty on the Gothic hero-villain.

The contrary lines of argument of these essays demonstrate that for the writers, as for Abel, critical dissent suggests not so much the fragmentation of Babel as a fortunate fall into languages. Although Abel is as pessimistic as Hawthorne, the ruined Eden of the present world is for him and for the contributors to this collection no critical wasteland. Nevertheless, despite Abel's lifelong receptivity to critical disagreement over texts and critical strategies, the fallen Eden of the present is for him not merely a fall into the languages of criticism, but, simultaneously, a fall into doubt about the possibility of any certitude. Never "merely" a formalist critic, Abel concerns himself with the fundamental epistemological, ontological, and axiological bases of existence itself. At the heart of this concern is the perplexity of time, of the eternal and the finite. Abel is fascinated with "Hawthorne's sense of 'a timeless continuum'. . . that. . . erased the distinction between past and present." Such "timelessness," however, "really amounts to being lost in time, rather than lifted out of time." Abel observes that "Hawthorne lost some sense of being fully alive in his own moment" and that in "this tension between the present and eternity there is a dilemma for the man and the artist." The "artist's solution to the dilemma of being either lost in the confused timelessness of time, or being confined in the shell of his own moment or crushed under the heaped up shells of past moments, is to fill the shell of time's moment with the life of eternity's instant."

What fills the present in a ruined world, after all, and therefore also bears the burden, are words—for the critic, the fiction of criticism. Long before Abel wrote his essay "Robert Frost's 'True Make-Believe,'" his work demonstrated that in a fallen Eden, wherein all certitude has fled, the only alternative is acceptance of Frost's dictum: "All virtue in 'as if.'" The critic—and any speculative mind, for that matter—must believe all primary propositions into existence. Such a recognition renders undogmatic all dogmatic utterance within this volume.

G. R. T.
V. L. L.
West Lafayette, Indiana
April 1979

Acknowledgments

Several people have been instrumental in the publication of this volume. Cherylynn Knott helped with the preparation of the manuscript. Purdue University Press, especially its managing editor, Verna Emery, offered much encouragement during the various stages of the project. Colleagues in the Department of English and the Program in American Studies at Purdue, most notably Jacob H. Adler, William Stafford, William J. Stuckey, Chester Eisinger, and Martin Bertram, offered encouragement in the initial stages. Donald A. Seybold helped us with critical problems in the latter stages. Many American literature scholars who were unable to contribute an essay expressed in other ways their desire to celebrate the career of Darrel Abel.

Darrel Abel: A Memoir

Chester E. Eisinger

"In the Heart of the Heart of the Country" is Bill Gass's excoriating hymn of hate to Brookston, Indiana, a small town some eleven miles north of West Lafayette and Purdue University, where Gass taught philosophy for many years. Darrel Abel and his family also lived in Brookston, but he never saw the place through Gass's eyes. Darrel's move from West Lafayette to Brookston, I always thought, was his effort to find the happy rural seat that lived its enchanted life in his memory; it was a return to a past that never existed for him but that could be imagined and therefore improved upon. Darrel grew up on an Iowa farm. He had an American childhood in which he never learned to play the games that American children play, as he often said, but he never said he resented his deprivation. When we were in graduate school together, another student once said to me of Darrel, he looks and acts as though he were never young. It's true that as a young man he had a staid and slightly stiff demeanor, a formal comportment that

1

belied his years and suggested a foreshortened youth. He had the look of a person from the farm who knew how to plow but not to play. (But it must also be said that Darrel continued, almost preternaturally, to look like a young man until well into his fifties.)

Darrel's life was indelibly marked by his growing up in that place and in that time—he was born in 1911—but unlike so many people, he fled back to his past and not away from it. It lived warmly in his consciousness. A few years after we had both come to Purdue, the dietitian at the Purdue Memorial Union retired. She said in an interview that she had been happy to provide good, healthy farm fare for the students of the university over her long tenure of service. When I remarked to Darrel that I had found her culinary practices heavy and unappetizing, he disagreed with me vigorously, told me in effect that I did not know a good thing when I ate it, and regretted her departure.

What he cherished from his rural heritage—and, in a way, food was part of this—was the simplicity of an unadorned life that allowed one to seek purity in a variety of its forms, the kind of Thoreauvian purity that made for a stripping away of nonessentials. It was not simply that Darrel rejected the artificial, it was that he sought for himself and his family ways of thought and feeling and behavior that were open and natural. The source of these values was in the myth of the farm and the small town, the myth of rural America, which Darrel pursued all of his life. It was always a source of wry, ironic amusement to him that I, the urban Jewish son of immigrants, should have made a scholarly investigation of the early American agrarian concepts and myths that he was legitimate heir to and had experienced in the bone and the flesh. Like Thoreau, he was proud of the number of things he could get along without. He did not want to clutter his life with what was unnecessary or distracting, and certainly not with anything that was ostentatious or pretentious. Like Thoreau, he yearned for a minimal or subsistence standard of living, although, also like

Thoreau, he sometimes enjoyed somewhat more than
that. Late in his career at Purdue, he built a little place in
the Maine woods which, from all accounts (I have never
seen it), in its bareness and crudity satisfied his appetite
for simplicity more fully even than his Brookston life.
The Abels, incidentally, moved out of Brookston, driven
away, Darrel said, by the poor quality of the public
schools.

I think it fair to say that while Darrel has a mind
capable of dealing with sophisticated ideas, he was always
leery of worldly sophistication. When he finished his
dissertation at the University of Michigan, he was invited
to join the Department of English there. He refused and,
instead, returned to Purdue where he had been teaching
since 1942, with time out for graduate study. Most young
scholars, I should guess, would have found Michigan a
more prestigious and more attractive appointment than
the Purdue English department in the years just after the
Second World War. Purdue could have been described at
that time (with no great inaccuracy) as a cow college. The
Department of English was a service department. It had
no graduate program. The teaching of composition was
the principal mission of the department, and we all taught
a great deal of it, especially as there was little else to
teach. Professional and scholarly achievement, despite
the presence of scholars like Herb Muller and Harold
Watts, was not valued in the department as highly as
compatibility and loyalty. The Purdue English
department of that time, in short, bore a startling
resemblance to the English department at Cascadia
University in Bernard Malamud's *A New Life.* But Darrel,
who knew what the department was like, preferred it to
Michigan's, in part at least because it had no intellectual
pretensions and no swollen image of itself as a
professional body with a professional responsibility. Just
so, he preferred Purdue to the University of Michigan
and West Lafayette (and even Brookston) to Ann Arbor,
because they were closer to the rural ideal and less
sophisticated.

He very kindly thought that I too would like Purdue, and he recommended me to the department head, Dr. Herbert Creek, a man who was invariably referred to by that title and who bore it with quiet dignity. In a sense, then, Darrel brought me to Purdue. A few years later, in 1947, he left the university to take a post at Franklin and Marshall College. In January 1950, if my memory serves, he wrote to me saying that he had had enough of Franklin and Marshall and had resigned his position there; then he added, almost incidentally, that he had no other job for the coming fall. It was a typically impractical and imprudent action. Shortly after receiving the letter, I told Dr. Creek that Darrel was leaving Franklin and Marshall and that I believed he would like to return to Purdue. Dr. Creek, despite the high valuation he placed on loyalty, saw (as well as I) the wisdom and advantage of inviting Darrel to rejoin the Purdue English department. The arrangements were quickly made. In a sense, then, while he had brought me to Purdue, I brought him back. Although I played a minor role in this as in other appointments to the faculty, it was the best personnel decision that I have ever made.

The transformation of the Purdue English department that began about the time of Darrel's return was not entirely of his making, of course. The university itself was changing and growing and coming to a kind of maturity with the inevitability that marks the development of a natural organism. While the institution has never surrendered its emphasis upon agriculture and engineering—it is, after all, a land-grant school, as its administrators point out on almost any occasion—it could not fully control, if indeed it wished to, the development of other divisions within it, such as science and the humanities. Barriss Mills, the man who succeeded Dr. Creek as head of the English department in 1951, understood that the force of this unplanned growth would make irresistible the expansion of the English department and the initiation of graduate work there. In time, the department grew to a senior staff of some seventy-five members and about two hundred teaching asistants, who constituted the bulk of the students in the graduate program. And the School of Humanities, Social Science, and Education, of which the department was a part, grew until it had the largest enrollment of the eleven schools in the university.

Chance played its role in determining the direction and proportions of the English department, as it had of the university as a whole. No one willed or planned the concentration of teachers and publishing scholars and critics in American literature that soon became a special mark of the Purdue English department. And Darrel was preeminent among all these teachers and scholars. In my opinion, to go a step further, he had the finest mind in the entire department. He made, through his studies in the American renaissance, a major contribution to the reputation of the department. I am not concerned with the publications themselves; the essays that follow in this volume will discuss their method and substance and attest to their value. I wish to emphasize, instead, what it meant to the department to have among its members a man who clearly was establishing a national reputation and a place for himself among the leading students of the American renaissance. If it was an irony that, through his efforts, the Purdue English department was now striving toward the same goals that the Michigan department, which he had rejected, had already achieved, it was an irony of which Darrel took no notice, so far as I could tell. I do know that, at a minimum, Darrel was one of very few at that time who was bringing professional and scholarly respectability to a department that had never owned or seemed to aspire to that order of achievement. He helped to legitimate that sort of activity in the Purdue English department and thus to make it possible for others to pursue their studies with a view toward publication. He began to effect a change in the image of the department, not only for the profession as a whole outside it but also for those of us within it; in short, he helped to alter for the better our self-image.

More important was the fact that Darrel was a presence in the department as a scholar, a teacher, and, if I may so put it, a citizen. Among the many matters that I might comment upon with regard to Darrel as a student of literature, I want to remark only three. He had an extraordinarily tenacious memory; he could always tell you, if there were any doubt about the matter, the details of the action in an Irving story or the point of view from which a particular episode had been written in a James novel. He had also, as his publications testify, a great capacity for penetrating a text, a complex vision of the potentialities that lay within a work of literature. He brought the ample intellectual powers of a triple-thinker to the task of literary analysis. Finally, he had wide range and catholic tastes. It goes without saying that he was profoundly engaged with English literature, but the fact is that he was engaged with and committed to other literatures and to the entire Western cultural tradition, as a *bona fide* intellectual must be. He was just as capable of teaching a course in literary methods as he was of teaching a Great Issues course that ranged from Aristotle to Freud.

What do we know about a colleague's teaching? The public facts: Darrel drew students to the department, built up courses when he taught them, directed a large number of dissertations. He attracted the best students. Another kind of knowledge came from remarks that Darrel or his students made to me about his teaching (I trust it need not be said, unsolicited remarks). He was a competitive teacher; he wanted to teach a course better than others taught it. But of course he was generally competitive in his professional life. Yet he was also, so far as I know, uncompromising; he never did anything simply to gain popularity and thus be regarded as a "good" teacher. He kept his standards high, and he never resorted to fashionable gimmicks. He made considerable demands upon students, and it is clear that they responded to him. He doesn't seem to have lectured. He spoke to them, and furthermore he spoke in a low voice which made a special claim on their attention and their concentration. They gave him what he deserved.

Darrel never aspired to administrative status, but he had a strong desire to make policy, in the department and in the university as a whole. He believed that most important decisions in the department should be made by members of the faculty, and he played an important role in moving us toward that participatory goal and away from domination of policymaking by the head. I don't believe I ever heard him say that the faculty is the university, but I think that was one underlying principle of his thought and action as a citizen of the department. He had a strong sense that the faculty of the university would more readily act in the interest of education and the students than the bureaucracy of the university, which he felt was more likely to act in its own interest. He therefore understood that in the department as well as in the university it was necessary to increase the power of the faculty at the expense of the administration to as great a degree as possible. Darrel was suspicious of authority and resentful of institutional and bureaucratic power in what I always took to be a complex of populist attitudes that derived from his agrarian heritage. In departmental staff and committee meetings, these assumptions about the power relationships in academic life guided his thinking. For as long as I can remember, he spoke out on every issue that faced the department, and on almost every occasion he spoke first, incisively and persuasively. For what it is worth, on almost every occasion I thought he was right; I cannot recall disagreeing with him on any important policy decision.

I don't wish to give the impression that Darrel was aggressive or contentious. Despite his anti-establishment views, he never treated administrators with scorn or disrespect. He got on well with them and had their confidence; they trusted him and looked to him for advice and guidance. They appointed him to innumerable committees; in the seven or eight years before his retirement, for example, he served as chairman of the

search committees for head of the English department
and for dean of the school. The members of the
department also trusted him. He was an acknowledged
leader whose sanction to speak first came from his peers.
When they had the opportunity to elect someone—to
the school senate or the university senate or to anything
else—they elected Darrel. He never lost an election. He
was, not to put too fine a point on the matter, simply the
most widely trusted man in the department and,
probably, in the School of Humanities. Yet he never
made what might be regarded as an overtly political
gesture. It would be a gross mistake to call him a campus
politician. He never campaigned for any elective position,
and I have the strong impression that he never voted for
himself in any election. It was a charming paradox, that
this modest and diffident man should be, and should want
to be, so preeminently a public man.

But he was. He was one of that select group, a
citizen of the university community. His cause was not
only a defense of the rights and responsibilities of the
faculty but also a defense of humane education. This
latter was not an easy cause to speak for at Purdue
University. While Darrel in a general way took the
opportunity to make the case for liberal education, his
particular battlefield became, some fifteen years ago, the
condition of the university library. The library is the
smallest and, one can fairly say, the worst in the Big Ten,
that group of universities to which Purdue regularly
compares itself in every way. It is the single greatest
handicap to scholarship in the humanities and social
sciences at Purdue. It is disheartening for a teacher of
American literature to have to work with this library.
Here was an issue of the highest educational importance:
what was needed was a new building and a massive
increase in holdings. Darrel fought for these goals at
every level in the university—in committees, in
departmental meetings, in the offices of provost and
deans. He was pretty thoroughly defeated. But it must be
added that if today, after his retirement, the library is

being improved, as in some small measure it is, some of the credit belongs to him. One of the most memorable scenes in my thirty-five years of association with Darrel came at a meeting where he was asked to report on the status of negotiations over the library. Darrel was always quietly in control of himself. But as he stood before us on this occasion, he recited his frustrations in so impassioned and broken a voice that he made his losses ours.

Another memorable scene occurred during the time of troubles at Purdue. The student rebellions of the sixties came to Purdue late and little, but we did have a student sit-in at the Executive Building. While the students were inside, occupying the president's office, a large crowd milled about outside. The Indiana State Police were called in. It was considered necessary that some faculty gain admission to the building and interpose themselves between the students and the police, in order, by their presence, to prevent violence or unjust, summary action on the part of the police or university authorities. In the chaos outside the building, the thought suddenly occurred that a side entrance to the building might provide access to the occupiers, and a surge toward that entrance developed, among the police and "others." Among the latter was Professor Abel, a tall, dignified, but somewhat unathletic figure, who rushed for the door, was tripped or knocked down, rose and was pushed back, and stood panting, his face red and his trousers torn at the knee.

Instinctively, Darrel was on the side of the students, because he regarded them as the underdogs and because he opposed the administration. The students knew it, and he was one of several faculty members whom they telephoned, around four o'clock one morning during this period, when they were being evicted from the Purdue Memorial Union, where they had been conducting a sleep-in for several days and nights. Again, it was necessary to interpose faculty between students and police. When Darrel arrived at the union, all the doors were locked. With others, he found an open window and climbed through, in order to confront the police and university officials. But Darrel's actions also had a rationale; they were not the automatic reflexes of bleeding-heart liberalism. They were his response to the autocratic exercise of power by the university establishment, acting out of fear and contempt for students and faculty alike.

The president had summarily fired the editor of the student newspaper, in an action so ill considered that he reversed it shortly thereafter. The trustees had altered the *University Code* by depriving the faculty of powers to discipline students, which the faculty had exercised for years before. This latter action in particular infuriated Darrel. At one of the numerous high-pitched meetings that marked those days, he presented a petition for our signature which announced that unless the trustees restored faculty rights, the signatories would withhold the final grades of students. The student newspaper published the petition with some of the signatures. I believe that Darrel thought he might be challenged about this matter in the university senate, of which he was a member at the time. I saw him leafing through Mill's *On Liberty* shortly before a senate meeting, clearly preparing a defense for principled civil disobedience. He was not challenged. The trustees did not reverse themselves. We did not withhold grades.

Yet by no means was all lost—Darrel was engaged, in the largest sense, in defining and acting out a role for the faculty in the modern university. He was asserting the place of the faculty in the governance of the university. At Purdue University, as at so many others, it was necessary for the faculty to learn its role, to explore its potentialities. It had to teach itself as well as the administration what could be done to shape and share the decision-making processes. As a citizen of the university community, Darrel made a large contribution to a necessary and ongoing process.

This is, of course, *my* Darrel Abel. Others will have a very different view of him. That goes without saying, in a day when we have come to recognize the partiality of all truth and all facts. But I have the feeling that Darrel may be a particularly elusive man. I have not touched upon aspects of his personality and certain of his actions which I have never understood. In addition, there are, naturally, large areas of his life about which I have no knowledge.

I do understand that some people have a quite different Darrel. Some years ago, when the English department was in the midst of one of those bitter internal crises that every once in a while grips academic departments, Darrel was on leave. The assistant head of the department and I were on opposite sides in this matter, but on good terms personally. One day, when we were talking about our troubles, he said to me with great intensity, "How I wish Darrel were here." I was astonished. Did he think Darrel would have sided with him? I knew that Darrel would have sided with me. Let us say simply that my Darrel, the one I have described here, would have been on my side. And my side would have been the better for it.

The Critic
in the Context of His Time

Virgil L. Lokke

The preface to Darrel Abel's three-volume survey of American literature announces his literary, historical, and critical intentions with direct and clear statements of his objectives:

> This account of American literature attempts to describe and interpret American writing in relation to the characters and personal circumstances of the men who wrote it and to the social and political tendencies which conditioned their writing. It assumes that a work's meaning is not all contained in its form and its specific content, but includes also its significant reference to things going on outside of it when it was written.

Such an announcement implies much about Abel's assumptions concerning literary history and criticism. He is an eclectic, a contextualist and a textualist, an intrinsic and extrinsic analyst. He looks intently at the biographical, social, and political data for relevancies, for significant references in all the extrinsic data that can be brought to bear upon any given text. At the same time, he is willing to make use of, even central use of, New Critical strate-

gies. For example, when he states that "a work's meaning
is not all contained in its form and its specific content," he
is simultaneously admitting that a significant portion is
embedded in its form and specific content. In short, Abel
is an unabashed eclectic with a specific goal.

For the specific purposes of the American literature
survey, he is, of course, seeking to recover particular and
identifying aspects of American writing, but even in this
work, and more obviously in the body of his critical essays, he points toward a more embracing objective. It is
not so much that Abel is interested in recovering the
American mind, or in demonstrating the uniqueness of
American literature, or—for that matter—in bolstering
the virtues of any particular ideological stance or any
political trend. It is rather that Abel seems to be more
centrally concerned with viewing literature as a reflection
of the human mind and psyche itself. Such a concern explains his interest in Jungian psychology and myth criticism generally. Jung, for example, was appealing not
only for his attempts to discover basic aspects of the
human psyche as revealed in texts, but also for the literary style of Jungian discourse. Abel is profoundly concerned with revealing basic patterns in the mind of an
author, but such an interest seems always related to a
more comprehensive concern with the mind of man himself. This objective is not overtly stated but the evidence
is strong, particularly in his emphasis upon dichotomies,
binaries, and general patterns of opposition. Abel's concern, however, differs importantly from the interests and
concerns of structuralists, who seek both technical and
overtly scientific goals.

When I speak of Abel's concern with the human
mind, I do not mean the concern is limited to cognitive
structures only, for he seems ever attentive to emotional
and feeling patterns. As a humanist, Abel believes in reason, and in logic, but only up to a point. His logic is a
classical kind, not a mathematical one. Still, he believes in
logic more than in an empiricism which attempts to re-
duce the world to measurable units, especially in litera-

ture and the arts. He puts reason in search of complete and enduring structure rather than in the service of the fragmentary, countable, and evanescent. Abel is never impressed by the counting of images, nor is there much evidence of enthusiasm for stylistic studies which depend upon the accumulation of statistical evidence. For Abel, the critic looks for structures and patterns in a text, but the patterns which emerge are recognized as being only loosely analogous to what might be defined as a mathematical structure. It is quite apparent that Abel is never beguiled by hopes that criticism could become a science. Among the critical works on Hawthorne, those which Abel finds promising employ a mythic approach. Such an approach is at least compatible with his tendency to accept an analysis which does not lay claim to dispelling the ultimate mystery of a significant text.

Abel's interest in myth is also compatible with his attention to the moral and theological structures of a work. For Abel, I suspect, all aesthetic questions are, in the final analysis, moral questions. In his Hawthorne criticism, we do, of course, find a theology or philosophy operative in Hawthorne's mind and work. But for Abel, like Hawthorne, all philosophical and theological problems embrace the aesthetic. The aesthetic is not for him isolatable, and any attempts at isolation of the aesthetic yield only trivialities. Aesthetics is a subcategory of ethics. While it is not unfair to describe Abel as essentially a moral critic, it must be understood that Abel, like Hawthorne, is not "moralistic." What Abel tends to reveal in his criticism is a moral vision of life, which, like Abel's comment on Hawthorne's view, does not present any specific moral or utilitarian instruction for influencing conduct.

One important aspect of Abel's criticism is his suspicion of the pretensions of New Criticism. His admiration for an older mode of criticism emerges in his strong respect for the "man of letters." Such a respect is linked with a general suspicion of all methodologies. Abel's work reflects his wide and careful reading, a strong sensitivity to human values, and the firm belief that the graceful turn of phrase is of central importance.

In his criticism of the New Critics, two aspects emerge. The first is his respect for tradition, which is overt and transparent; the second, less obvious feature is his belief in the need for self-evident values. In his arguments against New Criticism, Abel continually postulates a series of "values which belong to the poet and to sensitive men in society whose highest sensibilities and most inarticulate predilections he utters." Something has happened, however, in the twentieth century, namely, the emergence of "a more vociferous" group who are "literate but not intelligent." Abel concludes that "criticism which addresses itself to them translates into lower terms the real values of literature."

It is difficult to overlook the elitism in Abel's stance—an elitism which is employed to attack the narrower elitism of the New Criticism. There are, it seems, those educated, well-read, sensitive scholars who because of their qualifications are more responsive to real values. Real values, he contends, exist outside of the poem. Poets do not make values; values are "somehow imported from the outside." The poet "makes a permanent construction which holds them and makes them less elusive than they were in their free state." These values are like self-evident truths that can be denied only by blindness or forgetfulness or gross insensitivity. Such values can neither be objectified nor expressed. They float freely in the minds of men and are sensed as feeling and basic emotional response. These self-evident values are finally more important than objectivity or cognitive processes because they are more essentially human. Such truths are, like the difference between common and specialized knowledge, more available to more of mankind.

Abel's preoccupation with the revelation of moral stances in texts, along with his contextualist bias, is alien to the New Critical perspective within which he had been thoroughly indoctrinated through such mentors as Brooks, Warren, Tate, and others. Abel, however, has always been primarily concerned with recovering, by whatever means possible, the characteristic features of the mind of the author. Throughout his work on Hawthorne, Abel strives not so much to impose a mind on Hawthorne, but to discover the patterns of the mind he was exploring and to apply these patterns to the analysis and judgment of the work itself. For some of us, Abel succeeds so well that he seems almost to have *become* Hawthorne. Abel's total immersion in the works of Hawthorne leads him to a critical perspective in which he has become Hawthorne as critic rather than Hawthorne as author.

Abel's attack on the New Criticism focuses upon its excessive intellectuality—more specifically, its presumptive claims to detachment and objectivity. Furthermore, he rejects the claim of New Criticism that poetry, in particular, offers a special knowledge. He also rejects its formalism, its stress on technique, its appreciation of artifice, its delight in obscurity, and its elitist rejection of traditional literary forms which have had wide appeal. Abel finds New Criticism destructive in its implications, particularly in its skeptical denial of all but formal and analytic values. Basically, the New Critical argument and practice violates Abel's notion of the function of poetry itself, for Abel's idea of poetic and literary qualities rests upon his notion of the nature of human nature, upon human values as distinct from animal—indeed, from all else in the universe.

Abel's literary criticism is exemplified in his much praised article "A Key to the House of Usher." Two features are immediately apparent. The first is his willingness to employ some of the strategies of New Criticism. The second is his rejection of New Critical assumptions concerning the goals of such criticism. To Abel, close reading, careful attention to symbol and language, and concern with the formal unity of the text are necessary aspects of criticism. He believes that the best art will display a functional relation among all its parts, that the text itself is in part successful to the degree in which scene, theme, tone, character, and point of view can be demonstrated to exhibit internal and necessary causal relationships. Texts are finally significant, however, to the extent that they offer extra-literary meanings. Significant texts will offer some philosophical, theological, psychological, or (most importantly) moral truth. Literary texts are rendered significant in the extent to which they point to and illuminate an "extra-text," and that extra-text involves awareness of tradition, history, and, ultimately, the problematical nature of the human mind itself. The notion of literature as being self-referential, merely playful, escapist, and a fulfillment of man's need to dream is, for Abel, an irresponsible view. Good literature, literature worthy of serious attention, is always literature that illumines important aspects of the mind of man.

"A Key to the House of Usher" illustrates, in its very excellence, a problem which is not merely Abel's problem but which troubles the very heart of contemporary criticism. There is, on the one hand, Abel's concern with rationality, with unity as demonstrating an underlying and discoverable causality. In Abel's critical essay we see life/reason struggling against death/madness, order against disorder, coherence against incoherence, purpose against ultimate chaos. Abel seems to be describing the interior conflicts that Poe has presented. On the surface is the commonsensical affirmation of the positive values of order, coherence, and rationality. These are the positive values which lie within the mind of man. On the other hand, underneath these affirmations lies a contrary portrait of the heart of man, which seeks death, disorder, incoherence, and chaos. I refer to a deeper pessimism that speaks of the painful incompatibilities and eternal tension that lie within man's consciousness. Behind the self-evident, positive value lies its equally self-evident contradiction; behind the vision of the orderly, coherent, and rational man lie the positive values of the warm, spontaneous, and feeling man—natural man. Any satisfactory resolution of these values is a logical impossibility.

The doubleness of Abel's critical outlook can be

found throughout the works of Hawthorne—both the doubts and the somewhat precarious affirmations. An especially fruitful text for evidence of Abel's total immersion in Hawthorne and his acceptance of a Hawthornean view of the world can be found in his analysis of *The Marble Faun.* What seems central here is Abel's version of Donatello as the Natural Man. In one sense, although Abel does not stress the point, Donatello is prelinguistic man. Here we encounter a problem—a general problem about the nature of language itself.

It is both difficult and dangerous to try to speak about a theory of language in Abel's work. In one sense, he seems to accept a simple referential theory, but that acceptance is merely for the pragmatic purposes of his criticism where he demonstrates grave respect for the potential exactitude of language. Yet clearly, Abel knows that language, in its efforts to be exact, generates illusion; that language simultaneously distorts as it reveals; that it reifies the rock and also takes the place of the rock, so that word and thing must be forever isolated.

While Abel may seem at times to be literal minded about language, he operates comfortably within an Emersonian theory of language, wherein we see that the goals of language run through words to things to pre- or non-linguistic Platonic forms. What is revealed in the portrayal of Donatello is the search in Hawthorne, and also in Abel, for the archetypal prelinguistic man. Both Hawthorne and Abel find the myth of the Natural Man attractive. Before man's fall into language, he was warm, innocent, sensuous, earthy, spontaneous, joyous, unreflective, honest. He had no sense of time or history, no self, no sense of the other, no perception of cause and effect, and no consciousness. But that Edenic state could not last. Now the question is whether this portrait is merely a character created by Hawthorne and a portrait of the portrait by Abel.

More is involved. It seems possible that Abel is following the very paths of Hawthorne, seeking, as it were, the recovery of the source of those basic values, those

self-evident truths (perceptions, feeling states, and response patterns) that underlie all linguistic fabrications.
He discovers that at the source they are indeed unutter-
able, because they are prelinguistic in nature. Such values
do indeed lie outside history and time. He recognizes, as
Hawthorne did, that language conceals as it reveals; but,
for Abel, the central significance and value of a text is its
momentary ability to catch the universals, to give them
momentary luminescence. Man in culture is always conscious of the norm of prelinguistic man, of the Natural
Man. But he has no existence in the present, except as a
critical perception of the ruined Eden. Archetypal man
floats behind the work of Hawthorne and, again, behind
Abel's criticism of Hawthorne. Abel and Hawthorne remind themselves and us that the only existence possible
for Natural Man is within literature, within fiction. He
does not exist because he cannot exist. As a metaphysical
postulate, his invoked image is a constant reminder of
man's separation from himself and from his physical and
social world. Given the breadth and depth of Abel's reading and research, the scrupulous care for accuracy of
presentation, the avoidance of radically quirky or modish
readings, the respect for the work of scholars who preceded him, and finally the grace and skill of his style, one
can expect his work to stand against the standards of
time. That there is evidence within his work of basically
irreconcilable contradictions—contradictions of which he
is patently aware—is not a defect. Rather, it is evidence
of his awareness of the problematic and troubled state
that literary criticism finds itself confronting in the present moment.

Abel's work only occasionally focuses directly upon
problems of literary theory or critical methodology. His
work does not express directly the current interest in
finding new and more solid foundations for literary
studies through the development of a new poetics. But
examination of his practice, his techniques and assumptions, reveals two positions which illustrate his awareness
of the disturbing problems that have brought theory of

literature into such a central focus. Abel is concerned
with the "truth value" of critical utterances about the
text: he knows full well the problematic status of both
text and meta-text. At the same time, he postulates an "as
if": there are extra-textual truths to which both text and
meta-text can constantly and confidently refer. There are
these self-evident truths and self-evident values—sensed,
felt, understood—which, in the last analysis, are beyond
articulation.

Two positions emerge. One is skeptical, even pessimistic, about the possibility of other than impressionistic, idiosyncratic criticism; the other rests on an "as if"
which seeks powerfully to provide the precarious hope
that the known impediments can be surmounted. Such
double knowledge creates a tension which surfaces particularly in some of his exploratory essays on Hawthorne—not in all, of course, because Abel wrote many
different kinds of essays. His essay on Hawthorne's attitudes on social reform differs in its approach from that in
"Who Wrote Hawthorne's Autobiography?" and these,
again, are quite different from "Hawthorne's House of
Tradition." They are all well and carefully argued, and
illustrate Abel's capacity to adapt a problem to a more or
less conventionally acceptable form. Characteristically,
Abel accepts the conventions of each mode of critical or
historical discourse with a polite bow. He is, in turn, a
historian of ideas, an accepter of the notions of the
presumed unity and coherence of a given text, a re-
coverer of myths, an explorer of moral truths, a believer
in the need for self-evident truths, a theological exegete,
and an aesthetician.

Since Abel is so much an eclectic, it is difficult to
find in this present period of aggressive attention to literary theory any theoretical school that embraces Abel's
finest work. Among such contenders as the deconstruc-
tionists, the semioticians, the reception theorists, or the
structuralists and the Geneva school, perhaps the
theories, if not the practice, of the Geneva group come
closer to expressing some of the basic notions exhibited

in Abel's work. Abel consistently denies exclusive precedence to the text itself. He draws what he needs from the
whole body of the writer's work to bear upon his
exegesis. What he seems concerned about is entry into
and reconstruction of the mind of the author. Like the
Geneva theorists, Abel regards literary criticism as a
literary act in itself, and what he seeks are the themes and
vision of the author. Abel seeks not merely external objectivity but rather the interior system of patterning, and
the processes of the author's consciousness.

What remains to be reemphasized is the extent to
which language itself becomes more and more an interesting and difficult problem in Abel's work. His work
indirectly expresses and anticipates the current concern
with the mysteries of language, literary and otherwise,
pointing to the attention language has received in the
work of structuralists and phenomenologists. Articles
such as "Black Gloves and Pink Ribbons: Hawthorne's
Metonymic Symbols," "'This Troublesome Mortality':
Hawthorne's Marbles and Bubbles," and "Giving Lustre
to Gray Shadows: Hawthorne's Potent Art" illustrate
Abel's sensitivity to the implications that current theories
about language, and specifically literary language, are now
foregrounding. Where the problems of language were
gracefully implicit in the work of Abel, they have now
become a noisy scandal. Exegesis has not found solid
ground. It can only spin frantically in its effort to levitate.

The reason for such fervent theorizing is to be found
not in the stars but in the nature of language itself. What
I am suggesting is that Abel, having immersed himself in
American nineteenth-century literature, becomes, particularly with respect to and because of his entry into the
mind of Hawthorne, more and more suspicious of the
dominant and imprisoning aspects of language. As I read
Abel, I suspect that he has become increasingly aware of
the distances between author, text, and critical reader. In
this sense, Abel's work moves beyond the context of the
time of his formal training in criticism, from his early in-
doctrination in romantic theories of language toward the

current mode of linguistic skepticism. Yet, in another sense, he has not had to move an inch, since in Hawthorne himself such doubts about language had already been articulated.

In Abel's work, insights into the fluidity and instability of language are reflected in an ambivalent response to the perennial problem that confronts literary criticism: What is the nature, the status of the literary text? With Abel, respect for the recoverable text as processed through all the available "scientific" strategies and the tracing of all the processes of revision and counter-revision are not really a central concern. His response is pragmatic. He is willing to accept whatever text that scholarship of the moment has awarded the highest degree of authenticity. It is as if Abel recognizes that to become too involved in textual authenticity is to foreground too powerfully his suspicion that textual facts are never quite neutral. Further, the notion of the scientific neutrality of the true text and its processes of transformation and retransformation strained his simultaneous realization that the critic cannot in principle overlay his interpretation as some kind of grid upon the certainties of each textual fact. Such literary scientism, in its overall objectives, inescapably alters or warps interpretative responses. What seems to be the case is that while Abel dealt with the given text with high respect, he simply accepted it as a given fact (or rather as a given fiction) from which analysis might proceed.

In this attempt to identify some of the critical voices that speak within Abel's texts, it is easy to find evidence in the productive life of a critical commentator of those critical modes that are tied to the period in which they emerge. Abel's entry into the debate between New Criticism and older modes of response, historical and moral modes, binds him to the middle of the twentieth century; but at the same time, his aggressive speculation about, and intense immersion in, the texts of the nineteenth century and his wide-ranging eclecticism provide us—not with a theory of literature—but rather with a practice of criticism which contains within itself those competing voices that struggle for our attention in the present moment. Underneath nearly all Abel has written, however, lies uneasy melancholy—perhaps even a fundamental pessimism—about man, about his projects, about literature, and most surely about the future of literary studies and literary criticism.

The Chaotic Legacy of the New Criticism and the Fair Augury of the New Scholarship

Brian Higgins and Hershel Parker

It is easy enough to despair at the writing on American literature being published these days—criticism pieced together from earlier criticism, literary history which violates long-available facts, biographical studies gleaned from standard biographies, and even textual studies which derive from earlier editions or which skimp crucial evidence. Although New Criticism has been dead, folk say, for a decade or more, its legacy is omnipresent in the inability or unwillingness of critics to evaluate and employ scholarly evidence. Less noticed, perhaps, is the fact that would-be scholars have also lost sight of how to deal with documentary evidence and, in any case, turn out to have been sharing with the New Critics, all along, certain restricting attitudes toward the creative process and authorial intention. Yet we find ourselves cherishing a measure of genuine exuberance, not just cautious optimism, about a new blending of scholarly and critical approaches in writing on American literature.

A "New Scholarship" is emerging, distinguished not only by fresh vigor in the pursuit and analysis of historical, biographical, textual, and bibliographical evidence but also by the alert sophistication with which such evidence is probed for its aesthetic implications; or the trajectory of research can go in the other direction, as when a study begins with recognition of an aesthetic problem which turns out to be resolvable only by external evidence. In this survey we will first look at some of the limiting ways critics and scholars in the 1950s and afterward have thought about literature, with a consequent waste of effort. Then we will point out recent work on many American writers that strikes us not only as better than earlier work but often different in kind—writing by the new scholar-critics.

The combination of scholarship and criticism is hardly new, of course, and we would be loath to argue that such work makes up a higher percentage of total academic publication now than it did three or four decades ago. Even in the 1950s, the heyday of the New Criticism and the dark ages of scholarship on American literature, some people managed to interest themselves in textual-critical matters such as the processes by which works were composed, the purposes of authorial revisions, and the significance of information about how works were published. Good examples are Leon Howard in his books on Melville and Lowell[1] and William M. Gibson in his work on Howells, notably the introduction to the Riverside *A Modern Instance*.[2] But naturally enough, most textual-critical studies of the 1950s bear the impress of the dominant literary approach in what they leave undone if not also in what they set out to do.

A major mid-fifties study was George R. Stewart's elaborate hypothesis about the composition of *Moby-Dick*, a version of the earlier "two *Moby-Dicks*" theory, according to which the book was nearly finished in one form, then in large part rewritten.[3] Stewart knew the earlier attempts to array relevant external evidence, but he concentrated on amassing and analyzing a range of internal anomalies. Although he shrewdly brought to bear his own knowledge of how novelists work, he did not raise such questions as whether Melville customarily projected reliable completion dates for his books and whether surviving documents reveal that Melville customarily discarded large sections of manuscripts during one phase of composition or another. Not writing as a New Critic, Stewart nonetheless seems to have been influenced by the prevailing concern for internal evidence at the expense of external.

During the same years, writers interested in an author's demonstrable revisions, rather than hypothetical ones, were also restricted by the dominant critical methodology. Seymour Gross's influential study of Hawthorne's revisions of "The Gentle Boy" divided authorial revisions into two simplistic classes, "mere 'worrying' of material" and "consciously artistic revision," the latter sort presumed to lead to an improved aesthetic unity.[4] The maxim "To revise is to improve" also held sway, at least tacitly, over a spate of 1950s articles on Henry James's revisions. Indeed, well into the 1960s the same maxim governed not only holdover New Critics but people as disparate as rhetorical critics and followers of W. W. Greg. Wayne C. Booth set himself to justifying the Malcolm Cowley version of F. Scott Fitzgerald's *Tender is the Night* in a spirit like Gross's, never taking into account the aesthetic dislocations and outright destruction done by Cowley's misguided attempt to implement Fitzgerald's supposedly "final" desires.[5]

It is still more curious to discover that leading textual critics of the 1960s and 1970s were using the same rudimentary textual-critical vocabulary that served critics in the 1950s. Fredson Bowers's simplistic notion of "artistic revisions" was identical to Gross's, for instance, and Bowers and many others found in the term "author's final intentions" (which by definition were "artistic" intentions) a Celestial Railroad to editorial bliss.[6] As we can now see, parallel developments in literary criticism and textual theory had directed concern toward the ultimate product, not toward the processes by which a work achieves its completed form, or forms, and not toward the author's intentions as embodied in any first form or in any intermediate forms of a work.

Most critics and scholars, still blinded by one or both of these compatible critical and textual dogmas, have proved unable to pose some of the most basic questions any student of literature ought to ask. Recent writing on any important American author is full of the failures of critics to be scholars and of scholars to be critics, but the clearest cautionary example we can think of is the writing on *The Red Badge of Courage*. Crane's masterpiece has always been read in an expurgated and otherwise mangled form which, precisely because it does not make real sense in the published form, has spawned a number of contradictory and confused arguments over whether the main character matures and whether the ending is ironic. Most critics never mention the textual evidence at all, but those who do have always misrepresented it and drawn untenable conclusions.[7] But there is no need to seek examples from beyond the writers celebrated in this collection. We choose to look at what a scholar and a critic have done with Hawthorne's "The Gentle Boy" and at what several scholars and critics have recently done with Melville.

"The Gentle Boy" is one of the few tales that Hawthorne revised from printing to printing. After first publishing it in *The Token* (1832), Hawthorne shortened it considerably for *Twice-Told Tales* (1837), with no rewriting except for a few new transitions. He was still unhappy with it. Using the condensed version as the basis for a new, third printing in 1839, Hawthorne compared the story unfavorably to others among *Twice-Told Tales*, several of which, "on reperusal" affected him "less painfully with a sense of imperfect and ill-wrought conception." Given this situation, one would have expected some extended editorial commentary in the Ohio State edition, but Fredson Bowers offers no justification for following the 1837 text.[8] One has to consult the earlier Ohio State

volumes for a discussion of textual priciples which
suggest that in this instance Bowers was mechanically
applying W. W. Greg's rationale of copy-text, according
to which all later authorial readings are to be followed,
whether or not the editor thinks they are improvements.[9]
For any reasoning about what Hawthorne's revisions did
to the story, we are left with the 1954 essay in which
Seymour Gross makes his distinction between "mere
'worrying'" and "consciously artistic revision." Gross de-
clared stoutly that the deletions and slight revisions "exhibit how Hawthorne has managed to give his piece a
firmer point of view through the solidifying of a remarkably perilous balance between Puritan and Quaker." "In
short," he concluded, Hawthorne "has clarified the terms
of his tragedy" (p. 196).

We suspect, to the contrary, that any problems with
the 1832 version are lesser than the new problems
created by the excisions.[10] A maxim of our own would be
that any revision-by-excision is apt to produce discon-
tinuities in direct proportion to the coherence of the original version. Insofar as the 1832 version of "The Gentle
Boy" is the product of an imperfect and ill-wrought conception, we would say, it is because of Hawthorne's uncertain attitude toward the Puritans. He is at pains to
show how, given the historical circumstances, they could
have behaved as cruelly toward the Quakers as they did.
He is also concerned to show them realistically in their
worship and to suggest, through Pearson's household
furnishings, something of their day-to-day lives, their
husbandry, warfare, and domesticity. Yet he regards them
with bitterness that sometimes swings past irony into sarcasm. As he prepared the 1837 version, Hawthorne apparently felt that some of the historical passages were not
imaginatively assimilated into his story, for the bulk of
the changes consisted of deletions of just such passages.
He removed a long explanation of "extenuating circumstances" for the Puritan persecution of the Quakers, a
longish description of the furnishings of the Pearsons'
combination sitting room-kitchen and Dorothy's wel-

come of Ilbrahim, a description of the Puritan women
and men in church, a bitter characterization of the minister's derivative sermon, a description of the struggle between Puritanism and Quakerism in Pearson's soul, and a
final sarcastic comment on the dubious "better nature" of
the fathers of his native land.

The 1837 version is at least as imperfect and ill-
wrought a conception as the first version. In fact, it was
not reconceived; the conception is the old one. Hawthorne was merely hacking away at the story, not satisfying
himself and not solving the basic problem of how to balance historicity with imaginative creation. The historian's
impulse, which sometimes led to the inclusion of over-
abundant or extraneous-looking detail, persists into the
1837 edition, despite the deletions; it is just less con-
spicuous and more erratic than before. The text is certainly left less coherent. With the deletion of much of the
historical perspective on their motives, Hawthorne,
perhaps inadvertently, left the Puritans less comprehen-
sible than the complexly motivated beings of the original
story. Also, the original contrast of Puritan "polemic
fierceness" with Quaker fanaticism is weakened by deletion of the analysis of why the Puritans treated the Quakers as they did.

In smaller ways too, the 1837 text is unsatisfactory.
The deletion of the description of the Pearsons' furnishings weakens an otherwise moving section designed to
recapitulate the very passage which was deleted. In 1837,
when the reader learns that the "furniture of peace" has
disappeared from the Pearson house, as well as "the implements of war," he can only be puzzled, since he has
had no way of knowing that such implements had ever
been there. "But the Holy Book remained," we are still
told in 1837, although the earlier mention of the Bible's
presence is removed. Another excision, apparently designed to remove the account of Pearson's finding peace
at the end of his spiritual struggles toward Quakerism,
pulls out (along with it) a reference to Dorothy's not having been "the subject of a similar process, for her reason

was as clear as her heart was tender." This deletion seriously weakens the earlier equation of Dorothy with "rational piety." Any responsible editor or critic must grapple with such damage, caused by hasty though belated authorial excisions.

As a critic, Seymour Gross shirked some of his responsibility by contenting himself with the assumption that "consciously artistic revision" is always to be justified, even when, as he himself recognizes, a deletion "weakens a later passage in the tale" (p. 200). Here Gross's bias leads him into a contradiction: a change weakens the story, yet it must be artistic. Symptomatically, he seems not to visualize the 1832 version as a real text read by real people. Although he was using *The Token,* he treats its text almost as if it were hypothetical, as when (discussing the 1837 deletion of Ilbrahim's arrival at the Pearson house) he says: "In fact, the inclusion of the passage would have lent something to Hawthorne's portrayal of her [Dorothy] as the ideal of 'rational piety' and sensitive motherhood" (p. 200). But the passage *had been included in 1832* and *had already lent something* to that portrayal. Elsewhere, Gross says of another deletion that although the passage "would have served Hawthorne's purpose beautifully, he probably could not bring himself to be so unfair as to insinuate, even for artistic purposes, that the whole of the Puritans' religion was one monstrous distortion" (p. 202).

Apart from the fact that the 1837 version, lacking much of the original analysis of their motivation, does make the Puritans seem more monstrous, our point again is that, whatever its effects, the passage *had* appeared in 1832—Hawthorne *had* brought himself to include it. Gross knows this, of course; still, he seems so mesmerized by the concept of revision as necessarily "artistic" that he cannot quite bring himself to think in terms of two separate texts but, instead, thinks of the deleted passages in isolation from the entire 1832 text. Though some of his interpretations are perfectly sensible, he very rarely shows any sense of what the 1832 text meant as a whole. In the limited critical perspective from which it views the variant texts, Gross's is in truth a representative 1950s essay.

Aside from Jay Leyda, Leon Howard, and several students of Stanley T. Williams, Melville has had very few scholar-critics. For the past two decades, the field has been preempted by critics who are shaky about even the most documented periods of Melville's life and who, in any case, show only meager interest in how knowledge of Melville's life might affect our understanding of his works. That biographical studies have usually been almost as flimsy as purely critical essays is clear from a glance at the mutually contradictory studies which argue that *Moby-Dick* is a political allegory in which Ahab "is" Daniel Webster, John C. Calhoun, William Lloyd Garrison—whoever.

A persistent trap for scholars has been the old problem of the composition of *Moby-Dick,* most recently explored by James Barbour in two articles, one of which won the Norman Foerster Prize for the best article published in *American Literature* during 1975.[11] Barbour argues in his *American Literature* article that there were three main stages in the composition. According to this modification of the "two *Moby-Dicks*" theory, Melville in stage 1, from February to August 1850, pretty nearly completed a whaling story; in the following months of 1850, he wrote many of the cetological chapters and, perhaps, some whaling adventures; and beginning early in 1851, he revised the early whaling narrative and later interpolated material into it. Two of Barbour's unproven assumptions, repeatedly asserted, are that by the summer of 1850 Melville had all but finished one version of the book and that several months of 1851 were spent in "revising the early narrative"—rather than, as seems more likely, spent mainly in writing new chapters and parts of chapters. In repeating the old notion that Melville began the book as a mere whaling story, "romantic but truthful," Barbour quotes, without analysis, one of the main surviving documents, Melville's 1 May 1850, letter to

Richard Henry Dana, Jr. There, tailoring his comments to the factually-minded Bostonian, Melville warns that what he is writing will be "a strange sort of a book" because of the difficulty of getting poetry out of blubber; but he will cook it up with "a little fancy," while still giving "the truth of the thing." This is hardly a description of a simple whaling story.

Furthermore, Barbour constantly trips himself up by assuming that the "datable" chapters (such as the one referring to the collapse of Table Rock at Niagara Falls) were probably written almost immediately after each datable event. As for the much cited, unfulfilled predictions in *Moby-Dick,* they no more warrant belief that Melville wrote a now-lost conclusion to the book in 1850 than the unfulfilled predictions in *Pierre* warrant belief that Melville ever wrote a different conclusion to that book. In both cases we can reasonably assume that Melville's intentions changed as he worked and that he did not subsequently tidy up all the details of his manuscript for consistency. Nobody is apt to say a near-final word about the composition of *Moby-Dick* without first studying the compositional methods Melville employed in all his works. Meanwhile, even in Barbour's prize-winning essay in the major journal for studies in American literature, documentary evidence is still handled with the lack of rigor that has bedeviled scholarship ever since the New Criticism made attention to such evidence unfashionable.

In criticism on *Pierre* a long debate about the nature of Melville's intentions has been carried on with little recourse to biographical evidence, except for Harrison Hayford's analysis of some of the implications of Melville's letter to his English publisher, Richard Bentley, on 16 April 1852, and Leon Howard's much later argument that Melville wrote some 150 "unanticipated pages" after 20 February 1852, in a greatly altered attitude toward his plot.[12] Most critics simply ignored the evidence that the published book was much longer than it was first intended to be, but recently Robert Milder rejected Howard's belief that the belated enlargement was an

indication that during the composition Melville had been
led into psychological profundities at odds with his first
conception. Finding no serious "discontinuity" in structure and theme, Milder concluded that "Melville was in
command of his material from the very start—in command of his plot, which did not change substantially as he
labored on it, and in command of his complex and ironic
attitude toward Pierre, which also did not change. The
book Melville published, 'loathsome' as it seemed to
many of its first readers, is the book he set out to
write."[13]

With even greater facility (not having bothered with
earlier arguments about the late-stage enlargement),
Warwick Wadlington asserts that Melville, throughout the
book, was trying "to be directly (and scornfully) profound."[14] Still more recently, Richard H. Brodhead has
pronounced that Melville "was wise not to let a foolish
consistency keep him from exploring the subjects and
methods" of such chapters as "The Journey and the Pam-
phlet," "Young America in Literature," and "The Church
of the Apostles," since "they are among the most interesting in *Pierre*." Their inclusion "has a curious effect on the
book's narration," Brodhead recognizes, but he believes
that through them Melville "enormously expands his
book's frame of reference." Brodhead is determined to
find artistic purpose even in what seem to be "authorial
oversights," declaring that "in the spirit of *Pierre*'s conclusion such oversights seem to be pointed and pur-
poseful."[15] It would be hard to find better evidence of the
lingering power of the New Critical impulse to find an
artistic unity in every set of pages bound between two
covers.

Our own determination to write about *Pierre* sprang
(several years ago) from an uneasy feeling that justice had
not been done to the opening of the book—that the better half was the first half, despite the power of many passages late in the book. In 1974 we drafted a long essay,
"The Flawed Grandeur of Melville's *Pierre*," now contained, in revised form, in a British-American collection

of essays on Melville.[16] Writing this essay gave us a clearer understanding of where and how *Pierre* goes wrong in the second half; and in trying to account for the obvious disruption of Melville's intentions, Parker began assembling, in chronological order, all the known facts about the composition and publication. As it turned out, the evidence was far from exhausted. It was soon possible to prove that at least two major events, occurring almost simultaneously in the first days of 1852, led Melville to recast his manuscript—*then,* rather than weeks later, as Howard and others had assumed.[17] The biographical evidence supported our critical findings. No single pervading purpose impelled the book; instead, one major intention—that of portraying a young idealist's ambiguous awakening to tragedy—carried Melville through the Saddle Meadows section and survived (sometimes in altered form), still later, among passages written with another major impulse, that of recording his own struggles to maintain a literary career.

None of this is especially new, except the clarification of the causes and the timing of the altered purpose; many people had known that something had gone wrong and that it had to do with Melville's concern about his career. Now that the documentary evidence is laid out more elaborately and precisely than before, we will be curious to see whether critics continue to talk about Melville's single intention in *Pierre* and the unity of the book. If they are at all conscientious, they won't.

Recent criticism of *Billy Budd, Sailor* augurs ill, however, for any sudden critical conscientiousness with *Pierre.* The Hayford-Sealts edition of *Billy Budd* has been available since 1962,[18] yet only a handful of the many who have discussed the book have realized that the evidence in their Genetic Text might have interpretative implications. Critics most often ignore the textual evidence altogether, in fact, as when Robert Merrill declares that in the first half of *Billy Budd* "a very few incidents are made to yield a great deal of authorial analysis."[19] Correcting F. Barron Freeman, Hayford and Sealts show that, in general, the authorial analysis came first and the dramatic scenes grew out of the analysis.[20] Critics also regularly fail even to acknowledge the Hayford-Sealts evidence that, in Melville's manuscript, *Billy Budd* never began with a preface and that the passage so labeled in previous editions was a discarded fragment of chapter 19.

Milton R. Stern has made the fullest use of Hayford's and Sealts's work by preparing his own "edition" of the book from their Reading Text and Genetic Text, rather than from a fresh transcription and analysis of the manuscript.[21] Yet he has merely added textual confusion to critical confusion by placing the alleged "Preface" (leaves 229d–f in the Hayford-Sealts foliation) after leaf 238 (chapter 21 in Hayford and Sealts, chapter 22 in Stern). This textual decision of Stern's is based on his speculation that the superseded leaf 238a was preparing for the introduction of leaves 229d–f and on the critical judgment that they "follow perfectly" from leaf 238, which incorporated parts of 238a (Stern, pp. 154–155). But in leaf 238, Melville explains that the killing of Claggart occurs "close on the heel of the suppressed insurrections," a time demanding from English commanders "prudence and rigor," and then goes on to make a further point: "Moreover, there was something crucial in the case."[22]

In Hayford and Sealts, this further point is elaborated in the next paragraph, leaf 239. By interposing leaves 229d–f between leaves 238 and 239, Stern interrupts this logical progression at a point of great dramatic and psychological tension and has Melville explain, with garrulous redundancy, the historical background for a connection he has earlier established (in chapter 3) between the French Revolution and the Spithead and Nore mutinies (Melville had already satisfactorily recalled these "suppressed insurrections" in the previous paragraph, leaf 238). Further, the new idea (introduced at the end of leaf 229f), that the Nore mutiny "doubtless gave the first latent prompting to most important reforms in the British navy," has no bearing at all on Captain Vere's subsequent thinking and, in the Stern arrangement, merely adds a distracting element to the chapter.

More important, Stern's inserting the leaves after leaf 238 works against the purpose of Melville's late revisions in this part of the manuscript. These discarded leaves belonged to an earlier version, in which the narrator tended to support Vere unequivocally: "successful resistance" to the "inordinate and aggressive demands" of the men-of-war's-men at the Nore "was confirmed only when the ringleaders were hung for an admonitory spectacle to the anchored fleet." Melville's revisions of chapters 19, 20, and 21 (substituting leaves 230–237 for 229a–f) emphasize, on the contrary, the surgeon's profound discomposure at Vere's excited manner and surprise at his unusual proceeding and his insistence on secrecy; they even seem to raise the possibility that Vere is not in his right mind (see Hayford and Sealts, pp. 8–11). All in all, Stern's decision to place leaves 229d–f between leaves 238 and 239 seems merely willful.

Stern also reintroduces the discarded "Lawyers, Experts and Clergy" section which Raymond Weaver had included toward the end of his chapter 10,[23] and which Freeman had printed as chapter 12, thereby setting the pattern for all editions, until Hayford and Sealts omitted the section on the grounds that Melville himself had clearly rejected it. Stern appears more the impressionistic critic than the textual scholar when he argues: "Substantively the paragraph is so typically Melvillean, so obviously applicable to chapter 11, which precedes it and to chapter 13, which follows it, to the entire tone of Claggart's relationship with Billy, and to Vere's dilemma (especially to leaf 236, chapter 22, and to leaves 254, 255, 258, and 259), that the dubiousness concerning deletion would make omission a rather rigid act of editorial purism" (p. 170). Stern's mistake in this matter (aside from a rather winsome but irresponsible desire to put as much of what Melville wrote back in the book, whether Melville wanted it there or not) was in ignoring the Hayford-Sealts evidence that Melville had discarded the section only when he had used its material up, absorbing its essence into the manuscript in other ways (see Hayford and Sealts, pp. 36–38).

Given the persistence of an academic climate where historical, biographical, textual, and bibliographical evidence is routinely ignored or superficially employed, it is hardly surprising that the profession bungled its best chance for self-education in the relationship between scholarship and criticism, the chance to come to terms with the volumes published under the auspices of the Center for Editions of American Authors. This grand attempt to spread the benefits of the Great Society to the academic community went unreviewed, one might almost say, for very few commentators on CEAA volumes were equipped (or bothered to equip themselves) to judge the varying kinds of information presented or the formats chosen for presenting that information. On the occasions when the editors made shaky aesthetic arguments in support of their dubious textual decisions or made textual decisions in the face of contradictory evidence, most reviewers were too intimidated to make any challenge, or else couched their challenges in language that left in doubt the cause, place, and circumstances of the dispute. Again and again, CEAA editors got away with weighty sins of omission and commission.

One indomitable reviewer, John Freehafer, set out to understand just what Fredson Bowers had done to *The Marble Faun,* and discovered, all by himself, that the volume was so heavily and so erratically emended as to be unusable,[24] but the typical reviewer (who flourished in the pages of *American Literature*) purveyed superficial disapprobation or sychophantic praise. Still, because of the CEAA, a good many people around the country (however competent and however well known they already were) became better scholars and critics, and the initial lure or repellent of textual work proved the means by which a number of other people learned to put "criticism" into "textual criticism."

By the late 1960s, a group of scholar-critics, most of them associated directly or indirectly with one or more CEAA editions and most of them aware of some of each other's work, had begun writing what we call the New Scholarship, scholarly studies alert to critical implications and critical studies alert to aesthetic implications of scholarly evidence. Any listing may seem invidious as well as arbitrary, but we venture to cite a few of these studies which come most rapidly to mind. If most of these writers are associated with only a few universities, this is, presumably, as much a tribute to the intellectual activity at those institutions as to the presence or absence of major textual editions. (A revealing fact is that few of the new textual centers around the country have produced such writing; clearly, the mere availability of federal cash was by itself insufficient to educate either an older or an upcoming generation.) Here is our unabashed sampler of New Scholarly studies: Joseph McElrath's demonstration that biographers and critics of Anne Bradstreet have often drawn some of their major conclusions from highly dubious assumptions about the texts of her poems;[25] E. N. Feltskog's remarkably thorough study of the composition and publication of Irving's *Mohamet and His Successors*;[26] Alexander Hammond's work on Poe's tales of the Folio Club, an impressive attempt to reconstruct a text which was never completed and never published;[27] Joseph J. Moldenhauer's edition of *The Maine Woods,* which elegantly handles some complex problems of copy-text;[28] McElrath's review-essay on the first volumes of the Princeton Thoreau (especially his sensitive curiosity about the value of the Huntington final manuscript of *Walden*, a version considerably longer than the published book);[29] Robert H. Hirst's 1975 Berkeley dissertation, "The Making of *The Innocents Abroad*," a masterful accumulation and analysis of evidence about Mark Twain's shifting intentions for the book; Kenneth Sanderson's and Bernard Stein's acutely argued application of Greg's rationale of copy-text to the special problems of *Fables of*

Man;[30] James L. W. West's demonstration that the punctuation of the manuscript of *The Great Gatsby* creates greatly different aesthetic effects from those of the printed edition;[31] Thomas L. McHaney's textual-critical study of the Elmer papers, fine evidence of what sorts of knowledge are yet to be learned from Faulkner's manuscripts;[32] and Noel Polk's demonstration that Faulkner's shifting conceptions of the characters in his revisions of *Requiem for a Nun* show an increasing moral complexity.[33]

We could rest our case by saying that anyone who reads these works carefully will be convinced that scholar-critics are once again at work in the land, freed from the curse of the New Criticism and strengthened by the lessons of that great fiasco and great triumph, the CEAA. But we want also to point out that much recent work is not merely good but genuinely pioneering. G. Thomas Tanselle's study of authorial intention is a formidable attempt to reconcile the terminology and concepts of textual editors with those of aestheticians and speech-act theoreticians—a kind of article no one had ever written before.[34] And there are stirrings in quarters where scholar-critics have rarely been sighted. In a new collection of psychoanalytic criticism, the editor, Leonard Tennenhouse, proclaims his interest in "how the text was made, how it was perceived by the author, how it may have been read by its original audience, and how it is read by a particular reader.[35]

These are some of the preeminent questions of the New Scholarship, and if they are seldom or never raised in the actual essays in Tennenhouse's collection, the optimistic preface may lead psychoanalytical critics to raise them in the future. We look forward to the publication of studies which combine rigorous textual analysis with such once foreign approaches as creativity theory and reading conventions. There are even signs that reputation study, so long the monopoly of academic drones, may prove an invaluable testing ground for reader-response critics. We are convinced that a few years ago, when no one was looking, academic writing on American literature bottomed out. With the emergence of the New Scholarship, things are already getting better.

NOTES

1. *Herman Melville: A Biography* (Berkeley: University of California Press, 1951) and *Victorian Knight-Errant: A Study of the Early Literary Career of James Russell Lowell* (Berkeley: University of California Press, 1952).
2. Boston: Houghton Mifflin (1957), pp. v–xviii.
3. "The Two *Moby-Dicks*," *American Literature*, 25 (1954), 417–448.
4. "Hawthorne's Revision of 'The Gentle Boy,'" *American Literature*, 26 (1954), 196–208.
5. *The Rhetoric of Fiction* (Chicago: University of Chicago Press, 1961), pp. 190–195. For a fuller discussion of the Cowley version of *Tender Is the Night* (New York: Scribner's, 1951), see Brian Higgins and Hershel Parker, "Sober Second Thoughts: Fitzgerald's 'Final Version' of *Tender Is the Night*," *Proof: The Yearbook of American Bibliographical and Textual Studies*, 4 (1975), 129–152.
6. In his "Textual Introduction" to *Maggie* in *Bowery Tales* (Charlottesville: University Press of Virginia, 1969), Bowers argues, for example, that Stephen Crane was in general "sincerely intent on improving the style of *Maggie*" by the many changes in the 1896 edition (p. lxxiii), that some of the deletions of "described cursing" were for "artistic effect" (pp. lxvii–lxviii), and that the excisions which remove the gross fat man and Maggie's soliciting of two other repulsive men from chapter 17 were made to rid the chapter of "certain dissonances" (pp. lxxvii–xci). Blinded by the notion that revisions are necessarily artistic, Bowers ignores or minimizes the evidence that most of the changes and excisions in the 1896 edition were the result of editorial titivating and censorship. He resembles Gross in arguing that the revision of chapter 17 was artistic, even though it introduced a major flaw: in the 1896 version, Bowers admits, the "literal details by which Crane describes Maggie's journey are absurd"(p. lxxxiii). See our further discussion of Gross's article on "The Gentle Boy" below.
7. In "The *Red Badge of Courage* Nobody Knows," the lead article for the 1978 special issue of *Studies in the Novel* devoted to Stephen Crane, Henry Binder presents evidence that the book was expurgated, in violation of Crane's intentions, by the editor at Appleton's, Ripley Hitchcock. See also Parker's review of *The Red Badge of Courage: A Facsimile Edition of the Manuscript*, ed. Fredson Bowers (Washington D.C.: NCR Microcard Editions, 1972 and

1973), and *The Red Badge of Courage: An Episode of the American Civil War,* ed. Fredson Bowers, introd. J. C. Levenson, vol. 2 of *The Works of Stephen Crane* (Charlottesville: University Press of Virginia, 1975) in *Nineteenth-Century Fiction,* 30 (1976), 558–562.

8. *Twice-Told Tales* (Columbus: Ohio State University Press, 1974). In his "Textual Commentary," Bowers merely remarks that for the 1837 edition, Hawthorne "substantially revised" some of the stories "with which he had become dissatisfied, like 'The Gentle Boy'" (p. 536).

9. "The Rationale of Copy-Text," *Studies in Bibliography,* 3 (1950–1951), 19–36.

10. Otherwise hard to come by, the 1832 version of "The Gentle Boy" can be found in *Shorter Works of Hawthorne and Melville,* ed. Hershel Parker (Columbus, O.: Charles E. Merrill Publishing Co., 1972).

11. "The Town-Ho's Story: Melville's Original Whale," *ESQ,* 21 (1975), 111–115; "The Composition of *Moby-Dick,*" *American Literature,* 47 (1975), 343–360. See also James Barbour and Leon Howard, "Carlyle and the Conclusion of *Moby-Dick,*" *New England Quarterly,* 49 (1976), 214–224.

12. See Harrison Hayford, "The Significance of Melville's 'Agatha' Letters," *ELH* 13 (1946), 299–310; Leon Howard, "Historical Note," in *Pierre,* ed. Harrison Hayford, Hershel Parker, and G. Thomas Tanselle (Evanston and Chicago: Northwestern University Press and The Newberry Library, 1971), pp. 365–379.

13. "Melville's 'Intentions' in *Pierre,* "*Studies in the Novel,* 6 (1974), 186–199; the quotation is from pp. 192–193.

14. *The Confidence Game in American Literature* (Princeton: Princeton University Press, 1975), p. 116.

15. *Hawthorne, Melville, and the Novel* (Chicago: University of Chicago Press, 1976), pp. 182, 185.

16. *New Perspectives on Melville,* ed. Faith Pullin (Edinburgh: Edinburgh University Press, 1978, and Kent, Ohio: Kent State University Press, 1979), pp. 162–196.

17. See "Why *Pierre* Went Wrong," *Studies in the Novel,* 8 (1976), 7–23.

18. *Billy Budd, Sailor (An Inside Narrative),* ed. Harrison Hayford and Merton M. Sealts Jr. (Chicago: University of Chicago Press, 1962).

19. "The Narrative Voice in *Billy Budd,*" *Modern Language Quarterly,* 34 (1973), 283–291; the quotation is from p. 284.

20. See Freeman, *Melville's Billy Budd* (Cambridge, Mass.: Harvard University Press, 1948), pp. 69–71, and Hayford and Sealts, pp. 1–12, 17.

21. *Billy Budd, Sailor (An Inside Narrative),* (Indianapolis: Bobbs-Merrill, 1975).

22. Hayford and Sealts, pp. 102–103; Stern, p. 97.

23. *Billy Budd and Other Prose Pieces* (London: Constable, 1924), pp. 46–47.

24. *"The Marble Faun* and the Editing of Nineteenth-Century Texts," *Studies in the Novel,* 2 (1970), 487–503.

25. "The Text of Anne Bradstreet: Biographical and Critical Consequences," *Seventeenth-Century News,* 34 (1976), 61–63.

26. "Historical Note," *Mahomet and His Successors,* ed. Henry A. Pochmann and E. N. Feltskog (Madison: University of Wisconsin Press, 1970), pp. 517–559.

27. "A Reconstruction of Poe's 1833 *Tales of the Folio Club:* Preliminary Notes," *Poe Studies,* 5 (1972), 25–32. See also Hammond's "Poe's 'Lionizing' and the Design of *Tales of the Folio Club,"* *ESQ,* 18 (1972), 154–165.

28. *The Maine Woods* (Princeton: Princeton University Press, 1972).

29. "The First Two Volumes of *The Writings of Henry D. Thoreau:* A Review Article," *Proof: The Yearbook of American Bibliographical and Textual Studies,* 4 (1975), 215–235.

30. "Textual Introduction," *Fables of Man,* ed. with an introd. by John S. Tuckey, text established by Kenneth M. Sanderson and Bernard L. Stein (Berkeley: University of California Press, 1972), pp. 475–483.

31. "The SCADE *Gatsby:* A Review Article," *Proof: The Yearbook of American Bibliographical and Textual Studies,* 5 (1977), 237–256.

32. "The Elmer Papers: Faulkner's Comic Portraits of the Artist," *Mississippi Quarterly,* 26 (1973), 281–311.

33. "The Textual History of Faulkner's *Requiem for a Nun,"* *Proof,* 4 (1975), 109–128. Two of the earliest pieces of the New Scholarship were James B. Meriwether's "Notes on the Textual History of *The Sound and the Fury," Papers of the Bibliographical Society of America,* 56 (1962), 285–316, and Michael Millgate's *The Achievement of William Faulkner* (New York: Random House, 1966). Meriwether shows acute sensitivity to the aesthetic damage done by corrupt texts, and Millgate succinctly indicates the aesthetic implications of surviving textual evidence.

34. "The Editorial Problem of Final Authorial Intention," *Studies in Bibliography,* 29 (1976), 167–211.

35. *The Practice of Psychoanalytic Criticism,* ed. Leonard Tennenhouse (Detroit: Wayne State University Press, 1976), p. 8.

The Significance of Plot in Hawthorne's Romances

Nina Baym

In the 1950s, Darrel Abel published a series of important readings of Hawthorne's four long romances. These articles were part of the remarkable renaissance of interest in Hawthorne during that decade and helped establish him firmly as one of the great American authors. Inevitably, the analysis took its color from the leading critical theory of the time, New Criticism. New Criticism expressed a conservative, Christian-oriented ideology and an aesthetic developed for close readings of brief, lyrical texts. As a result, Hawthorne's romanticism or radicalism was denied, and his fictions were read as though they were poems, eloquent but plotless expressions of feeling and attitude.

Prior to the resurgence of critical interest in Hawthorne in the late 1940s and 1950s, most discussion of the author had centered on *The Scarlet Letter,* which was widely agreed to be a glorification of Hester and the impulse of romantic individualism she supposedly represented. Abel participated in the revisionary work that quarreled with this reading. In "Hawthorne's Hester"[1] he argued that Hawthorne portrayed Hester as woefully inadequate, and in "Hawthorne's Dimmesdale: Fugitive from Wrath"[2] he maintained that Dimmesdale was the novel's true protagonist. In "The Devil in Boston"[3] he appeared to suggest, through an analysis of possible sources for Roger Chillingworth, that Hawthorne held the religious views of a seventeenth-century Puritan. Except for the Chillingworth essay, Abel's work rests on a conviction of Hawthorne's social rather than religious orthodoxy. Such a conviction pervades his essays on *The House of the Seven Gables,*[4] *The Blithedale Romance,*[5] and *The Marble Faun.*[6]

Although the earlier view of Hester and *The Scarlet Letter* was oversimple, it attended to an aspect of Hawthorne's work that critics of the 1950s overlooked. It considered *The Scarlet Letter* not as an agglomeration of discrete poetic units—an assemblage of symbols, metaphors, images, or verbal ironies—but as the representation of a complete action whose shape controlled the possible interpretations of character and significance within the boundaries of the novel. Abel's work, however, like that of other critics on Hawthorne during the decade, tended to overlook or minimize the importance of plot. My focus here will be on the significance of plot in Hawthorne's fiction and the incompleteness of a criticism that ignores it.

I

One impulse appears to animate two of Abel's articles on *The Scarlet Letter,* "Hawthorne's Hester" and "Hawthorne's Dimmesdale" (the Chillingworth essay represents a sources and analog approach to the novel and will not be considered here): the wish to diminish the significance of Hester. The impulse works itself out in two ways: Hester is shown to be seriously flawed and then (since flawed characters are, after all, the staple of tragedy) her flaws are shown to be of a nature to disqualify her from meriting the attention of a serious reader. It is Dimmesdale, we are told, who is the true center of the romance; *The Scarlet Letter* is his story.

From a structural point of view, this position is untenable. Of the romance's twenty-four chapters, thirteen are "about" Hester, three are "about" Hester and Dimmesdale both, and eight are "about" Dimmesdale. In "The Custom-House" the scarlet letter is associated entirely with Hester, and Surveyor Pue charges the author to tell Hester Prynne's story. "The Custom-House" says not a word about Arthur Dimmesdale. At the most, one could make an argument for a divided focus in the romance between Hester and Dimmesdale; but if a single protagonist is to be chosen, the identity of Hester as protagonist is established, through "The Custom-House," before the romance begins, and in the first two chapters of the romance proper. It follows, then, that to represent Hester as an auxiliary character and Dimmesdale as the protagonist, Abel must alter or ignore the emphasis that Hawthorne gives to events in *The Scarlet Letter.*

I have asked myself over and over why it is that critics of the 1950s were almost unanimously concerned to deny Hester her place as protagonist of *The Scarlet Letter.* To some degree, the answer is to be found in the overt social ideology of New Criticism. Within important constraints, Hester and her behavior are associated with the ideals of passion, self-expression, freedom, and individualism against ideals of order, authority, and restraint. If she were in fact the heroine, then Hawthorne would have to be understood as a kind of romantic: exactly what the New Critics were trying to disprove. Hence, she had to be relegated to a subordinate role and seen as the object of Hawthorne's disapproval.

Beyond this, however, I have come to the regretful conclusion that some of the unwillingness, perhaps much of it, to recognize Hester as the protagonist came from a more covert aspect of the New Critical social ideology, its strong sense of appropriate male/female roles and its consequent conviction that it would be improper for a woman character to be the protagonist in what might well be the greatest American book. It is for this reason, I believe, that so many of the arguments "against" Hester's importance in the book focus on the assertion that during the course of the romance she steps out of her proper woman's place, defeminizes herself, and ceases to be a woman in some conventional sociobiological definition of the term.

These were certainly Abel's arguments in "Hawthorne's Hester." At various places in the article he asserts that she typifies romantic individualism, that "in her story Hawthorne endeavored to exhibit the inadequacy of such a philosophy," that "the larger tendency of the book subordinates her and exposes her moral inadequacy," and that "her role in the story is to demonstrate that persons who engage our moral compassion may nevertheless merit moral censure." In concluding sentences, he asserts that Hawthorne believed and showed through Hester that all sinners, even those who are victims of circumstances, must be held accountable for their actions. If they are not, says Abel, we have to repudiate the moral ideas which give man his tragic and lonely dignity; therefore the "doctrine," though hard, is inescapable.

In order for statements like these to be applicable to *The Scarlet Letter,* the plot would have to (1) show that romantic individualism is an effort to evade moral accountability, (2) present Hester as a representative of romantic individualism, and (3) represent an action that brings out the inadequacies of romantic individualism as a philosophy. Now, if the plot had contained nothing but Hester's act of passion and her subsequent disgrace—if, that is, the second chapter had ended the novel instead of effectively commencing it—we might be able to fit it to these conditions. But in fact, as is repeatedly brought out in analysis of the romance, the act of "romantic individualism" has occurred before the plot of *The Scarlet Letter* begins. The plot that Hawthorne designed centers on quite different issues.

Nothing in the plot shows Hester attempting to evade responsibility for her actions. Of course, she cannot deny what has happened, but she makes no attempt to plead for diminished responsibility in the act. More importantly, she fully accepts the responsibility she has toward the human being who has been created as a result of it. In comparison to her, Dimmesdale's refusal to recognize any obligation to Pearl is strikingly irresponsible. Whatever philosophy Hester represents, it is not one that entails an attempt to escape accountability for her actions.

Almost nothing that she does in *The Scarlet Letter* can be labeled as an example of romantic individualism. During the entire length of the romance her behavior is self-effacing, unassertive, hard-working, disciplined. Only twice in the novel does she speak out in what might be called an individualistic way. First, she argues to keep her child. Whatever her motives here may be, they cannot be those of a self-indulgent, pleasure-seeking romantic. On a second occasion she utters her famous sentence, "What we did had a consecration of its own." This certainly looks like a passionately romantic utterance, but observe the context of action in which the idea is expressed. Hester is talking to Dimmesdale in the forest, urging him to leave the settlement, trying to imbue him with the energy and self-trust that will enable him (as she perceives it) to save himself from annihilation. Her words are romantic indeed, but she speaks them to help another, not to help or justify herself.

It is only in her secret thoughts that Hester might be called a romantic individualist—and there, I suspect, "romantic individualist" is far too soft a phrase. We are led to believe that Hester's brooding thoughts aim at the overthrow of the entire Puritan establishment. But in what way does Hawthorne demonstrate the "inadequacy" of such a philosophy? In answering this question, Abel moves to the second argument, the antifeminist argument: Hawthorne demonstrates the inadequacy of Hester's philosophy by showing how unwomanly she becomes in her years of solitude.

Problems with this argument appear, however, in its very formulation. "Unfitted by her intense femininity for intellectual speculation," Abel writes, "as well as by her isolation from the common experience of mankind, which rectifies aberrant thought, she unwomaned herself and deluded herself with mistaken notions." The first problem is that, insofar as Hester's loss of womanliness resulted from her isolation, it was the community, rather than she herself, that did the "unwomaning." This point reaches deeper than Abel's argument takes it, for the idea of "woman" implicit in the argument is one that depends, profoundly, on a "place" in the community. If the community that makes woman's place excludes a given woman, then of course she will be "unwomaned."

A second point, of greater importance, is the confusion between Hester's particular thoughts and her act of thinking. Is it her fault that she thought unwomanly thoughts or that she thought at all (an unwomanly activity)? The implication of the phrase "unfitted by her intense femininity for intellectual speculation" seems to suggest that it is not so much the content of her thought that is judged—her thoughts, if entertained by a man, might be appropriate—as her act of thinking. Her error is not an inadequate philosophy, but the unwomanly attempt to formulate a philosophy for herself. If this is the butt of Hawthorne's criticism, then he is condemning not romantic individualism but would-be thinking women, and *The Scarlet Letter* shrinks measurably in thematic significance.

Finally, how do we understand the nature of a femininity at once so intense as to unfit a woman from engaging in intellectual speculation, and yet so fragile as to be destroyed by the very attempt to speculate? It cannot be both ways: either woman's mind is resistant to thought, or thought is resistant to woman's mind. These confusions all point to a distaste for the idea of a thinking woman—a distaste, however, which is not Hawthorne's but Abel's. I would not suggest that Hawthorne demonstrates what we call today an "androgynous" view of human nature in *The Scarlet Letter*. On the contrary, he manifests a clear idea of "womanliness" and shows throughout the romance that Hester is, and remains, a true woman in his sense of the phrase. The only way in which she becomes less womanly is superficial; she no longer "looks" so womanly as she had before her suffering. But the forest scene shows, among other things, that all along Hester has in fact remained as beautiful and as much a woman as ever; her womanly side is simply hidden from public view by the severe garb she wears.

Nevertheless, we do not need to "see" that Hester is still the beautiful physical woman she was at the story's outset, although it is immensely satisfying when we do. Throughout the story, Hester acts according to certain clear principles of womanliness. At the beginning, when she refuses to name Pearl's father, Dimmesdale exclaims, "Wondrous strength and generosity of a woman's heart! She will not speak!" Measured against the criteria of strength and generosity, Hester remains a woman throughout. She brings up a child. She earns a living for two by needlework. She tends the sick and the poor. She suffers abuse in silence. She refuses to leave Boston so as to be near the man she loves. When she sees that man sick almost to dying, she urges him to escape from his morbid situation and does not offer to go with him until he virtually solicits her company. According to Hawthorne's criteria, she is a woman from first to last; but these criteria do not exclude the capacity, or the right, to indulge in "intellectual speculation."

Let us, finally, consider whether it would have been more feminine in Hester if seven years of solitude had left her unmarked. What would we say of a woman who was made to endure what Hester endured and who, after seven years, remained blooming, ebullient, and full of sexual enchantment? There, I think, would have been evidence of a *true* moral incapacity. Hester might have turned to witchcraft; she might have seized the opportunity to rid herself of Pearl; she might have run away to the Indians, or with sailors—Hawthorne had many opportunities to plot a story of loss of femininity or moral inadequacy for Hester. However, he invented a plot that shows her persevering in strength and in womanliness until the very end.

The morally inadequate character in the story is Dimmesdale, of course. The defect, however, lies not in his philosophy but in his psyche, for his need for social approval is such that he cannot live up to the high ideals he professes. Although I cannot agree that Hester is un-womaned by her ordeal, I would maintain that Dimmes-dale is unmanned by his. He enters the romance with a simple, childlike aspect and totters out of it like an invalid. Much too much has been made, in the criticism, of the minister's ordeal with his "God," a Being who may be supposed to know what has happened and from whom there can be no hiding, and much too little of the minister's neglect of his human family—his true, human family, rather than the parish whose shepherd he figuratively is. In the scaffold scene in chapter 12, the minister makes the one acknowledgment of preeminent human importance—that he is responsible for a "family," that he has made a mother of Hester, that he has participated in the creation of a child. He never makes that acknowledgment again; his last thoughts on the scaffold are for himself, for dying with a clean conscience, for the institutions rather than the human beings he has failed.

Abel makes the best case he can for Dimmesdale as protagonist in "Hawthorne's Dimmesdale," necessarily at the expense of order, proportions, and emphasis in the plot. In fact, Abel goes so far as to assert that, for all practical purposes, *The Scarlet Letter* has no plot at all. "The situation is presented . . . in exposition and spaced scenes which picture the positions that the exposition prepares. Hawthorne's narrative does not have the dramatic continuity of a moving picture; it has the static consecutiveness of a series of lantern slides, with interspersed commentary." Because there is no plot per se, it is permissible for the critic to infer a plot from the sequence of lantern slides, and Abel infers that the "plot" of *The Scarlet Letter* consists of the "struggle between God and the Devil for the soul of Arthur Dimmesdale." The series of events which lead Dimmesdale to take his place by Hester's side on the pillory constitutes "the dynamic substance of the story."

As I have suggested above, more than half of the story has nothing to do with Dimmesdale; and if one focuses on those events which lead Dimmesdale to his dying confession, one is limited to even a smaller segment of the story: the episode in the forest and the sequence immediately following it. To the extent that the earlier parts of the story concern Dimmesdale, they mostly demonstrate the occasions on which Dimmesdale *resists* taking his place on the pillory—the feints, placations, and hypocrisies that help him to save face. Trying to make a plot for Dimmesdale that includes all twenty-four chapters of the romance, Abel proposes a four-part sequence. In this sequence, Dimmesdale is passive, acted upon by others, who are, in order, society (chapters 1–8), Chillingworth (9–12), Hester (13–19), and God (20–23). This is an ingenious expository structure, but it is not a story; and this brings us to the "slide show" metaphor used above: the purpose of insisting that Hawthorne does not have a true story in *The Scarlet Letter* is precisely to permit the critic to invent a form in which Dimmesdale might be the focus.

Thus far I have pointed to particulars of the action; let me take an overview of the plot that permits us to see how Hester and Dimmesdale are involved in a single story, initiated at the outset and resolved at the conclusion. Although *The Scarlet Letter* has a simple line of action, it achieves complexity, depth, and irony because its events are susceptible to integration within more than one plot structure. One of these plot structures is the story of star-crossed lovers, whose union, for one reason or another, is forbidden within their society and who, hence, are separated. Throughout, the possibility is implicit in *The Scarlet Letter* that Hester and Dimmesdale may escape the confining society and assert their love, but, as in the tradition of such fables as Tristan and Isolde and Romeo and Juliet, this possibility emerges as a likelihood only to be tragically aborted.

A second kind of plot is suggested in the opening scenes of the novel, when Hester is shown in disgrace on the scaffold and Dimmesdale in a place of honor on the balcony. This scene puts emphasis on the two characters' places in society, each in comparison with the other. A reader quickly comes to feel that one character is unfairly ostracized, the other unfairly celebrated. Here is a plot of exclusion and integration into society and a plot of "false appearances": the characters are in the wrong places, and it is in the nature of plots to rectify such situations. At the conclusion, Dimmesdale dies on the scaffold and Hester becomes part of society. False appearances have been righted.

Whether we look at it as a plot of forbidden love or a plot of false appearances, we must see that Dimmesdale is the less weighty of the two characters. He is responsible for the failure of the lovers to escape, just as he is the "poseur" in the drama of false appearances. Ultimately, it is not Dimmesdale but Hester who is truly concerned with society and human relations. Her return, still wearing her letter, to a community that accepts her and comes to love her, represents a compromise between self and society, a resolution of the problems of the story less glamorous than the lovers' elopement would have been, but more durable. For society to accept Hester at her own valuation means that it has begun to make a place for the human heart and its private needs. For Hester to return at all, however, means that she has abandoned her radical forest thoughts, when she brooded on the overthrow of society, and come to accept the human community, however imperfect, as the necessary habitat of the individual. On the other hand, Dimmesdale thinks of no one but himself, and to perceive him as one in Hawthorne's long line of obsessed egotists is to clarify the relationship of *The Scarlet Letter* to Hawthorne's earlier fiction.

II

To minimize Hester's significance in *The Scarlet Letter,* it is necessary to minimize or ignore the plot which points so unequivocally to her importance. The method accords with the intention. Abel's studies of the other three romances also disregarded plot; but they develop ideas that could have been enhanced by plot analysis. It is evident, however, that the difficulty of Hawthorne's later plots and the general critical tendency to downgrade the importance of story have come together in an odd *apologia* for Hawthorne: the author was asserted to be a poor storyteller but is defended for doing something better, more artistic. In "Hawthorne's House of Tradition," Abel took this line toward *The House of the Seven Gables.* This romance, he writes, "cannot be understood as a history of particular persons in a specific place at a definite time; it is, instead, a series of *tableaux vivants et parlants* showing phases and types of humanity embodied in different generations of two families who live in significantly revelatory relationship with each other within an ancient but changing tradition. . . . The book is considered not as a narrative organized by the strict concatenation of events, but as a kind of prose symphony organized in five stages or movements." The fact that this model brings the romance to a conclusion at chapter 14 (it has 21 chapters) does not appear to be a defect, although Abel remarks that, after the "poem" essentially ends at chapter 14, "in concluding chapters [Hawthorne] ties up loose ends of the realistic level of his narrative in his usual arbitrary and inept fashion." To point out that fully one-third of a novel is "arbitrary and inept" would appear to be a severe criticism, but from the vantage point of a critic who finds the author writing a symphony or a poem (a superior activity to novel-writing), it is not so intended. On the contrary.

Citing Hawthorne's preface to *The House of the Seven Gables,* Abel suggested that Hawthorne was a bad plot-maker because his concept of romance implied a wish to escape from the strictures of a story. The devices of ro-

mance, refusing to occupy themselves with the history of
particular persons in specific places at definite times, are
"expedients to evade present and palpable circumstance
and to reveal what lies beyond it." But plot per se is not
identical to the particularized, temporally definite entity
that Abel sets up as a straw man; this straw man is the
manifestation of plot in the form of a nineteenth-century
realistic novel. That Hawthorne did not intend to—
indeed, intended *not* to—write such a novel is patent; but
to say that he therefore intended to get away from plot is
an unallowable inference. The rhythms and rhetorics of
the world's fables, myths, legends, and fairy tales—the
quintessential shapes of fiction that underlie all storytell-
ing, including nineteenth-century realistic novels—are
not particularized in time or space. I would argue that,
rather than wishing to free himself from story, Hawthorne wished to free himself from the very narrow understanding of story that controlled the expectations of his
audience, in order to return to the basics of fable.

This would appear to be his intention in the plot of
The House of the Seven Gables, for the premise of the work
is that, beneath the deceptive appearance of the modern,
everyday world, an older, hidden, magical story is working itself out according to its own inherent time scheme.
Without the key provided by that story, the events of
daily, modern life are an incomprehensible jumble.
Abel's strategy for ordering this jumble is to take the
symbol of the house in its permutation through generations as the story of the romance. The house rises, falls,
and rises again with the union of Pyncheon and Maule,
Phoebe and Holgrave, in the garden in chapter 14. But I
would say that the significance of the house is defined by
the events in which it figures: the events which precede
its building and the events (after the garden scene) that
lead to its abandonment. In other words, the house does
not give meaning to the story, but is given meaning by it.

In order to understand a plot and its significance, we
must begin at the beginning and end at the end. It begins
some two centuries before the romance's present time,

when the settler Maule takes a tract of wilderness and makes it into a garden. The house comes later, after Pyncheon has legally murdered Maule in order to get possession of his property. Built for this Pyncheon by a son of Maule, the house is the realization of Pyncheon's crime. On Maule's part, it represents his unwilling and ultimately subversive cooperation in a system that he cannot openly withstand. By virtue of his subversion, the house becomes the channel of a destructive force that victimizes its owners. In a word, Maule has cursed the house and, through it, cursed the Pyncheons.

Like other curses, this one is no respecter of persons, and over the years it falls alike on the guilty (Jaffrey Pyncheon, in the story's present time) and the innocent (Clifford, Hepzibah, and Phoebe). At the climax, which runs from chapter 16 through chapter 20, the story demonstrates the awful power of the curse at the same moment that it shows the agent of the curse, Maule, retracting it. The "Governor Pyncheon" chapter, in which the dead man is mocked and reviled, is as fiendish and macabre as anything Hawthorne wrote; although the house does not split asunder and subside into a dank tarn, the author is not far behind Poe in his dramaturgics of storm and fury.

The story comes to an end, however, not because the curse has melodramatically claimed one more victim, but because its power ceases to operate. Otherwise, there would be nothing to keep the story from endless repetition through historical time. It ceases to operate simply because Maule—in the present, Holgrave—has lost his taste for vengeance. Why has he done so? To put the climax, as Abel has done, at the garden love scene is to overlook the later sections of the plot, where Holgrave actually changes. He is changed by the night he spends with the judge, when he witnesses the curse in action. He may have regretted what the curse has done to Hepzibah and Clifford. He may have fallen in love with another of its victims; but the event that takes away his animus is participation in the death of his enemy.

Why should this be so? In psychological terminology, we may say that he has incurred guilt; in the archaic terminology of the story, he has made himself vulnerable to the curse of the man he killed, precisely as Pyncheon had been made vulnerable to Maule. In moral language, we may say that Holgrave realizes that to return crime with crime is to become a criminal oneself. The lifting of the curse, then, is not a purely joyful event, because the avenger perceives that he is, after all, implicated in the corrupt system he had thought to redeem. The story ends on a double, hence an ironic, note of both reconciliation and separation. The mood of *The House of the Seven Gables,* as Hawthorne wrote to a friend, "darkens damnably towards the close."

III

Abel's article on *The Blithedale Romance,* "Hawthorne's Skepticism about Social Reform, with Special Reference to *The Blithedale Romance,*" made clear by its title that it did not propose to elucidate the principles of coherence in the work. Rather, it used the work to draw out Hawthorne's views on a chosen subject because *The Blithedale Romance* is the only novel "in which attitudes toward specific reforms are expressed." To study a work for its authorial attitudes on a particular matter is difficult because the expression of attitudes is necessarily limited by the scope of the individual work. The special temptation that a critic must resist is to abstract essayistic commentary on the subject, whether spoken by the narrator or a character, and treat it as though it were taken from a piece of expository prose. Attitudes must be derived only from the whole story.

The specific reforms with which Abel dealt are organized philanthropy, feminism, and communal socialism, and he avoided the temptation noted above by locating each of these reforms in a character and then analyzing that character for its strengths and weaknesses. Philanthropy is embodied in Hollingsworth, feminism in Zenobia, and communal socialism in Blithedale Farm. But the problem with Abel's method is that he considers these characters independently of what they do; he centers, rather, on certain key descriptive passages about them and takes these static presentations of the character, at a certain point in the action, for the whole.

It is unquestionably true that the story shows all three individuals in question (counting Blithedale itself as an individual, as does Abel, for the moment) to be misguided and mistaken. To the extent that each deserves the reformer label that Abel affixes to them, one might agree that Hawthorne is skeptical about the given social reforms. It is also true that these characters, in entering the action, lay claim to the label that is given in Abel's discussion. But does the story demonstrate the shortcomings of the movements they purport to represent? Or does it, rather, show the unfitness of each for the reform he or she or it claims to personify? That is, Hollingsworth is no philanthropist, Zenobia no feminist, and Blithedale Farm is not a socialist community. All three are shams. At the outset, however, their shamming is not evident. We take them at their own valuation, but the action unmasks them.

As the story proceeds, we get repeated signs that Hollingsworth lacks the principle of brotherly love. The blind egotism with which he pursues his pet project and the callous use he makes of others demonstrate this, as does the project itself, predicated on the assumption of basic human criminality while assuming his own exemption from error and guilt. Zenobia's behavior toward Priscilla shows no feelings of sisterhood, while her behavior toward Hollingsworth shows no goal more spacious than to be owned by a powerful, patriarchal male. Her final speech of self-exculpation, falling back on all the traditionally attributed faults of her sex as excuse, and bitterly complaining that men have not been nice enough to her, reveals a profound immersion in conventional feminine ideology. Abel himself observes that Zenobia fails because her doctrines were nothing more than rationalizations for her mistakes—but is this not to say that she is only a pretender to feminism?

Blithedale Farm is not really an active character, although Abel treats it so, for its fate is inseparable from the actions of those who operate within its boundaries. In itself, it is only a piece of ground—the focus of much of the conflict—and dependent on the significant characters for its significance. Their significance, in turn, depends on the plot. Blithedale is supposed to support a community that exemplifies the ideals of honesty, altruism, and equality; since each of the main characters at Blithedale is deceitful, selfish, and snobbish to some degree, they can in no way come together to form a community that is better or different from themselves. The plot is in many ways like a mordant comic drama in which nobody is what he seems to be and everybody is plotting to deceive everybody else. But it has a measure of moral earnestness or pathos because the characters are, above all, self-deceived.

I think it is fair to conclude from this discussion that *The Blithedale Romance* cannot be used as a source for statements about social reform. Properly to contain such statements, it would have to involve characters who actually represent the reforms they identify themselves with. Hawthorne could certainly have invented such characters had he wished to. The only possible statement that he might be making about reform in the romance is particularly sour: people who are attracted to reform movements are likely to be least fitted to represent them. A power-hungry, manipulative man may find philanthropy appealing; a conventional but self-seeking woman may find a facade in feminism; a group of egoists may set themselves up as a "commune" and enjoy feelings of moral superiority to their neighbors. To the extent that reform movements are to be equated with the hypocrites who populate them, Hawthorne criticizes them severely.

Indeed, "skepticism" is too kind a word; his attitude is more properly labeled "disgust."

But we may want to follow a suggestion implicit in Abel's investigation. What is the function of social movements in *The Blithedale Romance*? Since they are not there for the purpose of allowing Hawthorne to comment on them, we must find a fictional reason for their presence. The plot of *The Blithedale Romance* rectifies false situations, as wrongly identified characters get their proper labels. It is a plot of reversals, since the rectifications involve putting all the characters in places opposite to where they began. The most vital character is dead, the hopeful man has lost hope, the autocrat is dependent, the subservient is dominant. We are alerted from the beginning to the fact that no one is what he appears, through the multiform imagery of masks, veils, secret names, mysterious pasts, and the like.

The initial labels are false because each presents the character as much better than he or she really is. Each presents the character's self-romanticization, his misapprehension concerning his own nature. Each character draws a complacent sense of security—undeserved and unfounded, as it turns out—from the flattering self-image. An important aspect of the flattery is, of course, the character's perception of himself as a radical reformer, as a person involved in progress, in bettering the world, in humanitarian concerns. Yet none of the characters' actions bring reformist or humanitarian motives into play, or are directed toward the furthering of the movements they claim to believe in. Hence the social reform movements cited by the chief characters become one of the tests by which they are judged and found lacking. Had Hollingsworth not pretended to be a philanthropist, his tyrannizing over others would not be so pointed a comment on his character. If Zenobia had not claimed to be feminist, her dismissal of Priscilla and truckling to Hollingsworth might be judged less severely than they are. The rhetorical adherence to social reform movements makes the gap between profession and performance very evident.

IV

The moral of this analysis of *The Blithedale Romance* is that when a block of "real material" is worked into a fiction, it does not so much give meaning to the story as absorb meaning from it. In the confrontation scene beneath Eliot's pulpit, Hollingsworth throws off his "mask" of philanthropist and assumes his "true identity" as Puritan judge. Yet even the Puritans are a figure in Hawthorne's writing, whose meaning must be assessed by the context in which they appear rather than by any presumed connection between the historical beings and Hawthorne's interest in them. In some stories, Puritans are the oppressors; in others, they are the liberators; and depending on which role they play, Hawthorne assesses them differently. And as the Puritans may assume either of these roles, other figures may assume roles we commonly associate with Puritans in Hawthorne's work. Despite a superficial contrast made by Hilda, in *The Marble Faun,* between Catholicism and Puritanism, the structure of that romance places the church in the same role that the Puritan oligarchy played in *The Scarlet Letter.* That Hilda, a "daughter of the Puritans," as she so often calls herself, should ally herself with the church is not a travesty (as her deluded lover Kenyon believes) but a natural alignment, given the deployment of roles within the story. Our key to the story is the problem or conflict established at the outset, and the path taken to a resolution.

Like *The Blithedale Romance, The Marble Faun* opens with a knot of four characters, friends and colleagues engaged in a communal life of work and leisure, and concludes with the separation and fragmentation of the group. In the face of a threat to one of its members, the cohesion of the group begins to soften. That threat is obscurely personified in the "model," who emerges from the catacombs and mysteriously attaches himself to Miriam. His shadowy nature informs us that we are in the world of romance rather than realism, and that the story will play itself out in types and symbols. Abel made this assumption in "A Masque of Love and Death." The novel is a "symbolic narrative," he writes. His means of getting at the narrative was to detach the symbols—in particular, the characters—from the actions which define them. Putting plot aside, he isolated the characters from their behavior, labeled them, and then hypothesized a story in which these types could be characters. The critical method guarantees that there can be no plot-related observations, and hence the tangled plot of *The Marble Faun* looks more like a hindrance than a help to Hawthorne's expression of his vision.

In preparation for his analysis, Abel devised a hierarchy of character modes in Hawthorne's works, including individuals (human beings presented), types (human beings classified), and symbols (human beings analyzed). The characters in *The Marble Faun* are symbols, representing an abstracted human trait or complex of traits. According to this scheme, Donatello represents natural, hedonistic, impulsive man; the Model represents intellectual man; Kenyon represents detached, observing, aesthetic man; and Hilda represents Puritanism, naive nineteenth-century Americanism, and Victorian womanhood—conventional or conformist man, let us say. Miriam is actually a metacharacter or a metasymbol, in that she represents not a set of abstracted traits but the very idea of the human being, the entire scope and range of human capacities and possibilities. The story is designed, Abel maintains, to test each of the four types against their experience of the wholeness and variety embodied in Miriam.

This scheme offers a perceptive entree to some of the complexities of the story, and one looks to see what test Abel will discover Hawthorne using to judge the characters. But since he does not look at the plot, he has no way of moving from the typology to the text, and so says only that "the action of the romance is designed to exhibit the characters which I have distinguished." In other words, the starting point of the novel, the definition of four stances toward a major character, becomes its end point as well. And the scheme itself has problems. The Model, for example, does not play a role in the fiction comparable to that of the other three characters and hence should probably not be given equal significance. Nor is there anything in his characterization to suggest that he is an "intellectual." Even more important, the scheme does not allow for changes in the other three characters as they live through their experience of Miriam. Perhaps Donatello is a "natural man" at the outset, but he certainly does not remain one. Kenyon may represent artistic detachment to some degree at first, but he immerses himself fully in his friends' dilemmas and works to influence their lives. The only character who is hardened by the action, rather than altered by it, is Hilda, but she undergoes a period of mental anguish and turmoil before the mold is set.

Then, even if we were to grant that Hawthorne invented a story designed to display fixed characters rather than to change them through an action, what is the explanation for the particular story that he invented? Even if it serves only for purposes of illustration, one story is different from another. Rightly perceiving that the story portrays the inadequacies of each character by showing that each character fails Miriam, Abèl does not ask *how* each character fails Miriam. I have argued elsewhere that the story chronicles a failed rescue. Ensnared in some hideous oppression by the mysterious Model, who is associated with history, the church, and her family, Miriam is "rescued" by Donatello, who then abandons her; is "rescued" again by Kenyon, who negotiates a reconciliation between her and Donatello; but finally is abandoned by all, when Hilda fails to sanction the morality according to which Kenyon has intervened.

For each character successively, the psychological consequences of championing Miriam become more than they can bear. Like the characters in *The Blithedale Romance,* those in *The Marble Faun* take on more than they can achieve. The motif of unfulfilled promise runs through all four major romances, though it is most strongly articulated in *The Marble Faun.* In all four, a beautiful ideal is set before the reader by characters who cannot achieve it, and their failure results because they are partly or wholly in thrall to the very forces they must overcome if the ideal is to be attained.

Although Abel's intentions with *The Scarlet Letter* precluded close attention to plot, his readings of the three other romances might have been broadened and strengthened had he included plot analysis among his critical methods. Additionally, he would have avoided giving the impression that plot did not matter to Hawthorne or that he was not a good storyteller. But Abel clearly believed—as did many critics of the 1950s who were reviving his influence and reminding us of his significance—that plot did not matter to Hawthorne, that he was not a good storyteller, and that his shortcomings in this regard were not artistic defects. The critical tradition within which Abel was working saw story as a kind of necessary evil in fiction, as the truly lowest common denominator. Accordingly, critics turned their attention to other aspects of Hawthorne's achievement. It is probably true that Hawthorne would not be a major artist without his characters, his symbols, his images, his vivid pictorialism, his style. But all of these are made orderly and compelling by the stories, which, even at their most obscure, provide the impetus that keeps us reading through to the end of each romance. This underlying fact about Hawthorne's fiction should not be forgotten.

NOTES

1. *College English*, 13 (1952), 303–309.
2. *Nineteenth-Century Fiction*, 11 (1956), 81–105.
3. *Philological Quarterly*, 32 (1953), 336–381.
4. "Hawthorne's House of Tradition," *South Atlantic Quarterly*, 52 (1953), 561–578.
5. "Hawthorne's Skepticism about Social Reform, with Special Reference to *The Blithedale Romance*," *University of Kansas City Review*, 19 (1953), 181–194.
6. "A Masque of Love and Death," *University of Toronto Quarterly*, 23 (1953), 9–29.

Hawthorne's Literal Figures

Roy R. Male

In the last decade, one of the best articles on Hawthorne's fiction was by Darrel Abel, titled "Black Glove and Pink Ribbon: Hawthorne's Metonymic Symbols." I am pleased to report that this is not an occasion-serving judgment, prompted by this festschrift, but an opinion first offered when I reviewed the year's work on Hawthorne for *American Literary Scholarship* in 1969. In that article, after showing how Hawthorne's historical imagination worked in *The Scarlet Letter* and "Young Goodman Brown," Abel persuasively sums up the author's most insistent theme: "Every reading of facts, every version of 'truth,' is an arbitrary determination." His point is not simply that Hawthorne admits this epistemological uncertainty; he deliberately and artfully exploits it in his tales.[1]

In support of his claim, Abel collects a batch of quotations which, as he says, could be expanded into a volume. One passage that he omits comes from the *American Notebooks* and leads into the thesis of this paper. Here is

the passage: "Letters in the shape of figures of men, etc.
At a distance, the words composed by the letters are
alone distinguishable. Close at hand, the figures alone are
seen, and not distinguished as letters. Thus things may
have a positive, a relative, and a composite meaning."[2]
This passage seems seminal for interpreting Hawthorne's
work because (1) it suggests that our epistemological uncertainty is rooted in the mystery of language; (2) it indicates his characteristic emphasis upon the graphic rather
than the phonetic aspects of language; (3) it affirms that
words do not have meaning; people, depending upon
their perspective, have meanings for words; and (4) it
suggests that language has more than two dimensions.

One would think that, given the original image of
this passage, Hawthorne would have used the terms
"figurative" and "literal" rather than "positive" and "relative" in describing the different meanings supplied by dif-
fering perspectives. But he was probably wise in avoiding
"literal," since it immediately plunges us into a curious
semantic thicket. We usually think of literal meaning as
language taken at its simplest representational or descriptive level, but, as Northrop Frye has observed, "this
conception of literal meaning as simple descriptive meaning will not do at all for literary criticism." After all, "'literal' surely ought to have something to do with letters. . . .
And if a poem cannot be literally anything but a poem,
then the literal basis of meaning in poetry can only be its
letters, the inner structure of interlocking motifs."[3]

This attempt to restrict and even reverse the usual
meaning of "literal" is significant in revealing Frye's critical position, but it is doomed by the heavy weight of
convention (I shall continue to use "literal" the way it has
been used before) and by Frye's view (which he shares
with the New Critics) that literary texts are privileged by
having semantic autonomy. He attempts to define a literary text as one whose final direction of meaning is inward
or reflexive. "In literature, questions of fact or truth are
subordinate to the primary literary aim of producing a

structure of words for its own sake, and the sign-values of symbols are subordinated to their importance as a structure of interconnected motifs. Whenever we have an autonomous verbal structure of this kind, we have literature" (p. 74). Or as Wolfgang Iser puts it more bluntly, what is peculiar to all literary texts is that "they permit no referral to any identical real-life situation."[4] Fine. But what happens to Aristotle's *Poetics,* the Bible, Boswell's *Life of Johnson,* Bradford's *History of Plymouth Plantation,* Milton's *Areopagitica,* Franklin's *Autobiography?* The Declaration of Independence? The Gettysburg Address? Capote's *In Cold Blood?* Mailer's *Armies of the Night?* Is the "final direction of meaning" in *The Education of Henry Adams* centrifugal or centripetal? Anthologies of English and American literature would have to be radically pruned if we adhered strictly to this definition.

In short (and somewhat reluctantly), I am now convinced that the question of whether or not a given text is literary depends upon the attitude of the audience or reader. Literature, like the other arts, is a disjunctive category.[5] We recognize literary texts the way we recognize members of a club, not by any identical traits but by the social acceptance of their membership, attested to, if need be, by their membership cards. Whether or not a text is literary is a social convention, culturally determined. If John Smith's *Generall Historie of Virginia* is contained in a book whose cover proclaims it to be an anthology of American literature, then Smith's writing is literature. (In this connection, it is instructive to compare the *Cyclopedia of American Literature,* edited by the Duyckinck brothers in 1855, with any modern anthology.)

Another difficulty with Frye's distinction, and one which is shared by Michel Foucault's analysis in *The Order of Things,* is that it is two dimensional. Language is viewed as being either representational or reflexive—neither aspect, of course, being exclusive. A richer model, it seems to me, can be based on M. H. Abrams' familiar diagram, orienting critical theories, and will emphasize four interrelated aspects of language.[6]

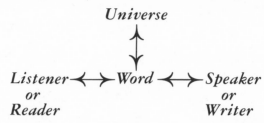

1. *Mimetic* or *copy* theories, emphasizing the relation between language and the universe. The notion that the word is one with the thing is, in one sense, naive. Any literate, sophisticated person knows that the connection between words and things, whether considered phonically or graphically, is arbitrary, conventional, culturally transmitted. Exceptions—phonic imitative devices like onomatopeia and graphic imitative devices like shaped verse—are trivial in English and all nonpictographic languages. A tree is a tree, whether we call it "tree," "*Baum,*" or "*arbre.*"

Yet this arbitrary connection—the fallacious assumption that language and the world are isomorphic—has the same functional solidity as other human reifications. Without it, our kind of civilization would have been impossible. To insist obsessively, as the general semanticists used to do, on the gap between word and thing is a form of linguistic paranoia. Probably the essential point here is that the most representative language is the most conventional. Writers who see their task as the recording of ordinary life will not be linguistic deviates.

2. *Pragmatic* or *incantatory* theories, emphasizing the relation between language and the reader or listener. In its primitive form, the notion that the primary function of language lies in its effect upon others can be seen as verbal magic. "Open Sesame" and "Abracadabra" make things happen. On a somewhat more sophisticated level, we know that mantras, chants, shouted slogans, and imprecations do function affectively. Some speakers can use

words or mere sounds as if they were rubber hammers or oscillating objects to hypnotize their audience. Graphic devices, like screaming headlines (NEW YORK: DROP DEAD), boldface or colored type, catchy titles, exclamation points, and dashes, are less potent but capable of much wider communication in time and space. On a more sophisticated level, of course, the pragmatic category would include all linguistic devices that are used primarily to persuade.

3. *Expressive* theories, emphasizing the relation between the speaker or writer and his language. Note that here the stress is upon the ways in which an *individual* articulates his thoughts, images, and emotions: expression is thought to be *self*-expression. Staccato rhythms of speech, a nasal drawl, mumbled fillers, and silences all serve as an index to a person's supposedly unique identity. His or her style is linguistic physiognomy, words the dress of thought, verbal timing the pulsation of inner being. Graphically, the simplest assumption is that a person is identified by his signature, that his character is expressed by his penmanship. On a higher level of abstraction, even if his words are translated into print, his character can be deduced by his favorite words, his unusual syntactical devices, his images and metaphors. Whether spoken or written, language is perceived as an utterance, an externalization of the internal.

4. *Objective* theories or language per se. The most impressive achievements of modern linguistic study resulted from the decision to cut language loose from the relationships listed above and treat it as an autonomous system, made up of parts whose significance depended upon their internal relations. Like physicians who were trained to identify and treat the disease, not the patient, linguistic scientists abstracted themselves as much as possible from individual cases. Primarily interested in speech as a channel of communication, they have developed an elaborate but functional set of terms defining phonological systems: the identification of phonemes as the units of such a system, the classification of those

phonemes in various ways, including the way their al-
lophones are produced. Thus we all now know that [*f*] is
a voiceless labial fricative, no matter who utters it.

More recently, we have witnessed greater interest
among linguists (or literary critics with a linguistic orien-
tation) in graphological systems. Edmund Wilson once
scornfully (but correctly) remarked that the New Critics
were a bunch of young men who had discovered that
poetry is written in words. It might be said that Derrida,
Lacan, and Foucault, and especially their excited disciples,
have discovered that literature is written in letters.[7] (My
tone may sound derisive but, as will be apparent later, I
think we can all learn something from this discovery.) It
must be admitted, however, that despite their spectacular
success in describing both phonological and graphological
systems, the linguists have not been very helpful in de-
ciphering some of the central riddles of language: the
mysteries of metaphor, the strange relation between literal and figurative meaning, the fact that man is the animal who can say *A* is and is not *B*.

This brief outline is, of course, highly schematic and
artificial in that it simplifies the multiple and interrelated
aspects of language. (I have also never mastered the art of
willful obscurity that so often makes critical investigation
of these matters seem profound.) But we can use the
chart to orient Hawthorne's verbal performance in relation to that of his leading contemporaries. For our purposes, Emerson, Thoreau, and Whitman can be easily
placed; they all believed in an expressive theory of language, with Emerson and Whitman placing heavy emphasis upon its oral aspects. Since Matthiessen and others
have thoroughly discussed their efforts to achieve a
"radical utterance" and since they wrote little or no fiction, we can move quickly to a comparison of Poe and
Hawthorne.[8]

Poe, obviously, had little use for a mimetic theory of
language. Why copy a decaying, doomed world or the
social structures of a society run by boobs, idiotic businessmen, or used-up generals? His primary interest, as

everyone knows, was in the incantatory effect of words. Devoted to spectacular chiming effects and metronomical rhythms in verse, he loved liquid consonants and the long *o* sound, yearning to achieve the purity of music by distancing words from their referents. The supposition, as Richard Wilbur puts it, is that "a melodious and rhythmical destruction of the earthly must be heavenly."[9] In the tales of terror, Poe's typical style is perhaps best described as a closet monologue. His narrators, cut off from the community of everything, including speech, write their breathless confessions, compose and bottle up their accounts of murder, suffocation, and madness. As Robert Crossley points out, the "essential horror in the narration of 'Berenice' resides not in Egaeus' act of perverse dentistry (which is, after all, not narrated but left to the reader's lurid imagination), but in the awful ability of Egaeus to dissociate himself from his action and to write so 'clean' and literate a version of such dreadful experience."[10] Instead of opening up an intercourse with the world, Poe's tales of terror are sealed letters to an unknown or potentially hostile audience.

Of course, as he often insisted, Poe wrote other kinds of fiction besides the tales of terror. Many of them hinge upon a conception of language per se, an autonomous game with its internal rules: the simple substitution cipher in "The Gold Bug," the inside jokes in "The Duc de L'Omelette," the phony sources and relentless insertion of phrases in foreign languages, the experiments with type ("X-ing a Paragrab")—all of them indicating his closeness to the "printer's devil" but offering a lighter side of his basically demonic or grotesque perspective.[11]

Hawthorne's attitude toward language was basically expressive, with heavy emphasis on its graphic dimension. His art has long been recognized as essentially pictorial. But no one, so far as I know, has really concentrated on the fact that he was, quite literally, a "man of letters" (not as obscure as he once claimed, and not without great skill in reading aloud, but basically a man doomed—or blessed—to spend much of his life in *furor scribendi*).[12] From the "owl's nest" in Salem to the study at the top of The Wayside, there was no mistaking or shirking where his vocation lay. He was a writer, not an orator or bard—a person who wore a writing gown embroidered by his wife, who knew that his unique manuscripts would or could be translated into a medium where "the letter is the atom of the printed language."[13] In a sense, he was born too late or too soon. Too late, in that he must have envied the glorious illuminated manuscripts of medieval scribes; too soon, in that he might have seen *The Scarlet Letter* adapted to color TV or shared a modern writer's awe at letters painted by light. "Do you wonder that I was late for the theatre that night, when I tell you that I saw two club-footed Egyptian A's . . . walking off arm-in-arm with the unmistakable swagger of a music-hall comedy team? I saw base-serifs pulled together as if by ballet shoes, so that the letters tripped off literally *sur les pointes*."[14]

Characteristically, when Hawthorne thought of the superb book that he might have written during his years in the Salem Custom-House, he said that he might "find the letters turn to gold upon the page." This was the ideal. The harsh fact was that his profoundest thoughts would be transmuted into small black marks on dried woodpulp, drastically limited in visual range and appeal. "It is a singular thing," he wrote in his *American Notebooks,* "that, at the distance, say, of five feet, the work of the greatest dunce looks just as well as that of the greatest genius—that little space being all the distance between genius and stupidity." Similar remarks dot his prefaces and journals, including the famous and ironic comment about the Custom-House marker, which carried his name to faraway places where his stories had never gone. (In the context that I am presently examining, C. E. Frazer Clark's use of that marker on the cover of *The Nathaniel Hawthorne Journal* could not be more appropriate.)

A man makes his mark—a signature, a letter, a story, an epitaph. At least it is more durable than the ephemeral vocables of speech. Though Hawthorne chafed at the limitations of writing and print, he was fully conscious of their power. Toward the oral aspects of language, his attitude ranged from mild curiosity to contempt and suspicion.[15] A sympathetic listener, alert to nuance, dialect, and word play, he noted in his journals that conversation depends more upon tone, body language, and other impressions than upon the actual, spoken words. And his orators, like Old Stony Phiz (modeled after Daniel Webster) in "The Great Stone Face," are usually described as wonderfully eloquent but often deceptive. "Wrong looked like right, and right like wrong; for when it pleased him, he could make a kind of illuminated fog with his mere breath, and obscure the natural daylight with it." In a particularly pessimistic mood, he commented that "language—human language—after all, is but little better than the croak and cackle of fowls and other utterances of brute nature; sometimes not so adequate."[16] True, the evanescent babble of human speech must have been preceded in some Edenic age by the "original voice and utterance of the natural man," sympathetically in tune with his environment. But because that natural utterance has been irrevocably lost, to Hawthorne the oral aspect of man's evolution seemed less important than his markings on stone, canvas, and paper.

As Hawthorne viewed it, that evolution can be most clearly described as a series of translations, in each of which something is gained and something lost. Sensations and conceptions are converted into signs, spoken words are "feebly substituted in the place of signs and symbols," speech is transmuted into written words, and manuscript is set in print. At each stage, what was gained was intelligibility, extension or portability in time and space, and thus speed and efficiency. What was lost was some portion of "the natural man," the human as creature. Of this loss as it applied to manuscript and print, Hawthorne wrote: "Strange, that the mere identity of paper and ink should be so powerful. The same thoughts might look cold and ineffectual, in a printed page . . . the original manuscript has always something which print itself must inevitably lose."[17] The "something" which is lost has to do with lack of uniformity—a blot, an erasure, "a casual irregularity of hand"—all of which "bring us close to the writer." He made a somewhat similar comment about translation from a foreign language: "Sentiments in a foreign language, which merely convey the sentiment without retaining to the reader any graces of style or harmony of sound, have somewhat of the charm of thoughts in one's own mind that have not yet been put into words. No possible words that we might adapt to them could realize the unshaped beauty that they appear to possess. This is the reason that translations are never satisfactory—and less so, I should think, to one who cannot than to one who can pronounce the language."[18]

Though something is lost as well as gained by translation, it at least is a transaction, and, as such, may produce a sense of reality. In a world of epistemological uncertainty, where everything depends on relationships and all attribution of meaning is arbitrary, determining the process and outcome of a transaction is one way of keeping in touch with the reality of ordinary life without being engulfed by it. This is the stance that Hawthorne whimsically adopts in his preface to "Rappaccini's Daughter." By referring to his works as productions of M. de L'Aubepine, he is able to give them weight and volume: the minute sketch "Fire Worship" becomes "'Le Culte du Feu,' a folio volume of ponderous research"; "The Artist of the Beautiful" becomes "L'Artiste du Beau; ou Le Papillon Mécanique, 5 tom., 4to, 1843"; and so on. The gentle self-irony in this preface should not conceal the fact that even Hawthorne's lightest pieces usually *are* profound, because they express in various ways his concern with man's central dilemma. He is the translating, interpreting, paraphrasing animal, but his symbol-making ability is precisely what alienates him from his environment, while at the same time making civilization possible.

Thus Hawthorne's fiction is full of guides, interpreters, translators, and gossips, while at the same time he uses all the devices at his command to achieve an authentic vision, undimmed by custom, preconceptions, and prior interpretation. Along with talent, the artist's most precious asset is his ability to see the world as if for the first time. Though this kind of vision is usually impossible, there are, as Walker Percy has noted, "many measures which may be taken to overcome the opacity, the boredom, of the direct confrontation of the thing or creature in its citadel of symbolic investiture."[19] Among these measures are the Inside Track, the Familiar Revisited, the Accidental Encounter, and the Disaster. Percy's chief example is the effort of the tourist to recover the wonder of the Grand Canyon; Hawthorne's examples include his trip to Niagara Falls, his exploration of Fort Ticonderoga, his visits to the Berkshires and the Notch of the White Mountains—even his walks from Salem to Swampscott.

Here, for instance, is Hawthorne's effort to regain what Tony Tanner has called the "reign of wonder": "Oh that I had never heard of Niagara till I beheld it! Blessed were the wanderers of old, who heard its deep roar, sounding through the woods, as the summons to an unknown wonder, and approached its awful brink, in all the freshness of native feeling." His first stratagem is to get off the beaten path, finding a solitary vantage point on Table Rock. A second device is, as Percy puts it, a recovery of the thing from familiarity by means of an exercise in familiarity. "Our complex friend stands behind his fellow tourists at the Bright Angel Lodge and sees the canyon through them and their predicament, their picture taking and busy disregard. In a sense, he exploits his fellow tourists; he stands on their shoulders to see the canyon" (p. 49). So Hawthorne observes the falls through the eyes of his fellow travelers, "watching the varied impression, made by the cataract, on those who disturbed me, and returning to unwearied contemplation, when left alone." No disaster is recorded, but the hint of terror is introduced early in the sketch with the reference to a madman plunging into the falls, and recurs with the brief description of a young man who stands close to the edge of the rock, deep in contemplation of Horseshoe Falls. "His whole soul seemed to go forth and be transported thither, till the staff slipped from his relaxed grasp, and falling down—down—down—struck upon the fragment of the Table Rock."

We need not specify in detail Hawthorne's use of the accidental encounter and the disaster in familiar stories like "The Ambitious Guest" and "Ethan Brand." Suffice it to say that his effort toward the renewal of perception is summed up in "The New Adam and Eve," which begins with a doomsday vision in which all living creatures have been destroyed but (as if in anticipation of the neutron bomb) human artifacts remain untouched. The opening sentences cannot be bettered as a statement of Hawthorne's ambivalent attitude toward man's symbolic transformation of his environment: "We who are born into the world's artificial system can never adequately know how little in our present state and circumstances is natural, and how much is merely the interpolation of the perverted mind and heart of man. Art has become a second and stronger nature; she is a stepmother, whose crafty tenderness has taught us to despise the bountiful and wholesome ministrations of our true parent. It is only through the medium of the imagination that we can lessen those iron fetters, which we call truth and reality, and make ourselves even partially sensible what prisoners we are."

I said that this statement could not be bettered, but as a compulsive interpreter I must add two comments. The first is that in Hawthorne's view, man is imprisoned by art (defined broadly here as his symbol-making capacity); yet the only partial exit from this prison is through that same image-making activity. Second, it seems significant that Hawthorne sees this creatureless, symbol-cluttered world not from the perspective of a man from another planet (as a modern writer might) but through the eyes of traditional biblical characters recast as the new Adam and Eve.

I agree completely with Hyatt Waggoner that Hawthorne admired the faith of the "old-time" Christian authors—Dante, Spenser, Bunyan—that he "held on as best he could to a faith he honored and, as he hoped, shared in its essentials." But even more to the point is Waggoner's comment that Hawthorne deliberately blurred his eye on some matters of belief because, for him, humanly significant truth "was more given than achieved, given in the epiphanies and revelations of symbols."[20] I would only add that for Hawthorne this gift was also the primal curse; it gave man consciousness, but separated him from the other animals and his environment. As an artist, he was peculiarly sensitive to the "joys and sorrows of symbol-mongering" (Percy, p. 45). This is why labels like "Christian," "Puritan," "skeptic," "transcendentalist," and "naturalist" seem ultimately unsatisfactory in defining his beliefs. Not a systematic thinker, he nevertheless anticipated the findings of Jung, Cassirer, and Langer. But he put much more emphasis than they on what man has lost in symbolically transforming his world.

To overstate the case slightly, Hawthorne's characters err insofar as they "become symbolical of something"; yet without this identifying tag they blur away into nothing. If we view the corpus of his fiction as if it were a puppet show or an open-air theatrical performance (to use two of his analogies), what would we see? A series of figures: a woman wearing a scarlet letter, another wearing pink ribbons, another a mantle, a young man in a forest, brandishing a staff, another inside a laboratory, surrounded by scientific equipment, another resembling the statue of a marble faun. Here is a series of processions, with people carrying cards labeled "Mr. Gathergold," "Mr. Wind-of-Doctrine," and so on. Another set of performances would show the artist at work, creating his illusions of life: a mechanical butterfly, a wooden figurehead, a scarecrow, a snow-image, a miniature. But as Leo Levy has observed, concisely summing up a familiar problem, the aesthetic image has a precarious existence. The essence of its being is metamorphosis, just as the familiar objects in the author's parlor are transformed by moonlight and firelight. Yet, existing as it does between the two poles of the actual and the imaginary, the artistic creation either moves "too far toward the actual, so that the distinction between the beautiful and the real is blurred or lost; or it may swing toward the other boundary, in which case the beautiful becomes unreal, involving itself in the life of dreams, fantasies, or wishes."[21] The showman's dilemma dramatizes the old war between spiritual and materialistic explanations of the human condition. As consistent systems, neither is satisfactory alone; yet efforts to combine them are incoherent or delusive.

But Hawthorne was not a puppeteer, a sculptor, or a carpenter (though in a moment of despair he reportedly said to Elizabeth Peabody, "If I could only make tables . . . I should feel myself more of a man".[22] Insofar as he escaped from the dilemma described above, he did so by being crafty in his craft. Poe said that Hawthorne's style was "metaphor run-mad"; Taylor Stoehr has aptly commented that he used "a heavily metaphorical style in which whatever is described seems always on the verge of turning into its metaphorical description."[23] I would go further and suggest that, for Hawthorne, language was at once a kind of disease (the "plague of letters" is purified in "Earth's Holocaust") and also a cure. Catachresis, fully understood, is catharsis; that is, as its Greek roots suggest, it means both to misuse and to make complete use of words or phrases. In the same way, a metonym both names and misnames. One can see Hawthorne's typical way with language in this notebook passage: "To make literal pictures of figurative expressions;—for instance, he burst into tears—a man suddenly turned into a shower of briny drops. An explosion of laughter—a man blowing up, and his fragments flying about on all sides. He cast his eyes upon the ground—a man standing eyeless, with his eyes on the ground, staring up at him in wonderment &c &c &c." (*American Notebooks*, Centenary Edition, VIII: 254). These examples, even though they hint at a link in Hawthorne's mind between linguistic analysis and fragmentation, may seem unpromising, the kind of fanciful conceits that so irritated F. O. Matthiessen. But they point to what Hawthorne does at his best as well as at his worst; observing the fluid dialectic between literal and figurative is the way into and out of his stylistic labyrinth.

This dialectic is a dynamic and continuous process in which the recognition of either literal or figurative meanings depends radically on our recognition, at nearly the same time, of the one, the other, or both.[24] The situation is further complicated by the fact that, especially with innovative metaphors, the reader is not always sure which is the tenor and which is the vehicle—that is, which is the local term and which is the imported term.[25] To use Morse Peckham's example, the apparently ridiculous metaphor, "chocolate kilowatt," can be meaningful if one pictures a person, tired after driving many hours, entering a store and buying a candy bar. He returns to his car with new energy and says, "That was a chocolate kilowatt." Here "chocolate" is the local term, "kilowatt" the imported term. He is saying that the candy bar gave him a charge (to use a paler metaphor). Suppose, on the other hand, our man has been suffering through a power outage, his apartment dark and cold. The outage is repaired and he flips the light switch, enjoying the sweet sensation of the power coming back on. Now "kilowatt" is the local term and "chocolate" the imported term. The verbal host and guest have changed places (reminding us that both "host" and "guest" go back to Latin *hospes,* meaning both guest and host). All we know is figure and ground, but the figure may be a shape shifter (the word goes back to Latin *fingere,* just as "fiction" does, and thus is both a shaping and a feigning). And as we have just seen, the context or ground may change as well.

Hawthorne grounds his fictions in this groundlessness, constructs his castles in the air out of this paradox. What would happen, he wonders, if various citizens of the actual world entered "The Hall of Fantasy"? One group consists of sagacious businessmen and technologists who assume that their words are firmly linked with objects. Theirs is the language of the bottom line; they are like Bottom in *A Midsummer Night's Dream,* "trapped in a world of wild fantasy to which his literalism makes him eminently vulnerable" (McCanles, p. 283). As Hawthorne puts it, there "was a character of detail and matter of fact to their talk which concealed the extravagance of its purport." They are dangerous because they mistake words for things, fantasy for brick and mortar. The fiction writer, like the poet, "knows his whereabouts, and therefore is less likely to make a fool of himself in real life." He knows that the literal meanings of his words are constantly turning into metaphors and thus is able to exploit the hypothetical or "as if" nature of his discourse.

A somewhat similar point is made in "A Virtuoso's Collection." The virtuoso has gathered a large number of objects that, it turns out, are words that have literally become things. Thus the narrator observes Spenser's milk-white lamb, Shelley's skylark, Coleridge's albatross, and so on. Even the device of listing or cataloging seems to give them some degree of solidity. The sketch is primarily just a game, and one that Hawthorne shared with his friends for years before publishing the piece. But it has its serious side too, for the virtuoso is a particular kind of literalist, a man who has cut through the mysteries of language by reifying fictive discourse, solidifying imaginative writing into the crudest kind of realism. The ironic result is that he has grown to despise all these things that have been ripped from their fictive context; his packaged guided tour ends in cynicism and despair. For Hawthorne he is the symbol of alienated man, the Wandering Jew.

One could point almost everywhere in Hawthorne's work to variations of this theme, including some of his difficulties in fusing the literal actions of his plots with the metaphorical meanings he wants them to assume. But I prefer to conclude with a brief examination of the book that best exemplifies the oscillation between the literal and the figurative. This, of course, is *The Scarlet Letter.* Two passages from the sketches we have just examined lead into Hawthorne's accomplishment in his masterpiece. At the end of "The Hall of Fantasy," he observes that one should move back and forth from the actual world to the world of fantasy in order to spiritualize "the grossness of this actual life." The other item is one that, according to Lathrop, Hawthorne composed but did not use in his virtuoso's museum: "A few of the 'words that burn,' in an old match-safe (very rare)." The flaming words become the central metaphor of *The Scarlet Letter,* a book that progressively spiritualizes the grossness of ac-tual life. [26]

The book begins with a leisurely but acute analysis of the Custom House, showing how the reality of ordi-nary life is socially constructed through custom, routine, role playing, institutionalization.[27] Hawthorne lingers, with considerable relish, over his portrait of the Inspec-tor. "Looking at him merely as an animal—and there was very little else to look at—he was a most satisfactory ob-ject." By the end of the book, virtually all the stuff of the Custom House and the carnality of mankind have been purified by Hawthorne's words of flame, so that we are left with only a point of light, the letter glowing against its sable background.

Hawthorne's notebook entry, cited at the beginning of this paper, imagines letters as figures of men. In this book, of course, the letter *A* is imagined as a child; it is incarnate in Pearl, the "character of flame," who has learned the "great letter *A*" in the horn-book. What other literary work has been so successful in breathing life into a letter? In *Mardi,* Melville devoted a chapter to *A, I,* and *O;* Wallace Stevens asserted that "*A* is an infant . . . stand-ing on infant legs," and convinced us that the Comedian could be seen as the letter *C.*[28] Several writers, including Poe, have given prominence to *O,* Omega, the end, the object whose story is finally pornographic. But *The Scarlet Letter* is the only fictive work that perfectly fuses the ex-pressive, representational, and objective aspects of lan-guage, transforming even its fragments into capital.

I mean "capital" literally. The Decapitated Surveyor gets his revenge not only in the quietly murderous pref-ace but in the text of the novel itself. There are the numerous references to heads, beginning with the comment about the ignominy of being pilloried and including the description of Governor Bellingham, whose elaborate ruff made his head look like John the Baptist's on a platter. The book is studded with capitals: all the explicit and implicit associations that cluster around the letter A; a profusion of proper names, places, and institutions, some of them historically based, some not, some debatable in their origin;[29] capitalized abstractions, like Love, Passion, Shame, Despair, Solitude, Remorse, Cowardice. And, of course, there is the capitalization of the book's guiding metaphor, the Tongue of Flame.[30]

The book gracefully achieves its truth by affirming and dissolving, concealing and revealing the supposed boundaries of matter and spirit, outer and inner, time and space. Metonym, the trope archaically known as "the Misnomer," is one of Hawthorne's ways of being true by naming and misnaming. Pearl's name, chosen by Hester as the emblem of her inner being, is regarded as a misnomer by John Wilson, who judges the "scarlet vision" only by her external hue. "Pearl?—Ruby, rather! or Coral! or Red Rose, at the very least." But we know that Pearl's name matches her inner significance, and, unlike most of the characters in the book, we literally and figuratively know her origins. She is based upon Hawthorne's daughter Una, who is named after Spenser's Una, who is based upon an abstraction called truth, which is based on language, which is based on internal relationships. (This is the Quaker Oats Box Effect in action.) So when Hawthorne has Hester ask Pearl "Art thou my child, in very truth?" he knows what he is doing.

Out of the warped, deformed figures that make up our catachrestic language, Hawthorne weaves his inspired personification of secret guilt. "Under the appellation of Roger Chillingworth, the reader will remember, was hidden another name," and as I noted two decades ago, the other name is not only Prynne—it is Guilt. If the identity of Pearl's father is the first secret, the identity of Roger Chillingworth is the second, and on the figurative level it seems to be one that is still unrevealed to some readers. Consider first, on a commonsense level, the accuracy of Hawthorne's personification. As the wronged husband, Chillingworth would seem to be the innocent party in this triangle. But this is only true if we see him from inside, from his point of view; and we don't. Instead, we see him as the adulterers do. And what person is more likely to produce feelings of guilt in the errant wife and her lover than the wronged husband?

Moving closer to Hawthorne's text, we notice that our perception of the literal and figurative levels is cumulative rather than instantaneous. After Chillingworth moves into Dimmesdale's house, we read in chapter 10 that he groped with a stealthy, cautious tread into the minister's dim interior. Later, in chapter 18, we read this familiar passage, which clinches Chillingworth's figurative identity:

> And be the stern and sad truth spoken, that the breach which guilt has once made into the human soul is never, in this mortal state repaired. It may be watched and guarded; so that the enemy shall not force his way again into the citadel, and might even in his subsequent assaults, select some other avenue, in preference to that where he had formerly succeeded. But there is still the ruined wall, and, near it, the *stealthy tread* of the foe that would win over again his unforgotten triumph. [My italics.]

Hawthorne's characteristic method is to use a simile or metaphor on one page and make it part of the literal action elsewhere. So Chillingworth is described on one page as digging into the poor clergyman's heart "like a sexton delving into a grave"; a page or so later, the old man has gathered some herbs that he found growing on a grave. Or we are told that Dimmesdale's "converse" with Chillingworth afforded him some temporary relief: "It was as if a window were thrown open, admitting a freer atmosphere." A few pages later, the two men perceive Pearl in the graveyard, with Dimmesdale "looking instinctively from the open window." Interesting in his own right as a kind of heartless psychoanalyst, Chillingworth's figurative role is even more important. As a symbol of secret guilt, he is a leech, draining away Dimmesdale's will and energy. But as the ending of the book demonstrates, he is also the healer.

The book's plot turns, then, on riddles of origin (who is Pearl's real father?) and relationship ("Who is that man, Hester?"). And, given his purposes, Hawthorne's heavily Latinate diction and artfully chosen New England archaisms provide the perfect channel for expressing "the highest truths through the humblest medium of familiar words and images." The book's structure is fearless symmetry; distilling its language patterns of utterance and vision, its themes of origin and relationship, it ends with the one word that fuses the Letter of Scarlet with the Tongue of Flame. "Gules" in its heraldic context or relationship means "scarlet," but its origin is the Latin *gula,* meaning "throat." This is the perfect capstone for a book that capitalizes upon the guilty heart's native language.

NOTES

1. *New England Quarterly,* 42 (1969), 163–179.
2. Centenary Edition of the *Works of Nathaniel Hawthorne,* ed. Claude M. Simpson (Columbus: Ohio State University Press, 1972), pp. 8, 183.
3. *Anatomy of Criticism* (Princeton: Princeton University Press, 1957), pp. 76–77.
4. "Indeterminacy and the Reader's Response to Prose Fiction," in *Aspects of Narrative,* ed. J. Hillis Miller (New York: Columbia University Press, 1971), p. 8.
5. For disjunctive categories, see Jerome S. Bruner, *A Study of Thinking* (New York: John Wiley, 1956), p. 159, and Morse Peckham, *Man's Rage for Chaos* (New York: Chilton, 1965), pp. 47–49.
6. *The Mirror and the Lamp* (New York: Oxford University Press, 1953), pp. 3–29.
7. See, for example, Jacques Lacan's "Seminar on 'The Purloined Letter,'" trans. Jeffrey Mehlman ("French Freud"), *Yale French Studies,* 48 (1972), 38–72, and Jacques Derrida's response in "The Purveyor of Truth," trans. Willis Domingo, James Hulbert, Moshe Ron, and Marie-Rose Logan ("Graphesis"), *Yale French Studies,* 52 (1975), 31–113. The insights of the French deconstruction workers

parallel in some ways those of Kenneth Burke. Both have been put to good use by J. Hillis Miller and Geoffrey H. Hartman. For current examples of what this kind of criticism can do, see Miller's brilliant article, "Stevens' Rock and Criticism as Cure," *Georgia Review,* 30 (1976), 5–31; Homer O. Brown, "The Errant Letter and the Whispering Gallery," *Genre,* 10 (1977), 573–599; Jacob Korg, "Hopkins' Linguistic Deviations," *PMLA,* 92 (1977), 977–985; and Philip Furia and Martin Roth, "Stevens' Fusky Alphabet," *PMLA,* 93 (1978), 66–77.

8. F. O. Mathiessen, *American Renaissance* (New York: Oxford University Press, 1941), pp. 5–43, 83–99, 517–531. See also my "Whitman's Radical Utterance," *ESQ,* no. 60 (1970), pp. 73–75.

9. Introduction to his edition of Poe's poetry, Laurel Poetry Series (New York: Dell, 1959), p. 19.

10. "Poe's Closet Monologues," *Genre,* 10 (1977), 225.

11. The difficulty of reconciling the serious and comic aspects of Poe's fiction is notorious. The best full-length treatment of this problem is G. R. Thompson's *Poe's Fiction* (Madison: University of Wisconsin Press, 1973).

12. Tony Tanner has some brief but suggestive comments on this aspect of Hawthorne in *City of Words: American Fiction, 1950–1970* (New York: Harper and Row, 1971), pp. 23–25.

13. Quoted from Morris Eaves, "Blake and the Artistic Machine: An Essay in Decorum and Technology, *PMLA,* 92 (1977), 905.

14. Beatrice Warde, *Alphabet,* quoted by Marshall McLuhan in *Understanding Media* (New York: McGraw-Hill, 1965), p. 171.

15. Matthiessen, in *American Renaissance* (pp. 211–212), points out that "Hawthorne had quite as good an ear as Thoreau had, or Melville. . . . Yet Hawthorne's ripest work, to say nothing of his sketches, contains hardly a trace of conversational idiom."

16. *American Notebooks,* Centenary Edition, VIII:294.

17. "A Book of Autographs," in *Complete Works of Nathaniel Hawthorne* (Cambridge, Mass.: Riverside Press; Boston: Houghton Mifflin, 1882), XII:88–89.

18. *American Notebooks,* Centenary Edition, VIII:16.

19. *The Message in the Bottle* (New York: Farrar, Straus, and Giroux, 1975), p. 51.

20. "Art and Belief," in *Nathaniel Hawthorne,* ed. J. Donald Crowley (New York: McGraw-Hill, 1975), pp. 133–143.

21. "'Lifelikeness' in Hawthorne's Fiction," *Nathaniel Hawthorne Journal, 1975,* p. 142.

22. George P. Lathrop, *A Study of Hawthorne* (Boston: Houghton-Mifflin, 1876; reprinted New York, 1969), p. 181.

23. "'Young Goodman Brown' and Hawthorne's Theory of Mimesis," *Nineteenth-Century Fiction,* 23 (1968), 395.

24. See Michael McCanles, "The Literal and the Metaphorical: Dialectic or Interchange," *PMLA,* 91 (1976), 279–290.

25. I am indebted here to Morse Peckham, "Metaphor: A Little Plain Speaking on a Weary Subject," in *The Triumph of Roman-*

ticism (Columbia: University of South Carolina Press, 1970), pp. 401–419.

26. For the best discussion of the book's attenuation of reality, see Charles Feidelson's article on *The Scarlet Letter* in *Hawthorne Centenary Essays,* ed. Roy Harvey Pearce (Columbus: Ohio State University Press, 1964).

27. For a modern sociological discussion of this process, see Peter L. Berger and Thomas Luckmann, *The Social Construction of Reality* (New York, 1966).

28. See the article in *PMLA* by Furia and Roth, cited in note 8.

29. Did Hawthorne, with his well-known interest in Archbishop Laud, derive Chillingworth's name from the English theologian William Chillingworth (1602–1694), who reputedly informed to Laud against Alexander Gill (who was tried and sentenced to lose his ears)? Did he get the name of Prynne from the English Puritan pamphleteer William Prynne (1600–1669), who was Laud's relentless enemy and who was punished by having his cheeks branded with the letters *SL* (Seditious Libeler)?

30. See chapter VI of my *Hawthorne's Tragic Vision* (Austin: University of Texas Press, 1957).

Romantic Iconology in *The Scarlet Letter* and *The Blithedale Romance*

Donald A. Ringe

Because it is so firmly grounded in the social world of nineteenth-century America, *The Blithedale Romance* has often been seen as markedly different from the three symbolic romances that surround it in the Hawthorne canon. Critics from Henry James to Arlin Turner have emphasized its realism and closeness to actuality,[1] and Richard H. Fogle has seen in this fact a major artistic problem for its author: because he "is dealing with contemporary life," Fogle writes, Hawthorne has some difficulty in "wresting from its confusion and phenomenal chaos the kind of design and meaning which alone interest him."[2] Many critics, of course, have found design in *Blithedale,* as, for example, such scholars as Hyatt H. Waggoner, who describes a pattern involving the veil/fire imagery that runs through the book, or Robert Stanton, who perceives a form and theme based on the interrelation of nature and the human spirit.[3] All such interpretations, however, leave the reader with the uneasy feeling that the problem of form in the book has not really been solved. Its strong contemporary quality has not been properly reconciled with its romance elements, and its relation to Hawthorne's other major work has not been fully shown.[4]

Most, if not all, of these problems can be solved if we approach *The Blithedale Romance* from the point of view of romantic iconology and examine the book in terms of the moral geography implied in the spatial metaphor that informs the book. It is clear, for example, from the first five chapters, that Hawthorne, in setting up his romance, is arranging his spatial elements as carefully as he had done in *The Scarlet Letter* and *The House of the Seven Gables*. Miles Coverdale leaves the city, presumably Boston, to join the Blithedale community in the midst of a wintry blast that impinges significantly on his consciousness. He plunges "into the heart of the pitiless snow-storm, in quest of a better life," and travels along the road past stone fences, "half-buried in the wave-like drifts," while "snow-spray" blows about him. The storm in these passages seems to have taken on the quality of the sea, and it even appears, after he has arrived at Blithedale and the evening lowers, to warn him and his companions back from the adventurous enterprise on which they are embarked to "the boundaries of ordinary life."[5]

As the evening wears on and they sit near the blazing hearth of the Blithedale kitchen, Coverdale increasingly envisions the storm in terms of the sea and Blithedale itself as an island within it. The firelight is so cheering that he and his companions care "not what inclemency might rage and roar, on the other side of [the] illuminated windows" (III, 23), and he hopes that their "blazing windows will be visible a great way off. There is nothing so pleasant and encouraging to a solitary traveller, on a stormy night, as a flood of firelight, seen amid the gloom. These ruddy window-panes cannot fail to cheer the hearts of all that look at them. Are they not warm and bright with the beacon-fire which we have kindled for humanity?" (III, 25). Developed even thus far, the spatial metaphor has three distinct elements in it: the city, which symbolizes the boundaries and conventionalities of everyday life; the storm or sea, into which the characters move in quest of a higher life; and the island, Blithedale, set in the sea and providing a beacon light for others who are embarked on a similar enterprise.

This concept is strongly reinforced in the fifth chapter of the book, when the inhabitants of Blithedale retire to the sitting room after their first supper at the farm. Priscilla has also arrived from the city, and as Coverdale observes the group, he brings to a focus the spatial image he has been developing since he left the city and applies it to Priscilla:

> The sense of vast, undefined space, pressing from the outside against the black panes of our uncurtained windows, was fearful to the poor girl, heretofore accustomed to the narrowness of human limits, with the lamps of neighboring tenements glimmering across the street. The house probably seemed to her adrift on the great ocean of the night. A little parallelogram of sky was all that she had hitherto known of nature; so that she felt the awfulness that really exists in its limitless extent. [III, 36]

All three elements—city, sea, and island—combine in Coverdale's imagination as he perceives the apprehension of the city-bred girl in the face of the violent and seemingly limitless storm.[6]

That the image has application as well to both Coverdale and the other inhabitants of the community is made clear by additional comments that both he and they make. "The evening wore on," he writes, "and the outer solitude looked in upon us through the windows, gloomy, wild, and vague, like another state of existence, close beside the littler sphere of warmth and light in which we were the prattlers and bustlers of a moment" (III, 37). This image is extended by others who have gathered in the Blithedale parlor. As they try to invent a name for their farm, some suggest that it should be called "'The Oasis,' in view of its being the one green spot in the moral sand-waste of the world" (III, 37). This suggestion adds a new dimension to the spatial image that Coverdale has been developing. The oasis is the symbolic equivalent of the island, for each is a place of refuge in a surrounding waste of sand or water. Blithedale is therefore an oasis/island in a desert/sea, represented here by the threatening chaos of the wintry storm.

In the complex, extended metaphor of the opening chapters of his book, Hawthorne is creating his version of a romantic iconology that appears in the works of many artists. Coverdale's plunge into the storm as he leaves the city is analogous to the plunge of the *Pequod* into the Atlantic as it sails from Nantucket on its romantic quest, and the withdrawal of warmth and life into the farmhouse serves much the same function as the similar withdrawal that John Greenleaf Whittier was later to describe in *Snow-Bound*. The sea/storm thus has both a positive and a negative value. As W. H. Auden has pointed out in *The Enchafed Flood,* the sea is the place of freedom, solitude, openness, and potentiality, where one may escape the confines of community life, but it is also the place of primitive—and frightening—power. The romantic island, then—and, of course, the oasis, too—is a private place, set apart from both the city and the sea. It is "the earthly paradise," the place of innocence, where one may pause temporarily on the romantic voyage.[7] In Hawthorne's version of the spatial metaphor, it is the "cold . . . Arcadia" that Blithedale becomes to Coverdale's perception that first night on the farm, when he wakes from disturbed sleep and looks out across the snowy, moonlit landscape (III, 38).

Some crucial aspects of Hawthorne's metaphor are immediately apparent. Though Coverdale says he is seeking a new life when he enters the sea/storm world, and thus seems about to embark on romantic voyaging, he does not pursue the figure. He stresses instead the danger and threat of that world in the sitting-room scene, and converts it into a frozen waste when he looks out the window at night. From this point on, Coverdale all but drops the image of infinite space and concentrates instead on the remaining elements of the metaphor: the city and the oasis/island. The latter soon turns out not to be an earthly paradise—it is, after all, "a counterfeit Arcadia" (III, 21)—nor a place of innocence, where, in Auden's words, "there is no conflict between natural desire and moral duty."[8] There is conflict aplenty in Blithedale— between Coverdale and Hollingsworth, between Zenobia and Priscilla, and between Hollingsworth and Zenobia— and the community turns out to be, perhaps, not the Oasis that some would have named it, but the Saharah, which, at the same moment, others had whispered it might become. Thus if Coverdale did indeed conceive that he, and perhaps the others, were embarked on a voyage to a better life, that journey is soon frustrated by human passion, and the oasis/island turns into a moral wasteland.[9]

Coverdale does not, of course, immediately recognize this truth. When he reads the transcendentalists during his convalescence from the cold he caught on his journey to Blithedale, he thinks them "well adapted . . . to pilgrims like ourselves, whose present bivouâc was considerably farther into the waste of chaos than any mortal army of crusaders had ever marched before" (III, 52), and he later sees the little band of reformers as carrying the "high enterprise" of their Pilgrim forebears "to a point which they never dreamed of attaining" (III, 117). Shortly thereafter, however, he reaches the moment of crisis in his relations with Hollingsworth, when he refuses to enlist in his philanthropic cause, and he immediately withdraws to the city. Coverdale feels at first like "a traveller, long sojourning in remote regions, and at length sitting down again amid customs once familiar" (III, 145), and though he experiences a strange sensation, in which the city and Blithedale seem alternately unreal, he settles at last into the cold conventionality of city life. The other major characters either die or move away from Blithedale, and by the time he writes the romance— twelve years after the events he recounts—the Blithedale community has long ceased to exist.

That Coverdale thinks of the Blithedale experience in terms of his Pilgrim forebears is highly suggestive and directs our attention back to *The Scarlet Letter,* where a similar community of devoted reformers is presented through much the same spatial metaphor. Seventeenth-century Boston, in Roger Chillingworth's words, is a "wild outskirt of the earth" (I, 76), begirt on one side by the sea and on the other by a forest wilderness, which serves the same symbolic function. Like Blithedale, Boston is an island in a desert waste, but, unlike the latter community, it embodies a value and purpose that allows it to exist and go forward in spite of the threatening chaos that surrounds it. The Puritan settlers are not only convinced of the righteousness of their actions but foresee as well, in Dimmesdale's vision, "a high and glorious destiny for the newly gathered people of the Lord" (I, 249). From their point of view, the forest and the sea are wild and lawless regions, and the forest in particular is a heathen place that has never been "subjugated by human law, nor illumined by higher truth" (I, 203). It is, on the one hand, the abode of the Black Man, the embodiment of evil, but it is also, on the other hand, the area of possibility, from which their New Jerusalem will be carved.

Hawthorne maintains the relative values of forest/sea and island throughout the book. The Puritan community glories in its enforcement of both civil and religious law as the story opens, and the final scene reaffirms the principle of organized society in its description of the New England holiday in honor of the election of the new governor. The forest and sea, on the other hand, are consistently depicted as chaotic and lawless wastes, from the moment that Chillingworth, who eventually turns himself into an incarnation of evil, arrives in the city with his Indian captor, until he arranges with the buccaneer captain to accompany Hester and Dimmesdale in their flight. Mistress Hibbins, the reputed witch, constantly reminds the sinners that they have made a compact with the Black Man in the forest, and Hester once admits to little Pearl that she had met him there and that the "scarlet letter is his mark" (I, 185). Though Arthur Dimmesdale will not concede to Mistress Hibbins that he has done the same (I, 221), his denial rings false. In the forest, in fact, he has just agreed to flee with Hester across the sea to Europe.

Hester, perhaps, stands in a closer relation to the forest than any other character. Because of her sin and ignominy, she is placed in a unique relation to her environment, "as if a new birth . . . had converted the forest-land, still so uncongenial to every other pilgrim and wanderer, into Hester Prynne's wild and dreary, but life-long home" (I, 80). Not that Hester becomes, like the Indians, a creature of the forest: her relationship with Pearl keeps her in a miniature society, apart, but not totally divorced, from the greater one in Boston. Her situation is well symbolized by her home. Though "not in close vicinity to any other habitation," the thatched cottage to which she moves, after her ordeal on the scaffold, is "within the verge of the peninsula," and near enough to Boston to lie within the order of society. But it also stands "on the shore, looking across a basin of the sea at the forest-covered hills, towards the west" (I, 81). It too is a kind of island, set apart from the larger one of the Puritan community, but also distinctly separated from the forest/sea that encompasses them both.

Though the spatial metaphor in *The Scarlet Letter* is much the same as that described by Auden (the "city," of course, is the European community from which the settlers have come), it cannot be called romantic in the strictest sense. Rather, Hawthorne seems to have used the spatial pattern to establish the moral geography of the book largely in terms of the manner in which the Puritans in Boston might have seen their relation to the world that surrounded them. Yet this is not his only use of the metaphor. He employs the image toward the end of *The Scarlet Letter* in a manner more consonant with its usual romantic function. On one occasion—the famous forest scene, in which Hester and Dimmesdale meet alone as lovers after more than seven years apart—the pattern of imagery shifts and the forest takes on a meaning related to, but nonetheless markedly different from, what it usually signifies in the romance. The "island" of Boston becomes the constricting town; the unlimited forest and sea are transmuted into places of freedom, where the self may explore and grow;[10] and the forest dell, where the lovers meet, is transformed into a truly romantic island.

This "island" is, of course, completely surrounded by forest, but as the scene develops, the image of the sea is also kept before the reader. Both the forest and the sea had early been presented as alternatives for Hester's escape from Boston, if she had not chosen to remain (I, 79), and now that she has reestablished the bond of faith with her lover by revealing the only secret she had kept from him—the identity of her husband—she offers the same alternatives to Dimmesdale: the "forest-track," which, she says, can lead him to freedom and happiness, or "the broad pathway of the sea," on which he can return to Europe (I, 197). Thus both are means of escape from the crippling Puritan environment, where, Hester believes, his "better part" had been kept "in bondage too long," crushed beneath a "seven years' weight of misery." But, she says, "thou shalt leave it all behind thee! It shall not cumber thy steps, as thou treadest along the forest-path; neither shalt thou freight the ship with it, if thou prefer to cross the sea." He can, she believes, "begin all anew," and as a pledge of her support she promises to go with him (I, 197–198).

Once this decision is made, the effect is immediate. The minister feels "a glow of strange enjoyment" as he breathes "the wild, free atmosphere of an unredeemed, unchristianized, lawless region"; his spirit rises with a bound, and he feels as if he had been born anew (I, 201–202). Hester removes the letter from her breast and lets down her hair, feeling at once a great sense of relief. "Her sex, her youth," and her beauty return to cluster "themselves, with her maiden hope, and a happiness before unknown, within the magic circle of this hour" (I, 202). Indeed, even nature itself seems to respond to their decision. "All at once, as with a sudden smile of heaven, forth burst the sunshine, pouring a very flood into the

obscure forest, gladdening each green leaf, transmuting
the yellow fallen ones to gold, and gleaming adown the
gray trunks of the solemn trees" (I, 202–203). This is,
without question, the paradisaical interlude on the
romantic island, where, freed, at least for the moment,
from the moral and legal constraints of the city, the seek-
ers may pause before they continue their quest for happiness across the open sea.

But the interlude cannot last. It is, after all, a kind of
everlasting present, freed from time and all the constraints of the past, and opening up before them the illusion of a future unrelated to what has already occurred.
Hester believes that she can leave the past behind, that
Dimmesdale, on his voyage, will not be freighted with his
burden of misery, that—by simply removing the scarlet
letter from her breast—she can "undo it all, and make it
as it had never been" (I, 202). The scarlet letter is not,
however, the only physical sign of the adultery, there is
also Pearl; and if Hester intends to "undo it all" by
merely throwing the letter away, she must also reject the
child, that other physical sign of the sin. Neither, however, is so easily disposed of. Hester cannot reject the
child—who, rather, rejects her mother, until she takes
up the letter again—and though Hester thinks to be rid
of the sign in either forest or sea, the implication is
strong that neither course is possible. The romantic island, therefore, is only an illusion—a moment out of
time, when acts no longer seem to have their natural consequences.

Dimmesdale learns this truth long before Hester
does. On his way back to the town, he perceives the forest path as "wilder, more uncouth with its rude natural
obstacles, and less trodden by the foot of man, than he
remembered it on his outward journey" (I, 216); the
town and its inhabitants look different to his eyes; and he
is filled with a desire to do gratuitous evil to those he
meets. If the forest has seemed to him to be liberating, it
is also the place where he has sinned again and been
made aware of its consequences. Such knowledge cannot

be ignored by a man like Dimmesdale, and he soon decides that there can be no flight for him. Hester, on the other hand, maintains her belief that escape is possible, and she makes arrangements with the captain of the ship for their passage to England. Her enlightenment comes when she learns that Chillingworth has detected their purposes, and that he plans to accompany them wherever they go. Hester is brought to an impasse by this knowledge, and only the confession and death of Dimmesdale on the scaffold resolves the problem for her. The romantic interlude ends, therefore, not with a voyage into space but with a return to the confines of the city.

With that return, the city again becomes the Puritan island, set in the lawless wilderness of forest and sea. Now, however, elements from both these regions encroach upon it in a way they had not done earlier. "Rough figures, whose attire of deer-skins marked them as belonging to some of the forest settlements" (I, 226), appear for the first time, and the town is invaded not only by Indians, the wild and "painted barbarians" of the forest, but also by the even wilder mariners from the Spanish Main. They are "rough-looking desperadoes, with sun-blackened faces," whose eyes, "even in good nature and merriment, had a kind of animal ferocity" (I, 232).[11] The colony of saints has clearly changed from what it had been during the first scaffold scene. Even the Puritan settlers, harking back to the pleasures of the merry England from which they came, engage in "wrestling-matches" and a "bout at quarterstaff"; even "on the platform of the pillory . . . two masters of defence [begin] an exhibition with the buckler and broadsword," but are stopped by "the town beadle, who had no idea of permitting the majesty of the law to be violated by such an abuse of one of its consecrated places" (I, 231–232).

Thus if Puritan Boston seems freer, more open, more expansive at the close of the book than it did at the beginning, it is clear that much of this appearance has been purchased by the entry of lawlessness, which is rep-

resented by the forest and the sea, and the island com-
monwealth no longer maintains the principles on which it
had established itself, as a region apart from both the
cities of Europe and the forest/sea wilderness in which it
is set. No less than the romantic island on which Hester
and Dimmesdale briefly rest in the forest, the island of
Puritan Boston is not permanent. It too is involved in
time and change, so that it cannot be maintained for long.
Worse, it cannot progress or improve, and its dream of
establishing a New Jerusalem in the wilderness is mere
fantasy. Hawthorne makes the point on the first page of
his romance. "Whatever Utopia of human virtue and
happiness" the settlers might project, they must always
recognize the practical necessity of establishing, at once,
both a cemetery and a prison (I, 47). In other words, man
is fallible and mortal, and on these rocks the utopian society will always founder.

But if seventeenth-century Boston comes to grief on
these shoals, so does nineteenth-century Blithedale. The
utopian community starts with a vision no less millennial
than that of their Puritan forebears, and Coverdale even
looks forward to a time, a century or two in the future,
when later generations will look back on them as the
founders of a new and better way of life. In almost the
same breath, however, Coverdale expresses the opinion
that their "system of human life" will never seem real and
"practical, as well as poetical," to him, "until somebody
has sanctified it by death," and he suggests to Hollingsworth that it might be well "to fix upon a spot for a
cemetery" (III, 130). Hollingsworth, however, has no
patience with Coverdale's view of a millennial future at
Blithedale; he refuses to believe him serious and suggests
instead that Coverdale join him in his "scheme for the
reformation of the wicked by methods moral, intellectual,
and industrial, by the sympathy of pure, humble, and yet
exalted minds, and by opening to his pupils the
possibility of a worthier life than that which had become
their fate" (III, 131).

Coverdale and Hollingsworth, of course, reach an

impasse when Coverdale refuses to join the philanthropist's cause. But more important is the fundamental
issue that each has raised. The cemetery and the prison of
the first chapter of *The Scarlet Letter* are repeated here in
terms of a nineteenth-century utopian society, and the
problem of sin and death is as real and as inimical to the
millennial dreams of the later society as it was to those of
the earlier. Human passion drives the major characters
apart, and Zenobia, rejected by Hollingsworth, ends by
drowning herself in the river. With her death, Blithedale
finds at last "the necessity of a burial-ground" (III, 238),
and Hollingsworth gives up his scheme for the reformation of criminals, concentrating instead on "a single
murderer" (III, 243). Hollingsworth takes on himself the
responsibility for Zenobia's death, and both his philanthropic scheme and that of the inhabitants of Blithedale
come to nothing. In a sense, Blithedale repeats the experience of Puritan Boston: setting out in the beginning
with high hopes for a glorious future, but failing in the
end because of the incurable weakness and fallibility of
human nature.

Seen in these terms, *The Scarlet Letter* and *The
Blithedale Romance* read almost like a double novel, each
part commenting significantly on the other. But there are,
of course, important differences. Puritan Boston has an
intellectual and moral strength that its successor, just two
hundred years later, sadly lacks. In *The Scarlet Letter,* the
sense of a mission into the wilderness is strong, and the
basic moral geography of the book is more obvious and
more significant than that of the latter. The forest and the
sea are real, and if they are the places of freedom and
exploration, so also are they lawless, threatening regions
which, from the point of view of the Puritan island, must
be kept first at bay and at last subdued. The island falls
far short of what it was intended to be, however. Death
was present almost from the first moment, with the passing of Isaac Johnson, whose land supplied the burial plot;
and both the collective sin of the community, whose

judgments are harsh and unchristian, and the particular sins of the individual inhabitants must always prevent the fulfillment of the original, utopian dreams.

Two hundred years later, things are, if anything, worse. Though a small group of people congregates on the Blithedale farm to set up a nineteenth-century version of the utopian colony, there is much less true belief and firmness of purpose among these descendants of the Puritans. Coverdale tends to sentimentalize their mission, few are willing to devote themselves wholeheartedly to the cause, and the summer at Blithedale seems, in the final analysis, to be hardly more than a masquerade. The moral geography of the book, therefore, is less substantial. The forest and the sea, against which the Puritans had to contend, have been reduced to an April storm that soon blows over, and from that point on, there seems to be little outside the community for them to contend with. Indeed, the characters can enter and leave the Blithedale island at will and with little effort. It is only a short trip back to the city—a trip that three of them make toward the end of the Arcadian summer: a clear indication that Blithedale demands, and the characters are willing to make, very little moral commitment. Small wonder, then, that the Blithedale experiment is so early aborted.

The Blithedale Romance, therefore, is more closely related in content and theme to Hawthorne's normal practice than has generally been observed, and its contemporaneous quality serves a real and important function—not to satirize the experiment at Brook Farm, as has sometimes been contended, but to show the inevitable collapse of those millennial ideas that had haunted the New England mind for a full two hundred years. The smallness and thinness of the contemporary characters is obvious when they are compared with those in the earlier book. Coverdale and Hollingsworth lack the moral agony of Dimmesdale, Zenobia lacks the strength of Hester Prynne, and the magician, Westervelt, seems almost trivial beside the satanic Chillingworth.

Blithedale is only a game for some rather ineffectual nineteenth-century intellectuals and reformers, who lack the purpose and passion of their ancestors.

The Blithedale Romance is indeed the dark and somber book that a number of critics have taken it to be, but it is not a failure. Its relation to *The Scarlet Letter* in both content and imagery is so clear and so precisely drawn—it complements that book so closely—that it must be seen as accomplishing exactly what Hawthorne intended.

NOTES

1. Henry James, *Hawthorne* (Ithaca: Cornell University Press, 1956), p. 105; Arlin Turner, *Nathaniel Hawthorne: An Introduction and Interpretation* (New York: Holt, Rinehart and Winston, 1961), pp. 79, 81–82. James, in fact, regrets that as the book progresses, "we get too much out of reality" (p. 108). For a more recent, and rather extreme, statement of this position—that the book should have been more realistic—see Robert C. Elliott, *"The Blithedale Romance," Hawthorne Centenary Essays,* ed. Roy Harvey Pearce (Columbus: Ohio State University Press, 1964), pp. 103–117.

2. Richard H. Fogle, *Hawthorne's Fiction: The Light and the Dark* (rev. ed.; Norman: University of Oklahoma Press, 1964), p. 189.

3. Hyatt H. Waggoner, *Hawthorne: A Critical Study* (rev. ed.; Cambridge, Mass.: Harvard University Press, 1963), pp. 191–205; Robert Stanton, "The Trial of Nature: An Analysis of *The Blithedale Romance,"* *PMLA,* 76 (1961), 528–538. More recent interpretations have generally concerned themselves with the problem of the narrator, the interrelations among the characters, or the ideological meaning that the critic discerns in the book.

4. A. N. Kaul touches briefly on the relation between *The Scarlet Letter* and *The Blithedale Romance,* but in different terms from those in which they are discussed below. See A. N. Kaul, *"The Blithedale Romance,"* *Hawthorne: A Collection of Critical Essays,* ed. A. N. Kaul (Englewood Cliffs, N.J.: Prentice-Hall, 1966), pp. 153–155. This is a reprint of part of the Hawthorne chapter in Kaul's *The American Vision: Actual and Ideal Society in Nineteenth-Century Fiction* (New Haven: Yale University Press, 1963).

5. Nathaniel Hawthorne, *The Blithedale Romance* and *Fanshawe* (Centenary Edition; Columbus: Ohio State University Press, 1964), III:10, 12, 18. All citations of Hawthorne's works in my text are to volume and page numbers in this edition.

6. This important passage has seldom been commented on, and never in any detail, but see Leo B. Levy, *"The Blithedale Romance:* Hawthorne's 'Voyage Through Chaos,'" *Studies in Romanticism,* 8 (1968), 5, where it is briefly touched upon.

7. W. H. Auden, *The Enchafèd Flood; or, The Romantic Iconography of the Sea* (New York: Vintage Books, 1967), pp. 6–25.

8. Auden, *The Enchafèd Flood,* p. 20.

9. Cf. Roy R. Male, *Hawthorne's Tragic Vision* (Austin: University of Texas Press, 1957), p. 141.

10. The forest scene has, of course, been much commented upon, and the many interpretations need not be repeated here. The relative values of city and forest are briefly and correctly noted, however, in R. W. B. Lewis, *The American Adam: Innocence, Tragedy and Tradition in the Nineteenth Century* (Chicago: University of Chicago Press, 1955), pp. 113–114.

11. Cf. Leslie A. Fiedler, *Love and Death in the American Novel* (rev. ed.; New York: Dell, 1966), pp. 435–436.

Art and Illusion:
COLERIDGEAN ASSUMPTIONS IN HAWTHORNE'S TALES AND SKETCHES

Richard Harter Fogle

Nathaniel Hawthorne had a considerable acquaintance with Coleridge's poetry and prose. He encountered Coleridge's poems in the early 1830s, if not earlier, and invested in a three-volume edition of his poetical works later on, as the foundation of a "select library." His book borrowings from the Salem Athenaeum included James Marsh's famous edition of Coleridge's *Aids to Reflection,* the *Biographia Literaria,* and other Coleridgean prose. Casual references here and there— for example, a reference to the Ancient Mariner's albatross in "A Virtuoso's Collection"—indicate his familiarity with the Coleridge canon. More important is what I believe to be the pervasive influence of Coleridge's theoretical criticism upon Hawthorne's literary theory, and even upon his imagination and sense of unity. Hawthorne's notable prefaces constantly track with Coleridge's subtle speculations on "poetic faith," "willing suspension of disbelief," and poetic and dramatic illusion, as does his general sense of "the picturesque," with its values of harmony and contrast.

One of Hawthorne's most Coleridgean statements occurs at the end of his tale "The Antique Ring": "'You know that I can never separate the idea from the symbol in which it manifests itself.'" In "Ethan Brand," the peculiar use of "Idea," though in general both Platonic and transcendental, corresponds with Coleridge's careful discriminations. An idea is not a mere concept, which belongs to the limited realm of the understanding, but a vital and creative organization of the whole mind. The unhappily inspired Brand is possessed by the Unpardonable Sin, an Idea that "had operated as a means of education; it had gone on cultivating his powers to the highest point of which they were susceptible; it had raised him from the level of an unlettered laborer to stand on a star-lit eminence, whither the philosophers of the earth, laden with the lore of universities, might vainly strive to clamber after him." One doubts that Coleridge would have agreed with Hawthorne's application of the term, since the effect of Brand's Idea is absolute separation of his intellect from his heart, which Coleridge does not envision. There is a likeness, however. Unlettered men (by Coleridge's standards), like Boehme and George Fox, have risen to great and star-lit eminence by the living ideas of the reason (*Biographia Literaria,* ch. IX). They are unbalanced. It would have been better if they had been learned, but they have hit upon truth. "Jacob Behmen was an enthusiast in the strictest sense, as not merely distinguished, but as contra-distinguished, from a fanatic." So Hawthorne portrays Ethan Brand, but probably with this difference: Brand *is* fanatic. His mind "has wrought itself by intense and solitary meditation into a high state of *enthusiasm*" (italics mine); but it is doubtful that Hawthorne distinguishes the enthusiast from the fanatic, and Brand's half-truth is in effect false and destructive.

So also is it with the Quaker Catharine in "The Gentle Boy," whose countenance is "wild with enthusiasm and strange sorrows," and who "had strayed from duty in following the dictates of a wild fanaticism." As elsewhere, Hawthorne's interpretation of "symbol" is in application not precisely at one with Coleridge. Yet the line is not easy to draw, since he portrays both Ethan Brand and the Quaker woman with much imaginative sympathy. It is true of them that he "can never separate the idea from the symbol in which it manifests itself." As to theory of character, "The Gentle Boy" suggests, among other matters, a further resemblance between Hawthorne and Coleridge, who explained the relative colorlessness of Shakespeare's heroines not as a defect but as representative of a more complex harmony than is given to men. The strongest character in Hawthorne's tale is Dorothy Pearson. "Her mild but saddened features, and neat matronly attire, harmonized together. . . . Her very aspect proved that she was blameless . . . in respect to God and man; while the enthusiast, in her robe of sack-cloth and girdle of knotted cord, had as evidently violated the duties of the present life and the future, by fixing her attention wholly on the latter." A further statement is definitely un-Coleridgean: "The two females, as they held each a hand of Ilbrahim, formed a practical allegory; it was rational piety and unbridled fanaticism contending for the empire of a young heart." Hawthorne is not distinguishing between symbol and allegory, as Coleridge would have.

"The Gentle Boy" is a long and weighty tale. As such, it contains a number of Coleridgean motifs, along with other suggestions of romanticism. In its opening tableau, the child Ilbrahim is discovered in "the dim moonlight" beneath a tree, like Christabel under her oak. The child, like Coleridge's heavenly maid, is nearly an apparition, with "eyes that seemed to mingle with the moonlight": as in *Christabel,* the story commences with a powerful image of the weird, beautiful, and remote. Later on, Ilbrahim is the romantic imagination. He "would derive enjoyment from the most trifling events, and from every object about him; he seemed to discover rich treasures of happiness, by a faculty analogous to that of the witch hazel, which points to hidden gold where all is barren to the eye." Thus he possesses the imaginative genius that Coleridge discovered in Wordsworth, who gave "the charm of novelty to things of everyday," and excited "a feeling analogous to the supernatural, by awakening the mind's attention from the lethargy of custom and directing it to the loveliness and the wonders of the world before us."

Ilbrahim is a romantic Coleridgean artist, too. As imagination perceives the unusual in the usual, so it presents it in artistic imitation, harmonizing difference with sameness. The child has the faculty of "reciting imaginary adventures," which are "curious on account of a vein of human tenderness which ran through them all, and was like a sweet, familiar face, encountered in the midst of wild and unearthly scenery." Still another resemblance may be glanced at. Briefly, Coleridge uses *harmony* to link his aesthetics with his ethics; it is the common factor in beauty and goodness alike. Ilbrahim is a harmonizer, while the evil child who betrays him and destroys him is a living discord. "The countenance of the latter immediately impressed a beholder disagreeably, but it required some examination to discover that the cause was a very slight distortion of the mouth, and the irregular, broken line, and near approach of the eyebrows." Furthermore, this little scoundrel is also endowed with "an almost imperceptible twist of every joint," not to speak of an "uneven prominence of the breast"—all of these attributes betraying "a moral obliquity which grated very harshly against Ilbrahim's instinctive rectitude." As Christabel, completely good, is an easy victim of the evil Geraldine, so Ilbrahim is shattered by contact with malevolence. "Perhaps, among the many life-weary wretches then upon the earth, there was not one who combined innocence and misery like this poor, broken-hearted infant, so soon the victim of his own heavenly nature."

It has been remarked that Ilbrahim symbolizes the Coleridgean romantic imagination (it need hardly be said that the relationship is general). Imagination, however, is so comprehensive a theme that it implicates a great many others. Thus, for example, Hawthorne's self-comment in "Rappaccini's Daughter" is a confession of his "inveterate love of allegory," but this allegory is imaginative too. His fictions sometimes, he says, "have little or no reference either to time or space." Coleridge had specified that imagination, though not free of time and space, is able to command them arbitrarily. Hawthorne's tales, "with a very slight embroidery of outward manners," endeavor "to create an interest by some less obvious peculiarity of the subject." Imagination seeks a deeper-than-outward truth; it fuses usual and unusual. Correspondingly, "occasionally a breath of Nature, a raindrop of pathos and tenderness, or a gleam of humor, will find its way into the midst of his fantastic imagery, and make us feel as if, after all, we were yet within the limits of our native earth."

"Rappaccini's Daughter" is among other things, a study of incomplete and perverse imagination. Young Giovanni Guasconti starts off as a promising hero of romance, but he is not up to it, and gets lost in "the wild vagaries which his imagination ran riot continually in producing." He is basically a man of fancy; and he does not bring into play his whole soul, according to Coleridge's prescription. "Guasconti had not a deep heart— or, at all events, its depths were not sounded now; but he had a quick fancy, and an ardent southern temperament, which arose every instant to a higher fever pitch."

Guasconti's material is the scene of Rappaccini's garden, and he faces it with the best intentions. "The young man rejoiced that, in the heart of the barren city, he had the privilege of overlooking this spot of lovely and luxuriant vegetation. It would serve, he said to himself, as a symbolic language to keep him in communion with nature." One thinks of the "gardens bright with sinuous rills" of "Kubla Khan"—and Giovanni also has his dreams, which are "fertile of mysteries." But he can achieve no fusion: the vision of morning is not the vision of dusk. He swings helplessly between "his wonder-working fancy" and "a most rational view of the whole matter." The garden is the symbol of the beautiful Beatrice, and the two are revealed before him in various lights and points of view; the elements of the problem, in fact, are all presented to him one by one, as are the elements of imagination in the haunted chamber of "The Custom-House" sketch. Like Hawthorne in the chamber, Giovanni sees the parts but not the whole.

Schematized, Coleridge's critical and aesthetic system is made up of a series of oppositions, in which the first term (as presented here) is superior to the second, for example, imagination-fancy, organic-mechanical, imitation-copy, illusion-delusion, and genius-talent. All are akin; indeed, all are really one opposition viewed from varying angles. Thus imagination, an attribute of genius, produces "imitation," or genuine and original art as opposed to copy, which is literal and derivative. From the point of view of truth—of religion, of science, of history—art is a justifiable illusion, whereas false art aims at delusion, confusing the criteria of art and truth. Coleridge's most noticeable figure for "imagination" is imaginative portraiture, which catches the essential traits of its subject by means of the organic workings of imagination. He uses the literal wax-work effigy, such as Mme. Tussaud's, as his figure for copy.

Picture, especially portrait, is also a highly prevalent figure with Hawthorne, to symbolize the values of artistic creation; and he distinguishes, much as Coleridge does, between genuine and counterfeit art, imitation and copy. The painter of "The Prophetic Pictures" is, if anything, too well endowed. It is said that "he paints not merely a man's features, but his mind and heart. He catches the secret sentiments and passions, and throws them upon the canvas, like sunshine—or perhaps, in the portraits of dark-souled men, like a gleam of infernal fire. It is an awful gift. . . ." The artist himself reechoes the statement. "'The artist—the true artist—must look beneath the exterior. It is his gift—his proudest, but often a melancholy one—to see the inmost soul, and by a power indefinable even to himself, to make it glow or darken upon the canvas, in glances that express the thought and sentiment of years.'" His success is almost total. "He had pried into their souls with his keenest insight, and pictured the result upon their features with his utmost skill, so as barely to fall short of that standard which no genius ever reached, his own severe conception." One may remark this difference, that Coleridge shows no trace of Hawthorne's dread of art's possible effect. It may be that his doctrine of illusion keeps it at a safe distance, or that he aligns sympathy (always beneficent) with imagination more closely than Hawthorne could or desired to link them.

Hawthorne's "illusion" sails closer to the wind of imposture, as evidenced by the showman's art in the long sketch "Main Street," which needs to be seen in precisely the right perspective. Similarly, "Edward Randolph's Portrait" is severely challenged by an important viewer, Lieutenant-Governor Hutchinson: "'Have you brought hither your painter's art—your Italian spirit of intrigue—your tricks of stage effect . . . ?'" He finds it more difficult than Coleridge to accept the "difference" in the sameness-in-difference that constitutes artistic imitation. At any rate, he feels the necessity of justifying the conventions of art to the literal minded.

"Feathertop: A Moralized Legend" furnishes an entertaining study of artistic illusion. The witch, Mother Rigby, makes for her own amusement "a mere thing of sticks, straw, and old clothes, with nothing better than a shrivelled pumpkin for a head." She has, however, unusual creative ability. "Nevertheless, as we must carefully hold in remembrance, Mother Rigby was a witch of singular power and dexterity; and, keeping this fact duly before our minds, we shall see nothing beyond credibility in the remarkable incidents in our story." She equips her scarecrow with a magic pipe, which is "the breath of life" to him—an animating principle, equivalent to imaginative, organic unity. As illusion, like the showman's art in "Main Street" the scarecrow sails close to the wind. He is "merely a spectral illusion, and a cunning effect of light and shade so colored and contrived as to delude the eyes of most men." Hawthorne explicitly raises the question of his art: "Shall I confess the truth? At its present point of vivification, the scarecrow reminds me of some of the lukewarm and abortive characters, composed of heterogeneous materials . . . with which romance writers (and myself, no doubt, among the rest) have so overpeopled the world of fiction." Against this disillusioning, however, the phrase "present point of vivification" is to be noted. In this genially ironic tale, poor Feathertop somehow achieves a genuine life and feelings.

Romantically, he acquires a heart, which at first is an ironic cliché. "'With all thy heart!' cried the old witch, setting her hands to her sides and laughing loudly. 'Thou hast such a pretty way of speaking. With all thy heart! And thou didst put thy hand to the left side of thy waistcoat as if thou really hadst one!'" It is all too true, however. Feathertop falls in love, is deceived by his own illusion, and turns out to be more human than the human beings around him. Finally he sees through himself, with an insight beyond his creator, and flings aside the life-giving pipe. At the end, Mother Rigby reflects: "'His feelings are too tender, his sensibilities too deep. He seems to have too much heart to bustle for his own advantage in such an empty and heartless world. Well! well! I'll make a scarecrow of him after all.'" It would be humorless to pursue the relation too closely, but the witch at least suggests the romantic, Coleridgean creator who mysteriously achieves more than he consciously intends. "The unconscious," says Coleridge, "is the genius in the man of genius."

The sculptor of "Drowne's Wooden Image" also, and once only, creates more than he knows. Drowne is a skillful carver of ships' figureheads, "on the best of which might have been bestowed the questionable praise that it looked as if a living man had been changed to wood, and that not only the physical, but the intellectual and spiritual part, partook of the stolid transformation. But not in a single instance did it seem as if the wood were imbibing the ethereal essence of humanity." Drowne's work is invariably characterized by "mechanical and wooden cleverness."

Through love, however, he achieves a true work of art, a figure of the beloved object herself. It receives significant praise. "'Here,'" says the painter Copley, "'is the divine, the life-giving touch. What inspired hand is beckoning this wood to arise and live?'" He hails the carver as "'a man of genius.'" The figure is at once distinct and imaginative; it reconciles totality with minute detail, by virtue of an inherent harmony that transcends artistic rules. Coleridge, it may be remarked, persistently contrasts *principle* with *rule,* along with his other oppositions. "Principle" is ranged with the imaginative, the organic, with imitation; the rules with mechanical copy. Drowne has been able for once to bring his whole soul to bear upon his work: "'A well-spring of inward wisdom gushed within as I wrought upon the oak with my whole strength, and soul, and faith.'" Like the Ancient Mariner, he has been vouchsafed the living vision. The Mariner, to whom the creatures of the calm had been only "a thousand, thousand slimy things," beholds them transfigured.

> O happy living things! no tongue
> Their beauty might declare:
> A spring of love gushed from my heart,
> And I blessed them unaware.

Drowne, like poor Feathertop, is only momentarily inspired. Deprived of his beloved, he relapses into "the mechanical carver in wood," a mere copyist. But here Hawthorne's reflection is optimistic. "Yet who can doubt that the very highest state to which a human spirit can attain . . . is its truest and most natural state, and that Drowne was more consistent with himself when he wrought the admirable figure of the mysterious lady, than when he perpetrated a whole progeny of blockheads."

The external cause was not all; there was something in Drowne that responded to it.

In this story Drowne was saluted, we recall, as a man of genius. The distinction between genius and talent is a commonplace, but Coleridge read the word "genius" heavily, attaching to it its root meaning of birth and creation and organic activity. Thus when he speaks of "a genial criticism" he is not talking merely of good humor. On one occasion he got himself in trouble with Charles Lamb by using Lamb to exemplify talent, while crediting himself with genius. He took Wordsworth as an instance of predominant genius, without proportional talent; while Wordsworth once commented that Coleridge remarkably evidenced the fusion of the two. Coleridge also, though less frequently, distinguished between "absolute" and "commanding" genius, the genius of the poet and the man of action. Absolute genius is whole and self-contained, demanding no further satisfaction than contemplation of itself. The commanding genius needs to complete himself in external action and its impact on the world outside. Shakespeare exemplifies the former, Napoleon the latter.

These distinctions are frequent and interesting enough to be worth mentioning in Hawthorne's tales. Hawthorne uses an ironic phrase about Dumas in a note to "Dr. Heidegger's Experiment," in reply to a charge of plagiarism. Pointing out the early date of his own story, he remarks that M. Dumas is heartily welcome to it; "nor is it the only instance, by many, in which the great French romancer has exercised the privilege of commanding genius by confiscating the intellectual property of less famous people to his own use and behoof." The obsessed hero of "Peter Goldthwaite's Treasure" is a comic example of absolute genius. Devoid of worldly wisdom, he has nevertheless the divine spark: ". . . the essential Peter was a young man of high hopes, just entering on the world. At the kindling of each new fire, his burnt-out youth rose afresh from the old embers and ashes." Peter's relation to his old partner John Brown, "portly and comfortable," has also a Coleridgean tang. Just as Coleridge interpreted *Don Quixote* as an allegory of the transcendental reason (the Don) and shrewd but limited common sense (Sancho Panza), so Brown is Peter's opposite and foil.

Hawthorne hints at the genius-talent distinction in a passage of his sketch "The Procession of Life." In his procession is a great multitude of those mortals who "have lost, or never found, their proper places in the world." Along with many other callings, "Authors shall be ranked here whom some freak of Nature. . . had imbued with the confidence of genius and strong desire of fame, but has favored with no corresponding power." Complementing these are "others, whose lofty gifts were unaccompanied with the faculty of expression, or any of that earthly machinery by which ethereal endowments must be manifested to mankind." The first group suggests Coleridge's "general talent determined to poetic composition by accidental motives, by an act of the will, rather than by the inspiration of a genial and productive nature." The phrases occur in his important discussion of "the characteristics of original poetic genius" in *Biographia Literaria* (ch. XV), as one instance among many. Hawthorne's second category, the mute, inglorious Miltons of inarticulate genius, are perhaps more Wordsworthian than Coleridgean.

Coleridge, that is, would ordinarily not have accepted a separation of genius from its expression except as an abstraction of logic. His dialectic reconciles oppositions by using terms in two senses, moving from limited to comprehensive meanings. The distinction of genius from talent is essential to him, and his first step in defining them is by stating their differentiae; he goes on, however, to expand the meaning of "genius" until it fuses with the lesser term "talent" by absorbing it. The highest genius implies the greatest talent as its necessary intermediary. Thus in his thinking, Wordsworth's genius, as an abstraction, is lofty. In reality, however, its imbalance with Wordsworth's talent impairs it. This synthesizing habit of thought is very infrequent in Hawthorne, on the other hand. The limited antitheses of the "Procession of Life" passage are more characteristic of him.

Nevertheless, he is capable of conceiving and effectively presenting the Coleridgean synthesis. In his wonderfully evocative "Artist of the Beautiful," the hero, Owen Warland—creative, imaginative, and idealistic—uses mechanism as the base of his supremely organic creation. Owen is an "irregular genius" who detests "the stiff and regular processes of ordinary machinery," but he has an "intuitive comprehension of mechanical principles" and "the hidden mysteries of mechanism." Indeed, the story presents the organic development of the artist, successfully struggling to create the perfect symbol and to achieve the height of mental beatitude, against a multitude of difficulties. Briefly, the tale's movement of thought is transcendent, rising through plane after plane of opposition to a final, triumphant resolution. The oppositions in question are many. Beauty conflicts with utility; Coleridge-wise, imagination in Warland is balked by the lower faculty of "understanding" in his old master Peter Hovenden, and, correspondingly, Warland's idealism is opposed by Hovenden's remorseless materialism. Regularity and irregularity, copy and imitation, temporal and eternal, earthly and spiritual are ranged against each other. Possible relationships with Coleridge's thought are too numerous to canvass, but "The Artist of the Beautiful" is at any rate a very Coleridgean story, while deeply representative of Hawthorne too. One discrimination might be made: Warland, though triumphant, renounces a great deal to gain his victory. Coleridge would have emphasized the happy self-sufficiency of the creative mind rather more than the struggle to achieve its happiness.

Perhaps, however, there is also one point at which Hawthorne is particularly Coleridgean, in a slight but most interesting touch of resemblance. This is the picture revealed of the blacksmith Danforth in his shop, amid "red glare and alternate dusk." He is "well worthy to be viewed in so picturesque an aspect of light and shade,

where the bright blaze struggled with the black night, as
if each would have snatched his comely strength from the
other." Here the emphasis is on the productivity of the
struggle, since it *does* picturesquely display the
blacksmith's "comely strength." Its effect is to unify. Similarly, to Coleridge, "in Shakespeare's *poems* the creative
power and the intellectual energy wrestle as in a war embrace. Each in its excess of strength seems to threaten the
extinction of the other. At length in the DRAMA they
were reconciled, and fought each with its shield before
the breast of the other" (*Biographia Literaria,* ch. XV).

This same chapter of Coleridge contains another
parallel, this time suggesting the causes of mental aliena-
tion and decay. Arguing that the licentiousness of *Venus
and Adonis* is sanitized by the energy and distinctness of
Shakespeare's portrayal of it, he asserts that "the reader is
forced into too much action to sympathize with the
merely passive of our nature. As little can a mind thus
roused and awakened be brooded on by mean and indistinct emotion, as the low, lazy mist can creep upon the
surface of a lake, while a strong gale is driving it onward
in waves and billows." Coleridge is vitally concerned with
the dangers of "the low, lazy mist," and often for himself.
Its atmosphere is the Death in Life to which he fears himself condemned. Thus the soul-destroying acedia of his
"Dejection: An Ode" is

> A grief without pang, void, dark, and drear,
> A stifled, drowsy, unimpassioned grief,
> Which finds no natural outlet, no relief
> In word, or sign, or tear.

This is a "wan and heartless mood" that separates him
from the life and beauty and meaning of nature. A vital
link is broken.

> It were a vain endeavour,
> Though I should gaze for ever
> On that green light that lingers in the west:
> I may not hope from outward forms to win
> The passion and the life, whose fountains are within.

Hawthorne's most extreme "isolato," Wakefield, is "the Outcast of the Universe," and, as in Coleridge, his downfall is passivity. The tale in which he appears is hardly more than a sketch, though haunting; and it is frankly speculative. "In some old magazine or newspaper I recollect a story, told as truth, of a man—let us call him Wakefield—who absented himself for a long time from his wife." What is remarkable about this is that the man went to live in the next street, unbeknownst, for twenty years. Then, long presumed dead, "he entered the door one evening, quietly, as from a day's absence, and became a loving spouse till death." From these circumstances Hawthorne tries to imagine what sort of man this Wakefield was. He does not accept the happy ending, but leaves his protagonist just as the latter returns: "We will not follow our friend across the threshold." His own advice is "Stay, Wakefield! Would you go to the sole home that is left you? Then step into your grave!" As with Ethan Brand and his Unpardonable Sin, Wakefield is damned by the mere conception of his act. But Brand is tremendous, while Wakefield is lost from sheer frivolity and negation.

He is pervaded with "a certain sluggishness"; he is reflective but passive and mentally indistinct. He cannot encompass genuine relationships. "He was intellectual, but not actively so; his mind occupied itself in long and lazy musings, that ended to no purpose, or had not vigor to attain it; his thoughts were seldom so energetic as to seize hold of words. Imagination, in the proper meaning of the term, made no part of Wakefield's gifts." With conflicting qualities, he has no active principle in him to bring them together. He is vaguely conscious of his situation, but the vagueness is fatal. "Such ideas glimmer through the mist of Wakefield's mind, and render him indistinctly conscious that an almost impassable gulf divides his hired apartment from his former home." This sounds like Coleridge's "mean and indistinct emotion," and his "low, lazy mist."

Coleridge asks in his "Epitaph,"

> O, lift one thought in prayer for S.T.C.;
> That he who many a year with toil of breath
> Found death in life, may here find life in death!

Hawthorne uses the phrase "death in life" in "The Christmas Banquet," where, by his will, a certain old gentleman has established a fund for an annual Christmas banquet in perpetuity "for ten of the most miserable persons that could be found." Among these, year after year, is Gervayse Hastings, who seems an inappropriate guest, since he is handsome, healthy, and apparently fortunate in general. But he is "chill and unsubstantial—a mere vapor." Through some "deficiency of his spiritual organization," he is afflicted with "a sense of cold unreality." His miserable companions have "the privilege of a stricken heart," by virtue of which they are at least real, and resent his presence. One, a misanthropist, remarks to him that "my companions and myself must seem no more than shadows flickering on the wall. And precisely such a shadow are you to us."

Nevertheless, Gervayse Hastings is indeed the most unfortunate man in this wretched company. After many years, he is at length the oldest among them. Asked for his secret, he replies, "'You will not understand it. . . . None have understood it—not even those who experience the like. It is a chilliness—a want of earnestness—a feeling as if what should be my heart were a thing of vapor—a haunting perception of unreality.'" Roderick Elliston, who tells the story, avows that his portrayal is unsuccessful "'because the characteristics are all negative.'" Such men as his protagonist "'seem to be on the outside of everything; and nothing wearies the soul more than an attempt to comprehend them within its grasp.'"

There is perhaps some difference between Coleridge's state in "Dejection" and the negative of poor Hastings, apart from Hawthorne's failure to rescue his character from the abstraction he avows. He is closer to the "Limbo" of Coleridge's fragmentary poem of that name, which is "a mere horror of blank Naught-at-all," or "growthless, dull Privation," less impressive than the hell of "positive Negation." A resemblance remains, however. The plight portrayed in "Dejection" is a deficiency in imagination, a grief "void, dark, and drear," from the living connections' failing, the drying of the fountains within. The poet is left with only an "inanimate cold world," and heartless. Such is assuredly the situation of Hawthorne's Hastings.

In "The Wedding Knell," the aged bridegroom charges that his late-won bride "took away all the substance of my life, and made it a dream without reality enough even to grieve it." This opposes dream to reality, as is often the case in Hawthorne. In a further complication, Coleridge writes in "Dejection" of "Reality's dark dream," with a sudden transposition. As we have noted, Hawthorne's dreams, artistic or literal, may be the fictive metaphors of truth. The narrator of "The Celestial Railroad" passes through the gate of dreams to reach his story, a traditional dream-vision like its prototype, *The Pilgrim's Progress.* At the end, he is rescued from imminent disaster, as from a nightmare, by waking. But his dream is a warning of what may well eventuate. "Young Goodman Brown," which Melville called "as deep as Dante," is a complex dream of evil, though Hawthorne preserves his artistic illusion by leaving the question of its reality ambiguous.

> Had Goodman Brown fallen asleep in the forest and only dreamed a wild dream of a witch-meeting?
> Be it so if you will; but, alas! it was a dream of evil omen for young Goodman Brown.

Since this ending has provoked much critical discussion, I will utter the last word on it (*my* last word, that is). A sensitive reader, who understands that he is reading fiction, will draw no conclusion at all, but take pleasure in the ambiguity that Hawthorne intended. There is much profit in speculating in either direction, and none in tak-

ing a stand. Many highly intelligent readers are not interested in fiction but only in the "stand" they can find in it.
Hawthorne's illusions are complex and delicate; they
tremble gracefully on the verge of the fanciful. A playful
mystification is part of the game for him, and his frequent
juxtaposition of the playful and the serious or tragic is
original and unique. The enigma of Donatello's ears is
probably not one of his successes in this vein, along with
other mystifications in *The Marble Faun.* But he did not
wish his mysteries to be taken literally, and they are, in
the main, self-justifying.

To Coleridge, artistic illusion is analogous to dream.
In "The Custom House," Hawthorne, establishing the
conditions of illusion, writes: "At such an hour, and with
this scene before him, if a man, sitting all alone, cannot
dream strange things, and make them look like truth, he
need never try to write romances." Dream and reality or
truth are traditionally opposed, but just as traditionally
associated. Dream as prophecy has immemorially been
acceptable as belief and as an artistic convention, and in
modern times as unconscious psychological process. So,
to return to "Young Goodman Brown," Faith has already
dreamed Brown's nightmare and gives him sage advice:
"Prithee put off your journey until sunrise and sleep in
your own bed to-night. A lone woman is troubled with
such dreams and such thoughts that she's afeard of herself
sometimes." This contains the germ of the whole narrative, and Brown duly reemphasizes it. "She talks of
dreams, too. Methought as she spoke there was trouble
in her face, as if a dream had warned her what work is to
be done to-night." It is part of the story's irony that the
young "goodman" fails to associate the dream with Faith's
ambiguous role in the action. He doesn't, as it were,
know the half of it.

"The Birthmark" repeats the speculations of "The
Haunted Mind," in which dream overflows the bound-
aries of sleep and becomes torment, as in Coleridge's
"The Pains of Sleep." One wonders if Melville had "The

Birthmark" in mind in the tortured nightmares of Ahab. "The mind is in a sad state when Sleep, the all-involving, cannot confine her spectres within the dim region of her sway, but suffers them to break forth, affrighting this actual life with secrets that perchance belong to a deeper one. Aylmer now remembered his dream." He has fancied that, in trying to remove the birthmark, he has cut to his wife's heart, and gone on cutting. The dream figures forth his real desires. "Truth often finds its way to the mind close muffled in robes of sleep, and then speaks with uncompromising directness of matters in regard to which we practise an unconscious self-deception during our waking moments."

Through metaphor, Aylmer's dream conveys a psychological truth, and also it is a prophecy of what is actually to happen as a consequence of the mental state it portrays. Coleridge's *Christabel,* like "Young Goodman Brown" and "The Birthmark," is pervaded by the dream motif—elaborate, elusive, and most resonant. Christabel gets in trouble, in the first place, from dreaming, though the nature of these dreams is not clear. A happily abandoned early addition would have underlined them more heavily as "Dreams, that made her moan and leap,/As on her bed she lay in sleep."

Since, however, like "Young Goodman Brown," *Christabel* is a tale of innocence entrapped by inexplicable evil, the state of dream is peculiarly appropriate, symbolizing an experience utterly strange and overpowering. Yet (and here Coleridge perhaps anticipates too plainly) the dream concludes in comfort, though a strictly psychological and solipsistic interpretation will identify Geraldine and the mother as the warring principles of Christabel's psyche. Preferably, this is—as it would be in Hawthorne—a mere overtone, a proffered but subordinate dimension. More simply, it prophesies the happy ending that Coleridge intended.

A more complex prophetic dream comes later: the symbolic dream of the poet's imagination, which pierces to essential truth. This is the vision of Bard Bracy, in which Christabel, as a dove, is enlaced by a snake (Geraldine), "bright green" and therefore camouflaged amid green foliage, and inextricable from its captive. Characteristically, Christabel's father, Sir Leoline, pays no attention to Bracy's warning dream. The baron does not understand how to get the truth out of poetry.

His heedlessness is perhaps suggestive of Hawthorne's problem—to "dream strange things, and make them look like truth"—and to find readers who detect the verisimilitude.

"Rappaccini's Daughter" and the Nineteenth-Century Physician

Seymour L. Gross
for Bernard Levatin, M.D.

Rappaccini's Daughter" (1844) has invited a substantial number of commentaries which emphasize Hawthorne's distrust of science, most particularly its materialistic epistemology, which denies, in the words of the story, that "there is something truer and more real, than what we can see with the eyes, and touch with the finger." Only recently, however, has the relationship of the story to the contemporary medical situation been touched upon. M. D. Uroff, in "The Doctors in 'Rappaccini's Daughter,"[1] contends that "the frame of the tale is a medical dispute between Rappaccini and Baglioni which, although set in ancient and far-off Padua, actually raged in Hawthorne's own day in Massachusetts." The dispute was between the advocates of allopathic medicine, who believed in bleeding, purging, and large doses of medication, and the advocates of homeopathic medicine, who believed in small doses of drugs which spurred the body's "vital principle" to expel the disease. Allopathy, the orthodox position, is advocated by Baglioni; homeopathy by Rappaccini. Uroff is certainly correct in contending that Hawthorne does not take sides in the medical dispute and that the story displays a marked antipathy toward the doctors of his time. It is my view, however, that "Rappaccini's Daughter" is a more extensive treatment of the medical profession than Uroff has indicated.

When Hawthorne was writing "Rappaccini's Daughter," what we have come to call the "image of the medical profession" occupied a median position in American culture, between the earlier view of the doctor as an object of almost pure ridicule and the later one of veneration and adulation. By about 1820, medicine had clearly emerged from what Benjamin Rush called its "slavish rank." A fine literary portrait of the early doctor is Cooper's comically ignorant Dr. Elnathan Todd of *The Pioneers* (1823). Cooper's novel is set in a 1797 backwoods settlement; the physician it depicts reflects the medical practitioner of several decades earlier in the developed urban centers. Another kind of evidence of the earlier position of the medical doctor is afforded by Theodore Greene's *America's Heroes: The Models of Success in American Magazines* (1970). His tabulation of role-models in the gentlemen's magazines through 1820 reveals that whereas about 25 percent of the essays were devoted to such professions as statesman-politician, military man, and clergyman, only 5 percent were devoted to physicians.

But although the medical profession had been elevated during the period about 1830 to 1850 above the place it had earlier occupied, it was still a long way from that "priestly" rank which it was to enjoy later in the century, when the "triumphant march" of chemical and technological discoveries, coupled with the commendable record achieved by the medical profession in both South and North during the Civil War and the decline of the influence of the clergy as moral guides and arbiters, served to create not only a more competent profession but one which felt itself capable of prescribing for all areas of life. Dr. Andrew Smith, for example, argued in an essay in an 1889 issue of *Harper's Magazine* that the family doctor must not only care for the health of his patients but should also be in charge of directing their educations, occupations, and places of residence.[2]

Several years later, with even greater arrogance, Dr. Paul Gibier, in the *North American Review,* advocated that the medical "priest" ("minister," "apostle") must be at the forefront of the movement from "sentimental" to "scientific" religion (a position adumbrated earlier, but with more tact and discretion, in Holmes's *Elsie Venner* in 1860). This meant that the physician should be heeded not only in matters medical but in social ones as well, for he alone could "diagnose" such diseases as socialism and anarchy and, through marriage counseling, based on his knowledge of genetics, "contribute to the purification of the race"—an antidote to "the blind evolution of the present period."[3]

The hubris of these two physicians is patent, and I do not mean to imply that their statements betokened full cultural compliance with their views, but the confidence with which they addressed the readership of general magazines must surely indicate some cultural hospitality to the view of the doctor-as-God. Be that as it may, a Smith or a Gibier would have been impossible fifty or so years earlier. Finally, it is significant to note that when Henry James chose to depict his most confidently tyrannical manipulator of another person's life, he made him a physician: Dr. Sloper of *Washington Square* (1881).

The criticisms leveled against the medical profession in early nineteenth-century America were primarily aimed at city practitioners—those who enjoyed economic success and an elevated social position, often because of more or better formal medical education. The country doctor was another matter, as Henry Clay Lewis points out in his *Louisiana Swamp Doctor* (1846); *he* was deservedly exempted from the strictures and sarcasms laid upon the more "regular" urban doctors. James

Thomas Flexner's *Doctors on Horseback* (1937), for example, describes a number of nineteenth-century rural doctors who labored selflessly, with little reward, and who were revered (if not remunerated) for their services. The "myth" of the country doctor has its source in such actions as traveling by horse for twenty miles to deliver a baby, sitting up all night with the mother, and then getting a chicken and a dozen eggs for payment, along with undying gratitude.

Criticism of the early nineteenth-century medical profession comes in various forms.[4] Some, like accusations of ignorance or coldness and conceit, are either too vague to be useful or can be subsumed under larger categories. Some, like claims of sexual improprieties, are too eccentric to be taken seriously as constituting a significant part of the cultural image of the doctor. As for charges of irreligion, a central feature of the European medical man's image, these were rare in the America of the 1830s and 1840s; Americans' criticism was aimed primarily at the "impiety" of dissection. By my analysis (others might group them differently), the negative view of the physician breaks down into six categories, four of which impact "Rappaccini's Daughter"—a remarkably high proportion for so short a work, which is not *centrally* concerned with medicine in America.

One of the two criticisms which does not find its way into "Rappaccini's Daughter" has to do with money. The feeling that there is something wrong, or at least not quite decent, in making too much money from the ills and sufferings of the race is a conviction that Hawthorne's time shares with our own. Henry Clay Lewis speaks for this conviction when he points with disgust to the costly clothes ("his hat reads 'Paris'"), "comfortable dwellings," and generally elegant lifestyle of the urban doctor. Although Dr. Rappaccini is wealthy and Dr. Baglioni evidently well off, the story gives no indication that their comfortable economic status has been inappropriately achieved through their medical practices. Neither their actions nor their attitudes are ascribed to greed, a traditional criticism of the medical profession which goes back at least to Chaucer, whose physician "lovede gold in special." Hawthorne knew the moral ruin that could be caused by lust for money (witness Judge Jaffrey Pyncheon of *The House of the Seven Gables*); but neither the doctors in "Rappaccini's Daughter" nor those in his other fiction (Chillingworth, Aylmer, Heidegger) suffer this kind of criticism. One can only guess that Hawthorne felt avarice is too universal a quality to be of particular significance in his characterization of physicians.

The other contemporary criticism of the medical profession that we do not find in "Rappaccini's Daughter" is the accusation that physicians exhibited "sacrilegious disrespect to the dead." This was essentially, though not exclusively, an objection to the mutilation of the body through dissection, the most bizarre expression of which occurred in 1788, when a crowd in New York (the Doctors' Mob, as it came to be called) attempted to lynch a number of medical men who were teaching anatomy by means of dissection. By Hawthorne's time, public censure of "disposing of people anatomically" had begun to wane but had not wholly disappeared. But even where there was growing acknowledgment of the need for doctors to learn anatomy through dissection, there was a residual distrust of their attitude toward the dead—they were thought more apt than not to treat "the house of the soul" without the reverence it deserved. Something of this is caught metaphorically in Melville's *White-Jacket* (1850), where, in the chapter titled "The Surgeon of the Fleet," Melville contrasts the feelings of the narrator with those of Dr. Cadwallader Cuticle toward the plaster casts of human parts which fill the doctor's stateroom. One in particular, the head of a "singularly gentle and meek" elderly woman, from whose forehead protrudes a horrible growth in the shape of a horn, evokes heart-bursting sorrow in the narrator for the fate this disfigured woman suffered. The surgeon, however, feels "no pang of pain, not the slightest touch of concern," for the life of this wretched woman; when he retires for the night, he invariably hangs his cap "upon the upward curling extremity of the horn."

A Boston physician lamented in 1831: "As a community, physicians are, more than most classes of men, made the butt of ridicule, and not infrequently the subjects of sweeping and unsparing censure." One of the most frequent and serious forms that this "censure" took was a perception of the medical profession, despite its avowed calling, as "indifferent to human life." Whether justifiable or not, there was a distinct belief that patients who came to doctors in fear and pain were no more significant to them than so many pieces of wood to a carpenter. Doctors might tell each other and medical students that an aloof, seemingly cold and uninvolved manner was beneficial to the practice of medicine since it disposed patients to believe in the curative powers of the practitioners of in what, in effect, was a mystery to laymen. It undoubtedly was helpful in many instances (we know the efficacy of the "placebo effect"), but a significant part of the image of the physician was his indifference to the sufferings of mankind and imperviousness to the ordinary emotions of humanity. What mattered to the doctor was not the patient *qua* patient but the opportunity to enhance his reputation, at whatever risk to the patient. There was fear that doctors would "try things" on them; that patients, in short, were used, not treated. It is obvious that just such a view informs Hawthorne's conception of Dr. Rappaccini, though it is raised to the level of nightmare.

Rappaccini exists outside the normal parameters of human feeling. His garden is a symbol of the estrangement of its creator from the moral and emotional lives ordinary people live. When Giovanni, upon first seeing the garden, asks if it is part of the house in which he is living, Lizabetta, that utterly ordinary human being, replies in horror, "God forbid, Signor!" and we can imagine her crossing herself. In the figure of Rappaccini—tall, emaciated, garbed in black, "cold and purely intellectual"—we can see (from the perspective of this essay) a Gothic magnification of the cultural view of the physician as one who is isolated from humanity. To think of him as "Adam," as Giovanni does when he first sees him, is to emphasize that aloneness. Throughout the story, even when Rappaccini is literally with other people, he is utterly alone, with that kind of aloneness that is generated by a man who has never "expressed much warmth of heart" for other people. His relationship to the two youngsters in the story is solely that of doctor to patient, not to their well-being but to his success as a medical scientist. To the end, his only response to his daughter-patient is irritation that this "foolish girl" has not appreciated the remarkable scientific gift he has given her. At the sight of the dead Beatrice, Hawthorne tells us, Rappaccini was "thunder-stricken"—but whether at the end of his experiment or at the loss of his child, Hawthorne does not say.

"Visionary theories," as applied to early nineteenth-century medicine, is a broad-spectrum term. It was applied, most obviously, to radically unorthodox theories of sickness and health which sprang up in the third and fourth decades of the century, in opposition to the standard view of medicine held by "regular" (or allopathic) practitioners, which involved mostly dosing, purging, and bleeding. "Water-cures," homeopathy, Thomsonianism (using only "botanic drugs"), and a wide variety of "health cults," which promised well-being from the observance of certain "rules of life" and eating specified foods, flourished, each with its substantial number of "bigoted" adherents. But the term was also applied to phenomena which were not quite "theories"—to the cures and cure-alls with which people in the early nineteenth century were assailed at every turn. No reader of nineteenth-century newspapers and periodicals can fail to be struck by the incredible number of advertisements for catholicons and panaceas (total health from one nostrum), as well as specifics for the curing of gout, stone, tuberculosis, hydrophobia, dyspepsia, and all other ills that flesh is heir to.

To a degree, the situation in the medical profession grew out of the same forces which impelled analogous radical departures from orthodoxy in other parts of the cultural life of the United States—in politics, philosophy, theology, ethics, and so on. But it had its more immediate, concrete causes as well. Although medical science was making progress in diagnostics, in learning the human body, in distinguishing one disease from another (such as typhus from typhoid), its growing knowledge had no immediate effect on the practice of medicine. The brutal fact was that the doctor still could do nothing about most illnesses. In such a situation, it is not surprising that sincere men and charlatans, orthodox practitioners and empirics ("quacks," the disapproving called them), were encouraged to try for fame and fortune where standard medicine had failed. It should be remembered, too, that the United States, unlike several European countries, made very little attempt to restrict the practice of medicine to duly licensed and adequately educated persons. Irregular practitioners abounded and graduates of the one-year proprietary medical schools (unattached to a university), which came into existence after 1820, were in some instances inferior in knowledge to "quacks." Thus the medical game was not a hard one to play, nor, according to some, should it be made difficult in a country committed to the principles of Jacksonian democracy. An attempt to form a national body of physicians in the 1830s failed. The result was a chaos of competing claims and theories, with few successful results. Small wonder, then, that the public was disposed to view the profession as characterized by "a bigoted devotion to visionary theories."

Dr. Baglioni recognizes that Rappaccini cares nothing for mankind: "His patients are interesting to him only as subjects for some new experiment." But for all his apparent conviviality and openness of manner, Baglioni's relationship to Beatrice and Giovanni is finally no more human than that of his seclusive and silent enemy. Though he masks his actions in avowed concern for the son of an old friend, diminishing Rappaccini's reputation is his only concern. In his response to the death of the girl, whom he has helped to kill, there predominates, despite an element of horror, an exhilarating sense of victory. He "called loudly, in a tone of triumph . . . 'Rappaccini! Rappaccini! And is *this* the upshot of your experiment?'" Neither Beatrice nor Giovanni, as people to whom terrible things have happened, enters his mind.

The hostility between the two doctors in the story is a dramatic rendering of one of the dominant impressions of the medical profession in Hawthorne's time. Internecine squabbles, often reaching vilification and vituperation and sometimes even physical violence, by members of a profession theoretically dedicated to reason and science, were part of the reason why doctors were often "made the butt of ridicule." As the author of "Character and Abuses of the Medical Profession" admitted, "physicians exhibit a sensitiveness and jealousy of temper, especially in their intercourse with each other, far greater than is met with among other educated men."

Because the efficacy of so few medical procedures and therapies was certain, factionalism was far more prevalent than it is now, and it was common for doctors to "abuse each other with unsparing violence" in the name of their medical commitments. Moreover, the contemporary physician was perceived as hypersensitive in matters of "professional etiquette." Criticisms of a doctor's procedures by a colleague, lack of a respectful attitude of one physician toward another, a bluntly given opposing medical view—anything, in short, that smacked of "patient-grabbing" or even remotely implied an unfavorable estimation of one practitioner's skill by another—doctors were constantly, and often neurotically, on watch for. The result was that "the intercourse between [physicians] is but too often disturbed by personal rivalry, if it be not even wholly interrupted by feelings of actual hostility." Such a situation, the author of "Character and

Abuses" goes on to say, "embitters the happiness of medical men, and not infrequently impairs their usefulness."

Early in the story we learn that there was "a professional warfare of long continuance" between Baglioni and Rappaccini and that it has been generally conceded that Rappaccini has had the better of it. This has resulted, on Rappaccini's part, in the cold contempt of a superior medical intellect for the "sober imagination" of a practitioner whose fingers are apt to stink "of some vile apothecary drug" and, on Baglioni's part, in a consuming envy. Although Baglioni nods in the direction of admitting Rappaccini's medical skill, he is gnawed by a jealousy that corrupts his judgment. He refuses to acknowledge that anyone in Italy has more medical science than himself, ascribes Rappaccini's apparently "marvelous cures" to "the work of chance" and his failures to his mistaken theories, and denigrates his colleague's inhumanity, without recognizing how much he himself resembles his enemy in this regard. How neurotic this professional rivalry has made Baglioni is revealed by his conviction that Rappaccini is preparing Beatrice to take Baglioni's chair in the medical faculty, which we know is absurd, since Beatrice is utterly ignorant of medical science.

All of Baglioni's actions are driven solely by a desire to "thwart" Rappaccini—not from any humane hope of freeing the two youngsters from a cruel destiny but from a craving to become in actuality what he wants to believe he is: the most illustrious doctor in Italy. "Perchance, most learned Rappaccini, I may foil you where you little dream of it!" is the mad cry of a doctor whose professional jealousy has emptied the precepts "of the divine art of medicine" (his own words) of all meaning. Caught in the pincer of professional enmity, Beatrice and Giovanni are cruelly crushed, the former losing her life, the latter his reason for living. From the cultural-historical perspective, the disaster in which the rivalry culminates can be viewed as the ultimate emblem of what physicians' propensities for "frequent jealousies and quarrels" can come to.

"Readiness to take offence for slight causes," which in the view of Hawthorne's culture characterized the medical practitioner, was aggravated in the 1830s and 1840s by the breakout of what R. H. Shryock—in *Medicine and Society in America: 1660–1860* (1960)—calls "medical sectarianism": fragmentation of the profession into opposing medical philosophies. This split gave rise to two additional criticisms of physicians, which the public "charged upon them as a body." The first of these, in the words of the author of "Character and Abuses," was "bigoted devotion to visionary theories"; the second was "bigoted attachment to authorized modes of practice, [which] renders physicians unwilling to receive information, or to adopt improvements in practice, however valuable, unless they come through the regular channels of scientific investigation, or established theories." That these charges tend to be contradictory, accusing doctors of being both radical and reactionary, is not remarkable; it seems to be traditional. In our own time, doctors are accused of being unscientific in prescribing tests and therapies for which no clear proof has been established, and of being *too* scientific in their approach to medicine at the expense of "the whole person."

In the figure of Dr. Rappaccini, Hawthorne embodied "a bigoted devotion to visionary theories" in such a pure, almost abstract form as to make him into the very paradigm of what Hawthorne's culture censured. Apart from his dream of creating a race which would be, so to speak, impervious to the "diseases" of life—"to be endowed with marvellous gifts, against which no power nor strength could avail,"—Rappaccini simply does not exist. As with all true fanatics, nothing intercedes between the man and his vision. Without even a thought to their consent, he arrogates to himself a total biological control over the lives of Beatrice and Giovanni. In this, Hawthorne predicts the figure of the doctor-as-God (which the symbolism of the story continuously supports) that was to emerge later. Hawthorne, it seems, sensed tendencies in the medical profession's relationship to the culture which, if allowed to develop unchecked, would allow it to become what in fact it became—a profession unwilling "to brook criticisms by God or man," as Alan Gregg puts it in *For Future Doctors* (1957).

One of the most interesting aspects of the story, from the medical point of view, is that Hawthorne makes Rappaccini's theory both right and wrong. When we first meet him, he has already deviated, in Baglioni's words, from "the good old rules of the medical profession" and so has become, in the language of the nineteenth century (and the story), an "empiric." His practice of limiting his materia medica to medicines distilled from plants and "his theory, that all medicinal virtues are comprised within those substances which we term vegetable poisons," ally him with both the "botanics" and the homeopaths. But his unorthodoxy has been eminently successful—he is a "famous Doctor," known throughout Italy for his marvelous cures. Even the "therapy" he has practiced on his daughter has been wholly effective, insofar as it has accomplished what he set out to do: remove her from "the limits of ordinary nature." But Dr. Rappaccini has not thereby created for her an Eden, but rather "an Eden of poisonous flowers." In insulating her from human ills, he has, at one and the same time, removed her from life itself. Her actual death, then, is merely a formality, a grim instance of a grim saying—the doctor cured the disease but killed the patient.

As I have indicated, although there was cultural antipathy toward that segment of the medical profession which was perceived as being visionary theorists, there was also, paradoxically, a condemnation of doctors as being "unwilling to receive information or adopt improvements" unless they came through the channels of orthodox medicine and established theories. On the face of it, this makes little sense, since it condemns the refusal of knowledge from sources that it has defined as "crackpot." There is, however, no law which says cultures, or for that matter individuals, must be logical in their aversions. The illogic shows how pervasive was the negative view of the profession. Surely people went to both kinds of doctors, and almost certainly exempted their personal practitioners from the general onus of the profession; but when they looked at the profession as a whole, they were apt to say, "A plague on both your houses."

It is entirely appropriate, then, that Hawthorne, with impartial aversion, presented both types of doctor in his story. Baglioni is obviously a "regular" practitioner, who has followed "the good old rules of the medical profession." From Rappaccini's heterodox approach to medicine, he will learn nothing, despite the evidence of "miraculous cures." To this man of "sober imagination," Rappaccini is a "vile empiric," which by definition means that his "views of the healing art" are unsound. Baglioni's practice is immutably what it has always been—dosing with "some vile apothecary drug."

Beatrice's terrible condition, which is the result of her father's visionary theory, and its promised cure, which is Baglioni's chemical antidote ("almost divine in its efficacy"), collide in her body. The result is the ultimate irony: iatrogenic death. Criticism of the medical profession can hardly go further.

When Hawthorne was in college and thinking about a career, he rejected the prospect of becoming a physician, because, as he wrote his family, "I should not like to live by the diseases and infirmities of my fellow creatures." On the evidence of "Rappaccini's Daughter," he had found, in the intervening twenty years, more compelling reasons for rejection. But as I have tried to show, Hawthorne's antipathy to the medical profession was not merely personal; it was, as well, a remarkably precise reflection of the image of the physician in early nineteenth-century America.

"Rappaccini's Daughter," of course, is not *about* the medical profession. Its central concern is with certain moral and metaphysical ambiguities, the various permutations of which there is no need to repeat here. But it is also a remarkable, if tangential, revelation of a significant aspect of the culture of its time. Years ago, T. S. Eliot reminded us that every *serious* writer, no matter what his subject, will convey truths about his culture. "Rappaccini's Daughter" seems to me to be a very fine example of that precept.

NOTES

1. *Nineteenth-Century Fiction,* 27 (1972), 61–70.
2. "The Family Physician," *Harper's Magazine,* 137 (1889), 722–729.
3. "The Physician and the Social Question," *North American Review,* 160 (1895), 461–469.
4. The materials for arriving at the "image" of the medical profession in early nineteenth-century America are scattered through letters, diaries, and the more public writings of the period. The best source I have found (though it must be augmented by other contemporary materials and the researches of later social histories of the profession) is "Character and Abuses of the Medical Profession" in *North American Review* (32 [1831], 367–386), an unsigned essay by a Boston physician. Because the essay is polemical, setting out to explain (or explain away) the various "abuses" his profession has suffered from a misunderstanding public, it affords the reader an excellent summary of the culture's view of the doctor. Although the essay appeared thirteen years before Hawthorne's story, I had no hesitation using it, since there is no evidence that the medical situation had changed much in the intervening years.

Eve's Bower:
HAWTHORNE'S TRANSITION FROM PUBLIC DOCTRINES TO PRIVATE TRUTHS

William H. Shurr

The most important question in the minds of the writers of the American renaissance was nothing less than the fundamental nature of reality. Was it mean? Then publish its meanness to the world. Was it sublime? Then give a true and adequate account of its sublimity.

Melville and Emerson determine the outer edges of the intellectual spectrum of the times, perhaps defining the known limits of the mental universe in ways that are still valid and interesting. Pessimism and optimism furnish initial, tentative categories. As landscape painters, for example, they live in Hell and Paradise, respectively. The vegetation of the Galapagos would not have nodded to Emerson, could one even imagine him in such an uncongenial setting. In poetry, "Shiloh" and "Malvern Hill" oppose Emerson's "Concord Hymn" on nearly every fundamental option concerning war, patriotism, the intelligence of the common man, and the nature of the Over-Soul. One author affirms that "evil is merely privative, not absolute. It is like cold, which is the privation of heat. All evil is so much death or nonentity." Surely we are at the other end of two extremes of some hypothetical mental spectrum when we find Melville affirming, almost as classic rebuttal late in his life, that in seeking an understanding of the positive agency of evil, at work in a realistically presented Claggart, we arrive finally at the mysterious "depravity according to nature."

Where does Hawthorne stand in this field of moral and metaphysical forces? Somewhat ambiguously, apparently, depending on the texts chosen. He is a participant in transcendentalism who then steps out to become its dark satirist. He is the American who writes of England as our old home. He is Protestant with a love-hate relationship to Catholicism. He immerses himself in Puritan history, to find it horrible, yet the only workable regime of life, as in "The Maypole of Merry Mount." He undoubtedly admires Hester, but shrinks, in the end, from the strength of her sexuality, purified and sublimated though it has become.

Although his friends found him "unknowable," as do many of his readers, there is at least one critical moment that can be clearly discerned in Hawthorne's writing where he underwent a profound change in direction. The moment is characterized by a firm and controlling intuition of his relation to transcendentalism, by moral understanding of the personal meaning of the myth of Edenic bliss and the Fall, and by a survey of the ground he occupied as a short-story writer and would occupy as (mostly) a writer of longer romances. His values suddenly clarify, as do also the devices for extending his narrative situations to greater length. Not surprisingly, he enjoyed the honeymoon years with Sophia at this same time. The record of this transitional moment is found in *Mosses from an Old Manse*. Three pieces in this volume, the preface and the two Garden stories, together form a significant record of Hawthorne's thoughts on questions raised by New England transcendentalism in relation to sexual fulfillment and the myth of the lost Garden Paradise.

I

"The Old Manse," which introduces the collection of stories and sketches, is one of the important writings of New England transcendentalism. Most of the major figures appear here, inventoried by Hawthorne. The historian Bancroft, he says, might have written more vividly and more philosophically had he lived at the Old Manse, as he once proposed. Emerson wrote *Nature* in the manse, though the author of *Mosses* prefers to admire him as "a poet of deep beauty and austere tenderness" rather than as a philosopher or prophet who could tender him the word of life. One of the most typical stories about Thoreau is here recorded: how he told Hawthorne of watching beds of pond lilies "unfolding in due succession as the sunrise stole gradually from flower to flower." Ellery Channing joins with Hawthorne, as he had with Thoreau, for fishing expeditions along the Concord River, and Hawthorne records the impression of "golden" lumps of conversation that were never to be transmuted into his poetry. Margaret Fuller seems present in this preface, as one "on whose feminine nature had been imposed the heavy gift of intellectual power . . . , and with it the necessity to act upon the world." Perhaps the seeds of Holmes's "statlier mansions" can be found in a sequence of phrases from this preface. And there appear to be hints taken up by Melville, in the "exquisite delight" mentioned in a passage rhythmically similar to the conclusion of Father Mapple's sermon, and in the boy whose ax stroke—"it must have been a nervous impulse, without purpose, without thought, and betokening a sensitive and impressible nature rather than a hardened one"—foreshadows Billy Budd's fatal blow. At least Hawthorne, in imagination, "sought to follow that poor youth through his subsequent career" and found that "this one circumstance has borne more fruit for me, than all that history tells us of the fight."

To move from historical personages to theory, there is much in Hawthorne's essay that furnishes commentary both on the transcendental intellectual ambience and on the literary methodology of its authors. Hawthorne, while living among transcendentalists, perceives himself to be linked, by his presence in the Old Manse, with generations of the older Calvinist ministry. Though the essay, at moments, exudes the honeymoon bliss of the first three years of the Hawthornes' marriage, the dominant impression upon the reader is that he has been invited to share the musings of a calm and fairly solitary individual, oppressed by the heft of clerical musings. The essay begins with a strong evocation of the spiritual quality of the house, retired, separated from the mundane cares attended to in the village and along the road outside. Whether rummaging through the old religious tomes in the house, or imagining the life of a young divinity student in his "Saint's Chamber" in the garret, or meditating on the long fruitful life of the clergyman who has planted the garden and orchards adjacent, Hawthorne finds in retrospect that his three years in this house were subtly dominated by an atmosphere of theological probing. Still, it has been a good place for him, where stories came to maturity like great apples, "falling without a breath of wind, from the mere necessity of perfect ripeness." And he has made advances upon the thought of the previous theological tenants. Their massive books are "too corpulent a body, it might be feared, to comprehend the spiritual element in religion." The problem is that they were works of intellect: "Thought grows mouldy. . . . The works of man's intellect decay like those of his hands." He reflects on the many sermons written there, chastising himself as heretofore merely a "writer of idle stories," and senses his own presence in the house as the first time "the Old Manse had ever been prophaned by a lay person." He is conscious of the need to extend their work into a more secularized world. In such a heavy atmosphere, Hawthorne would prefer to work in his garden, tending the summer squashes; he would find there, much as Thoreau had in his bean patch, not only "love of the beautiful," but "a hearty enjoyment," "something worth living for." In such an atmosphere, transcendentalist perceptions come readily: "An orchard has a relation to mankind, and readily connects itself with matters of the heart." But he is conscious also that the garden he tends is the same one that was established generations ago by the intense New England clergymen who lived there before him.

In assessing the discoveries of transcendentalist literary methodology, Hawthorne finds himself fascinated, as Thoreau is at the same time, with the triple capacities a sheet of water has; to delimit a physical surface, to reflect the trees about and even the heavens above, and at the same time allow suggestive glimpses of darker things below. Nature, in this instance, does not present opacities; its surfaces are at once transparencies and mirrors. Preference inclines to what is above: "Surely the disembodied images stand in closer relation to the soul." But Hawthorne, unlike Thoreau, leads the image off into allegory that is fairly Puritanic while still recognizable as transcendental:

> We will not then, malign our river as gross and impure while it can glorify itself with so adequate a picture of the heaven that broods above it; or, if we remember its tawny hue and the muddiness of its bed, let it be a symbol that the earthliest human soul has an infinite spiritual capacity and may contain the better world within its depths.

But something else is actually perceived in these depths: "The mud-turtle, whom continual washing cannot cleanse . . . the very same black mud out of which the yellow lily sucks its obscene life and noisome odor." Hawthorne places himself among the transcendentalists; he employs their typical method of progression from natural image to spiritual insight; but he is also their strongest link with the older Calvinist tradition.

The most individualistic trait of the preface, "The Old Manse," is the sense Hawthorne conveys—to his "friends," he prefers to think, rather than to "the public"—of having arrived at his private inner garden, "my garden . . . of precisely the right extent." Hawthorne came relatively early to cultivate his garden. And a perceptive young writer works the garden of the Old Manse, home of generations of New England clergy, at some hazard. It evokes an Eden, such as that enjoyed "by natives of summer isles." It is, as well, the biblical Eden before the fall, since he plucks ripe fruit from trees he has neither sown nor tended. For the rivers of Paradise he has "the Concord—river of peace and quietness." His garden, however, will not hold stable, either as a mythological place in the mind or as reality in the present world: during a rainstorm, "Eve's bower in Paradise must have been but a cheerless and aguish kind of shelter. . . . The idea of sleeping on a couch of wet roses!" This garden has its demon too: "The summit of a wooded hill, about a mile distant, was enveloped in a dense mist, where the demon of the tempest seemed to have his abiding place, and to be plotting still direr inclemencies." Nor, his reflections continue, does any kind of certainty result from allegorizing on the garden in the present stage of human history. It is more a vehicle for exploration than a pattern of certainty: "Some persons [like flowers] assimilate only what is ugly and evil from the same moral circumstances which supply good and beautiful results—the fragrance of celestial flowers—to the daily life of others." The murkiness of human will and human circumstance intrudes to wrap the present allegorical garden in further mystery; still, we shall find him allegorizing at great length on the Garden during this period.

Hawthorne's preface to *Mosses from an Old Manse* thus reveals a great deal about his conceptions of the literary and intellectual atmosphere of the times and his relationship to them. He knows the major figures personally and lives among them. He describes their particular method of literary generalization and finds it congenial. Influences are mutual. He is aware of some collapse in the authority of New England religion, yet senses in himself the capabilities, which he shared with Emerson and Thoreau, for examining and restating the older concerns in newer terms, more valid in an increasingly secularized world. Hawthorne thus sees himself, for the moment at least, as full participant in the major literary movement of his time. His role, as he acts it out here, is to record and evaluate the work of his fellow transcendentalists, to restate their literary methods, and to add (in his probings of a typical transcendentalist metaphor) corrective expansions to their body of insight. "The Old Manse" is a moment of light, of relative calm and emotional security. It may be that the surface tensions that support his earlier ambiguities are momentarily slackened, when introspective semi-recluse had become ardent lover and truster. The garden he cultivates is at once the one which the old clergymen cultivated, his own present bliss as newlywed, and the allegorical garden which stands at the beginning of Christian history. It is worth puzzling over the fact that his own Eve is unmentioned in the essay.

II

It is at this point that the preface leads directly to one of the stories in *Mosses from an Old Manse:* "Rappaccini's Daughter." Hundreds of pages have been written on this story; but seen in a context of New England Calvinism, established by the place where he wrote it and the preface to the collection in which he published it, the allegory suddenly clarifies in interesting new ways. There are several discernible Christianities, and much of what one takes to be Christianity depends upon how one reads the simple dynamics of the archetypal Garden story, what happens in the transition from imagined ideal state to actual fallen state, from myth into history. What the figures in the Garden represent and how their relationships are perceived, both before and after the fall, largely determine both the theology and the institutions of life that follow.

Hawthorne appears to disarm such serious analysis of his story by lightly introducing it as the work of "M. de l'Aubépine" (Hawthorne), and diagnosing his lack of popularity as caused by "an inveterate love of allegory." But he shifts to a more serious intensity as he charges the reader to find exactly "the proper point of view" intended in the allegory. The introduction then goes on to cite Eugene Sue for comparison, an author whose religio-sexual romances had recently excited French readers and censors. Apparently the library at the Old Manse was supplemented in interesting ways.

Hawthorne solicits the reader's serious meditations on his allegory of the Garden. Among the allusions that abound in the story are more or less explicit references to Dante, Genesis, Ecclesiastes, Samuel, the Song of Solomon, the Gospels, Revelations, Ovid (for the Vertum-nuus-Pomona legend), Edward Johnson's *The Wonder-Working Providence of Scion's Saviour, Faust,* Emerson's *Nature,* Hamlet's most famous soliloquy, Sir Thomas Browne, and possibly Jonathan Edwards. All these concern fundamental religious problems and many are cast in the form of allegory. They press the reader to consider Hawthorne's story in the same genre. They suggest, as the garden ironically does for Giovanni, as Hawthorne's garden had for him, "a symbolic language to keep him in communion with Nature."

The story concerns a beautiful girl who tends a botanical garden of poisonous flowers, and who has imbibed their poisons from birth. The question is started early in the story: "Was this garden, then, the Eden of the present world?" The answer is given later by Beatrice: "This garden is his [Rappaccini's] world"; and the answer is confirmed still later, when in answer to Beatrice's call Giovanni "hastened into that Eden of poisonous flowers."

But the allegory is complex and some work is required before it clarifies. A second question is asked along with the first; the father, Dr. Rappaccini, is seen cautiously tending the garden: "Was he the Adam?" It becomes obvious, as the story progresses, that this question is misleading, that Giovanni and Beatrice are the Adam and Eve of this historical garden, the actual fallen garden.

Serious problems occur in determining the identities of other allegorical items. The tree of life is easily identified as the poisonous plant of death in the center of the garden; the spring from which the rivers of Paradise flowed is now the broken bowl of the fountain; the serpent, no longer the necessary tool of Satan, is reduced to "a small orange-colored reptile," easily killed by the woman. But further identification makes it necessary to summon to mind a particular variety of Christianity, the older American Calvinism, which, as Channing had said, made a great deal more of the hints and fragments of the Genesis story than other Christian traditions thought necessary.

The Calvinism that Channing referred to must be the key to this allegory. The world, in this reading, is now totally under the domination of Satan and redemption is only a marginally successful operation, involving the few elect. Rappaccini dominates the garden of the present world. He is sick with his long absorption in the study of poisonous evil, but still immensely powerful. He always wears the color of death and embodies the worst of Hawthorne's evils by sedulous cultivation of intellect over "warmth of heart." He assumes divine prerogatives in a fallen world, looking into the "inmost nature" of his creations, "making observations regarding their creative essence." Like the Calvinist deity, he gives his creatures no choice, but preordains the poison which will take over his daughter's body from the moment of her birth. The demonic and the divine merge into one after the Fall: as Adam and Eve no longer enjoyed intimacy with God when he walked in the cool of evening, so "there was no approach to intimacy between [Rappaccini] and these vegetable existences. On the contrary, he avoided their actual touch." The world too is fallen, in addition to mankind, "as if all this beauty did but conceal a deadlier malice." The most concentrated center of this evil is carefully specified later in the story, where all of Beatrice's attractive power is "girdled tensely . . . by her virgin zone"; the woman is the devil's child and her specific evil for Giovanni is precisely her sexual attraction. She is "sister" to the poisonous shrubs which exhale death. Her rich Oriental beauty is "the deadliest poison in existence" in the fallen world. And Giovanni, the fallen Adam, is superficial and sensuous, robbed of the angelic gifts he enjoyed before the Fall. In this world, sexual love leads not to marriage and consummation but to convulsive death.

In the Christian economy, it is Christ whose special care is humanity. But the truly Divine is hard to discern in a fallen world. The only major figure still left unaccounted for in the story is the clumsy, rather foolish old man, Dr. Pietro Baglioni, who is presented as striving with Rappaccini for eminence in the healing arts. It may be difficult to discern the Christ in him, but there are some clues to this identity. He claims to be "a teacher of the divine art of medicine." He offers good advice to save Giovanni. From on high he renders final judgment on the action in the last words of the story. He offers the grace of a precious liquid, "almost divine in its efficacy," which actually kills the sinner. His role is that of an ineffective Christ in a fallen world, whose mostly reprobate figures move in utterly predestinated patterns. To Giovanni, the divine healer can offer only his impotent tears, in the glass of "Lachryma Christi." And the allegorical significance of the two authorities becomes transparent, for a moment, when Hawthorne writes "that there was a professional warfare of long continuance between [Baglioni] and Rappaccini, in which the latter was generally thought to have gained the advantage." Calvinist piety is one of the few forms of Christianity in which this last assertion could be made, that the probabilities are in favor of Satan, in his war with Christ for domination of the world. It is the "awful doom" of the two lovers to be caught between the two larger forces.

Behind the rivalry between Baglioni and Rappaccini, in a more mundane sense, may lie the bitter fight between Galenic and Paracelsan medicine. Rappaccini obviously prefers naturally grown herbs; Baglioni's preference for drugs derived from chemical experiment seems indi-

cated by the liquid he gives to Giovanni in the silver vial.
Significant in this battle between the schools of Galen
and Paracelsus was the cultivation of botanical gardens,
and the earliest seems to have been established at the
University of Padua in 1545. Padua, its university, and a
botanical garden also provide the setting for "Rappaccini's Daughter," and in 1545 John Calvin was prominently
engaged in the trials of witches and sorcerors, as well as
reframing the Genevan *Ordinances Concerning Marriage.*
Calvin's decade of the 1540s had recently been described
by Balzac as his "reign of terror," in *The Human Comedy,*
where Calvin was compared to another demonic figure,
Robbespierre. But Hawthorne's native Calvinism provided a sufficient frame within which to paint this particular version of the Garden, whether he had read this
section in Balzac or not.

The story touches human flesh and nerve endings.
For many thinkers in the last century, the gods turned
mean the moment before they disappeared. What if "the
sacred" no longer existed? What if the most rewarding
and necessary human relationships were blighted and
suspect, incapable of providing the needed comfort they
promised? What if, in the last act of the play, grace
turned into viciousness, paternity and divinity into sadis-
tic experimentation, the moment before all actors and
their shams disappeared from the stage? This would indeed be the end of religion: "Calvin's last extreme," in
Melville's words; the triumph of the "Conqueror Worm"
in Poe's. This would indeed be blight and torment for
Hawthorne, the new bridegroom cultivating the Garden
of his Calvinist predecessors.

As in some of his other works, it is difficult to determine the exact degree of "distance" Hawthorne was
able to put between himself and his subject. In "Young
Goodman Brown," the intrusive author writes of "the instinct that guides mortal man to evil," and he will not
allow the reader to minimize Brown's experience as a
mere dream. In another story, where "the saddest of all
prisons [is one's] own heart," a minister wears a peniten-

tial veil for the whole of his life in order to gain the authority, at the end, to declare all human beings infected with hidden sin. The intrusive author of "The Birthmark" asserts "the fatal flaw of humanity which Nature, in one shape or another, stamps ineffaceably on all her productions." And in the preface to *The House of the Seven Gables,* he proclaims "the truth, namely, that the wrongdoing of one generation lives into the successive ones, and, divesting itself of every temporary advantage, becomes a pure and uncontrolled mischief."

So Hawthorne, at least when he is the self-conscious author who manages the narratives and molds his readers' responses, frequently assumes a rigorously primitive kind of Calvinism. Such a Calvinism is the lens which clarifies the distortions of the Garden allegory in "Rappaccini's Daughter." But the question of shifting distances between the author and his material reasserts itself. The reader may take the story as a grotesque parody of the Calvinist point of view: in the introduction to the story, Hawthorne presents it as a translation of a tale originally published in a French journal which "has for some years past led the defense of liberal principles and popular rights." One can speculate that parody is working if a rigorously Calvinist allegory appears in a liberal journal—though this is a slender peg upon which to hang the whole interpretation of a story. Particularly is this true when the magazine he mentions is a slight disguise for *The Democratic Review,* in which Hawthorne originally published the story, and it may well be that he merely intends a whimsical compliment to the editors. And in view of other authorial statements (just cited), it is equally arguable that the grotesque features are to be taken as a straightforward allegory of things as they truly are, as Hawthorne sees them.

Hawthorne is hard on his world here—hard on his Eve and Adam, on God, on the impotent old Christ, on the nature of the fallen Garden of the world. Some original sin has quite literally poisoned the scene and all its mechanisms for wholeness and salvation. The new garden, the world, is distorted here far beyond the changes required by a more moderate and traditional Christian orthodoxy. Clearly, the reader is left dissatisfied with the warped *bizarrerie* of "Rappaccini's Daughter," because of the conflicting authorial clues to intention. One wishes for more aesthetic resolution, for some sense of further personal settlement. What one senses in the story is a savage stereotype of the classic American religion—the Calvinism to which writers, particularly of the nineteenth century, have granted almost canonical status, and departure from which was always delicious heterodoxy. It may perhaps have to remain moot—whether Hawthorne intends to see the world here as a horribly Calvinist distortion or whether he parodies the view. What can be asserted is that Hawthorne takes a serious view of his role as New England writer, conscious equally of the Calvinist past and the ethical intensity of the present transcendentalism. He probes for truth as the artist should, through creative manipulation of the symbol, the myth, exposing their latent powers for the reader's meditative enjoyment. For himself, he emerges with a new sense of the Garden and its prototypical figures.

Hawthorne's mind on these matters seems to have clarified suddenly with the stark allegory of "Rappaccini's Daughter." It may even be that the multiple interpretations allowed by the author show exactly how rich the allegory is as a matrix for contemplating American stereotypes. The story looks backward, as a frame through which Hawthorne's classic short stories can be viewed. From here on, Hawthorne has the forces, the concepts, and his own evaluations, even his own ambivalencies, more consciously under control. He has found the groundwork of values, symbols, and narrative patterns for the three great novels that follow. But first, it is interesting to find still another Garden story, consciously placed later in *Mosses from the Old Manse* (though it may have been written earlier), where alternative possibilities, with new beginnings and new freedoms, are explored.

III

The story is called "The New Adam and Eve," and Hawthorne's Eve seems undoubtedly present. In this piece, Hawthorne frames human history, with an allegory for its end to match the allegory of its beginning. The old Adam and Eve had explored a perfect Paradise before their abrupt expulsion to a fallen world and the necessity of fashioning a life with their fallen perceptions. The new Adam and Eve are still unfallen, their natures innocent and their vision new. But they are dropped into a world that has existed for thousands of years as corrupted. The fallen human inhabitants have suddenly been removed and the fresh world they now explore is Rappaccini's Garden: the actors have vanished but the poisons they cultivated remain. Hawthorne has here created the moralist's ideal vehicle, and though the use he makes of it is relatively slight (compared, say, to Mark Twain's later use of the figures), the inventory is fairly complete and the points are telling.

Hawthorne is careful to lay out his intentions in the first sentence: "We, who are born into the world's artificial system, can never adequately know how little in our present state and circumstances is natural, and how much is merely the interpolation of the perverted mind and heart of man." In the second sentence, two controlling concepts, Art and Nature, are presented as the positive and negative criteria for the vignettes that follow. The idea will recur that Art is crafty, a deceptive parent, under whose tutelage the former human race had perverted the goods of the earth; Nature, on the other hand, still guides the new Adam and Eve to react in disgust (for example) to the fancy banquet foods which "steam with a loathsome odor of death and corruption." The human race, since the fall of its first parents, has followed Art more frequently than Nature, and in every instance human Art has led to further corruption of the once-beautiful world; Nature remains the uncorrupted source of purer inspirations.

For an artist, Hawthorne presents an amazing list of the products of stepmother Art. The first thing that impresses the new Adam and Eve as they awaken in the city of Boston is an unnatural squareness and regularity, and "the marks of wear and tear, and unrenewed decay, which distinguish the works of man from the growth of nature." Stylish clothes seem bizarre and useless. They hear bells from a church tower tolling the hour, but don't understand their import: "Nature would measure time by the succession of thoughts and acts which constitute real life." The court of Justice ("Thou art the very symbol of man's perverted state"), the hall of Legislature, the prison and its scaffold, all are incomprehensible institutions to the new and innocent humans. The only man-made thing of beauty that they encounter is that favorite instrument of the romantics, an Aeolian harp, a kind of primitive receiver of the harmonies of Nature.

Just past the midpoint of the story, the analysis rises to a generalized statement about the Fall of man in this still-lovely world. For the narrator, who becomes a personalized version of Hawthorne in the course of the story, man's Fall results from "his revolt from Nature." The forms that this revolt have taken are then examined in the remaining pages: "those mighty capitalists" of the Exchange, who pursued the "most artificial of the sciences," according to one example. Following in this line are those who store their money in banks and those who prefer jewelry to roses ("these lovelier gems of nature"). The unfallen Adam and Eve puzzle over signs that there had been an enormous gulf between the wealthy and the crushingly poor; they are unable to imagine the horrors of war, symbolized by the Bunker Hill monument.

The allegory becomes more personal. They enter a library, where Eve notices a certain pensive and "dismal" mood come over her new Adam. Hawthorne's trade, the vocation he had pursued with near monomania for many years, comes under harsh and negative scrutiny here. The Tree of Knowledge holds the fatal apple to this new couple. What are books? "All the perversions and sophistries, and false wisdom so aptly mimicking the true; all the narrow truth, so partial that it becomes more deceptive than falsehood; all the wrong principles and worse practice, the pernicious examples and mistaken rules of life; all the specious theories, which turn earth into cloud-land, and men into shadows; all the sad experience, which it took mankind so many ages to accumulate, and from which they never drew a moral for their future guidance—the whole heap of this disastrous lore would have tumbled at once upon Adam's head."

A pitying transcendentalist might have reflected here that Hawthorne had never read Plato well and thus would remain a mere moralizing storyteller. But a more deeply personal consideration was running concurrently with this phase of transition in Hawthorne's work. The tirade above caps another and more important theme, stated just earlier. One recalls that "The New Adam and Eve" dates from early in the honeymoon years at the Old Manse, years when Hawthorne felt that Sophia had rescued him from his miserable preexistence: "'My dear Adam,' cries Eve, 'you look pensive and dismal! Do fling down that stupid thing [a 'bulky folio'].'" Hawthorne had a profound sense of the newness of his life with Sophia. He recounted in his notebook a brief visit back to Salem, alone, early in their marriage: "I went alone to Salem, where I resumed all my bachelor habits for nearly a fortnight, leading the same life in which ten years of my youth flitted away like a dream. But how much changed was I! At last I had got hold of a reality which never could be taken from me. It was good thus to get apart from my happiness for the sake of contemplating it."

This new consciousness is mirrored in "The New Adam and Eve." It begins with the birth to full adulthood of the new couple: "They find themselves in existence, and gazing into one another's eyes. Their emotion is not astonishment; nor do they perplex themselves with efforts to discover what, and whence, and why they are. Each is satisfied to be, because the other exists likewise; and their first consciousness is of calm and mutual enjoyment, which seems not to have been the birth of that very moment, but prolonged from a past eternity. Thus content with an inner sphere which they inhabit together, it is not immediately that the outward world can obtrude itself upon their notice."

The new couple here is not Giovanni and Beatrice, already infected by distrust and living in a society withered by envy and ambition, but—it seems—Nathaniel and his Sophia, finding lovely innocence in a world where the seeds of corruption do not yet "obtrude." The moment is as overtly erotic as publishing conventions of the 1840s would allow. The lovely sensuality of the naked couple is emphasized, is heightened, when Eve teasingly covers herself with "a remnant of exquisite silver gauze." The nakedness of the body heals the natural shame of the soul. They idealize their emotions of the moment and project them as panacea: "Man never had attempted to cure sin by LOVE! Had he but once made the effort, it might well have happened, that there would have been no more need of the dark lazar-house [the prison] into which Adam and Eve had wandered." Adam's speculative mind generates questions about the nature of the world and why they have been placed in it; Eve's instinctive answer is "Why?—To love one another!"

As mentioned, these three pieces—the preface and the two garden stories in *Mosses from an Old Manse*—constitute the record of Hawthorne's thoughts on the questions raised by New England transcendentalism and his relationship to that movement. In his view, the natural world is still the unfallen Garden, where grass breaks through and the sun beams down to offer man the still-pure influences of a benevolent Nature. But man is the frail element. Eve's consciousness grows inward, to questions of motherhood and children—woman-questions which she can't share with Adam. Adam's consciousness likewise grows inward, but apart from her, to speculate on the male mysteries which books are written about. Here are the beginnings of what Hawthorne calls, with his fellow transcendentalists, "his revolt from Nature," the retreat into the frail human consciousness where dark questions are asked and people are separated from one another. A robust self-reliance may be available to Emerson, but his personal force places him far above the ordinary man's capabilities. Hawthorne thought of those who made pilgrimages to Emerson as "uncertain, troubled, earnest wanderers."

Hawthorne expressed himself dissatisfied with the slightness of these short works at the end of "The Old Manse" preface. He had produced, he said, "no profound treatise of Ethics, no philosophic history, no novel even." Apparently, the twenty-one new tales he published during this period seemed insufficient because he had resolved, as a product of these three years, to write "a novel that should evolve some deep lesson and should possess physical substance enough to stand alone." These novels were to come, of course, fairly soon and in rapid succession: *The Scarlet Letter, The House of the Seven Gables,* and *The Blithedale Romance,* all between 1850 and 1852. The Old Manse period stands as entrance to the period of the great novels, with the term in the Salem customs house as fallow space between. And it is quite clear that the substance he looked for, the body of ideas and sustaining primary images that allows these books to stand alone, drives from the mental and emotional work of the three years at the Old Manse.

IV

Linking these pieces, as we have done, we seem to find a critical moment: Hawthorne's moving to a higher stage of maturity as a writer. In "Rappaccini's Daughter," the young suitor is gifted with no great mental perception. He senses guilt and shame as he pursues his relationship with the devil's daughter. He identifies the Other, the woman, with evil and the forces of darkness. He is insecure, and his insecurity leads him to mistrust her and himself. He readily submits to authority figures for solutions to his personal problems. In "The New

Adam and Eve," the young male has obviously moved into a position of mental strength, security, and self-possession. He is in touch with the flesh and happy with that touch. Problems still intrude, problems of truly cosmic import; the true nature of the world is still not known and the future is uncertain. But the problems are now at some remove, and speculative. He no longer senses the investment of dark emotions in them. He has come to trust the Other, the woman, and metaphysics can no longer scare him. Hawthorne can be seen in the process of taking the advice Poe offered when he read the book: "Let him mend his pen, get a bottle of invisible ink, come out from the Old Manse, cut Mr. Alcott, hang (if possible) the editor of 'The Dial,' and throw out of the window to the pigs all his odd numbers of 'The North American Review.'" But he does even more: he finds a sense of wholeness and mental health in his new relationship with Sophia. The public battle ends in private resolution.

The personal and artistic discoveries in *Mosses from an Old Manse* extend into the trilogy of great American novels. In *The Scarlet Letter,* the two male antagonists are tempted by the lure of books, and overlove of scholarship is diagnosed as at least partially the cause of the decline of each. Part of Hester's office is to woo Dimmesdale into the open air; part of Chillingworth's strategy is to involve himself and Dimmesdale more deeply in study and introspection. The opening chapter of the book presents Nature in opposition to the artificial and corrupting institutions of society, the same strategy which directed the new Adam and Eve in their evaluations. The diabolism of Rappaccini is also strong in Hawthorne's mind, when he employs a familiarity with Paracelsus and Sir Kenelm Digby as an item of his characterization of Chillingworth, the herb gatherer. The transcendentalist image of a reflecting sheet of water figures in the scenes when Pearl is at the seashore and when the brook reflects the scarlet *A* which Hester has momentarily cast off.

The major thematic conflict in *The Scarlet Letter* starts early in the book, with placement of the antinomian Ann Hutchinson in contrast to the rigidly legalistic Calvinism of the village people—the private mind against public institutions. Throughout the book, one comes upon powerfully connotative statements concerning "the black flower of civilized society": "the great law," "iron framework," "reverence for authority," "the whole system of ancient prejudice . . . of ancient principle," "stern tribunals," "the Puritan establishment," "human institutions, and whatever priests or legislators had established." The embodiment of these values is Dimmesdale, "a true priest, a true religionist, with the reverential sentiment largely developed, and an order of mind that impelled itself powerfully along the track of a creed. . . . In no state of society would he have been called a man of liberal views." Contrasted with this set of ideals are those associated with "the wild rosebush" of the first chapter: Hester and Ann Hutchinson, "natural dignity and force of character," "free-will," "freedom of speculation." Hester embodies these antinomian values, "little accustomed, in her long seculsion from society, to measure her ideas by any standard external to herself."

Hawthorne sets the issues in clear contrast to each other, though as "intrusive author" he is by no means unambivalent in his evaluations of each. Hester's actions remove her from "the ordinary relations with humanity." Representative of antinomianism, she becomes "a being, whose elements were perhaps beautiful and brilliant, but all in disorder." Even the sainted Ann Hutchinson must be suspect: elsewhere, in an early "Biographical Sketch," Hawthorne had placed her among "the ink-stained Amazons," the militantly feminist writers whom, in an earlier phase, he detested.

Seen from this view of the issues, the story offers the opportunity to meditate on the perennially expressed problem of regulation of human life from within or without, from Saint Paul's declaration of freedom from the Law through the Reformers' freedom from Rome. Seen from this viewpoint, the story offers Hawthorne's most profound setting for consideration of Emerson's neoantinomian doctrine of self-reliance. Hawthorne's consistent "yes but" style, his even-handed praise and condemnation of Hester, aid the reader to probe more deeply into the complexities of this human dilemma.

There are traces in *The Scarlet Letter* which indicate that the new freedom, security, and wisdom, gained by his marriage and explored in "The New Adam and Eve," are at work to clarify the issues of the novel. Chillingworth's early plea to Hester is that his world had been "lonely and chill, without a household fire." Hester would relieve his cramped scholarly loneliness, and bring him the genial gift of "simple bliss." But Hester's instincts are to offer this bliss to Dimmesdale instead. There are two points when her antinomianism flowers into action: "What we did had a consecration of its own" is her Emersonian evaluation of the action that lies outside the book, but without which the book does not exist. She offers the gift again at the peak of the forest scene: "She took off the formal cap that confined her hair; and down it fell upon her shoulders, dark and rich, with at once a shadow and a light in its abundance, and imparting the charm of softness to her features. There played around her mouth, and beamed out of her eyes, a radiant and tender smile, that seemed gushing from the very heart of womanhood. A crimson flush was glowing on her cheek." The antinomian offers sexual therapy to the Calvinist. She presents freedom, wholeness, the Garden as innocent and natural as it was for the new Adam and Eve. But Hawthorne vacillates again. However satisfactory he finds this as a private solution, the world is not ready for it. On the last page of the romance, Hester is not exactly condemned, but is judged inadequate as a public carrier for this new freedom by reason of her "sin," her "shame," her "sorrow."

These matters are once again an issue, in *The House of the Seven Gables*. An exchange between Hepzibah and Phoebe culminates this way:

> "But if Mr. Holgrave is a lawless person!" remonstrated Phoebe, a part of whose essence it was, to keep within the limits of law.
>
> "Oh," said Hepzibah carelessly—for, formal as she was, still, in her life's experience, she had gnashed her teeth against human law—"I suppose he has a law of his own!"

Phoebe, as one who prefers "the well-worn track of ordinary life," and the "lawless" Holgrave preserve the thematic materials that we've used for characterization in the previous story, though the roles are reversed and manipulated in different ways. The Garden is once again the setting for the major vignettes of *The House of the Seven Gables*. Hawthorne's "summer squashes" and other vegetables grow there, as they do in the garden of the Old Manse; the garden around Maule's well is "like a bower in Eden." Functionally, Phoebe and Holgrave are the most important characters in the plot—they reunite the separated families, foreclose the operation of the curse, and marry in rural bliss. Their conversations, which are their courtship dance, are spoken in the garden, secluded behind the rotting family mansion. The scene had been poisoned by a multitude of evils imposed by human artifice: the legalized stealing of Maule's home and property; his treacherous execution, with collusion of a corrupt legal system; the curse he uttered from the gallows; and finally what the Jeffersonian Hawthorne calls the "absurd delusion of family importance." The house itself embodies these evils down into the present: "It was itself like a great human heart."

Once again, Hawthorne sharply confronts a transcendentalist idea, seems to sympathize with it, then reverses himself completely. This happens in the garden, when Holgrave presents his tirade against entailments and hereditary property: "Shall we never, never get rid of this Past!. . . It lies upon the Present like a giant's dead body!" But this is a truth only for the Garden—as Hester's sexual liberation is—an ideal for "the future condition of society." Hawthorne manipulates Holgrave to a sudden abandonment of this Emersonian ideal, on the

eve of his marriage. Even Phoebe remarks with surprise
and wonder at her converted Adam: "'How wonderfully
your ideas are changed!'" But Holgrave is a Fourierist
and has been a mesmerist; both are excesses which
Hawthorne condemned in letters to his wife. The other
promoter of transcendental wisdom is Clifford, proposing
the gradual spiritualization of matter during his frantic
train ride. But he is "a porcelain vase, with already a
crack in it," flying against a granite column. In the mean-
time, though, Hawthorne has exploited these transcendentalist themes, as if they were truths, to undermine
poor Hepzibah's delusions of aristocracy, to depoliticize
and deradicalize his new groom, and to give a sense of
the effect of liberation on Clifford. At least one consistent technique in Hawthorne—the chop on the surface
of his prose, the tension which holds the reader's interest
and promotes his evaluations—in this constant oxymoronic treatment of major matters. Even a minor buffoon,
Uncle Venner, is introduced as "rather deficient, than
otherwise, in his wits"; yet, at the end, Clifford and
Phoebe, at least, bestow on him "wisdom and pleasant-
ness" with "not a drop of bitter essence at the bottom."

The garden in *The House of the Seven Gables* is similar
to Hawthorne's other gardens: in the center is the fountain, not quite poisoned but at least brackish. Flora and
fauna have all declined miserably under human husbandry, as has the decayed garden-house where the decayed
Clifford sits. From a window in an upper gable, Holgrave
has a view of Phoebe working in the garden below, as
Giovanni had spied on Beatrice, and both enter the garden by an obscure door. When Phoebe laments that she
feels she has given her youth to the aged tenants of the
Pyncheon house, Holgrave's consoling speech contains
echoes of Hawthorne's reflection on his own marriage:
"'You have lost nothing, Phoebe, worth keeping, nor
which it was possible to keep. . . .Our first youth is of no
value; for we are never conscious of it, until after it is
gone. But sometimes—always, I suspect, unless one is
exceedingly unfortunate—there comes a sense of second

youth, gushing out of the heart's joy at being in love.'"
Clifford, on the other hand, remains emotionally and intellectually a child, because he "had never quaffed the
cup of passionate love." Significantly, Hawthorne called
the chapter next to the last, in which "the miracle" of
emotional transition is wrought for Holgrave and
Phoebe, "The Flower of Eden." Phoebe and Holgrave
again become the new Adam and Eve: "They transfigured
the earth, and made it Eden again, and themselves the
first two dwellers in it." Clifford pronounces the bene-
diction, at the end of the chapter: "'And so the flower of
Eden has bloomed, likewise, in this old, darksome house,
to-day!'" Large philosophical and historical issues of Calvinism and transcendentalism, with their emotional
entailments of guilt and doom and high moral imperative,
are once again reduced by the private solution of marriage and sexual fulfillment. The flower of Eden can still
be plucked from the ruined garden.

The final novel of the American trilogy brings these
materials from *Mosses from an Old Manse* into still another
synthesis. Transcendentalism was institutionalized in only
a few ways: the *Dial*, Bronson Alcott's various educational enterprises, Brook Farm. This latter is the setting
for *The Blithedale Romance,* which is Hawthorne's most
extended confrontation with practical transcendentalism
and his final test of its theories. The fanaticisms of those
who surrounded Emerson or associated in other ways
with transcendentalism are brought to a dismal end:
suicide for the militant feminist Zenobia, childish and
imbecilic dependency for the reformer Hollingsworth.
Each had been meant to discharge the aberrant energies
of the other. The Garden possibilities are betrayed and
no satisfactory marriages take place.

Hawthorne has heeded Poe's advice: in *The
Blithedale Romance* "the writers of *North American Review*"
are classified among "all those respectable old blockheads." Transcendentalism is sharply satirized: "She beholds the Absolute" is said of an underfed seamstress,
and the speaker is a mountebank "wizard." But the

critique is not limited to satiric thrusts; it pervades the plot of the novel.

The garden of Blithedale has Puritan roots, and the prying narrator brings his famous Reformation name into its midst. The original Miles Coverdale was responsible for the first complete English translation of the Bible, just as Eliot, under whose pulpit the most dramatic clash of the novel takes place, was the first to translate the Bible for his Indian converts. In a scene that recalls "The Maypole of Merry Mount" revels, the fanatic Hollingsworth is dressed as a Puritan, and is wearing the costume at the moment he betrays his most personal loyalties for his "cause."

The clash between Calvinism and antinomianism is again prominent: as Coverdale views the enterprise, "we had left the rusty iron frame-work of society behind us; we had broken through many hindrances that are powerful enough to keep most people on the weary tread-mill of the established system . . . for the sake of showing mankind governed by other than the false and cruel principles on which human society has all along been based." But in this book, again, neither the Calvinist-Puritan cause nor the antinomian-transcendentalist prevails against the other. Both are defeated by the forces that carry each embodiment to a tragic end. Coverdale enters Blithedale with "Brotherhood" as his most frequently expressed ideal, and ends as the most solitary of men. Zenobia embodies the cause of female freedom, and dies because she cannot subordinate her wealth and her person to a male. Priscilla is a "lamb" who seeks protection in the fold of the new Utopia, and is thrown back to the wolves. Hollingsworth would subordinate all the socially conceived ideals of others to his purely personal version of reform, yet he ends parasitically, dominated by "a seamstress."

Hawthorne's Garden solution, personal happiness through sexual liberation, comes under severe scrutiny here. Zenobia is powerfully sexual; she elaborates on the paradise they have sought to achieve, suggests herself as a

possible Eve to Coverdale's Adam, and even offers the
enticing possibility of presenting herself to him in "the
garb of Eden." But she is too powerful, too passionate;
she is flawed, like Hester, by having already given herself
to a man, and Coverdale is too shallow and despicable a
member of the species to carry the load of happiness
anyway. The historical Zenobia was a tragic queen of an-
tiquity who betrayed her close associates in order to survive. In Hawthorne's book she is almost a goddess, but
the telling figure in Coverdale's not imperceptive mind is
Pandora. Hawthorne's Garden is a private solution—not
one that powerful public figures can promote as a social
cause.

V

The ideological sacrifices that Hawthorne makes to
arrive at his private Garden happiness are considerable,
not to say massive and crippling, to the artist and to every
kind of reforming enthusiast. The new Adam must abandon the pleasures of art and introspection; Dimmesdale
remains flawed because he aspires to be nothing less than
a moving force in history, the saint of New England, who
leaves his permanent stamp on the culture, rather than
take Hester as his Eve; Chillingworth aspires to the pure
diabolism of Ethan Brand; Holgrave's visionary plans for
the alleviation of society are dropped with startling
abruptness for marriage to the conventional Phoebe;
transcendental enthusiasm for the progressive "spiritualization of matter" is parodied in the feverish aestheticism
of Clifford; Hollingsworth's specific and (for a transcendentalist) quite practicable plans for the reform of
criminals are cut short by the flaws of a fanatical man with
a fixed idea, who lapses under the control of an at-
tenuated "New England woman"; the strength and beauty
of Zenobia's feminist leadership are frustrated because
she is a woman who, like Hester, had experienced sexual
intercourse without the subsequent "flowering" of a
stable marriage.

All the idealism of the transcendentalists is undermined and rejected in the American novels, as Hawthorne systematically analyzes their social energies as functions of human flaws and proposes, as his alternative, the redemption of the individual and, consequently (by implication), the reform of society through sexual fulfillment. The figure of Miles Coverdale, unmarried and functionless at the end of Hawthorne's only novel with a first-person narrator, is his author's horrified image of what he might have become without Sophia to liberate him.

Clearly, another transcendentalist theme, the Carlylean-Emersonian line of speculation on the role of heroes in history, is preempted by Hawthorne's preference for private and individual salvation. The drama of the times is vividly portrayed and set in motion, and Hawthorne's massive mirror for society is clear, sharply focused, and stamped with his individual experience and the resolution to his own individual problems. The American trilogy builds on the enlightenment experienced at the Old Manse. It was at this moment that Hawthorne clearly discerned the historical clash between the Calvinist-Puritan and the antinomian-transcendentalist forces at work in the culture, and sensed his own involvement as an artist in clarifying these issues. He discovered, at the same moment, the basic myth (the Garden) and the longer vehicle (the romance) which would enable him to probe these issues. He ended with abandonment of all American "isms," whether Calvinism or transcendentalism, for the purely private solution.

The work of the trilogy, then, impressive and idiosyncratic, delights with an instructive critique of the culture. Hawthorne lamented, after his stay at the Old Manse, that he had as yet produced "no profound treatise of Ethics, no philosophic history." He did, however, go on to do just that.

Some "Mosses" from the *Literary World:*
CRITICAL AND BIBLIOGRAPHICAL SURVEY OF THE HAWTHORNE-MELVILLE RELATIONSHIP

Melville's wrongness, unsoundness or whatever we call it matters next to nothing at all in our judgement of him as a great story teller, one of America's splendors in art. . . .We may admire him more wrong than almost anybody but Hawthorne right.

—Robert Frost to Lawrance Thompson, 1952[1]

Buford Jones

f we consider Hawthorne's review of *Typee* as the beginning of his relationship with Melville and their talks among the sand dunes in Southport, England, as the end, their literary and social contacts spanned a period of slightly more than ten years—from March 1846 to November 1856.[2] It is perhaps coincidental that this decade is almost exactly coextensive with the most fertile and richly productive segment of American romantic literature. We may suppose that an "American renaissance," with its "classic American literature," blossomed independently of these two writers during the same decade; yet, from our contemporary perspective, their remarkable outpouring of nearly twenty books during these years—together with the fact of their meeting in August 1850—in large measure gives the period its definition and shapes our critical reactions to it. Just under half of F. O. Matthiessen's entries for this decade in his *American Renaissance* "Chronology"³ concerns Hawthorne and Melville. Their names were significantly linked for a brief period, beginning in 1850, separated for seventy years because of their diverse critical reputations, joined again in the Melville revival of the 1920s, and—exactly a century after their first meeting—bound together inextricably and permanently.⁴

To paraphrase Hawthorne, it would be a curious matter for speculation to study the nineteenth- and twentieth-century biographies of these men with an intent of defining the critical stances, aesthetic movements, and blind spots of our literary history. For example, Henry James's famous biography of Hawthorne (1879) cites more than forty writers from Dante (or Alcott) to Zola but mentions neither Melville nor any writer or publisher who was ever in Melville's circle. He defines Hawthorne's tales in terms of the fancy, instead of "the larger and more potent faculty" of the imagination, and relegates most of them to "the province of allegory."⁵ He later employs John Gibson Lockhart's youthful novel *Adam Blair* (1822) as a means of pointing up Hawthorne's "abuse of the fanciful element" in *The Scarlet Letter*. His discussion of *Adam Blair* is his only extensive comparison of a work by Hawthorne and by one of his contemporaries. But even if the purpose of James's book had been to seek out Hawthorne's similarities to other writers, he undoubtedly would have passed Melville by. And if Melville read James's *Hawthorne* in his later years, he might have concluded that biographers and literary historians (as well as the realities of regional proximity and assumptions about provincialism) significantly aid or hinder the shock of recognition that genius runs the circle round.

By contrast, almost exactly a century later, Edwin Haviland Miller's biography of Melville (1975)⁶ departs from strict chronology in order to emphasize that the unfolding relationship of Hawthorne and Melville foreshadowed the roles they would later uncomprehendingly play, Melville for the rest of his life. Miller's life of Melville begins and ends with Hawthorne. As the intended, and virtually exclusive, object of Melville's pent-up love, Hawthorne (in this view) became Melville's "Apollonian icon," fulfilling life-long needs and enabling him—from "Hawthorne and His Mosses" to *Billy Budd*—to shape more vividly the fable that had always haunted his writing: the struggle for supremacy "between father and son in the eternal warfare to determine succession" (p. 358). Accordingly, the book has, one might say, a lyrical structure: it begins with the famous Monument Mountain excursion (5 August 1850), when the two men first met, proceeds to the review of *Mosses* resulting from that encounter, continues with end-of-chapter refrains about Hawthorne,[7] and ends with the Melvillean code word for Hawthorne, "vine," describing the decorative motif on Melville's tombstone.

These are just two of many examples one could cite to demonstrate the range of contrasting attitudes that Hawthorne and Melville have evoked during a century of biological or (as James insisted) essayistic writing. The intention of James's "little book" was to encapsulate Hawthorne in his "little" province of New England; to do this effectively, he needed to assume that, having no Epsom or Ascot in his world, Hawthorne had no significant literary relationships in his life. Miller's volume stands at the end of a whole generation of studies that maintain that the Hawthorne-Melville relationship is one of the most tantalizing in the history of literature.[8] Diverse as the two volumes appear when juxtaposed, they may be viewed as links in a chain leading back to Monument Mountain, 5 August 1850, and to the subsequent effusions of that fictional personage: the Virginian spending July in Vermont.

With the publication of *The Scarlet Letter* a few months before their meeting, Hawthorne had emerged as possibly the most esteemed writer in America; Melville, according to at least one magazine editor, was considered the first or second most popular.[9] My recent survey of

Hawthorne-Melville criticism, 1846–1979, has led me to believe that Melville shrewdly sensed that Hawthorne's reputation would last, whereas his own popularity could satisfy neither himself, immediately, nor his audience in the future. Furthermore, my reading of "Hawthorne and His Mosses" from this perspective indicates that Melville keenly felt (in a sense, he *knew*), from the judgments his contemporaries had already made, what judgments posterity would render. The courses their reputations would follow for the rest of the century had been determined by the time they first met. Melville's review of *Mosses* was thus an inspired but frenzied attempt to alter the stark realities at which he had been staring a good many months before he met Hawthorne.

Summaries of the course of his reputation usually stress how the generous approval of *Typee* and *Omoo* became mixed with censure over *Mardi*'s extravagances, which the popular narratives *Redburn* and *White-Jacket* "corrected"; the wide range of reactions to *Moby-Dick* immediately preceded the strong condemnations of *Pierre*'s excesses, and these sent Melville, with only minor exceptions among his writings of the mid-1850s, on the road to oblivion.[10] Whatever "Hawthorne and His Mosses" reveals concerning Melville's assumptions about religion and philosophy or his intriguing, possibly strange, attraction toward Hawthorne the man, it also points up, with unwavering emphasis, his most deeply felt and disturbing need in July and August 1850: to align his faltering critical reputation as much as possible with the success that Hawthorne had so gradually but irreversibly achieved. He sought to accomplish this by first exaggerating the Indian-summer side of Hawthorne's writing, then understating the public's prior awareness of his Puritan gloom and Calvinistic "blackness." These aspects of Hawthorne's critical reputation are a matter of record. What critics have not yet clearly surveyed or adequately emphasized are the ways in which Melville's review extracts, then adapts to Melville's purposes, the key ideas, images, concepts, and even word motifs of "The Old Manse." The essay's hyperbole has made it easy for both nineteenth-

and twentieth-century critics to assert that Melville's words portray his own, disturbed condition far more than they describe Hawthorne's achievement in *Mosses*.

Edmund Wilson (1943) set the tone by using Melville's ringing sentence as both title and epigraph for his famous anthology: "For genius, all over the world, stands hand in hand, and one shock of recognition runs the whole circle round";[11] but his brief discussion of "this eloquent essay" maintains that Melville's remarks "must have been inspired by his sense of his own genius rather than by any clear perception of the quality of Hawthorne's" (p. 185). Why *"must,"* why *"rather than"*? one might ask every time he hears the critics echo Wilson's view. In this important respect, at least, twentieth-century criticism has so closely followed mid-nineteenth-century appraisals of Melville that it has never deemed a close stylistic and thematic comparison of "Hawthorne and His Mosses" and "The Old Manse" necessary or advisable. Not a single article has bothered to weigh the evidence in an effort to ascertain whether Melville wrote the essay before or after he met Hawthorne; the position taken on this matter usually reveals more about the critic's general presuppositions about Melville than about the ability of the Virginian Melville to review Hawthorne's *Mosses*.[12] William B. Dillingham (pp. 92ff.) skillfully relates such themes or motifs as enchantment, mosses, and verdancy in the review and in "The Encantadas," concluding that to place these two works side by side is "to glimpse the brightest and darkest hours of a man's soul."

A similar comparative study of the review and the preface to *Mosses* would, I suspect, reveal a rich texture of thematic and verbal interlocking. In addition to the enchantment theme, moss imagery, and green symbolism, it would include themes and topics evolving from such verbal motifs as sleep, gloom, brightness, melancholy, sweet, root, soil, flowers, foliage, fruit, mountains, depth (and plunge, profundity), breadth, (Indian) summer, and penetrate. More importantly—and explicitly—"The Old Manse" is filled, from beginning to end, with significant allusions to or discussions of "Melvillean" key words or concepts relating to black, truth, faith (and confidence), originality, Calvinism, planting seed, germination, and genius. If we look at a few phrases or sentences describing the last three items on the list, we see how the rich fecundity of Hawthorne's genius planted seeds in the Virginian's soul. Melville says: "Already I feel that this Hawthorne has dropped germinous seeds into my soul. He expands and deepens down, the more I contemplate him; and further and further, shoots his strong New England roots into the hot soil in my Southern soul."[13]

If the image is insemination (E. H. Miller, p. 32), it has ample precedence in Hawthorne's essay; and if we consider the Virginian as another of Melville's bachelor seedsmen, his literary progenitor is none other than the last clergyman at the Manse.[14] A "hoary-headed man" who presumably had outlived his wife and relatives, he planted an orchard and lived on to the age of ninety, harvesting its fruit: "He loved each tree, doubtless, as if it had been his own child." This Puritan minister was indeed "rooted" in his New England soil, and felt akin to "the quiet congregation of trees" along the Concord River, trees that "set their feet" in the moist, rich soil on the river's bed. After portraying the orchard trees as "humorists and odd fellows" (a passage that Melville liked), Hawthorne returned to the idea of bachelor seedsmen in a passage I shall again anachronistically describe as strikingly Melvillean:

> Childless men, if they would know something of the bliss of paternity, should plant a seed—be it squash, bean, Indian corn, or perhaps a mere flower, or worthless weed—should plant it with their own hands, and nurse it from infancy to maturity, altogether by their own care. . . . I used to visit and re-visit it, a dozen times a day, and stand in deep contemplation over my vegetable progeny, with a love that nobody could share nor conceive of, who had never taken part in the process of creation. It was one of the most bewitching sights in the world, to observe a hill of beans thrusting aside the soil, or a row of early peas, just peeping forth sufficiently to trace a line of delicate green. [pp. 13–14]

These lines, indeed the whole sketch, are a love letter, one might say, addressed to a select society—that
"circle of friends" whom Hawthorne defined at the end
of the essay as his ideal readers. Ideas of insemination
and gestation teem, along with the harvest of apples,
cherries, currants, pears, peaches, squashes, cabbages,
grapes, and various flowers and mosses: the pond lily
opens its "virgin bosom" to the sun, the river's "bosom"
reflects the teeming animal life, smoke from outdoor
cooking is "impregnated with a savory incense." As if this
fecundity is insufficient, Hawthorne alludes to the spontaneous growth of tropical fruits that offer "natives of the
summer islands . . . an ever-ready meal." In these genial
New England Indian summer days, all nature "overflows
with a blessed superfluity of love"; her blessings are
broadcast as seeds are sown: "flung abroad, and scattered
far and wide over the earth, to be gathered up by all who
choose."

The intellectual counterparts to this fertility in nature are the free-flowing discussions of the paradisiacal
bachelor Ti in Melville's *Typee* and the convocations of
men and demigods in *Mardi.* Hawthorne's "wild" and
"free" outings on the Concord and Assabeth with Ellery
Channing dramatically contradict the nineteenth- and
twentieth-century accounts of his painful shyness and
morbid insociability: Hawthorne seems to have incorporated into his being the "virgin gold" associated with
Channing's teeming thoughts, thus temporarily freeing
the two husbands from societal and domestic restrictions.
"My mind was the richer," he states, merely from the
knowledge that a deeper, as yet unarticulated wisdom lay
underneath the babble of talk: the chief profit was found
in "the freedom which we thereby won from all custom
and conventionalism, and fettering influences of man on
man. We were so free today, that it was impossible to be
slaves again tomorrow" (p. 25).

All this, I presume, Melville read and perceived: the
shock of recognition, like the two halves of the physical
sphere, has a bright side as well as a dark. If Melville

described the function of the American master genius in his review, Hawthorne provided a definition of it in his sketch. In several respects, Melville's oft-quoted lines seem to be more a reflection of the discussions on genius in "The Old Manse" than a projection onto Hawthorne of his own thoughts and psychological needs.[15] Melville adds to his comments about American Shakespeares along the banks of the Ohio this summary reflection on native genius:

> The great mistake seems to be, that even with those Americans who look forward to the coming of a great literary genius among us, they somehow fancy he will come in the costume of Queen Elizabeth's day; be a writer of dramas founded upon old English history or the tales of Boccaccio. Whereas great geniuses are parts of the times, they themselves are the times, and possess a correspondent coloring. [p. 126]

Hawthorne's definition arose from meditations on how the ponderous volumes of sermons and moral treatises he discovered at the Old Manse contained no "intellectual treasure." On the contrary, these have much less to teach about the spirit of an age than "a few old newspapers and still older almanacs," which had not the "remotest pretension or idea of permanence." All the painful mental rummaging and groping by the Puritan divines in no way constituted what Melville termed a "great, deep intellect" that drops "into the universe like a plummet." The newspaper and almanac scribblers wrote (like Melville rushing to complete his article for the *Literary World*) in "the effervescence of a moment":

> It is the Age itself that writes newspapers and almanacs, which therefore have a distinct purpose and meaning, at the time, and a kind of intelligible truth for all times; whereas, most other works—being written by men who, in the very act, set themselves apart from their age—are likely to possess little significance when new, and none at all, when old. Genius, indeed, melts many ages into one, and thus effects something permanent, yet still with a similarity of office to that of the more emphemeral writer. A work of genius is but the newspaper of a century, or perchance of a hundred centuries. [pp. 20–21]

Hawthorne sets up a complex analogy that Melville completes with explicitness: the truths of the traditional new England Puritan writings are to journalistic perceptions of the "real" as these are to literary works of true genius. Only the American literary Shiloh can adequately explore the Calvinistic profundities, a task that the ministers botched because they set themselves apart from their age—as did the writers and critics of mid-nineteenth-century America.

From Melville's perspective, his keen perception into Hawthorne's achievements was matched, inversely, by the obtuseness of the age in its unwillingness or inability to judge him except in terms of the ever popular *Typee.* The magnitude of this problem for Melville emerges from the fact that the name of his critic-reviewer-editor friend, Evert Duyckinck, must be added to the names of those who set themselves apart from their age. Though Duyckinck's major reviews of Melville's books were on the whole favorable, the numerous comments hidden away on back pages of the *Literary World* or buried in reviews of other writers' works form a steady undercurrent of opinion that ultimately explains more than the strident but short-lived denunciations of *Pierre*—for example, the general neglect that would last for the next seventy years. Duyckinck's offhand comments about both writers, but especially about Melville, constitute a kind of intelligible truth for all times (applying Hawthorne's assertion ironically) as to why the age could not significantly link its two geniuses of prose fiction. In this respect, at least, Duyckinck had a rare opportunity to immortalize himself as critic. Melville's review, of course, provided the most dramatic opportunity of all; but instead, Duyckinck followed (or accompanied) Melville's famous remarks with the uncomprehending verbal inanities of Cornelius Mathews.[16]

II

Duyckinck had known both men for several years when he arranged the Monument Mountain encounter;

he had favorably reviewed Hawthorne's works for nearly ten years. During the years the *Literary World* was published (1847–1853), the names of Melville and Hawthorne appeared in approximately one hundred thirty-five critical reviews, notices, borrowings from other publications, selections from their works, and "gossipy" literary announcements.[17] Of about one hundred twenty-eight items written by Duyckinck, his staff, or by other editors and contributors (Hawthorne wrote one review, Melville seven), their names were linked together in the same article only eight times, and these bore no meaning for which Duyckinck could subsequently claim much credit.[18] Melville's name appeared in sixty-seven articles or announcements and Hawthorne's in sixty-one. Significantly, however, fifty-three of Melville's appearances were in 1850 or before, whereas fifty-five of Hawthorne's were in 1850 or after. In two instances (31 January and 14 August 1852), Duyckinck mentioned their names together simply because he was reviewing a book and a lecture that had already done the same. On three other occasions (13 April, 6 July 1850, and 9 August 1851), he briefly gossiped about what his two literary friends might be doing, or chatted harmlessly about the pseudonymous nature of their names. He continued this superficial commentary after the August 1851 excursion in the Berkshires with the two writers. The third installment of his "Glimpses of Berkshire Scenery" (*Literary World,* 27 September 1851) sticks to its announced subject all too well: "Can we forget the day's excursion with two pleasantly named and to be named authors, whose Scarlet Letters and White Jackets are gleaming here and there about the world in the light of quickening fancies. . . ?" Duyckinck seems deliberately to avoid mentioning *Moby-Dick,* which Melville had just completed, though later he subordinated glimpses of Puritan Salem scenery to the more acceptable Berkshires. Near the residence of the renowned Miss Sedgwick "arose for the world, doubtless, first painted on the mists of the valley, the vision of The House with the Seven Gables." In the next sentence, the author of a wicked book about whaling hardly seems capable of further ontological heroics: "Herman Melville, in the vistas of his wood and the long prospective glances from his meadows to the mountains, blends the past and the future on his fancy-sprinkled pages." Duyckinck's first juxtaposition of their names, strongly indicative of his later treatment, occurred in the column "What Is Talked About?" for 23 June 1849. Whereas he felt that Hawthorne's removal from the Salem customhouse had already become a national political—and literary—issue, the best he could do to keep Melville before his reading public was to quote a paragraph from chapter 95 of *Mardi* on "Fat Men." If Hawthorne found *Mardi* deep enough to "compel a man to swim for his life," Duyckinck preferred such lines as these to present the true Melville: "Fat men are the salt and savor of the earth; full of good humor, high spirits, fun, and all manner of jollity."[19]

These Hawthorne-Melville references by the one person who followed both careers closely throughout the most remarkable years of the American renaissance offer no clues whatever to the interest that would shower on them a century later and lead to the opinion that even Melville's marginal jottings in Hawthorne's works provide evidence of "the most mysterious and fruitful friendship in American letters."[20] The reasons for Melville's artistic failures are undoubtedly easier to list than Hawthorne's reasons for success. The whole episode is full of ironies: Hawthorne laid the foundations for a reputation by writing anonymously; Melville never "recovered" from the unparalleled success of his first work. Hawthorne experimented anonymously with virtually every neoclassical and romantic genre of the short tale and the essay. Melville's public, in a sense, would never permit him another genre than *Typee*. The point is hardly exaggerated: Hawthorne was deeply respected before *The Scarlet Letter;* Melville was still taken lightly, even after *Moby-Dick.*

With far greater accuracy than the favorably slanted major reviews and lengthy quotations, the obscure pages of the *Literary World* pointed out how posterity would regard Melville. Regardless of what Melville attempted or achieved in a different mode, he was judged by *Typee*. Thus Duyckinck announced confidently (18 November 1848) that Melville's new work "is expected, from peculiar sources of interest, [to] transcend the unique reputation of his former works." A few months later (30 June 1849) he made it clear, by quoting European reactions to *Mardi,* that sections were astonishing, shocking, or monstrous. After the first volume (when the voyage has become chartless), the French reviewer saw only "monstrous vagaries." European reviewers, however, struggled for a while with what Melville had done, seeing him as a "Rabelais without gaiety, a Cervantes without grace, a Voltaire without taste." The London *Morning Chronicle* strained even harder for meaningful comparisons, viewing the book as "a wonderful and unreadable compound of Ossian and Rabelais—of More's 'Utopia,' and Harrington's 'Oceania, '—of 'Gulliver's Travels,' and 'Cook's Voyages,' spiced with rhetoric from Macauley's essays, and sarcasm from Mr. D'Israeli's perorations." Duyckinck indulged in no such perplexities; he simply ignored the book and continued to draw his comparisons from the more comprehendable *Typee*.[21] In reviewing W. S. Mayo's *Kaloolah* (23 June 1849), which along with *Mardi* was the "culmination [of] the vogue of the Oriental tale in the first half of the nineteenth century,"[22] he ignores *Mardi* completely, and remarks simply: "Not so imaginative as Typee, Mr. Romer is more 'forgetive,' though less full of delectable shapes; his variety is infinite."

These are just a few examples (from a potential list of dozens) indicating the reasons for Melville's fervor in attempting to change his image as "H. M. author of 'Peedee' 'Hullabaloo' & 'Pog-Dog.'"[23] As I have hinted, Duyckinck had every reason to treat him as kindly as he could. Melville, possibly, felt that lack of kindness hurt less than lack of perception. Cruelty could perhaps be expected from *Blackwood's,* even from the great Christopher North's belittling pronouncement in his long review of *Redburn* (17 November): "We can assure Mr. Melville he is most effective when most simple and unpretending; and if he will. . . curb the eccentricities of his fancy, we see no reason for his not becoming a very agreeable writer of nautical fictions." But Duyckinck's offhand commentaries remained imperceptive (and focused on *Typee*) as long as he edited the magazine.

A final example will bring us back to the review of *Mosses* and Sophia Hawthorne's discovery of its author, whom she did not consider either simple or unpretending, even in *Typee*. On 3 January 1852, a month and a half after the publication of *Moby-Dick*, Melville was intently at work on *Pierre* when Duyckinck reviewed Bon Gualtier's *Book of Ballads*. He was particularly fond of the "Lay of the Lovelorn," parodying "Locksley Hall." The narrator, having left civilized London for a tropical paradise, sees himself

> Feeding on the luscious berries and the rich cassava root,
> Lots of dates and lots of guavas, clusters of forbidden fruit. . . .
>
> There the passions, cramped no longer, shall have space to breathe, my cousin!
> I will take some savage woman—nay, I'll take at least a dozen. . . .
>
> Whistle to the cockatoos, and mock the hairy-faced baboon,
> Worship mighty Mumbo Jumbo in the Mountains of the Moon.

As Melville was possibly working out the finer points of Plotinus Plinlimmon's horologicals and chronometricals (or sullenly drafting the chapter "Young America in Literature"), Duyckinck asked delightedly, "Shades of Typee, is not this most 'admirable fooling'?" The "author of *Typee*" must remain simple and intellectually unassuming, even after his youthful, popular work had become a joke.[24] By contrast, the *Literary World* would not permit Hawthorne to be portrayed more simply than he was, even when the portrait was drawn favorably and by his old friend, James Russell Lowell. In order to satirize Lowell's claim in *A Fable for Critics* that nature filled out her model of a "full-sized man" in Hawthorne and John Sullivan Dwight with "some finer-grained stuff for a woman prepared," Duyckinck called on the wit of "Fidelius Bathos" (Cornelius Mathews), who as "Esteemed Correspondent" and "Humble Self" would later portray Hawthorne and Melville as "Noble Melancholy" and "New Neptune" in his accounts of the Monument Mountain excursion. Duyckinck prefaced "A Rhyming Review" (25 November 1848) with a comment worthy of Fidelius Bathos himself: "A clever correspondent (F.B.) has sent us, in the style of the original, some verses on the Fable for the Critics, which may pass around with the other luminous accounts of that valuable production":

> Hermaphrodites both, Dwight and Hawthorne he fancies;
> What a merry conceit to suppose *them* "Miss Nancies"!

Such verses as these frame the important first meeting of the two men.

III

For significant commentaries, we have to look through letters that were unpublished for the rest of the century and search through biographies and reminiscences for clues that someone had an inkling of what was going on. At the time, however, Melville knew that he had only two perceptive critics. Though Hawthorne's "joy-giving and exultation-breeding letter" on *Moby-Dick* has not survived, Sophia Hawthorne's discovery of the identity of the Virginian, as told to her mother in the early autumn of 1850, fortunately *did* surface, 103 years later.[25] After so much evidence of imperceptivity in the *Literary World*—and elsewhere on both sides of the Atlantic—Melville must have indeed been pleased if, during their talk when the two were sitting together "in the light of the setting sun," she told him what she later told her mother after rereading *Typee:*

> It is a *true history,* yet how poetically told—the divine beauty of the scene, the lovely faces & forms—the peace & good will—& all this golden splendor & enchantment glowing before the dark refrain constantly brought as a background—the fear of being killed & eaten—the cannibalism in the olive tinted Apollos around him—the unfathomable mystery of their treatment of him.

Melville, too, had a dark as well as a bright side from the beginning of his literary career. We shall never know whether Sophia thought of applying the dark refrain to the Hawaiian missionaries when she read the final paragraphs of chapter 26—or whether Hawthorne heard it in the Christian-cannibal motif in *Moby-Dick*. All in all, this letter raises more questions than it answers, one of the most puzzling being Sophia's explicit commentary pertaining to when "Hawthorne and His Mosses" was written:

> We have discovered who wrote the Review in the Literary World. It was no other than Herman Melville himself! He had no idea when he wrote it that he should ever see Mr. Hawthorne. I had some delightful conversations with him about the "sweetest Man of Mosses" after we discovered him to be the author of the Review. . . . He told me that the Review was too carelessly written—that he dashed it off in great haste & did not see the proof sheets, & that there was one provoking mistake in it. Instead of "the same madness of truth" it should be the *sane* madness of truth."

If we accept the weight of scholarly opinion since 1950 and assume that Melville wrote the review after the 5 August 1850 meeting, what kind of admirable fooling was taking place? Did Sophia wonder about the leisurely Virginian's urgency and haste to have it published, or how it might have differed had he written it more slowly? Furthermore, since the letter remained in the Peabody-Hawthorne families for a century, why did the knowledge of Melville's authorship disappear from all the nineteenth-century lives of both men? Julian Hawthorne seems to have had oblique motives when he sandwiched the following comments between an account of Mrs. Peabody's reaction to the review and an overt reference to Melville:[26] "It is certainly not necessary to the vindication of Hawthorne's fame to bracket him with Shakespeare; and to the man himself the idea must have appeared too absurdly monstrous to be understood otherwise than as covert satire, or at least as the ravings of well-meaning imbecility." If Melville read these lines in his later years, he must have been impressed by either gratuitous cruelty or their ill-informed malice. To my knowledge, no twentieth-century Hawthorne or Melville scholar has addressed himself, directly or adequately, to these matters, or to the history of how the essay was readmitted to the Melville canon.

Similarly, it was assumed for nearly a century that Melville wrote a review of *The Scarlet Letter* for the *Literary World,* even though, as Willard Thorp clearly demonstrated, the voice is unmistakably Duyckinck's.[27] But whether he had read all (or parts) of *The Scarlet Letter* when he sat down to write his review is still one of the unanswered questions relating to this famous essay. He alludes to but does not discuss *Twice-Told Tales* and *The Scarlet Letter,* both of which he says are excellent but full of "manifold, strange, and diffusive beauties." One of the "strange and diffusive" contrasts with the pervasive Indian-summer sunshine of "The Old Manse" is the germination and blossoming of the "unsightly vegetation" outside that "black flower of civilized society," Hester Prynne's prison. Among other things, Hester's dark labyrinth of mind led her to forget Roger Chillingworth's "old faith, long forgotten," and to plant the "germ of evil," out of which grew their dark necessity: "Let the black flower blossom as it may." In the forest chapters of *The Scarlet Letter,* she transplanted these germinous seeds in Dimmesdale's soul, with the inevitable result that he entered her "dismal maze," becoming further (but temporarily) lost beside a "mossy tree-trunk . . . near a melancholy brook." Still in this maze on emerging from the forest, the minister was sorely tempted to broadcast the evil further, to infuse poison into the elderly, pious widow and to "drop" a "germ of evil" into the "virgin soul" of his youngest parishioner—a germ that "would be sure to blossom darkly soon, and bear black fruit betimes." The language, of course, is so close to the Virginian's pronouncements and the content so precisely inverse as to invoke a suspicion of irony on Melville's part when he speaks of the "infinite height of loving wonder and admiration" that *Mosses* infuses into him.

In any event, even these few speculations on the compact stylistic and thematic texture of "The Old Manse" and "Hawthorne and His Mosses" provides some means for judging how much remains to be done in order to understand the seminal influences of each man on the other. The influence was by no means in one direction only: the tropical, paradisiacal passages in *Typee* doubtless affected "The Old Manse," as well as *A Wonder Book*.[28] It is a short step from Giovanni Guasconti's "distrust" of Beatrice Rappaccini, from his crises of "faith" and "confidence" in judging appearances, to similar crises in the metaphysical masquerade aboard the *Fidele*. Or again, if we link "canvas" to "pasteboard masks," Hilda's epistemological problem in *The Marble Faun* (chapter 37) is virtually identical to Ahab's—though some of the imagery is traceable back to "The Old Manse" by way of "The Apple-Tree Table":[29]

> Heretofore, her sympathy went deeply into a picture, yet seemed to have a depth which it was inadequate to sound; now; on the contrary, her perceptive faculty penetrated the canvas like a steel probe, and found but a crust of paint over an emptiness. Not that she gave up all art as worthless; only it had lost its consecration. One picture in ten thousand, perhaps, ought to live in the applause of mankind, from generation to generation, until the colors fade and blacken out of sight, or the canvas rot entirely away. For the rest, let them be piled in garrets, just as the tolerable poets are shelved, when their little day is over.

Similarly, the metaphor of germinous seeds blossoming into fruit becomes part of the epistemological framework of *Moby-Dick* when we compare Captain Ahab, the bachelor husband, with the seedsmen aboard the *Bachelor*. Ahab's physical and spiritual states present images of polar opposites: he resembles a man burned at the stake, who is still alive after the fire "has overrunningly wasted all the limbs without consuming them."[30] His lividly whitish, slender, rod-like scar "resembled that perpendicular seam sometimes made in the straight, lofty trunk of a great tree, when the upper lightning tearingly darts down it . . . ere running off into the soil." The dryness and sereness, somehow the result of his fruitless search for knowledge, is nowhere evident in the crew members of the *Bachelor,* a ship encountered "some few weeks after Ahab's harpoon [his steel probe] had been welded." Unlike the empty *Pequod,* the *Bachelor*'s hatches are bursting with sperm oil, barrels of sperm oil are lashed to the masts' baskets, and even the furniture has been replaced with containers for oil. In celebration, the seamen onboard the *Bachelor* dance on the quarterdeck with "olive-hued girls who had eloped with them from the Polynesian Isles," and we learn "that indeed everything was filled with sperm, except the captain's pantaloon pockets."

Melville could perhaps have made no stronger comment on how he had outgrown *Typee* and Fayaway. The focus of *Moby-Dick* is on the dark Ahab and on the germs of evil in his soul. Such a focus indicates some of the ways by which we may see Melville as Hawthorne's shrewdest critic and student in the nineteenth century. In contrast to Henry James's quick dismissal of Hawthorne's Puritan sense of sin, Melville confronted the problem directly in the *Mosses* review: "Whether Hawthorne has simply availed himself of this mystical blackness as a means to the wondrous effects he makes it to produce in his lights and shades; or whether there really lurks in him, perhaps unknown to himself, a touch of Puritanic gloom—this, I cannot altogether tell." The phrasing is subtly understated, as in his letter on *The House of the Seven Gables* (April [?] 1851): "In one corner, there is a dark little black-letter volume in golden clasps, entitled 'Hawthorne: A Problem.'" This diminutive Gothic volume seems today to be more substantial than James's "poor little *opusculum,*" which denied the existence of the problem by maintaining that the "grim precinct of Puritan morality" was merely a playground—Hawthorne "played with it. . . to make it evaporate in the light and charming fumes of artistic production." Melville felt that he knew better, and posterity has not proved him wrong: perhaps the only match for Hawthorne right is Melville right.

NOTES

1. In Thompson, *Selected Letters of Robert Frost* (New York: Holt, Rinehart and Winston, 1964), pp. 552–554.

2. They saw each other a final time in Liverpool on 4 May 1857, but apparently had nothing to say to each other. Edwin H. Miller has described this meeting as an "epitaph of silence."

3. *American Renaissance: Art and Expression in the Age of Emerson and Whitman* (New York: Oxford University Press, 1941), pp. 658–659.

4. In this last instance, I have in mind the indispensable biography and chronology by Leon Howard and Jay Leyda, *Herman Melville: A Biography* (Berkeley: University of California Press, 1951) and *The Melville Log: A Documentary Life of Herman Melville 1819–1891* (2 vols.; New York: Harcourt Brace, 1951).

5. *Hawthorne* (London: Macmillan [English Men of Letters], 1879). James in all likelihood has a punning intent in the word "province," the adjectival form of which was a favorite word for describing Hawthorne.

6. *Melville* (New York: George Braziller, 1975).

7. See, for example, the endings for the unnumbered chapters on *Moby-Dick, Pierre, Pierre* and *The Blithedale Romance,* the short stories and *Israel Potter,* and his lectures.

8. Ronald Mason, "Melville and Hawthorne: A Study in Contrasts," *The Wind and the Rain,* 4 (Autumn 1947), 93–100. Mason reasserted this opinion in *The Spirit above the Dust: A Study of Herman Melville* (London: John Lehmann, 1951), p. 99, where he also claimed that, together, the two men can be seen as "the authentic representation in great art of a great national consciousness."

9. See Evert A. Duyckinck, "Magaziniana," *Literary World,* 6, no. 6/158 (9 February 1850), 130. Duyckinck was quoting *Holden's Dollar Magazine,* 5 (February 1850), 123: "The two most popular writers among us, just now are Melville and [Joel T.] Headley; and much of their success is undoubtedly owing to the perfect fearlessness with which they thrust themselves bodily before their countrymen."

10. See, for example, G. Watson Branch, ed., *Melville: The Critical Heritage* (London and Boston: Routledge & Kegan Paul, 1974), 1–49, and Brian Higgins, *Herman Melville: An Annotated Bibliography. Volume I: 1846–1930* (Boston: G. K. Hall, 1979), pp. xi–xv and passim.

11. "Herman Melville," in *The Shock of Recognition: The Development of Literature in the United States Recorded by the Men Who Made It* (New York: Farrar, Straus and Cudahy, 1943), p. 199. Melville's review of *Mosses* appears on pp. 187–204 and Wilson's untitled critical headnote on pp. 185–186.

12. Many critics have commented on these matters, but, regardless of the side of the fence on which they land, their brevity (almost without exception) matches their assurance. Lawrance

Thompson, *Melville's Quarrel with God* (Princeton: Princeton University Press, 1952), pp. 12, 127, 135, sees Melville's review (written a few weeks before their meeting) in terms of its "unintentionally" but "extraordinarily revealing and dark confessions" about himself. Hubert Hoeltje, "Hawthorne, Melville, and 'Blackness,'" *American Literature,* 37 (1965), 41–51, attributes the essay's "sophomoric distortions" and ignorant tone to the hasty two-day reading Melville gave *Mosses* immediately after the Monument Mountain excursion. Leon Howard (pp. 158–160) and Perry Miller, *The Raven and the Whale* (New York: Harcourt, Brace & World, 1956), pp. 282–286, both draw up a week's calendar of Melville's reading of *Mosses* (beginning 6 August 1850), composition of the essay, revising it, and giving it to Duyckinck before he departed the Berkshires for New York on 12 August. Edwin H. Miller (p. 31) sees Melville writing it with a kind of germinous vigor and haste after his exciting contact with Hawthorne during the Berkshire idyll. William B. Dillingham, *Melville's Short Fiction, 1853–1856* (Athens: University of Georgia Press, 1977), pp. 92–103, while dealing with some of the subtleties of the Virginian's *persona,* states that when Melville wrote the essay, "probably in July 1850," he had never met Hawthorne.

13. Quotations are from "Hawthorne and His Mosses. By a Virginian Spending July in Vermont," *Literary World,* 7, no. 7/185 (17 August 1850), 125–127, and 7, no. 8/186 (24 August 1850), 145–147; also see p. 146.

14. Subsequent quotations are from "The Old Manse," in William Charvat et al., eds., *Mosses from an Old Manse* (Columbus: Ohio State University Press, 1974), pp. 3–35.

15. Terence Martin, *Nathaniel Hawthorne* (New Haven: College & University Press, 1965), p. 56, shrewdly notes that the presence of the Master Genius and Posterity adds ballast to the more fanciful imaginative creatures at the Select Party; the sketch, as Martin emphasizes (following Melville), "evinces a complex attitude toward the imagination."

16. *Literary World,* 24 (31 August–7 September 1850). See entries in the appendix.

17. My exact count is 136, including reviews by Melville and Hawthorne; I have tallied articles that discuss both men under both names. My survey has, I believe, uncovered virtually all the references, though subsequent studies may necessitate an upward revision of this number. My listing differs in a few details from those of Brian Higgins (1979) and Daniel Wells, "An Index to American Writers and Selected British Writers in Duyckinck's *Literary World,* 1847–1853," in *Studies in the American Renaissance, 1978* (Boston: Twayne Publishers, 1978), pp. 259–278.

18. Seven items, including Melville's review of J. Ross Browne's *Etchings of a Whaling Cruise* and Hawthorne's review of Whittier's *The Supernaturalism of New England,* appeared in 1847, when Charles Fenno Hoffman was probably the editor. The Duyckinck brothers assumed control of the magazine in October 1848. From that time on, the names of Hawthorne and Melville appeared more frequently. See Frank Luther Mott, *A History of American Mag-*

azines, 1741–1850 (New York: Appleton and Company, 1930), I, 766–768.

19. Note Melville's comment early in the first installment of his review: "No rollicking rudeness, no gross fun fed on fat dinners, and bred in the lees of wine—but a humor so spiritually gentle, so high, so deep, and yet so richly relishable, that it were hardly inappropriate in an angel." A few months later, he seems to revert to Mardian sentiments after reading *Twice-Told Tales*: "Some of the sketches are wonderfully subtle. Their deeper meanings are worthy of a Brahmin. Still there is something lacking—a good deal lacking—to the plump sphericity of the man." Letter to Evert A. Duyckinck (12 February 1851), in *The Letters of Herman Melville,* ed. Merrell R. Davis and William H. Gilman (New Haven: Yale University Press, 1960), p. 121.

20. Walker Cowen, "Melville's Marginalia: Hawthorne," in *Studies in the American Renaissance, 1978* (Boston: Twayne Publishers, 1978), p. 280.

21. Duyckinck's "favorable" review of *Mardi* (14 April 1849) has a tentative and uncertain tone throughout. After questioning the author's "intellectual stamina" and wondering whether he is "the comet of a season," he settles comfortably on renewed praise of *Typee.* The narrative of this "wondrous tale" is characterized by "its freshness, vivacity, the grace of the story, the humor and ease of the style. . . .Typee is constantly getting printed and going off in new editions, which it is quite too much trouble to put upon the title page." Nor does Duyckinck fail to mention that darling of the critics, Fayaway: "Poets took up Fayaway and turned capital prose into indifferent verse; the daily newspapers ran out their vocabulary on the spot."

22. Dorothee Melitsky Finkelstein, *Melville's Orienda* (New Haven and London: Yale University Press, 1961), p. 19.

23. Melville made this journal entry on 4 November 1849, on arriving in England to work out details for the publication of *White-Jacket,* much of which he wrote while reading proofs of his "little nursery tale," *Redburn.* The "expurgated" edition of *Typee* had recently been published. See *Journal of a Visit to London and the Continent by Herman Melville, 1849–1850,* ed. Eleanor Melville Metcalf (Cambridge, Mass.: Harvard University Press, 1948), p. 18.

24. In a review of Lieut. Henry A. Wise's *Los Gringos* (24 October 1849), Duyckinck had reprinted, again with unconcealed glee, Wise's deromanticized account of what had happened to Fayaway after an interval of several years: "I may mention having seen a 'nut brown' damsel named Fayaway . . . who apparently was maid of all work to a French Commissary of the garrison. She was attired in a gaudy yellow robe de chambre, ironing the Crapeau's trowsers! *Credat Judaeus!* There was also a diminutive young *oui oui* tumbling about the mats, so it is presumable she had become childish of late." At this time Melville had long since completed his portrait of Yillah, and Hawthorne was, undoubtedly, in the process of shaping the character of Hester Prynne.

25. Eleanor Melville Metcalf, *Herman Melville: Cycle and*

Epicycle (Cambridge, Mass.: Harvard University Press, 1953). Mrs. Metcalf's accounts of the discovery of this letter are on pp. vii–viii, 91. She sees the document as "the most important letter ever written about Melville" and, again, as "the most . . . perceptive letter any of his contemporaries ever wrote about Melville."

26. *Nathaniel Hawthorne and His Wife* (Boston: J. R. Osgood, 1884), I, 385–385.

27. "Did Melville Review *The Scarlet Letter?"* *American Literature,* 14 (1942), 302–305.

28. See Harold H. Scudder, "Hawthorne's Use of 'Typee,'" *Notes & Queries,* 187 (1944), 184–186.

29. William Charvat et al., eds. (Columbus: Ohio State University Press, 1968), p. 341.

30. Quotations are from the Norton Critical Edition, ed. Harrison Hayford and Hershel Parker (New York: W. W. Norton, 1967).

APPENDIX

MELVILLE AND HAWTHORNE IN THE LITERARY WORLD (1847–1853)

The entries are arranged for each year in three categories: articles treating both men jointly or significantly juxtaposing them (1850, 1851, 1852 only) and articles treating or mentioning each man separately. I have repeated the editor's title for each item, including reviews for which a separate title appears. For brief references and allusions, I have supplied the article's general heading with inclusive page numbers, and then indicated, by means of italicized numbers, the specific page(s) where Melville and Hawthorne are discussed (e.g., "Literary Intelligence," *15–16* or "Miscellany and Gossip," *481–483 [482]*). After the first volume, I have provided both the annual and cumulative issue numbers, separating the two numbers by a slanted line (e.g., 3, no. 42/04 [18 November 1848]).

1847

MELVILLE (6)

[Herman Melville]. Review of *Etchings of a Whaling Cruise,* by J. Ross Browne, 1, no. 5 (6 March 1847), *105–106.*

Review of The Prose Writers of America, by Rufus Wilmot Griswold, 1, no. 7 (20 March 1847), *149–151[Typee* should not have been omitted].

"Publisher's Circular. American Literary Intelligence," 1, no. 8 (27 March 1847), *185* [*Notice of the forthcoming Omoo*].
"Passages from Mr. Melville's 'Omoo,'" 1, no. 12 (24 April 1847), *274-275* [Includes highly favorable critical introduction].
Review of *Omoo: A Narrative of Adventures in the South Seas,* 1 no. 14 (8 May 1847), *319-321.*
Review of *The Monk's Revenge,* by Samuel Spring, 1, no. 19 (12 June 1847), 440-444 *(441)* [This tale of the later Crusades would improve if it were "a Typee novel" with a Fayaway].

HAWTHORNE (1)

[Nathaniel Hawthorne], Review of *The Supernaturalism of New England,* by J. G. Whittier, 1, no. 11 (17 April 1847), *247-248.*

1848

MELVILLE (2)

"What is Talked About," 3, no. 42/94 (18 November 1848), *834* [Melville's new work, *Mardi,* will "transcend the unique reputation of his former books"].
"Publisher's Circular. Literary Intelligence," 3, no. 47/99 (23 December 1848), *953* [Reference to forthcoming *Mardi*].

HAWTHORNE (1)

"A Rhyming Review," 3, no. 43/95 (25 November 1848), 854-855 [See essay].

1849

MELVILLE (21)

[Herman Melville]. Review of *The California and Oregon Trail,* by Francis Parkman, Jr., 4, no. 13/113 (31 March 1849), *291-293.*
"Melville's New Book—Mardi," 4, no. 14/114 (7 April 1849), *309-310* [Review and a reprint of chapter 84].
Review of *Mardi: and a Voyage Thither,* 4, no. 15/115 (14 April 1849), *333-336* [See essay].
Review of *Mardi: and a Voyage Thither:* Second Paper, 4, no. 16/116 (21 April 1849), *351-353* [See essay].
[Herman Melville]. Review of *The Sea Lions,* by J. Fenimore Cooper, 4, no. 17/117 (28 April 1849), *370.*
"Longfellow's New Romance," Review of *Kavanagh, a Tale,* 4, no. 21/121 (26 May 1849), *451-452* [Comparison of Schoolmaster Churchill with Queen Hautia and her perplexity].
"Glimpses of New Books," 4, no. 24/124 (16 June 1849), *519* [Quoted passages from *Mardi* on "Sharks and Other Sea Fellows"].
Review of *Kaloolah, or Journeyings to the Djébel Kumri,* edited by W. S. Mayo, 4, no. 25/125 (23 June 1849), 532-535 *(533)* [Jonathan Romer is not so imaginative as Typee].

"What Is Talked About," 4, no. 25/125 (23 June 1849), 539–540
[On fat men in *Mardi;* see essay].
[Correspondence], 4, no. 26/126 (30 June 1849), 556 [*European
views of Mardi's* extravagances].
"Reviews," 5, no. 1/127 (7 July 1849), 5–8 [The new edition of *Typee*
makes Harper's series of Melville's books complete].
"What Is Talked About," 5, no. 2/128 (14 July 1849), 31–33 (*32*) [A
correspondent comments on the industrialization of Melville's
Polynesian paradise].
"Parisian Critical Sketches," 5, no. 5/131 (4 August 1849), 89–90
[Philarète Chasles on "The Actual and Fantastic Voyages of
Herman Melville"].
"What Is Talked About," 5, no. 5/131 (4 August 1849), 92–93
[Notice of forthcoming *Redburn*].
"Parisian Critical Sketches," 5, no. 6/132 (11 August 1849),
101–103 [Concluded from 4 August].
"Scenes in the Pacific," Review of *Four Years in the Pacific,* by Lieut.
the Hon. Fred. Walpole, R. N., 5, no. 12/138 (22 September
1849), *248–249* [Melvillean descriptions and a Fayaway
character named Elekeke].
"What Is Talked About," 5, no. 15/141 (13 October 1849), *319–320*
[Melville on way to London with proof sheets of a new work].
Review of *Los Gringos: or an Inside View of California and Mexico,* by
Lieut. Wise, U.S.N., 5, no. 17/143 (27 October 1849), *355–356*
[See essay].
"Passages from New Books," 5, no. 19/145 (10 November 1849),
395–397 [Critical praise for *Redburn* by the "DeFoe of the
Ocean," with quoted passages].
"Mr. Melville's Redburn" [review], 5, no. 20/146 (17 November
1849), *418–420* ["The book belongs to the great school of
nature. It has no verbosity, no artificiality, no languor"].
"Reviews," 5, no. 22/148 (1 December 1849), 463–469 [Reference
to *Blackwood's* review of *Redburn* as an expression of the
"snobbish. . . London cockney school"].

HAWTHORNE (5)

"What Is Talked About," 4, no. 25/125 (23 June 1849), 539–540
[See essay].
"Correspondence," 5, no. 8/134 (25 August 1849), *158* [Praise of
"Great Carbuncle" and of Hawthorne as New England writer].
Review of *The Child's First History of Rome,* by E. M. Sewell, 5,
no. 11/137 (15 September 1849), 222–227 (*226*) [Hawthorne is
among the "best minds" who write in their later years books of
information for the young].
"Thoreau's Travels," Review of *A Week on the Concord and Merrimack
Rivers,* 5, no. 12/138 (22 September 1849), 245–247 (*246*)
[Alludes to Thoreau's comment on *Mosses*].
"Aesthetic Papers," Review of Aesthetic Papers, edited by Elizabeth P.
Peabody, 5, no. 13/139 (29 September 1849), 269–271 (*270*)
[Praise for "Main Street"].

1850

MELVILLE AND HAWTHORNE (7)

Review of *Ned Allen; or the Past Age,* by David Hannay, Esq., 6, no. 15/167 (13 April 1850), 373–374 [Hannay's sketches of Scottish character are boring, unlike the recent productions of Melville and "Hawthorne Redivivus"].

Review of *The Vale of Cedars; or, the Martyrs,* by Grace Aquilar, 7, no. 1/179 (6 July 1850), 8 [Like Aquilar, Melville and Hawthorne are among the "happily named authors" whose real names appear to be *noms de plume*].

[Herman Melville], "Hawthorne and His Mosses. By a Virginian Spending July in Vermont," 7, no. 7/185 (17 August 1850), *125–127* [See essay].

[Cornelius Mathews], "Several Days in Berkshire (From an 'Esteemed Correspondent'), Introductory," 7, no. 8/186 (24 August 1850), 145 [Account of the 5 August excursion on Monument Mountain].

[Herman Melville]. "Hawthorne and His Mosses. By a Virginian Spending July in Vermont [*Concluded from the last number*]," 7, no. 8/186 (24 August 1850), *145–147* [See essay].

[Cornelius Mathews], "Several Days in Berkshire (From an 'Esteemed Correspondent'). Part II. The Mountain Festival," 7, no. 9/187 (31 August 1850), *166* [See 24 August entry].

[Cornelius Mathews], "Several Days in Berkshire (From an 'Esteemed Correspondent'). Part III. The Grand Fancy Dress-Ball," 7, no. 10/188 (7 September 1850), 185–186 [See 24, 31 August entries].

MELVILLE (17)

Review of *Wandering Sketches of People and Things in South America, Polynesia, California, and Other Places,* by Wm. Maxwell Wood, 6, no. 1/153 (5 January 1850), 6–7 [Cites descriptive passages of the Marquesas that recall "the classic ground of Melville"].

"Dana's Geology of the Exploring Expedition," Review of *United States Exploring Expedition, during the Years* 1838–1842, by James D. Dana, 6, no. 3/155 (19 January 1850), 55–57 [The "apocryphal pages of Omoo the wanderer" are among the narratives that "familiarized to our fancies . . . the paradise of the Pacific"].

"Magaziniana: *Holden's Dollar Magazine,*" 6, no. 6/158 (9 February 1850), 129–131 (*130*) [See essay].

"Facts and Opinions," 6, no. 6/158 (9 February 1850), *134–136* [Back from Europe, Melville has completed publication arrangements for *White-Jacket*].

"International Copyright," 6, no. 8/160 (23 February 1850), 171–180 (*179*) [English view of Melville "hawking" the unpublished *White-Jacket,* seeking a publisher rash enough to copyright it].

"Mr. Melville and Copyright in England," 6, no. 9/161 (2 March
    1850), *205* [Richard Bentley and others stress that Melville did
    not hawk *White-Jacket* around London].
"Advance Passages from New Books," 6, no. 10/162 (9 March 1850),
    218–219 [A "characteristic chapter" from the forthcoming
    White-Jacket].
"Mr. Melville's White-Jacket," 6, no. 11/163 (16 March 1850),
    271–272 [Review with quoted passages].
[Herman Melville], "A Thought on Book-Binding," Review of *The
    Red Rover,* by J. Fenimore Cooper, 6, no. 11/163 (16 March
    1850), *276–277.*
"Mr. Melville's White-Jacket [Second Paper]," 6, no. 12/164 (23
    March 1850), *297–299* [Review with quoted passages].
"Mr. Colton's Cruise," Review of *Deck and Port,* by Rev. Walter
    Colton, U.S.N., 6, no. 14/166 (6 April 1850), *347–348*
    [Melville is brought in to discuss flogging and temperance in the
    United States Navy].
"Publisher's Circular," 6, no. 17/169 (27 April 1850), *427* [*Typee* and
    Omoo have appeared at one shilling each in cheap pirated
    editions].
"The Mexican War," Review of *El Puchero; or, a Mixed Dish From
    Mexico,* by Richard McSherry, 6, no. 20/172 (18 May 1850),
    491– 492 [Future writers on the Mexican campaign will need
    the touch of a Melville or Ik Marvel to compare with
    McSherry].
"American Copyright in England," 7, no. 11/189 (14 September
    1850), *213–214* [*Typee* is still involved].
"Facts and Opinions," 7, no. 15/193 (12 October 1850), 295–298
    (*296*) [On the unchivalric behavior of English publishers with
    reference to the copyright laws].
"Publisher's Circular. English Literary Intelligence," 7, no. 17/195
    (26 October 1850), *338–339* [References to Melville and the
    South Seas missions in the current *Eclectic Magazine*].
"Facts and Opinions," 7, no. 20/198 (16 November 1850), 393–395
    (*393–394*) [A missionary reviewer in *Eclectic Magazine* thinks
    Melville was a Jesuit in disguise when he wrote *Typee* and *Omoo*].

HAWTHORNE (9)
"Facts and Opinions," 6, no. 5/157 (2 February 1850), *108* [Praise for
    "The Great Stone Face"; Hawthorne has been invited to
    contribute to *Blackwood's* regularly].
"Publisher's Circular. Literary Intelligence," 6, no. 5/157 (2 February
    1850), 108–*109* [Announcement of the forthcoming *Scarlet
    Letter* by "a man of original and striking genius"].
"Advance Passages from New Books," 6, no. 11/163 (16 March
    1850), *270* [Hawthorne's forthcoming romance represents the
    "pure and delicate in literature"; lengthy quotation on the
    permanent Inspector].
"Nathaniel Hawthorne," Review of *The Scarlet Letter: A Romance,* 6
    no. 13/165 (30 March 1850), *323–325* [The book combines

"the present day in the sunshine" with the "dark agencies of evil" from the past].

"Correspondence," 6, no. 16/168 (20 April 1850), 397–398 [A Boston correspondent alludes to the immense sale of *The Scarlet Letter* and to a new romance scheduled for fall publication].

"Facts and Opinions," 6, no. 17/169 (27 April 1850), 425–427 (426) [A Louisville correspondent cites a contemporary Hester Prynne in western New York].

"New Version of Aesop's Fables," Review of *Aesop's Fables: A new version,* by the Rev. Thomas James, 7, no. 6/184 (10 August 1850), 111–112 [The ability to interest children by "original books" is the test of a great author, as evidenced by Hawthorne and others].

"Holiday Books," 7, no. 21/199 (23 November 1850), 407 [Reminiscences of Samuel Goodrich's *Token,* in which Hawthorne's works appeared anonymously year after year].

Review of *True Stories from History and Biography,* 7, no. 23/201 (7 December 1850), 455 [The volume demonstrates that "a man who can write well for children deserves to be listened to by any body"].

1851

MELVILLE AND HAWTHORNE (2)

Review of *Godfrey Malvern, or, the Life of an Author,* by Thomas Miller, 9, no. 6/236 (9 August 1851), *109* [See essay].

"Notes of Excursions.—No. III. Glimpses of Berkshire Scenery," 9, no. 13/243 (27 September 1851), 241–242 [Duyckinck's account of a second excursion with Hawthorne and Melville; see essay].

MELVILLE (8)

"The Earl of Carlisle's View of America," 8, no. 3/207 (18 January 1851), *41* [America rejects the *dolce far niente* of the Southern races, as in *Typee.* Americans are happy with the great amount of work they have to do].

Review of *Para; or, Scenes and Adventures on the Banks of the Amazon,* by John Esaias Warren, 9, no. 1/231 (5 July 1851), 5–6 [The author attempts to get up a Fayaway "after the style of the romantic nautical Herman Melville"].

"Literature. Literary Intelligence," 9, no. 14/244 (4 October 1851), *270, 273* [Announcement of Melville's forthcoming *The Whale* and of the prepublication appearance of "The Town-Ho's Story" in *Harpers'*].

Review of Peter the Whaler, by William H. G. Kingston, 9, no. 17/247 (25 October 1851), *328* [Comparison of Peter with Redburn; Melville surpasses Kingston in "humor and picturesqueness"].

"Literary Intelligence. American," 9, no. 17/247 (25 October 1851), *333– 334* [*Moby-Dick* is "now very nearly ready"].

"Melville's Moby Dick; or, the Whale" [review], 9, no. 20/250 (15 November 1851), *381–383* [Summary of the plot and lengthy quotations—"a natural-historical, philosophical, romantic account"].
"Melville's Moby Dick; or, the Whale. Second Notice," 9, no. 21/251 (22 November 1851), *403–404* [The story comprises three books: an account of the great sperm whale, the romance of Captain Ahab and crew, and a moral rhapsody of "quaint conceit and extravagant daring speculation"].
"The Old Guard of Napoleon," Review of *The Imperial Guard of Napoleon: From Marengo to Waterloo,* by J. T. Headley, 9, no. 25/255 (20 December 1851), *482–483* [This popular author is not like Melville's Sandwich island priests, who neglect their gods or allow them to decay].

HAWTHORNE (7)
Review of *Lavengro; the Scholar, the Gipsy, and the Priest,* by George Borrow, 8, no. 9/ 213 (1 March 1851), 168–170 (*169*) [The book's "principle of woe" bears comparison with Hawthornesque "struggles of the spirit"].
"What Hawthorne Says of Himself, and His 'Twice-Told Tales,' in His Preface to the New Edition Issued by Ticknor, Reed, and Fields," 8, no. 11/215 (15 March 1851), *210–211* [Preface reprinted].
Review Notice of *Twice-Told Tales,* 8, no. 12/216 (22 March 1851), *236* [The elegant new edition shows how the sensitive and retiring Hawthorne can speak of himself with candor and impartiality].
"The Founder of the 'House of the Seven Gables'," 8, no. 13/217 (29 March 1851), *249–250* [Quoted passages].
Review of *The House of the Seven Gables,"* 8, no. 17/221 (26 April 1851), *334–336* ["In tenderness and delicacy of sentiment, no writer of the present day can go beyond this book"].
"Publisher's Circular. Literary Intelligence," 9, no. 1/231 (5 July 1851), *13–14* [Quotes H. F. Chorley on *Scarlet Letter* and *House of the Seven Gables*].
"Hawthorne's Wonder-Book for Boys and Girls" [review], 9, no. 22/252 (29 November 1851), *424–425* [The author's moral influence on children is most salutary, as they drink in unconsciously "the wisest lessons" and the "purest. . . poetry"].

1852

MELVILLE AND HAWTHORNE (3)
"Marks and Remarks," 10, no. 1/257 (3 January 1852), *8–10* (*9*) [On personal movements of authors; see essay].
"Personal and Historical Reminiscences. From Dr. J. W. Francis's Address before the Typographical Society," 10, no. 6/261 (31 January 1852), *91–93* (*92–93*) [See essay].

"Literature. The Men of the Time," Review of *The Men of the Time; or Sketches of Living Notables,* by Justus Starr Redfield, 11, no. 7/289 (14 August 1852), 99–101 *(100)* [See essay].

MELVILLE (3)
"Bon Gualtier's Ballads," Review of *The Book of Ballads,* edited by Bon Gualtier, 10, no. 1/257 (3 January 1852), 6–7 [See essay].
"Huc's Travels in Tartary. [Second Paper]," Review of *Recollections of a Journey through Tartary, Thibet and China, during the years 1844, 1845, and 1846,* by M. Huc, 10, no. 15/271 (10 April 1852), 260–262 *(261)* [Though a Roman Catholic missionary, Huc "reminds us not a little of the mode of telling of Mr. Melville's Typee"].
"Pierre; or, the Ambiguities" [review], 11, no. 8/290 (21 August 1852), *118–120* ["We would rejoice to meet Mr. Melville again in the hale company of sturdy sailors. . . strengthened by the wholesome air of the outside world."].

HAWTHORNE (22)
"New Tales by Hawthorne," Review of *The Snow Image and Other Twice Told Tales,* 10, no. 2/258 (10 January 1852), *22–24* ["Another choice gathering of golden thoughts from the old placer," our country's "delicate genius"].
"Graduates of Bowdoin," 10, no. 4/260 (24 January 1852), *73* [An alumnus describes, among other things, the remarkable class of 1825].
"Miss Mitford's Literary Life," Review of *Recollections of a Literary Life; or, Books, Places, and People,* by Mary Russell Mitford, 10, no. 10/266 (6 March 1852), *165–166* [Cites Mitford's praise for "Aunt Hepzibah"].
"Mr. Cheever's Reel in a Bottle," Review of *A Reel in a Bottle, for Jack in the Doldrums; being the Adventures of Two of the King's Seamen in a Voyage to the Celestial Country,* by Rev. Henry T. Cheever, 10, no. 11/267 (13 March 1852), *183–184* [A "nautical paraphrase of Pilgrim's Progress," reminiscent of Hawthorne's similar journey by railroad].
"'Colored' Views," Review of *Uncle Tom's Cabin; or, Life among the Lowly,* by Harriet Beecher Stowe, 10, no. 17/273 (24 April 1852), *291–292* [Mrs. Stowe has created a frightful scarecrow, which, unlike Hawthorne's, is not given to reflection].
"Hawthorne," 10, no. 23/279 (5 June 1852), *391–392* [Preface to the forthcoming *Blithedale Romance,* reprinted from Boston *Transcript*].
"Literary Intelligence," 11, no. 1/283 (3 July 1852), *15–16* [Hawthorne rumored to be writing a life of General Pierce: "they were fellow-students at Dartmouth"].
"Hawthorne's Blithedale Romance" [review], 11, no. 4/286 (24 July 1852), *52–54* [Though the book is not sufficiently matter of fact, Hawthorne again proves himself to be "a delicate spiritual anatomist"].

"Marks and Remarks," 11, no. 6/288 (7 August 1852), *90–91*
    [Remarks on death of Hawthorne's sister on the *Henry Clay*].
"Miscellany and Gossip," 11, no. 8/290 (21 August 1852), *123–124*
    [Grace Greenwood's "sketch of a Bozzian interior," from the
    National Era, recounts how Dickens recently gratified her
    national pride by praising Hawthorne, Stowe, and Longfellow].
"False Tendencies in American Literature," 11, no. 9/291 (28 August
    1852), *139–140* [Hawthorne and others, according to the
    London *Atlas,* are following a bastard French school by
    dissecting diseased minds and unhealthy sentiments].
"Criticism Extraordinary," Review of *Lotus-Eating; a Summer Book,* by
    George William Curtis, 11, no. 10/292 (4 September 1852), *157*
    [Parodic review with a reference to "The Blithedale Mangle" by
    "Lobsterphagus"].
"Literary Intelligence," 11, no. 12/294 (18 September 1852), *188*
    [The life of General Pierce "is now ready at all booksellers"].
"Hawthorne's Life of Franklin Pierce" [review], 11, no. 13/295 (25
    September 1852), *195–196* [The book shows Hawthorne's
    abilities as chronicler of American history, a "field to which his
    genius certainly invites him"].
"Miscellany and Gossip," 11, no 13/295 (25 September 1852),
    201–202 [The Washington *Union* says the life of Pierce "is as
    pleasant as the BEST of the author's romances!"].
"Literary Intelligence. Foreign," 11, no 15/297 (9 October 1852),
    236–237 [Quotes from London *Times'* review of *Blithedale
    Romance* on American coming superiority in "intellectual labors"
    as well as material development].
"Literary Intelligence. American," 11, no. 16/298 (16 October 1852),
    252–253 [The life of Pierce is "being ordered by tens of
    thousands"].
"Literary Intelligence. American," 11, no. 18/300 (30 October 1852),
    285–286 [On copyright laws and the "handsome sum" ($1,000)
    earned by the English edition of *Blithedale Romance*].
"Homes of American Authors," Review of *Homes of American
    Authors; Comprising Anecdotical, Personal, and Descriptive Sketches,*
    by various writers, 11, no. 21/303 (20 November 1852),
    325–326 [Account of the Concord "Club of Philosophers"
    includes a description of the silent, mysterious Hawthorne].
"Books of the Week," 11, no. 21/303 (20 November 1852),
    328–329 [Hawthorne appears in the second series of *Essays from
    the London Times*].
"Literary Intelligence. American," 11, no. 21/303 (20 November
    1852), *332–333* [A Boston correspondent recently saw
    Hawthorne and James T. Fields visiting the new Boston Music
    Hall].
"Homes of American Authors. Second Notice" (See 20 November
    above), 11, no. 22/304 (27 November 1852), *341–342*
    [Hawthorne compared with Emerson and Simms].

1853

MELVILLE (5)

"Literature, Books of the Week, Etc.," 12, no. 12/320 (19 March 1853), 227–228 [A French view of the extremely popular Melville stresses that he should guard against eccentricities, prodigality, digressions, and superfluous erudition].

"Bourne's Captivity in Patagonia," Review of *The Captive in Patagonia; or, Life among the Giants. A Personal Narrative,* by Benjamin Franklin Bourne, 12, no. 15/323 (9 April 1853), 286–288 [Patagonia is not a Typee: no "damsels delicately arrayed in flowers" nor "philosophic Melvillian savages" lounging about with "the gentlemanly ease of Broadway club-men"].

"Literature, Books of the Week, Etc.," 12, no 18/326 (30 April 1853), 355–358 (356) [*Household Words* retells the story of Daniel Dash, a Virginian whose adventures in the Marquesas closely parallel Melville's].

[Antony Autograph, Esq. (pseud.)], "A Stroll through New Amsterdam," 13, no. 3/341 (13 August 1853), 40–42 [The sight of ships evokes Melville's writing and "many pleasing and romantic associations"].

"Litera[t]ure, Books of the Week, Etc.," 13, no. 17/357 (3 December 1853), 295–296 [*Putnam's Monthly* for December concludes "Bartleby, the Scrivener," a "Poeish tale, with an infusion of more natural sentiment"].

HAWTHORNE (5)

"Literature, Books of the Week, Etc.," 12, no. 3/311 (15 January 1853), 43–44 [An article on Hawthorne in the *North American Review* carries us back "to the spirit and felicity" of Longfellow's article fifteen years ago].

"Three Tales: Christine Van Amberg, &c.," Review of *Three Tales: Christine Van Amberg, Resignation, and the Village Doctor,* by the Countess d'Arbourville, 12, no. 21/329 (21 May 1853), 416–417 [In Maunsell B. Field's translation, the second tale is judged best because it resembles *Twice-Told Tales*].

"Miscellany and Gossip," 12, no. 24/332 (11 June 1853), 481–483 (482) [Announcement of consular appointment of Donald G. Mitchell and Hawthorne to Venice and Liverpool].

"Literature. Hawthorne's Tanglewood Tales" [review], 13, no. 6/345 (10 September 1853), 99–101. [Hawthorne's style is appropriate for children and adults; such writing "will be a treasure to the household for many generations to come"].

"Leaves from the Diary of a Dreamer," Review of *Leaves from the Diary of a Dreamer. Found among His Papers* [by H. T. Tuckerman], 13, no. 7/346 (17 September 1853), 117–118 [Section on Hawthorne is quoted in its entirety].

Nemo Contra Deum... :
MELVILLE AND GOETHE'S "DEMONIC"

Nemo contra Deum nisi Deus ipse.
—The Auto-Biography of Goethe. Truth and Poetry:
From My Own Life

Robert Milder

After Melville had contracted for the English publication of *Mardi* in March 1849,[1] his first intention was to read and to rest; his second was to venture on. "I am glad you like that affair of mine," he wrote Evert Duyckinck on 5 April 1849, responding to Duyckinck's comments on *Mardi*: "But it seems so long now since I wrote it, & my mood has so changed, that I dread to look into it, & have purposely abstained from so doing since I thanked God it was off my hands.—Would that a man could do something & then say—It is finished.—not that one thing only, but all others—that he has reached his uttermost, & can never exceed it. But live & push—tho' we put one leg forward ten miles—its no reason the other must lag behind—no, *that* must again distance the other—& so on till we get the cramp & die."[2]

If Melville seems petulant he is only mockingly so, as Duyckinck surely realized, for in the spring of 1849 nothing excited him more than the literary prospects which lay before him. *Mardi* had been an initiation, a preliminary excursion into philosophy and high romance, but since that time Melville had listened admiringly to Emerson in Boston, "made close acquaintance" with Shakespeare (*L,* p. 77), and purchased a set of Pierre Bayle. Returning to New York after a brief absence, he purposed "to lay the great folios [of Bayle] side by side & go to sleep on them thro' the summer, with Phaedon in one hand & Tom Brown in the other" (*L,* pp. 83–84). But Melville was not to do much reading that summer, or get much sleep. The sales of *Mardi* proved disappointing, and to support his family (now including an infant son) he was forced to undertake what he considered hack work. Writing with incredible speed through the heat of a New York summer and the excitement of a cholera epidemic, Melville "completed the manuscript of *Redburn* in less than ten weeks, under considerable financial and emotional pressure,"[3] and the manuscript of *White-Jacket* within two months of that, churning out three thousand words a day (by Leon Howard's count)[4] in a desperate attempt to regain his literary and philosophical independence. The big book would have to wait.

As it turned out, it was nearly a year before Melville returned to metaphysics and romance—longer still if one credits some version of the "two *Moby-Dicks*" theory. And when he returned, it was with a mastery of craft which redeems *Redburn* and *White-Jacket* from his impatient disparagement. Both books helped Melville toward a surer handling of characterization and point of view, and in *White-Jacket* Melville discovered a structure—a narrative action embedded in and elaborated by a mass of expository chapters at once factual and symbolic—which would serve as his organizing principle in *Moby-Dick.* Artistically, the year's delay proved immensely fortunate, and there can be no question that a sequel to *Mardi* begun in 1849 and completed in 1850 would have been a cruder, less satisfying book than the published *Moby-Dick.*

If these seem commonplaces, the fact remains that when we try to pass beyond them, and beyond a purely technical consideration of Melville's development, we are struck by two things: first, that virtually all the themes of *Moby-Dick* are broached in *Mardi* and, second, that no advance in craftsmanship alone could have transmuted *Mardi* into *Moby-Dick*. There is a qualitative difference in vision between the two books which cannot be accounted for by a difference in "ideas" or a newly achieved mastery of symbolism and narrative technique. In retrospect, Ahab's assault upon the heavens seems the logical culmination of Melville's entire intellectual and imaginative development through 1851. The vital question involves the elusive *how* of this development, and here we are concerned with a process of mind which expresses itself only peripherally in *Redburn* and *White-Jacket*, and whose main current flows subterraneously through Melville's reading of 1849–50, surfacing briefly and often cryptically in a marginal notation, a fragment from a letter to Duyckinck or Hawthorne, or a word, a phrase, or an allusion from *Moby-Dick*. More than any of his contemporaries perhaps, Melville drew his intellectual and mythic vocabulary from books. At the same time, no one better illustrated the Emersonian notion that "man is endogenous, and education is his unfolding."[5] In the twelve to eighteen months following the publication of *Mardi,* Melville read a number of the authors who would influence him most: Bayle, Shakespeare and the Jacobean dramatists, Aeschylus, De Quincey, Goethe, Hawthorne, and Carlyle. Seldom, however, can Melville be said to have learned something from his reading, if by "learn" we mean the appropriation to oneself of another man's thoughts. More commonly, what Melville found in his reading was an articulation of his own nascent self. F. O. Matthiessen's description of Melville's response to Shakespeare—"a man of thirty awakening to his own full strength through the challenge of the most abundant imagination in history"[6]—applies to Melville's response to a number of less abundant imaginations as well, many of which not only find discernible echoes in *Moby-Dick* but contributed in essential ways to the emergence of the mind which would create *Moby-Dick*. In the deepest sense, the books Melville read during 1849 and 1850 were the chemical agents which raised the invisible writing on his imagination.

The subject of this essay is one of those agents, Goethe's *Autobiography*, which Melville purchased in London in December 1849 and read either before or during the composition of *Moby-Dick*.[7] My thesis, which I offer as an instrument for investigation, not an argument to be proved, is that the latter sections of *Mardi* presented Melville with a literary and philosophical problem which he could not resolve, and which for a time (economics apart) effectually blocked his inclination to press "forward ten miles" to a book like *Moby-Dick*. Briefly stated, this problem involved Melville's inability to imagine an apocalyptic action for his hero to perform and a fictional world capable of sustaining it. In focusing on only one of Melville's readings, I am conscious of a disproportion between the impasse I describe in section I of this essay and the partial "solution" I suggest in section II. It should be understood, however, that my remarks about the influence of Goethe might be applied, with a different set of textual references, to other formative sources—to Bayle's discussion of some of the Gnostic sects, for example, or to Carlyle's *Sartor Resartus*. Melville's response to Goethe's concept of the "Demonic" was conditioned by what, as an artist and thinker, Melville was half-consciously "looking for" in 1849 and 1850 and by what, as a personality, he was disposed to find congenial. At the same time, Goethe's demonic was but one of the elements that Melville's imagination dissolved and reconstituted according to its current needs. What makes Melville's debt to Goethe particularly valuable for study is its paradigmatic quality. It helps illuminate the nature of *Moby-Dick*'s world and the relationship of Ahab's madness to Ishmael's sanity. But it is also a signpost to what, in the absence of journals and ample marginalia, must ever remain a mystery: the imaginative route by which Melville arrived at *Moby-Dick*.

I

When Melville began *Mardi*, sometime in 1847, he was in the world's eyes (and most likely in his own) a writer of quasi-autobiographical travel literature whose intention as an author "was to communicate, in familiar language and literary forms, materials which readers could absorb and understand without any special antecedent knowledge and without any great concentration or effort."[8] By the time he completed the book, during the fall of the following year, he had made his way through "the world of mind" and sounded most of the themes which would characterize his mature work. Inspired by his readings of 1848, and particularly by the examples of Burton and Rabelais, he had abandoned his plans for a romance of Polynesian adventure and cast the major portion of his narrative in the form of an anatomy or symposium "digestively including the whole range of all that can be known or dreamed," as he later wrote of Pierre's book.[9] The result was "a rich book, with depths here and there that compel a man to swim for his life" (as Hawthorne put it[10]) but a discursive and outwardly uneventful one which lacked both the interest and continuity of a fictional narrative and the concentrated power of a tragedy.

To a large extent, *Mardi*'s want of dramatic action was the inevitable casualty of Melville's intellectual awakening. The book was his *Bildungsroman*, and months after it had been published (and flayed by the critics) Melville was entirely right in remarking to Duyckinck, "Had I not written & published 'Mardi,' in all likelihood, I would not be as wise as I am now, or may be" (*L*, p. 96). Still, *Mardi* needn't have failed in quite the way that it did. Among its endless dialogues are some of the most searching passages Melville would ever write, and in the person of Babbalanja—a man who could "neither believe, nor be comfortable in his unbelief," as Hawthorne would later say of Melville himself[11]—*Mardi* had a character fully capable of tragic development. Melville's problem in the later chapters of his book was what to *do* with Babbalanja.

Thematically, after two false starts, *Mardi* had involved Babbalanja in an intellectual quest of ever increasing urgency and complexity, carrying him to the point at which some purgative action, some definitive forcing of events, was both psychologically necessary and (given *Mardi*'s world) metaphysically impossible. Through Babbalanja, Melville had gazed at what he would later call "blackness," yet, like Arnold in "Empedocles on Etna," he had contrived a situation "in which suffering finds no vent in action; in which a continuous state of mental distress is prolonged, unrelieved by incident, hope, or resistance; [and] in which everything is to be endured, nothing to be done."[12] Unable to resolve Babbalanja's quest either intellectually or dramatically, Melville had converted his character to the Christian humanism of Serenia, his Mardian paradise, in what amounted to an undisguised lowering of expectations. "My voyage is ended," Babbalanja tells his companions: "Not because what we sought is found; but that I now possess all which may be had of what I sought in Mardi."[13] Conversion was Babbalanja's alternative to despair and may well have reflected Melville's hope that reason and faith might yet be reconciled in a Channingesque ethical Christianity.

Yet, leaving Babbalanja in Serenia, Melville had abruptly reintroduced the nominal but long-obscured hero of the book, Taji, and propelled him onward toward a final act of "abdication," half defiant and half suicidal, an act which had neither dramatic credibility nor intellectual significance but which managed, nonetheless, to upstage Babbalanja's conversion and overturn the carefully wrought synthesis of "right-reason" and "Alma" (Christ) which seemed to follow inescapably from *Mardi*'s investigation of life. It is generally agreed that Taji's "abdication" was meant to suggest an implacable demand for the

Absolute which scorned the compromises of Serenia, and that Taji thus prefigures, however weakly, the "Enceladan" or heaven-defying heroes of *Moby-Dick* and *Pierre*.[14] If this was what Melville intended, he did not succeed in persuasively dramatizing it, for he was not able to transform Taji's action into anything more than the Byronic posturings of an adolescent; unlike Babbalanja, who plumbed life to its core, Taji has no perceptible depth of understanding, and, hence, no painfully won right to rebel. What is significant about the ending of *Mardi* is not its meaning, which remains problematic, but the sense of spiritual adventurousness it conveys. Having explored, through Babbalanja, what he would later describe as "the tragicalness of human thought in its own unbiassed, native, and profounder workings" (*L,* p. 124),[15] Melville seems to have been struggling, through Taji, toward some apocalyptic metaphysical action whose content and meaning he could as yet only dimly imagine.

Probably nothing short of drastic revision could have salvaged the strained and meandering opening chapters of *Mardi* or the ill-conceived Taji-Yillah-Hautia romance. Yet despite its palpable flaws of structure and characterization, *Mardi* might have been a surprisingly compelling book had Melville been able to unite Babbalanja's intellect and Taji's will in some grand cosmic gesture more strenuous than conversion and more heroic than suicide. What frustrated Melville in the final chapters of *Mardi* was his inability to conceive an action which followed from, and in its magnitude was commensurate with, the tragedy of human thought.

In some sense, Melville's problem was that of the mid-nineteenth century, an age too sophisticated to tolerate the old materials which afforded the tragic writer his plots and too committed to a literature of introspection to devise new materials of its own. Living in a time of martial heroism, with a century of dynastic war behind him, Shakespeare could not only draw upon Holinshed and Plutarch for actions which spoke to the moral and political imagination of his age, but could assume in his audience an unquestioned belief in the reality and importance of the outward events he chronicled. Not so, the nineteenth-century tragedian. With the progress of civilization, as Melville's contemporary Jones Very theorized, the interest of literature had shifted from the outwardness of physical life to the inwardness of the mind. Homer, whose heroes "were but children of a larger growth," was for Very a noble anachronism;[16] and if Shakespeare escaped a similar judgment, in Very's eyes and others', it was because the criticism of the time effected a rigid separation between the profundity of Shakespeare's thought and the crudeness of incident he borrowed from the Elizabethan stage. More writers than Emerson found in Hamlet an image of the "speculative genius" of the nineteenth century;[17] but what, after all, had swordplay and poisoned goblets to do with *Hamlet*'s theme? "Alas, Shakespeare had to write for the Globe Playhouse," Carlyle remarked in extenuation, adding sympathetically: "No man works save under conditions."[18] Melville's impatience with "Richard-the-Third humps and Macbeth daggers"[19]—with, in fact, the entire dramatic apparatus of Elizabethan tragedy—was the response of a generation which reverenced Shakespeare as "inconceivably wise" (Emerson's words) while shuddering at the puerility of some of his effects. It is hardly surprising, then, that the Shakespeare Melville honored in "Hawthorne and His Mosses" was neither the dramatist nor the poet, nor the protean creator of characters, but rather "the profoundest of thinkers" ("Mosses," p. 541), who, living in an age of drama, happened to write plays. "Great geniuses are parts of the times," Melville wrote in the "Mosses" essay (p. 543), less as an apology for Shakespeare's Elizabethan "coloring" than as a prophecy that the American Shakespeare would come in a different "costume" and design fictions more congenial to the analytic spirit of the age.

But what coloring *would* the American Shakespeare assume, and what stories would he tell? In Carlyle's *Sartor*

Resartus and Wordsworth's *Prelude*, Very found the beginnings of a literature of mind in which thought and action were synonomous; yet Very's ideal subject, the
development of the soul, belonged to the transcendental
expansiveness of the 1830s and early forties, a mood
which yielded by mid-century, even among the transcendentalists themselves, to the widespread experience
of intellectual frustration. With the romantics, the subject
of serious literature had turned irrevocably inward,[20] but
with a sense now of the limitations, not the amplitude, of
the human mind, and with a concomitant feeling of
homelessness and despondency in the presence of an unknowable physical world. In England, the poems of Arnold, Clough, and Tennyson struck this note; in America,
Emerson's "Fate" and some of the later journals of
Thoreau. On both sides of the Atlantic it was as if a
whole intellectual generation came simultaneously to the
conclusion which Ahab would later voice in *Moby-Dick:*
"The dead, blind wall butts all inquiring heads at last."[21]

In both the energy and ambitiousness of its will to
know and its reluctant admission of skepticism and intellectual defeat, *Mardi* reflected this precise cultural moment. It arose at the point where romantic exuberance
shaded into Victorian doubt, spiritual autobiography into
metaphysical lamentation, *Sartor Resartus* into "Empedocles on Etna"; and the debacle of its ending bore witness
to a literary and philosophical impasse which frustrated
more writers than Melville. For the postromantics of the
mid-nineteenth century, nothing less than a literature of
thought seemed adequate to the challenge posed by the
dissolution of traditional belief, and yet such a literature
promised little more than a bleak and repetitious survey
of all truth that could not be known, all evil that could
not be ameliorated, and all the wearying oscillations between faith and doubt. Arnold's deletion of "Empedocles" from his 1853 *Poems* was an admission not only of
the emotional morbidness of his subject, which was much
the same as Mardi's subject, but of its artistic sterility: it
lent itself to no dramatic action, allowed for no catharsis.

Tragedy as the Elizabethans had practiced it was out of the question, for no writer who could conceive a Babbalanja or an Empedocles would be content to clothe his vision in some contemporary cut-and-thrust melodrama or bury the intellectual problems of his hero in a clutter of Shakespearean carnage. A literature of thought demanded a resolution that was appropriate to it. It required its hero either to rise above his despair in some final affirmation (and in doing so, like Tennyson's persona in "In Memoriam," solve or transcend problems which the author himself could not) or "to take up arms against a sea of troubles, And by opposing end them," though in some dramatic fashion other than suicide. What it asked, in short, was that the artist look beyond experience to prophecy—that he reconcile man to the universe if he could, or, if not, that he purge man's frustration vicariously through symbolic action.

In *Mardi,* Melville had tried to do both these things and had failed. He could not make Babbalanja's conversion seem viable, only half-believing in it himself, and he could not give Taji's "abdication" sufficient content to make it cathartic. His two endings to *Mardi,* both unsatisfying, betokened a metaphysical neither/nor whose combined lesson was that the intellect can only acquiesce to the conditions of life and the will only resist. In retrospect, we know that resistance, not acquiescence, would provide Melville with the tragic action for *Moby-Dick.* Melville's problem in 1848 was what to have his hero resist, and how. Lacking the cosmic egocentrism of Ahab, Babbalanja could not but acknowledge that man had no rightful claim upon the universe and, in any case, no visible adversary to press his claim against: "No coward he, who hunted, turns and finds no foe to fight" (*M,* p. 621). Instead of cutting the metaphysical knot through action, Babbalanja was thus condemned to unraveling it as best he could through reason, asking the same questions, arriving at the same frustrating solutions, and all the while growing more desperate and bewildered. With the Hebrews' belief in a personal God, Job could rail against his fate and provoke a response; but for Babbalanja, as for Arnold's Empedocles, there was only the dialogue of the mind with itself, corrosive, debilitating, and without hope or relief.

In these terms, it seems fair to say that the failure of *Mardi's* ending was less a matter of craftsmanship than vision and that it derived (as Lionel Trilling wrote of Hawthorne's work) from "a conception of the artist's dealing with the world which [was] less bold and intransigent than it might [have been]," which submitted too readily to "the literal actuality of the world" and was only incipiently conscious of the powers and prerogatives of the imagination.[22] For all its inventiveness, the world Melville presented in *Mardi* was an allegorical transcript of his own world. This was its philosophical strength, indeed its reason for being, for Babbalanja's questions were Melville's questions. But it was also its dramatic weakness: in a world governed by the physical and metaphysical conditions of reality, there was nothing, save recantation, suicide, or passive endurance, for the hero of thought to do.

Trilling's foil to Hawthorne is Kafka, who created a fictional world unconfined by the probabilities of experience; and perhaps, had Melville's imagination been more "spontaneous, peremptory, and obligatory"[23]—had it, like Kafka's, imposed its vision upon the world, rather than yield to the tyranny of the real—Melville might have constructed a fictional universe in which Babbalanja could definitively act. To require this of Melville, however, is to demand something which mid-nineteenth-century American fiction was in no position to deliver. Accustomed as we have become to Richard Chase's distinction between the "great practical sanity" of the English novel and the freedom from verisimilitude, the "profound poetry of disorder," of the American romance,[24] we may too easily forget that it was largely Hawthorne and Melville who created the American romance, and that before 1850, with rare exceptions like *Wuthering Heights,* the conditions of experience and the

conception of the artist as an imitator of experience ob-
tained too strongly over the Anglo-American imagination
to permit the kind of fierceness of vision, the experimentation with fictional *worlds,* that has become almost
commonplace in the twentieth century. In *The Confidence-Man,* Melville would write that fiction "should
present another world, and yet one to which we feel the
tie."[25] Characteristically, however, Melville's fictional
world was the world of reality selected and arranged, distorted sometimes (as in "Bartleby the Scrivener" and
Pierre) or translated into apologue (as in *The Confidence-
Man* itself), but seldom emancipated from the restrictions
of the possible. A world different from our own was both
unimaginable to Melville the artist and undesirable to
Melville the thinker, whose commitment to truth bound
him closely to what he and his age regarded as the in-
tractably real.[26]

But if Melville could give no credence to the kind of
fictional world his impulse toward cosmic action required,
he could and eventually did come to imagine a character
who believed in that world—that is to say, a hero of
thought "gone mad." We do not know how or when
Melville conceived the idea of a monomaniac hunter and
his cosmic foe, but we may locate one of its earliest
adumbrations in a passage from Melville's 5 April 1849
letter to Duyckinck in which he expressed "shock" at the
derangement of their common acquaintance Charles
Fenno Hoffman, adding "What sort of sensation permanent madness is may very well be imagined—just as we
imagine how we felt when we were infants, tho' we can
not recall it. In both conditions we are irresponsible &
riot like gods without fear of fate.—It is the climax of a
mad night of revelry when the blood has been transmuted into brandy" (*L,* p. 83). As Melville presents it,
the "permanent madness" which overtook Hoffman was
something other than "the sane madness of vital truth" he
would later describe in "Hawthorne and His Mosses"; it
was that condition of psychic license in which the re-
straints of the ego and the moral sense, indeed of the

reality principle itself, gave way to the urgencies of buried desire, which played themselves out oblivious to the judgments of man and God. "Sane" (or tragic) madness, as in *King Lear,* was the blindness which came from too much light, from a full, unmediated, and potentially annihilating apprehension of the emptiness of things. "Permanent madness," in contrast, was a peculiarly exhilarating form of insanity which, freeing the sufferer from all psychic inhibitions and often from reality itself, permitted cathartic action.

Although the Hoffman passage is by no means a source or conscious "beginning" for the dramatic action of *Moby-Dick*, it represents one of those rare surfacings of thought and impulse by which we glimpse the hidden direction of a mind. Coming at a time when Melville was straining to push beyond the metaphysical blind walls of *Mardi*, the passage reveals a speculative fascination with the wild, unrepressed behavior madness allows and a curious affirmation of kinship with the victim. "This going mad of a friend or acquaintance," Melville wrote Duyckinck, "comes straight home to every man who feels his soul in him,—which but few men do. For in all of us lodges the same fuel to light the same fire. And he who has never felt, momentarily, what madness is has but a mouthful of brains" (*L,* p. 83). As a minor poet and novelist, Hoffman was enough of an artist to remind Melville that madness was something to which men of intellect and imagination were particularly liable—an idea Melville had already broached in *Mardi* and was beginning to find strikingly confirmed in his readings in Shakespeare. Nonetheless, Hoffman's "present misfortune—rather blessing" (and the reversal is significant) was "but the sequel to a long experience of unwhole habits of thought" (*L,* p. 83), and not, like Babbalanja's, the consequence of a too penetrating glance into the abyss. Indeed, to Melville in 1849, Babbalanja and Hoffman may have seemed strangely complementary, with Hoffman assuming the role Melville had fictionally assigned to Taji. Babbalanja could speculate to the verge of distraction, but he never fell—or rose—into the "permanent madness" which would allow him to act; Hoffman, like Taji, could act, but without the depth of reflection which would transform his "mad night of revelry" into a symbolic metaphysical protest. So long as the philosopher and the lunatic remained opposite poles of human development, Melville could only divide his allegiance, as he did in *Mardi*, between a profound but nondramatic exploration of life's blackness and an impassioned but callow defiance. If, however, "permanent madness" might be made to subsume "tragic madness" and involve a separation from reality so acute as to border on metaphysical delusion, then the apocalyptic cosmic action denied Babbalanja because of his sanity and Hoffman and Taji because of their "unwhole habits of thought" might become a vital dramatic possibility.

The realization that tragic and permanent madness might be synthesized in a single character is, it seems to me, what precipitated, certainly enabled, the dramatic action of *Moby-Dick*.[27] One might almost say that Ishmael recapitulates the progress from *Mardi* to *Moby-Dick* when he conjecturally traces the development of Ahab's malady from intellectual and spiritual frustration to cosmic rage to madness to his "final monomania" (*MD*, p. 160), the last two phases transforming Ahab from the seething impotence of Babbalanja to the metaphysical vengefulness of a Babbalanja-*cum*-Taji/Hoffman. What *Mardi* took for one of its principal themes—the discovery and articulation of the terrifying truth of the human condition—*Moby-Dick* assumes as a given and proceeds to imagine a symbolic action in which the hero, formerly cast down by his perception of the truth, rises again in uncompromising defiance. Ahab, resurrected from the delirium that followed the loss of his leg, is like Lear returned to strength but not to serenity, or Job unreconciled by the whirlwind; and his pursuit of "an audacious, immitigable, and supernatural revenge" (*MD*, p. 162) is a response to the hitherto unthinkable question, "What next?" Insanity in the clinical as well as in the "tragic" sense is the very condition for this revenge, as Ahab himself is keenly aware. "How can'st thou endure without being mad?" he asks the grief-stricken blacksmith Perth (*MD*, p. 403), clinging to his own madness not merely because it palliates an intolerable suffering but also because it allows him to incarnate "all the subtle demonisms of life and thought" (*MD*, p. 160) in a symbolic antagonist and so to take action when none would otherwise be possible.[28] "For this hunt," Ahab tells Pip, rejecting his "curing" influence, "my malady becomes my most desired health" (*MD*, p. 436).

For Melville, however, struggling to press beyond the dichotomized ending of *Mardi*, the literary implications of madness were not unmixed. A character who hallucinates a malevolent symbolic world and undertakes to defy it would have solved the problem which baffled Melville in *Mardi*—how a definitive cosmic action might be brought forth from a world in which there were no gods to be confronted and no symbolic antagonists to be slain—but it would have done so only at the cost of estranging the tragic hero from the audience and relegating his "audacious, immitigable, and supernatural revenge" to the status of a psychotic obsession. This of course is one of the *Moby-Dick*s that Melville might have written, but it is not the book he wrote or, apparently, the book he intended. Whatever process of moral disintegration Ahab may undergo during the course of *Moby-Dick*, it is important to remember that Melville's first allusions associate Ahab with heroes and redeemers (Christ, Prometheus, and Perseus), and that Moby Dick is repeatedly identified with a principle of chaos which presides over or is synonomous with the whole of Creation and which the Lord himself (or his agent, the Messiah) is destined to punish "with his sore, and great, and strong sword."[29] *Moby-Dick* is thus a reenactment of the "dragon-killing theme" which Northrop Frye describes as the "central form of quest romance";[30] and Ahab, who is linked to such dragon slayers as Perseus and St. George (*MD*, pp. 110, 305), is a would-be redeemer who "pile[s] upon the whale's white hump the sum of all the general rage and hate felt by his race from Adam down" (*MD*, p. 160). Ahab's "quenchless feud" seems Ishmael's, as it seems the crew's and is meant to seem the reader's, because it draws upon a latent resentment rooted deeply in man's collective unconscious, or, more empirically, in the universally perceived disparity between the world man requires and the world he is condemned to inhabit. Dramatically, Ahab had to be "mad," for without madness there could only be the futile questionings of a Babbalanja. And yet to command our sympathies and hold our literary belief, Ahab's "tragic madness" had to be made an intensification of (not a departure from) man's common bitterness over the conditions of life, and his "permanent madness" (particularly his understanding of Moby Dick) had to be given sufficient foundation in the world of the novel to free it from the taint of quixotic absurdity. Having imagined a character with the depth of Babbalanja and the uncompromising will of Taji, Melville had to design an appropriate fictional world for his character to inhabit, a world physically and metaphysically *like* our own and yet capable of supporting, with some degree of plausibility, an apocalyptic quest which belonged more properly to undisplaced myth than to the mainstream of nineteenth-century Anglo-American fiction.

II

In their long note on Ahab in the Hendricks House edition of *Moby-Dick,* Luther S. Mansfield and Howard P. Vincent locate possible sources or analogues for Melville's character in passages from Shakespeare, Milton, Goethe, Byron, Carlyle, De Quincey, and the Bible.[31] But among the most germinal passages both for Ahab and for the world of *Moby-Dick* may have been the one Mansfield and Vincent include as a gloss on the phrase "that certain sultanism of the brain," from the chapter "The Specksynder." The passage is from Goethe's *Auto-biography (Truth and Poetry: From My Own Life)*, and it

concerns the nature of the demonic as it appeared to
Goethe's character Egmont:

> He thought he could detect in nature—both animate and in-
> animate, with soul or without soul—something which man-
> ifests itself only in contradictions, and which, therefore, could
> not be comprehended under any idea, still less under one
> word. It was not godlike, for it seemed unreasonable; not hu-
> man, for it had no understanding; nor devilish, for it was benef-
> icent; nor angelic, for it often betrayed a malicious pleasure. It
> resembled chance, for it evolved no consequences; it was like
> Providence, for it hinted at connexion. All that limits us it
> seemed to penetrate; it seemed to sport at will with the neces-
> sary elements of our existence; it contracted time and expanded
> space. In the impossible alone did it appear to find pleasure,
> while it rejected the possible with contempt.
>
> To this principle, which seemed to come in between all
> other principles to separate them, and yet to link them to-
> gether, I gave the name of Demonic, after the example of the
> ancients and of those who, at any rate, had perceptions of the
> same kind. . . .
>
> Although this Demonical element can manifest itself in all
> corporeal and incorporeal things, and even express itself most
> distinctly in animals, yet, with man, especially does it stand in a
> most wonderful connexion, forming a power which, if it be not
> opposed to the moral order of the world, nevertheless does
> often so cross it that one may be regarded as the warp, and the
> other as the woof.
>
> For the phenomena which it gives rise to there are innu-
> merable names: for all philosophies and religions have sought
> in prose and poetry to solve this enigma and to read once for
> all the riddle which, nevertheless, remains still unriddled by
> them.
>
> But the most fearful manifestation of the Demonical, is
> when it is seen predominating in some individual character.
> During my life I have observed several instances of this, either
> more closely or remotely. Such persons are not always the most
> eminent men, either morally or intellectually; and it is seldom
> that they recommend themselves to our affections by goodness
> of heart; a tremendous energy seems to be seated in them, and
> they exercise a wonderful power over all creatures, and even
> over the elements; and, indeed, who shall say how much farther
> such influence may extend? All the moral powers combined are
> of no avail against them; in vain does the more enlightened
> portion of mankind attempt to throw suspicion upon them as
> deceived if not deceivers—the mass is still drawn on by them.
> Seldom if ever do the great men of an age find their equals

among their contemporaries, and they are to be overcome by
nothing but the universe itself; and it is from observation of
this fact that the strange, but most striking, proverb must have
risen: *Nemo contra Deum nisi Deus ipse.*[32]

The most obvious significance of this passage, which
has been cited by previous scholars but never sufficiently
explored,[33] is its presentation of a man like Ahab, with "a
tremendous energy" seated in him, who sweeps before
him "the more enlightened portion of mankind," hyp-
notizes the masses, seeks to extend his dominion beyond
the human to the natural world, and is finally overcome
by nothing less than "the universe itself." With hindsight,
one can see in the passage a foreshadowing of Ahab's relationship to Starbuck and the *Pequod's* crew, as well as to
the whole of Creation, but the more compelling point of
interest is how Goethe's remarks may have struck Melville as he read them in 1850, possibly before Ahab
entered his mind. In the Taji who rejected Serenia for the
open sea, Melville had experimented, however tentatively, with one demonic character; and in the sailor
Jackson in *Redburn,* he had more forcefully imagined another. Unlike Taji, Jackson was in no sense a hero but
rather "the foul lees and dregs of a man" who "had such
an over-awing way with him; such a deal of brass and im-
pudence; such an unflinching face," and above all such a
mastery of human nature that he reduced the crew of the
Highlander to virtual servitude.[34] In the teleology of
Melville criticism, Jackson has most often been interpreted as a forerunner of Ahab, for "he seemed to be full
of hatred and gall against every thing and every body in
the world; as if the world was one person, and had done
him some dreadful harm, that was rankling and festering
in his heart" (*R*, p. 61). Yet Jackson's is the hatred of the
cynic and the misanthrope, not of the tragic visionary,
and his "bitterness and disbelief" are neither an anticipation of Ahab's nor, as Newton Arvin has claimed, a
reflection of Melville's own.[35] To Melville in 1849,
Jackson was a literary and imaginative experiment whose

origin lay in the same fascination with demonic energy which prompted him to comment, beside a particularly audacious speech of Edmund in *King Lear*, "The infernal nature has a valor often denied to innocence."[36] "I can never think of him," Redburn says of Jackson in a passage which seems to mirror Melville's ambivalence, "but I am reminded of that misanthrope upon the throne of the world—the diabolical Tiberius at Capreae. . . . And though Tiberius came in the succession of the Caesars, and though unmatchable Tacitus has embalmed his carrion, yet do I account this Yankee Jackson full as dignified a personage as he, and as well meriting his lofty gallows in history" (*R*, p. 276). Redburn's ostensible point is that "there is no dignity in wickedness, whether in purple or in rags," and that "in historically canonizing on earth the condemned below, we do but make ensamples of wickedness" (*R*, p. 276). The irony is that in associating Jackson with emperors and immortalizing him in a lengthy epitaph, Redburn has performed a canonization of his own. It is not evil that has awed the mature narrator Redburn and led him away from his characteristic humanitarianism, but sheer demonic energy, regardless of its moral sign. Like Blake's Milton, Redburn has been seduced by the magnitude of his character and is of the devil's party without knowing it.

In the context of Melville's development, the characterization of Jackson is remarkable less for its direct prefiguration of Ahab than for its revelation of a bent of mind which in other circumstances might produce an Ahab. Although Jackson has only a cameo role in *Redburn*, his presence dominates the book far beyond what the sum of his narrated actions warrants. In the sordid world of sailor vice, Jackson's malice, like Iago's in *Othello*, appears so gratuitous, so inexplicable by all common theories of behavior, that it assumes an almost mystical quality, as if it belonged to a different order of reality. This was precisely its fascination both for Redburn, whom Jackson acquaints with a subtler, more diabolical evil than was to be found in the Liverpool slums, and for Melville himself, who within a month of portraying Jackson created Bland, the Master-at-Arms in *White-Jacket*—"an organic and irreclaimable scoundrel, who did wicked deeds as the cattle browse through the herbiage, because wicked deeds seemed the legitimate operation of his whole infernal nature."[37] It is as though, groping toward some conception of literary heroism, Melville came increasingly to associate this with the "valor" of the "infernal nature." "In some sort, Sin hath its sacredness, not less than holiness," Melville would later write in *Pierre*, and might, had he been bolder, have written in *Redburn:* "And great Sin calls forth more magnanimity than small Virtue. What man, who is a man, does not feel livelier and more generous emotions toward the great god of Sin—Satan,—than toward yonder haberdasher, who only is a sinner in the small and entirely honorable way of trade?" (*P*, pp. 177–178). In *Redburn* as in *Mardi*, however, Melville's impulses were frustrated by the limits of his imagination. Having created in Jackson a sinner equal to Tiberius, if not quite to Satan himself, Melville could envision no dramatic action for him to perform, certainly no cosmic action.[38] Where Ahab would be an earnest and austere thinker, Jackson was one who "according to his own account . . . had passed through every kind of dissipation and abandonment in the worst parts of the world" (*R*, p. 57). Far from "being a rebel against the universe," Jackson, as one critic has noted, was "a concrete manifestation of what is wrong with it."[39]

The quality which separated Goethe's demonic man from a reprobate like Jackson or a "Scamp Jupiter" like Emerson's Napoleon was the cosmological nature of his ambitions, suggested by his power "even over the elements" and confirmed by the Latin motto that moralized upon his fate: *Nemo contra Deum nisi Deus ipse.* Melville was sufficiently struck by "this wee scrap of latinity" to reproduce it in *Pierre* as a virtual epigraph on the career of his heaven-defying hero (*P*, p. 14). Whether the passage as a whole "aided Melville in arriving at his conception of Ahab," as Henry A. Murray has suggested (p. 438), we can never be sure; yet without a doubt the passage contained in embryo the dramatic action toward which Melville had been ineffectually struggling for two years. In *Mardi*, Melville had imagined a hero of thought, Babbalanja, and a hero of will, Taji—the one impotent, the other inconsequential. In *Redburn*, he had experimented with a villain of transcendent energy and spleen: And in *Redburn* and *White-Jacket* both, he had hinted at a motivation whose origins lay well outside the charted regions of the mind—indeed, which seemed to verge upon the theological. What he had not yet learned, and what Goethe among others may have helped to teach him, was how these elements might be united in a character of irresistible force and focused in a dramatic assault upon the universe itself.

If Goethe's demonic man is visibly an analogue to Ahab and possibly an important source, the more formative influence of Goethe's remarks lay in their discussion of the demonic in nature. As a "principle, which seemed to come in between all other principles to separate them, and yet to link them together," the demonic occupied an anomalous position in both a theistic and an atheistic scheme of the universe. It was not synonomous with Providence, fate, or chance, though it partook of the attributes of all three; and it was neither intelligent and manifestly purposive ("for it seemed unreasonable" and "had no understanding") nor arbitrary and blind ("for it hinted at connexion"). One thing which is certain from Goethe's invocation of "the example of the ancients" is that the demonic (often spelled "Daemonic," though not, significantly, in the edition Melville read) should not be confused with the diabolical.[40] Demons, for the Greeks, were by no means uniformly maleficent; the word itself comes from a Greek root meaning "apportioner" or "apportionment" (suggesting fate) and "had a good connotation, which was changed into an evil one when Christianity condemned the deities and spirits of paganism."[41] Nonetheless, one cannot interpret Goethe's principle of the demonic as imperturbingly neutral, much less benign. Departing from the thoughts of his character Egmont, Goethe tells how he "tried to screen [himself] from this fearful principle, by taking refuge, according to [his] usual habits, in an imaginary creation" (*Autobiography*, II, 157). Wayward and unaccountable, the demonic might have passed for a cosmological imp of the perverse had it not been for its tampering with "the necessary elements of our existence." As it was, the demonic represented a principle of obstinacy and caprice which, while inferior to a putative Supreme Being (just as the Greek demons were inferior to the gods), managed to have the final say in most matters concerning human life. It was a principle which could neither be worshiped nor propitiated, the former being inappropriate, the latter of no avail. And it was a principle which, as Goethe indicated, was all-pervasive and terrifying.

Melville had offered a comic version of the demonic in *Mardi* in his account of "certain invisible spirits, ycleped the Plujii," who, "with malice aforethought, . . . brought about the high winds that destroyed the banana plantations, and tumbled over the heads of its occupants many a bamboo dwelling"; who "cracked the calabashes; soured the 'poee;' induced the colic; begat the spleen; and almost rent people in twain with stitches in the side. In short, of whatever evil, the cause of which the islanders could not directly impute to the gods, or in their own opinion was not referable to themselves,—of that very thing must the invisible Plujii be guilty" (*M*, pp. 262–263). While King Media dismisses the belief as an ignorant superstition, Babbalanja is surprisingly drawn toward it as a metaphor or truth-giving myth. "For, Plujii or no Plujii," he tells Media, "it is undeniable, that in ten thousand ways, as if by a malicious agency, we mortals are woefully put out and tormented; and that, too, by things in themselves so exceedingly trivial, that it would seem almost impiety to ascribe them to the august gods" (*M*, p. 264). As inflictors of the various petty annoyances of life, the Plujii fill a "hiatus" in Babbalanja's "system of metaphysics" (*M*, p. 264).[42] They cannot, however, account for the graver evils of the universe, which Babbalanja, loath to invent an intermediate order of malevolent beings in the manner of Johnson's Soame Jenyns, must unwillingly lay at the hands of God himself. "Since evil abounds, and Oro is in all things," he reasons, "then he cannot be perfectly good; wherefore Oro's omnipresence and moral perfection seem incompatible" (*M*, p. 427).

Babbalanja's problem was of course one which Melville labored over through most of his literary career, apprehending it ever more profoundly but approaching no nearer a solution; within Christian orthodoxy, he rapidly came to feel, there *was* no solution. What Goethe offered him was what he had found previously, in more dualistic terms, in some of the ancient sects and heresies described by Pierre Bayle: a cosmology that separated the moral chaos of the experiential world from the will, perhaps the control, of the Supreme Being. For Goethe himself, the demonic served precisely this function; it was his "ultimate, most valid and characteristic conception for fitting his sense of evil into a vision of existence which [would] not admit anything 'radically evil' in human nature and [was] also unwilling to take the devil seriously or to entertain more than tentatively and transiently the idea of an evil God."[43] By "regarding *God* as good, but *the gods* as evil," as he "sometimes" tended to do (Mason, p. 51), Goethe was able to acknowledge his sense of cosmic disjunction without admitting it to be final. In some ways, perhaps, Goethe's solution was as appalling as the problem it addressed, for it seemed to abandon the world to the rule of the demonic while positing a God who, if He existed at all, was so removed from human affairs and so morally and spiritually indeterminate that belief in Him was not far from practical atheism. For a reluctant infidel like Melville, however, Goethe's theory had the advantage of recognizing the visible absence of Providence from the moral and physical world yet stopping short of outright disbelief. This is not to suggest that Melville

gave credence to some version of the demonic except as
an organizing metaphor for some of the disturbing and
initially disconnected thoughts toward which he had been
powerfully attracted during the preceding two years.
What is certain is that Melville found the demonic an
eminently *usable* idea which he drew upon significantly in
creating the fictional world of *Moby-Dick*.

A hint of the demonic appears in *Moby-Dick* in the
"unseen and unaccountable old joker" of "The Hyena,"
whose "sly, good-natured hits, and jolly punches in the
side" (*MD*, p. 195) seem, in Goethe's words, "to sport at
will with the necessary elements of our existence." But
more typically, where there is a mischievous and almost
spritelike perversity to Goethe's demonic, there is something ponderous and chillingly mechanical about Melville's. It expresses itself in the "broad firmament" of the
sperm whale's forehead, "pleated with riddles; dumbly
lowering with the doom of boats, and ships, and men"
(*MD*, p. 292), and in the person of the carpenter (a
"manmaker" or symbol of the gods), whose "certain impersonal stolidity . . . so shaded off into the surrounding
infinite of things, that it seemed one with the general
stolidity discernible in the whole visible world" (*MD*, p.
388). But above all, Melville indicates through his language, the demonic shows itself in Moby Dick: for Ahab,
he is the personification of "all the subtle demonisms of
life and thought" (*MD*, p. 160); for the crew, "the great
gliding demon of the seas of life" (*MD*, p. 162); and for
Ishmael, the evocator of an ontological terror which, like
the terror of the Vermont colt at the buffalo robe, arises
from "the instinct of the knowledge of the demonism in
the world" (*MD*, p. 169).

Ishmael's feelings toward Moby Dick require particular attention here, for they suggest most clearly how
the notion of the demonic may have helped Melville
bridge the worlds of realism and myth and establish a
continuum between Ahab's madness and Ishmael's sanity.
Objectively considered, the world Melville presented in
Moby-Dick is a naturalistic one[44]: life is "harsh, violent,

laborious, chancy, long, inequitable, fate-ridden, over-whelming; it appears profoundly disrespectful of persons and indifferent to private fortune or sorrow; it is tragic, and it is disinheriting."[45] It is not, however, malevolent, if only because it reveals no immanent intelligence and no perceptible design. In chapters like "The Hyena," "The Monkey-Rope," and "A Squeeze of the Hand," Ishmael responds to this world in what seems the most appropriate way possible, cultivating a "genial, desperado philosophy" founded upon existential humility and equally removed from resentment and despair. In contrast, Ahab's rage may be said to emanate from an anthropocentrism which projects human demands upon nature and "values to phenomena according to their contribution to [man's] well-being."[46] To the Ishmael of "Moby Dick," Ahab is "crazy Ahab," his hatred of Creation morbid, his monomania insane. Yet having dissociated himself from Ahab's vision of cosmic malice and offered in its place a world of whiteness, empty and indifferent, Ishmael gives voice to that remarkably Ahabian phrase: "the instinct of the knowledge of the demonism in the world." Though Ishmael professes to believe (and in many chapters evidently *does* believe) in a naturalistic universe, malignant to us only when we superimpose upon it our human ethics, in "The Whiteness of the Whale" he seizes upon metaphors which reveal a latently Ahabian outrage and abhorrence: an invisible world "formed in fright" (how and by whom? we are tempted to ask; fright at what?); "all deified nature" as a "harlot, whose allurements cover nothing but the charnel-house within"; the "palsied universe" lying before us like "a leper" (*MD*, pp. 169, 170). Confronted with the dread, soul-extinguishing prospect of whiteness, Ishmael cannot maintain the detachment which allowed him to take "this whole universe for a vast practical joke" (*MD*, p. 195). The universe appalls him—and not him alone, he takes pains to demonstrate, but men of all cultures and all ages, who recoil spontaneously at the thought of whiteness. To the behaviorist, this may indicate nothing more than that the threat of death and annihilation, the absence of cosmic meaning, and the apparent godlessness (indeed, ungodliness) of the created world are universally associated with whiteness and universally loathed. But Ishmael will not leave it at that. The presence of a universal response, he argues in Lockean fashion, implies the existence of an external stimulus: "Though neither [Ishmael nor the Vermont colt] knows where lie the nameless things of which the mystic sign gives forth such hints; yet with me, as with the colt, somewhere those things must exist" (*MD*, p. 169). It hardly matters to Ishmael that there is, or should be, no room for "demonism" in the world he has presented. Overwhelmed by a visceral sense of terror at the whiteness of the whale, Ishmael not only reverts to the anthropocentrism of Ahab, hating the world for its heartlessness and betrayal, but he locates the source of his terror as something in the Creation itself.

The imagined presence of a horrifying element in nature to be feared, hated, and if possible defied is what distinguishes the world of *Moby-Dick* from the world of *Mardi* and provides the metaphysical backdrop, indeed the stimulus and rationale, for Ahab's quest. One cannot say, however, that Melville's understanding of the world is deeper in *Moby-Dick*, or even that it has substantially changed. The fearful contingency of man's life that *Moby-Dick* dramatizes in encounters with "the full awfulness of the sea" (*MD*, p. 235), *Mardi* speculates upon, less vividly but in much the same vein, in the conversations of Babbalanja and his companions. One even sees in *Mardi*, in the long description of a calm, a hint of the annihilating cosmic emptiness which Ishmael would later find evoked by the whiteness of the whale (*M*, ch. 2). What separates the two books metaphysically is not so much their perception of experience as the categories through which they order and evaluate experience. Melville could never have brought Babbalanja to a phrase like "the instinct of the knowledge of the demonism in the world" because in *Mardi* the range of possible responses to life had been delimited by Melville's concern

with the objective nature of things. Thus Babbalanja
could agonize over the conditions of life, but he could
not "hate" them, much less ascribe them to a cosmic demonism, for like Melville himself he was too conscious
that he had no right to demand otherwise. As the philosopher Bardianna counseled, "'Though they smite us, let
us not turn away from these things, if they be true'" (*M*,
p. 577). This is not the case with *Moby-Dick*. Within the
world of verifiable experience, there is no objective cor-
relative for Ishmael's horror at the whiteness of the
whale, which proceeds from his own paralyzing sense of
non-being in the face of cosmic immensity. Yet rather
than accept this fact as it is, though it smites him, Ishmael
"projects his own frightened life experience upon the
universe,"[47] transforming its emptiness into "demonism"
and delusively positing a source for his terror in the
depths of the unknown. Although the world of *Moby-
Dick* is outwardly much the same as the world of *Mardi*,
Melville has permitted the subjectivity of his narrator—which is man's collective subjectivity or anthropocentrism—to shape the interpretation and appraisal of
that world, with profound consequences.

More sources than Goethe contributed to the world
of *Moby-Dick*, and finally of course it was the imagination
of Melville, working in ways we can only guess at from
the densely allusive prose of *Moby-Dick*, that synthesized
the ideas from his reading into a presentation of experience as comprehensive and original as any in our literature. Yet if Goethe supplied Melville with the notion of
the demonic, as seems likely, he may also have helped
suggest the literary use to which it might be put. As
Goethe presents it in his *Autobiography*, the perception of
the demonic is, significantly, not his perception but his
character Egmont's, and even that is problematical: Egmont only "thought he could detect in Nature" a principle of contradiction and perversity. Aside from its
definitional elusiveness, then, the demonic may at best be
only quasi-real. It gathers under one denomination and
causal scheme various undeniable elements of human ex-

perience, but whether it exists as anything more than a metaphor or frightened projection is a moot point. Egmont believes it does; Goethe himself, though he returns to the idea in his other writings, is here noncommittal.

To Melville in 1850, inclining strongly toward some heroic metaphysical action but inhibited by his stubborn sense of what was real, it may have been the very ambiguousness of the demonic which proved most liberating. In the madness of Charles Fenno Hoffman, Melville had found a freedom from the reality principle which allowed the sufferer to act out the necessities of his being and "riot like [the] gods without fear of fate." In Goethe's demonic he may have discovered something further—the necessary dramatic link between madness and sanity which restored the maddened hero to the community and made his outrage an extension of every man's. The demonic was not an ontological postulate and therefore did not affront belief, but neither was it the product of a morbid or pathological imagination. Rather, it originated at the point at which the heartlessness of the Creation impinged upon man's subjectivity and called forth a horror which was both involuntary and universal. A deeply felt sense of the demonic involved a madness of sorts, for it was a response in excess of the observable facts; but it was a madness which was inseparable from being human, or at least from viewing life, as we inevitably must, through the lenses of our personal and collective needs.[48] Seen in relation to the demonic, madness and sanity differed only in degree, with the madman displaying a particularly intense and single-minded form of man's common resentment and fear. Without transgressing Melville's sense of the real, the demonic offered the possibility of a mind-engendered world of terror fashioned from the unconscious imagination of the race and capable of nourishing, in selected individuals, a cosmic hatred which was "mad" only in its obsessiveness.

Partly by means of the demonic, then, Melville was able to create a fictional universe in which naturalism shaded into supernaturalism and sanity into madness in a way that linked Ahab securely to the world of common experience and established his revenge as a symbolic vehicle for all mankind's. In this sense the demonic helped Melville mediate between realism and myth; it made Ahab one of us, or at least one *for* us, and lent credit to a vision of cosmic malice which at first seemed merely paranoid. At the same time, however, the demonic, as described by Goethe and adapted by Melville, hinted at some predetermined necessity that separated the demonic man from the mass of mankind and defined his revolt in terms of an inverted filial allegiance to something which lay beyond him. That certain men should overawe their contemporaries and be broken "by nothing but the universe itself" was a phenomenon attributable (for Goethe) to a transcendent amoral willfulness which was the manifestation in man of the same demonic principle which penetrated the Creation. In some strange, fateful way, the demonic man was allied to the demonic in nature, his behavior flowing from the exigencies of an inner force which led him to "cross" the "moral order of the world," challenge the sovereignty of the gods themselves, and ultimately be destroyed by them. Goethe offers no explanation for the presence of the demonic in certain men, other than what is suggested by his curious phrasing: the "Demonical element can manifest itself," can "express itself," "is seen predominating"—his syntax implying that the demonic is an active principle which, like the Calvinist God, can infuse itself irresistibly into whomever or whatever it wants, whenever it wants. Through some inexplicable process of selection, the demonic man is singled out much like the Calvinist saint, though with reference to no overriding cosmic plan and with the promise not of beatitude but immolation. It is as if, for reasons of its own (or for no reason at all), the demonical element in the universe periodically generated in man a principle of uncompromising resistance to itself. Or, in the language of a myth obscurely present in *Moby-Dick* and regnant in *Pierre*, it is as if the gods, descending to earth, sired a race of semidivine sons whose nature impelled them to rebel against their fathers but whose relative impotence doomed them to defeat: hence the proverb, *Nemo contra Deum nisi Deus ipse.*

In *Moby-Dick*, Melville signifies this prophetic kinship through the "slender, rod-like mark, lividly whitish," which threads its way down Ahab's face and neck like a "perpendicular seam" made by lightning in a "great tree" (*MD*, p. 110), and which joins Ahab, the demonic man, in a peculiar intimacy with Moby Dick, the symbol of the demonic in nature. Two theories are offered to explain this mark. The first, that Ahab received his scar "not till he was full forty years old" and then "not in the fury of any mortal fray but in an elemental strife at sea" (*MD*, p. 110), is of considerable dramatic importance, for it is taken up again in "The Candles" in the suggestion that Ahab was literally or metaphorically struck by lightning during an act of worship. The second, that the scar is a birthmark which runs "from crown to sole," is significant not only because it is advanced by an old Manxman, "popularly invested . . . with preternatural powers of discernment" (*MD*, p. 110), but also because it has no dramatic function, is never mentioned again, and seems included here solely for the purpose of intimating some mysterious, preexperiential bond between Ahab and Moby Dick. If we read this hint with reference to Goethe's demonic, Ahab's character and motivation assume a new dimension. His cry "I'm demoniac" (*MD*, p. 147) is restored to its primary meaning, "I am possessed by a demon," supplementing the more common interpretation, "I am diabolical." And his agonized introspection in "The Symphony"—"What is it, what nameless, inscrutable, unearthly thing is it; what cozening, hidden lord and master, and cruel, remorseless emperor commands me; that against all natural lovings and longings, I so keep pushing, and crowding, and jamming myself on all the time . . ." (*MD*, pp. 444–445)—bids to be taken at face value.[49] On one level, Ahab's scar was Melville's way of emblematizing a temperament and intellect which pressed man's anthropocentric claims upon the universe to an extreme, which lived continuously with "the instinct of the knowledge of the demonism in the world," and which was enraged enough and bold enough not to cower before the demonic, as Ishmael does in "The Whiteness of the Whale," but to set out to defy it. On another level, the scar contributes an element of mystery which penetrates beyond all psychological explanations of Ahab and transmutes his defiance from a compulsion into a calling. Ahab becomes the one, chosen against all his "humanities," to "lay the world's grievances before [the] bar" (*MD*, p. 108)—and, necessarily, to be destroyed for it, since the same fatality that destines the rebellion of the demonic man destines his catastrophic defeat. It is all, from one point of view, a grisly cosmic joke which the demonic plays on man, just as Moby Dick plays with Ahab's whaleboat "as a mildly cruel cat her mouse" (*MD*, p. 449). But it is also, interpreted as myth, a kind of pageant in which the defeated hero vindicates himself and mankind and contemns the powers that destroy him. If the cards have been dealt and must be played, as Ahab feels, then Stubb's eulogy of Ahab—"thou actest right; live in the game, and die in it!" (*MD*, p. 413)—may point toward the only symbolic victory that is possible. Although no salvation will be forthcoming for the demonic man, he may nonetheless, through resistance, show himself worthy of being saved. The corollary to Goethe's "No one against God but God himself," Melville would later demonstrate in *Pierre*, is "whoso storms the sky gives best proof he came from thither!" (*P*, p. 347).

III

It would be too much to claim that all this was contained in Melville's immediate response to Goethe, much less in Goethe's remarks themselves. Unlike Melville's demonic man, Goethe's was not by primary intent a rebel against the universe, nor was he always among "the most eminent men, either morally or intellectually," and least of all was he a self-appointed redeemer. The passage on the demonic fell on imaginative ground well prepared to receive it; and Melville, who characteristically transformed his sources, would have understood Goethe in the light of his own intellectual preoccupations, just as he understood Hawthorne and Shakespeare. For Melville the artist, the demonic answered some of the crucial literary and philosophical problems which had frustrated him in *Mardi* and which he would have to solve before he could write *Moby-Dick*. But problems of art for Melville were rarely separable from problems of vision, and the influence of Goethe's demonic extended far beyond what is normally meant when scholars speak of a "source." For many of us, having the words for a thought often enables us to *think* the thought, to raise it from an inarticulate "sense" of something to a usable idea. In the rebellion of the demonic man against the demonic in the universe Melville found something more: an idiom or *mythos* around which to group not merely a series of perceptions and half-realized metaphysical truths, but a complex of emotions and temperamental needs. The fluidity with which naturalism passed by degrees into supernaturalism in *Moby-Dick* represents more than a triumph of Melville's art; it represents the way in which his imagination repeatedly dissolved the barriers between the naturalistic world his intellect forced him to acknowledge and the theistic world his spirit required. One sees this process at its most transparent in a letter Melville wrote to Hawthorne on 16[?] April[?] 1851 in response to *The House of the Seven Gables:*

> There is a certain tragic phase of humanity which, in our opinion, was never more powerfully embodied than by Hawthorne. We mean the tragicalness of human thought in its own unbiased, native, and profounder workings. We think that into no recorded mind has the intense feeling of the visable truth ever entered more deeply than into this man's. By visable truth, we mean the apprehension of the absolute condition of present things as they strike the eye of the man who fears them not, though they do their worst to him,—the man who, like Russia or the British Empire, declares himself a sovereign nature (in himself) amid the powers of heaven, hell, and earth. He may perish; but so long as he exists he insists upon treating with all

Powers upon an equal basis. If any of those other Powers choose to withhold certain secrets, let them; that does not impair my sovereignty in myself; that does not make me tributary. [*L*, pp. 124–125]

Writing nominally of Hawthorne, Melville is in fact speaking of himself, and the reference of the passage quickly changes from "Hawthorne" to the "sovereign nature" to the first-person singular. But equally important, the experiential world of the passage undergoes a concurrent change. Through some strange logic of emotional escalation, the "visable truth" is transformed first into a set of "present things" which may "do their worst" to the man of courage, then into the quasi-objective "powers of heaven, hell, and earth" amid which the "sovereign nature" stands, and finally into a series of haughty, personified "Powers" with whom (not which) the "sovereign nature" treats "upon an equal basis." Phrase by phrase, the naturalistic world of the "visable truth" is metamorphosed into a hostile, animated world whose refractoriness calls forth in man a corresponding assertion of his spiritual invincibility. It is quite beside the point that this final world is an ontological *non sequitur* or that Melville's bravado could not be further from the habitual self-effacement of Hawthorne, its professed subject. What we are witnessing here are the associational workings of a temperament which cannot sustain itself upon the scanty emotional fare of naturalism but must recast the world's emptiness into a conspiracy of antipathetic "Powers" which the soul thrives upon in the very act of resisting. As the exigencies of Melville's nature play themselves out in rhetoric, however, his mind tips back to sanity and the world again seems an empty collection of things: "And perhaps, after all, there is *no* secret. We incline to think that the Problem of the Universe is like the Freemason's mighty secret, so terrible to all children. It turns out, at last, to consist in a triangle, a mallet, and an apron,— nothing more!" (*L*, p. 125).

In the space of less than a paragraph, Melville has covered the entire spectrum, from the naturalism of chapters like "The Hyena" and "The Monkey-Rope" to the malevolent theism of a chapter like "The Candles." What makes the passage so fearfully compelling is the same thing that makes the world of *Moby-Dick* so fearfully compelling: it begins with experiential facts which cannot be gainsaid and seduces us by imperceptible degrees into a full sympathy with cosmic resistance, however "mad" or destructive we may know it to be.

It is this process of imaginatively transforming the world that I have been concerned with in this essay, though I have limited myself to the influence of only one of Melville's sources and, to this extent, may have given an impression of Goethe's preeminence that I do not think is warranted. In the progress from the naturalism of "The Hyena" to the supernaturalism of "The Candles," the demonic represents that stage at which the mind begins to lose its detachment and objectifies its sense of the "visable truth" in some half-credited external force or principle—thus Ishmael's "instinct of the knowledge of the demonism in the world" and Melville's own appeal to "the powers of heaven, hell, and earth." The demonic in Nature is shapeless and elusive, however; it produces anxiety, even terror, as in "The Whiteness of the Whale," but it offers the "sovereign nature" no specific antagonist to confront in action, in words, or even in thought. And so the imagination, wrought up in Ahab's case by physical and metaphysical injuries and in Melville's by its own self-generating rhetoric, *personifies* the recalcitrant "powers" into "Powers," or beings, or a "personified impersonal" (*MD*, p. 417). Here the influence of Goethe's demonic merges with that of other sources, such as Gnosticism and Zoroastrianism, which Melville was familiar with through Bayle and to which a full account of *Moby-Dick*'s world must give equal space. Together, these readings helped Melville transcend the problems which had impeded his progress toward a book like *Moby-Dick*, but their influence upon Melville the artist, we must always remember, sprang directly from their hold upon Melville the man. In Melville's response to Goethe (and, it might be demonstrated, to some of these other sources) we find the elevation into consciousness of a set of imaginative possibilities, a stance toward experience, a literary "vision." Nothing in Goethe's demonic would have attracted Melville had he not been inclining in that direction. On the other hand, nothing would have brought these inclinations so rapidly and dramatically into relief, or made them so accessible as literary material, as the discovery of something like Goethe's demonic. In the progress from *Mardi* to *Moby-Dick,* the demonic was one of several doubloons which mirrored back to Melville his own mysterious self.

NOTES

1. Although Melville completed *Mardi* some time in the fall of 1848, he did not conclude arrangements for its English publication until the first week of March 1849, when Richard Bentley contracted to publish the book. See Elizabeth S. Foster, "Historical Note," in *Mardi and a Voyage Thither,* ed. Harrison Hayford, Hershel Parker, and G. Thomas Tanselle (Evanston and Chicago: Northwestern University Press and The Newberry Library, 1970), p. 663.

2. *The Letters of Herman Melville,* ed. William H. Gilman and Merrell R. Davis (New Haven: Yale University Press, 1960), p. 83. Subsequent references to the *Letters* will be included in the body of the text and abbreviated *L.*

3. Hershel Parker, "Historical Note," in *Redburn: His First Voyage,* ed. Harrison Hayford, Hershel Parker, and G. Thomas Tanselle (Evanston and Chicago: Northwestern University Press and The Newberry Library, 1969), p. 315.

4. Leon Howard, *Herman Melville: A Biography* (Berkeley: University of California Press, 1951), p. 134.

5. Ralph Waldo Emerson, *Representative Men,* vol. IV of *The Complete Works of Ralph Waldo Emerson* (Boston: Houghton Mifflin, 1903), p. 8.

6. F. O. Matthiessen, *American Renaissance* (New York: Oxford University Press, 1941), p. 424.

7. See Merton M. Sealts, Jr., *Melville's Reading* (Madison: University of Wisconsin Press, 1966), no. 228.

8. William Charvat, "Melville," in *The Profession of Authorship in America, 1800–1870: The Papers of William Charvat,* ed. Matthew J. Bruccoli (Columbus: Ohio State University Press, 1968), p. 208.

9. Herman Melville, *Pierre; or, The Ambiguities,* ed. Harrison Hayford, Hershel Parker, and G. Thomas Tanselle (Evanston and Chicago: Northwestern University Press and The Newberry Library, 1971), p. 283. Subsequent references to *Pierre* will be included in the body of the text and abbreviated *P.*

10. Nathaniel Hawthorne, letter to Evert A. Duyckinck, 29 August 1850, in Jay Leyda, *The Melville Log* (New York: Harcourt Brace, 1951), I, 391.

11. Nathaniel Hawthorne, notebook entry, 12 November 1856, in Leyda, II, 529.

12. Matthew Arnold, "Author's Preface, 1853," in *The Poems of Matthew Arnold, 1840–1867* (London: Oxford University Press, 1913), pp. 2–3.

13. Melville, *Mardi and a Voyage Thither,* ed. Harrison Hayford, Hershel Parker, and G. Thomas Tanselle (Evanston and Chicago: Northwestern University Press and The Newberry Library, 1970), p. 637. Subsequent references to *Mardi* will be included in the body of the text and abbreviated *M.*

14. See, for example, William Ellery Sedgwick, *Herman Melville: The Tragedy of Mind* (Cambridge, Mass.: Harvard University Press, 1944), pp. 58–59, and Merlin Bowen, *The Long Encounter* (Chicago: University of Chicago Press, 1960), pp. 139–143. "Enceladan" is Bowen's term.

15. Chapter 135 of *Mardi,* "Babbalanja Discourses in the Dark," reads as an abstract of the philosophical problems which Babbalanja contends with throughout *Mardi.* It may also be taken as the best summary to that point of Melville's metaphysical reflections, indeed as the matrix for much of his thought until the time of *Pierre.*

16. Jones Very, "Epic Poetry," in *Poems and Essays* (Boston: Houghton Mifflin, 1886), p. 7.

17. Emerson, *Representative Men,* p. 204.

18. Thomas Carlyle, "The Hero as Poet," *On Heroes, Hero-Worship, and the Heroic in History,* vol. I of *Carlyle's Complete Works,* The Sterling Edition (Boston: Estes and Lauriat, n.d.), p. 337.

19. Melville, "Hawthorne and His Mosses," in *Moby-Dick,* ed. Harrison Hayford and Hershel Parker (New York: W. W. Norton, 1967), p. 541. Subsequent references to "Hawthorne and His Mosses" will be included in the body of the text and abbreviated "Mosses."

20. By "serious literature," admittedly a vague term, I mean primarily the poetry and nonfiction prose which Melville's contemporaries would have considered "intellectual." I do not mean the novel, which, "though increasingly popular [in the 1840s], still had in general a low status as an art" (Charvat, *The Profession of Authorship in America,* p. 215). Here I would agree with Newton Arvin that Melville's "springboard had never been the English or European novel, not at any rate in its characteristic mode, the mode of the social novel, the novel of manners, the novel of 'real life.'" See Newton Arvin, *Herman Melville: A Critical Biography* (New York: William Sloane, 1950), p. 152. Melville came to fiction by way of the tradition of travel literature, and until 1852 the quasi-autobiographical

travel narrative provided him with the outlines of his dominant fictional mode. In *Mardi* and *Moby-Dick,* however, Melville synthesized this form with the intellectual tradition of the Renaissance and modern anatomy, exploring a range of themes which were largely alien to the novel but common to much of the intellectual literature of the time, particularly in England. In this sense Melville's affinities were more with writers like Carlyle and Arnold than with contemporary novelists, Hawthorne excepted. In a recent book, *The Metaphysical Novel in England and America,* Edwin M. Eigner has described a subgenre of nineteenth-century fiction which may prove useful in defining the characteristics of Melville's work which distinguish it from the novel. My own feeling is that Melville is too much *sui generis* to bear extended comparison to Eigner's other "metaphysical" novelists, even Hawthorne. Melville's intellectual tradition was wholly eclectic and his literary form largely self-discovered.

21. Melville, *Moby-Dick,* ed. Harrison Hayford and Hershel Parker (New York: W. W. Norton, 1967), p. 427. All subsequent references to *Moby-Dick* will be included in the body of the text and abbreviated *MD.*

22. Lionel Trilling, "Hawthorne in Our Time," *Beyond Culture* (New York: Viking Press, 1968), pp. 200, 201.

23. *Beyond Culture,* p. 202.

24. Richard Chase, *The American Novel and Its Tradition* (Garden City, N.Y.: Anchor Books, 1957), pp. 2, ix.

25. Melville, *The Confidence-Man: His Masquerade,* ed. Hershel Parker (New York: W. W. Norton, 1971), p. 158.

26. In *The Theory of the Novel in England, 1850–1870,* (New York: Columbia University Press, 1959), Richard Stang quotes an 1853 article from the *Westminster Review* (ascribed by Gordon Haight to George Eliot) which bears upon the problem of the novelist's fictional world as it appeared to Melville and his mid-century audience: "'We feel the chasm which separates one age from another as completely in the style of fiction which has prevailed, as in the phase of religious belief, or of scientific knowledge, which has peculiarly distinguished each period. . . .' Since the present age, according to Comte's scheme, is no longer theological or metaphysical, but positive, modern novelists will restrict themselves 'more and more to the actual and the possible; and our tastes would be greatly offended were they greatly to overstep these limitations, for a scientific, and somewhat sceptical age, has no longer the power of believing in the marvels which delighted our ruder ancestors,'" pp. 146–147.

27. It is tempting to identify this moment of realization (if, indeed, there was a single moment) with the set of remarks which Melville inscribed on the fifth rear flyleaf of a volume from his 1849 set of Shakespeare, and which Charles Olson has commented upon in detail in *Call Me Ishmael* (New York: Reynal and Hitchcock, 1947). The passage reads:

Ego non baptizo te in nominee Patris et
Filii et Spiritus Sancti - sed in nomine
Diaboli. — Madness is undefinable —

It & right reason extremes of one.
—not the (black art) Goetic but Theurgic magic —
seeks converse with the Intelligence, Power, the
Angel

See Wilson Walker Cowen, "Melville's Marginalia" (Ph.D. dissertation, Harvard University 1965), IX, 524.

28. Henry Nash Smith makes a similar point in his recent book, *Democracy and the Novel* (New York: Oxford University Press, 1978). Ahab's insanity, writes Smith, "consists in a cognitive change that focuses hostility and resentment, previously directed against life and the universe in general, on the single tangible and accessible adversary," Moby Dick (p. 42). The point is fairly common in discussions of *Moby-Dick.*

29. Isaiah, 27:1. Melville establishes this context for Ahab's quest by including the verse from Isaiah as the last of the five biblical quotations in his prefatory "Extracts." The Oxford Annotated Bible (p. 653) identifies the Leviathan of Job as "not an ordinary crocodile, but the sea-monster . . . which was associated with chaos."

30. Northrop Frye, *Anatomy of Criticism* (Princeton: Princeton University Press, 1957), p. 189.

31. Luther S. Mansfield and Howard P. Vincent, "Explanatory Notes," in *Moby-Dick,* ed. Mansfield and Vincent (New York: Hendricks House, 1952), pp. 637–652.

32. Johann Wolfgang von Goethe, *The Auto-Biography of Goethe. Truth and Poetry: From My Own Life,* trans. John Oxenford (London: Bell and Daldy, 1871), II, 175–159. The Bell and Daldy edition is a reprint of the 1849 Bohn edition Melville purchased in London. All of the passage quoted here, with the exception of the fourth paragraph, is also reproduced by Mansfield and Vincent (pp. 674–679).

33. The passage was first mentioned as a source for *Moby-Dick* by Henry A. Murray in the "Explanatory Notes" to his Hendricks House Edition of *Pierre* (New York: Hendricks House, 1949), p. 438, and has been cited most recently by Henry Nash Smith (p. 48). Other possible sources for Melville's knowledge of demonism include an oft cited passage from Carlyle (*Sartor Resartus,* vol. I of *Complete Works,* Sterling Edition, p. 196), De Quincey's "Levana and Our Ladies of Sorrow," from *Suspira de Profundis,* which may have been bound with *Confessions of an English Opium Eater* in Melville's edition of De Quincey (Mansfield and Vincent, pp. 609–610), and scattered passages from Bayle's *Historical and Critical Dictionary.* Of the three, the Carlyle passage seems by far the most important, for it brings together madness, wisdom, and demonism (in the sense of diabolism) in something of the way that Melville does in his flyleaf notation in his volume of Shakespeare.

The most extended published discussion of Melville and demonism is Helen P. Trimpi's "Demonology and Witchcraft in *Moby-Dick," Journal of the History of Ideas,* 20 (1969), 543–562. Trimpi's "demonism" is equivalent to "diabolism," however, and her article does not touch upon demonism in Goethe's sense. Neither does the other published discussion on the subject, Don Geiger's "Demonism in *Moby-Dick:* A Study of Twelve Chapters," *Perspective,* 6 (1953), 111–124, which examines Melville's presentation of the "savagery" of nature in chapters 55–66. Leon Howard's *Herman Melville: A Biography* associates Ahab with Goethe's demonic man (p. 171), but only briefly and within the context of other sources Howard considers more significant.

Apart from Mansfield and Vincent's "Explanatory Notes," which are a veritable sourcebook for all studies of the influences upon *Moby-Dick,* perhaps the most useful general discussion of Ahab's madness is Smith's chapter in *Democracy and the Novel,* which assembles many of the relevant materials and is suggestive throughout, but is limited in length and scope. Smith makes only passing reference to Goethe's demonic.

34. Melville, *Redburn: His First Voyage,* ed. Harrison Hayford, Hershel Parker, and G. Thomas Tanselle (Evanston and Chicago: Northwestern University Press and The Newberry Library, 1969), pp. 57, 58. Subsequent references to *Redburn* will be included in the body of the text and abbreviated *R.*

35. Arvin, p. 105. "Bitterness and disbelief" are Arvin's words for Melville's state of mind in 1849.

36. Quoted in Leyda, I, 290.

37. Melville, *White-Jacket; or, The World in a Man-of-War,* ed. Harrison Hayford, Hershel Parker, and G. Thomas Tanselle (Evanston and Chicago: Northwestern University Press and The Newberry Library, 1970), p. 188.

38. William H. Gilman makes a similar point in *Melville's Early Life and Redburn* (New York: New York University Press, 1951), pp. 217–218: "But though Jackson's career is. . . almost completely evil, his malevolence does not beget dramatic action. He is simply the kind of character who fascinated Melville, the first in a line stretching through Bland in *White-Jacket* to Claggart in *Billy Budd,* written some forty years later, and including Captain Ahab."

39. John Bernstein, *Pacifism and Rebellion in the Writings of Herman Melville* (The Hague: Mouton, 1964), p. 65.

40. This is not to say that demonism in its more common sense is not also significantly present in *Moby-Dick.* See Trimpi, for example.

41. L. H. Gray, introduction to "Demonism," *Encyclopaedia of Religion and Ethics,* ed. James Hastings (New York: Scribner's, 1912), IV, 565.

42. Filling a metaphysical hiatus is in fact precisely what demons did for the Greeks. As Herbert J. Levine writes, "Daemons presided over various places as *genii loci,* lessening the awesome distance between man and the gods, and Plato goes so far as to say that daemons are the glue that prevents the universe from falling into two separate halves, gods and men" (Herbert J. Levine, "The Daemon and Yeats's Poetic," paper delivered at MLA Convention, New York, December 1978). According to the *Oxford English Dictionary,* a demon in Greek mythology was "a supernatural being of a nature

intermediate between that of gods and men" ("Demon," *Oxford English Dictionary*, III, 184).

43. Eudo C. Mason, "Goethe's Sense of Evil," *Publications of the English Goethe Society,* new series, 34 (Leeds: W. S. Maney, 1964), 52.

44. This is not entirely true of the final sections of *Moby-Dick* (chapters 106–135), where portents abound and nature seems animate in a way that lends support to Ahab's vision of the world. This change in the fictional universe of *Moby-Dick* derives from a profound alteration in Melville's emotional relationship to his narrative, a process one can see in miniature in the "sovereign nature" letter to Hawthorne, which I quote in section III.

45. Warner Berthoff, *The Example of Melville* (Princeton: Princeton University Press, 1962), p. 45.

46. R. E. Watters, "Melville's Metaphysics of Evil," *University of Toronto Quarterly,* 9 (1940), 172.

47. Edwin Haviland Miller, *Melville: A Biography* (New York: Venture/George Braziller, 1975), p. 213.

48. The only antidote for this kind of "madness"—and for Melville the cure was worse than the disease—lay in what Emerson called "intellect," a mode of vision which "separates the fact considered, from *you,* from all local and personal reference, and discerns it as if it existed for its own sake. . . . Every man beholds his human condition with a degree of melancholy. As a ship aground is battered by the waves, so man, imprisoned in mortal life, lies open to the mercy of coming events. But a truth, separated by the intellect, is no longer a subject of destiny. We behold it as a god upraised above care and fear" (Emerson, "Intellect," *Complete Works,* II, 326–327). For Melville, intellect, though perhaps a virtue in an angel, was presumptuous and withering in man. The greatest humanitarians were tragedians like Shakespeare and Hawthorne, whose compassion proceeded from a sense of the blackness of the human condition, not from a perception of the world's ultimate harmonies.

49. Helen P. Trimpi (pp. 550–551) also cites this passage, though in keeping with her presentation of demonism she interprets it as evidence of diabolical possession.

Nine Good Jokes:
THE REDEMPTIVE HUMOR OF
THE CONFIDENCE-MAN AND
THE CONFIDENCE-MAN

*Humor is, in fact, so blessed a thing, that even in the least
virtuous product of the human mind, if there can be found
but nine good jokes, some philosophers are clement enough to
affirm that those nine good jokes should redeem all the
wicked thoughts, though plenty as the populace of Sodom.*

—The Confidence-Man

Richard Boyd Hauck

Herman Melville's sec-
ond great and wicked
book, *The Confidence-Man: His Masquerade* (1857), has
resisted criticism because the behavior of the figure
named in the title cannot be understood if he is taken to
be a protagonist in an ordinary novel. The author presents his character in a series of disguises and withholds
all substantial information about the Confidence-Man's
intentions. The Confidence-Man in one disguise often alludes to himself in other disguises, a trick which seems to
hint that he is a single actor playing different roles, but
such connections are only apparent and are not supported
by other, more concrete, devices of plot. The best clue to
his being one person whose disguises are a continuous set
is the book's title, which refers to him twice in the singular and to his games as a masquerade. The character is a
quick-change artist playing tricks upon his marks as if he
were performing before audiences, but it is impossible to
tell whether he seeks to victimize them or to serve them.

He repeatedly says that he believes in man and wishes to elicit the charity of others; this claim may be either a straightforward declaration of his motives or one of the deceptions by which he keeps his motives hidden. The values he promotes are the fundamental values of religion and business in America; so if the Confidence-Man's purpose is to peddle lies, the book's satire is aimed at those values, but if his purpose is to expose his marks as hypocrites, the satire is aimed at America's failure to live up to those values. The gesture of confidence which he extends and for which he asks is the universal emblem of both charity and fraud; so rejecting the Confidence-Man as a faker is the same as denying the possibility that pure and simple faith can exist, while taking him at his word is the same as believing in an illusion. The Confidence-Man's game, which plays off appearance against reality, head against heart, dogma against faith, and behavior against belief, seizes every mark in a perfect double bind: withholding confidence may prove the mark to be a misanthrope or unbeliever; having confidence may prove him to be a fool or hypocrite. The readers of the book are in exactly the same bind when they try to find out who the Confidence-Man really is. He is as elusive as Proteus, which means that he is not the subject of the novel but the object of the novel's game. The game is the subject of the novel, and the novel itself reduplicates the game. In the game as subject, each mark has the role of Menelaus; in the game as novel, the reader plays Menelaus. This particular Proteus, however, always escapes, because one of the book's major didactic achievements is the reduction to absurdity of every system of proof. Moreover, there are no leaks in Melville's carefully designed excision of essential connections, which is a deliberate interception of the evidence most useful to a critic's proof. Instead of grasping the identity of the Confidence-Man, we grasp the complex indefiniteness of his identity, and it is his masquerade which is the behavior we must try to understand.

The novel compels the reader to pursue the Confidence-Man's masquerade instead of his actual identity
by offering perfectly ambiguous answers to the question
of who he is: he is Lucifer or he is Christ; he may be
Vishnu, who is both god and trickster; he could be a
swindler, but he is not very interested in making a profit;
he is a teacher whose lesson seems to warn us against
confidence while affirming its value. No part of the narrative examines the workings of the Confidence-Man's
mind or his private opinions of the society to which he so
nicely accommodates himself or the secret wisdom he
draws upon when he blithely converts the staggering
mysteries of the universe into truisms both simple and
benign. In short, we are denied all those revelations of
character we have learned to expect in a nineteenth-
century novel. The framework in which this extremely
interesting deception of the reader occurs is a unified sequence of dramatized scenes played upon the deck or in
the cabins of the *Fidèle,* a Mississippi River steamboat
chugging downstream on an April Fools' Day. Each scene
presents a comic confrontation between the Confidence-Man and one or more marks. The confrontations
rapidly evolve into satirical dialogues upon whether or
not charity, the redemptive quality of the heart, can exist,
and upon whether an appearance of confidence represents charity or fraud. Confidence is equated with faith
and opposed to skepticism and misanthropy, qualities
which corrupt trust and community but which are logical
responses to the world's deceptions. Often, the Confidence-Man tricks a mark into revealing that he does not
have charity though he says he does or that he has
foolishly misplaced his faith by having confidence in
skepticism. His favorite mode of enlightening his audience is ironic statement, but inverting his assertions,
which is a logical way to interpret irony, yields contradictory lessons: warnings against unexamined trust and warnings against that penetrating examination of the heart
which invariably discovers reasons for mistrust. Since we

cannot know his motives, we are left to accept or reject the paradoxical implication of all his games taken together, which is that charity can be known only emblematically, as a show of confidence, and can never be proved to be authentic.

This comedy of authenticity and playacting is for the most part presented as if it were being performed in a theater, while a number of specific jokes are designed strictly for the reader's eye. These two kinds of display bypass the fictional action, appealing directly to an audience of one. Such humor cannot effect a response in the world of the *Fidèle.* Among the well-executed jokes which can best be understood as theater are the Confidence-Man's second and third approaches, in different disguises, to a single mark; his numerous asides; and his carefully cultivated echoing of earlier scenes, such as his transfer of the role of Charlie Noble, a name taken by a lesser confidence man whom he has just exposed, to a new mark, Egbert. Jokes which can exist only in printed form include the sly chapter titles, puns such as the cosmopolitan's play upon rites-rights in chapter 39, and the three marvelously sarcastic essays on the credibility of fiction (chs. 14, 33, and 44). Melville's authorial voice often addresses the reader, commenting satirically upon the Confidence-Man's quick-change act and the marks' responses. In the essays on fiction and in deceptive descriptions such as the first sentence of the book, his authorial voice speaks in the impeccably ironic style of the con artist. As if mimicking the main character, the authorial presence thus becomes Proteus, surfacing repeatedly in the role of trickster-novelist. The confidence game is a paradigm which generates every scene, embedded story, or essay, and each of these parts speaks to the paradox of faith which is the theme of the whole. These recapitulations give the book an exceptionally compact unity. The trickster-novelist's deliberate interception of connections between the roles which make up the Confidence-Man's day-long masquerade actually supports the book's thematic and structural continuity. We are the audience in the pit, the marks in the trickster-novelist's confidence game, and the beneficiaries of his and his Confidence-Man's didactic humor.

In his role as the cosmopolitan using the name Frank Goodman, the Confidence-Man says to the lesser confidence man, Charlie Noble: "'Humor is, in fact, so blessed a thing, that even in the least virtuous product of the human mind, if there can be found but nine good jokes, some philosophers are clement enough to affirm that those nine good jokes should redeem all the wicked thoughts, though plenty as the populace of Sodom'" (ch. 29). The "wicked thoughts" are the Confidence-Man's ironic remarks, and the humbly offered "product of the human mind" is his quick-change act. These thoughts and the product can be perceived solely by the reader, so it is sensible also to apply the terms to the book itself. But are the nine good jokes to be equated with nine appearances of the Confidence-Man? Moreover, why is the number not ten? The allusion is to Genesis 18:23–32, in which God and Abraham strike a bargain over the fate of Sodom. Abraham challenges God by asking if He really intends to destroy the city without regard to the possibility that righteous persons—perhaps as many as fifty—might live there. God says that it is not His habit to sacrifice a few good men just to eradicate many bad ones, and if fifty righteous persons can be found in Sodom, He will of course spare the city. Well, asks Abraham, waffling now in the face of God's Self-confidence, suppose there aren't that many—suppose there are only thirty? Twenty? Abraham finally settles on ten, and God maintains His position. The outcome of the bargain is well known. What is the outcome of Melville's game with us? Are we spared if we discover nine appearances of the Confidence-Man? Is there an implied tenth avatar?

I propose that the shift to nine tells us there are nine significant disguises. Eight of them are appearances of the Confidence-Man and the ninth good joke is Melville's authorial presence in the role of trickster-novelist. While this *appears* to be the case (critics of this book tend to cultivate italicized disclaimers), counting the disguises of the Confidence-Man does not mean that he can be unmasked. The impenetrability of his masquerade compels us to deal directly with his and the author's ironic statements. Their humorous lesson lies with the surprising agreement between the Confidence-Man's argument that confidence is good because charity is unexaminable and the trickster-novelist's argument that fictional characters and real persons are analogous in that the mystery of their essential identity is impenetrable. Instead of supporting the principle of nineteenth-century optimism which said that understanding precedes faith, the Confidence-Man and *The Confidence-Man* both reverse the equation. But the design of the book forces the reader into engagement at the surface of things, and if, as in chess, development is to precede attack, our first move is to study the strategy of the Confidence-Man's masquerade.

I

We open by naming the disguises of the figure named in the title. Since the Confidence-Man thoroughly demonstrates that everyone is a con artist, more or less, almost any character could qualify, but there are ten who initiate at least one con and whose modes of operation make them prime suspects. Eight of these constitute the set which represents the Confidence-Man's genuine deceptions (the oxymoron is generative as well as humorous): the *lamb-like man* in cream-colors, who begins the set; *Black Guinea,* a crippled beggar; *John Ringman,* the man with the weed on his hat, which signifies mourning; the *philanthropist,* who solicits funds for the Seminole Widow and Orphan Asylum and describes his plans for a World Charity; *Mr. Truman,* the stock salesman for the Black Rapids Coal Company; the *herb-doctor,* who argues that there is no health without confidence; the *PIO man,* representing the Philosophical Intelligence Office; and the *cosmopolitan,* whose role occupies the last half of the book and whose games are aimed at the minds and beliefs of his marks rather than their wallets. These eight, taken as one character, win the title, the Confidence-Man. Setting aside for the moment the role of the trickster-novelist, another figure to consider would be Charlie Noble, whose moral and artistic defeat by the cosmopolitan verifies that the Confidence-Man is the one and only virtuoso performer, now appearing in a role which encompasses the qualities of all his previous roles. The tenth con artist is the boy in ragged clothes, who appears in the presence of the cosmopolitan during the final chapter, selling money belts and locks and giving away copies of the *Counterfeit Detector.*

There are several ways to make sense of this odd parade of motley characters. The simplest is to say the devil has come aboard the microcosmic ship of fools which drifts through the American Eden. His mission is to perpetrate fraud and thus undermine faith by making it dangerous. This association between a con man and the devil is the prevalent typology of traditional stories of the con game, whether medieval allegories or early nineteenth-century trickery yarns. But referring to these traditions alone does not illuminate Melville's whole accomplishment, and identifying the Confidence-Man only as the devil intercepts our perception of his act's didacticism. Elizabeth Foster, whose critical edition[1] is the cornerstone of recent analysis of the novel, shows that Melville drew not only upon the story of the Fall but upon the rich ambiguities in the symbolism of the Apocalypse. Subsequently, many critics have seen that the Confidence-Man's masquerade involves an allegory of the Second Coming and the seven appearances of the Anti-Christ, but there is little agreement upon which disguises represent which figure. Assigning roles to Charlie Noble or the ragged boy extends the possibilities by allowing for seven appearances of the Anti-Christ (Black Guinea through either Charlie Noble or the cosmopolitan) and two of Christ (the lamb-like man and either the cosmopolitan or the ragged boy). That there can be no closed determination of the precise allegorical values in the Confidence-Man's masquerade confirms that it is designed to reflect several Christian paradoxes instead of the Apocalyptic sequence alone: at the time of the Apocalypse, Christ is indistinguishable from the Anti-Christ; as the Creator of the history depicted in Genesis and Revelation, God can be thought of as the author of darkness as well as light; God permits Satan freedom so that he can test the saints as he tested Jesus in the wilderness; Doomsday's chaos clears the way for a new divine order. Unlike most religions, Christian doctrine separates the figure of evil from the figure of good, but residual ambiguities in Christian myth suggest that the distinction is not absolute. One of the devil's names, Lucifer, preserves the meaning, light-bringer.

The mythic interpretation of the masquerade has been expanded by H. Bruce Franklin[2] to include the avatars of the light-bringer in several other religions known to Melville. In these, the god is never just the sun but is his own antithesis as well. Often the god is a trickster. Both savior and devil appear and reappear to guide or beguile believers and nonbelievers according to the true condition of their souls. In Hinduism, for example, Vishnu the Preserver and Siva the Destroyer are two gods in one, representing the dialectic between belief and deception. Franklin's approach helps us understand one of *The Confidence-Man*'s primary lessons, which is that the meanings associated with objects and events are always ambivalent fictions, illusions characterized by interdependent, opposite moral conditions. All the myths evoked by Melville contribute to the ambiguity of the Confidence-Man's masquerade. Man's natural perceptions disallow the absolute penetration of illusions, binding him to the interpretation of appearances. The god of light and the god of darkness, whether one god or two, therefore adopt the strategy of acting out the part of the savior in order to elicit an authentic response from believer or nonbeliever. "To convert" someone is to persuade him to turn around, that is, to con him into being transformed according to his true belief.

Another approach which contributes substantially to our understanding of the book is one which takes the Confidence-Man literally to be an actor and his masquerade literally to be an act. The mythic possibilities can be subsumed into this reading because an actor could include allegorical suggestions in his characterizations. Leon Seltzer[3] offers that the Confidence-Man can be understood as an absurd creator, as defined by Albert Camus in *The Myth of Sisyphus* (1942). The absurd creator is that brave person who, having discovered that all experience proves the universe to have no referential meaning outside itself, elects to re-create the forms of meaninglessness by inventing illusions which confirm his ironic certainty that all is illusion. Camus's best example is the actor, who assigns value to his art by making it a radical declaration of its own temporality. The Confidence-Man's act educates us, if not his marks. Paul Brodtkorb, Jr.[4] extends the idea to its limit by saying that the Confidence-Man's masquerade shows us an actor who exists only in roles, the lesson being that there is no such thing as essential character. The evidence for this is, of course, entirely negative: if we think there is no one beneath the Confidence-Man's disguises, it is because Melville does not show us that anyone is. The most lucid interpretation of the Confidence-Man as actor is Helen P. Trimpi's fine article on Melville's use of the satirical tradition of *commedia dell'arte* and pantomime.[5] The clue is the storyteller's reply in chapter 33 to a hypothetical complaint from a hypothetical reader. "How unreal all this is! Who did ever dress or act like your cosmopolitan? And who, it might be returned, did ever dress or act like harlequin?" Thinking of the Confidence-Man as Harlequin allows us to perceive the novel's dramatic structure and to understand why its humor comes through to the reader without eliciting visible responses from characters in the fiction. Melville drew upon the universal types that are satirized in the tradition and, at the same time, gave the Confidence-Man's characters specifically American qualities. Trimpi recognizes that the first step in interpreting the masquerade is to set aside our expectations in regard to characterization as it is usually deployed in a novel. The Confidence-Man is literally a quick-change artist performing in a unified set of comic scenes.

The motivation for all interpretations which take the Confidence-Man to be a god or actor is a single feature of the novel, the storyteller's deliberate excision of the character's real identity. The reader finds himself trying to unmask a character who is presented only in masks. Two recent book-length studies devoted exclusively to those American novels which involve the reader in such authorial con games are Warwick Wadlington's *The Confidence Game in American Literature*[6] and Susan Kuhlmann's *Knave, Fool, and Genius*.[7] Both of these give due attention to Melville's definitive example. As I argued in *A Cheerful Nihilism*,[8] this kind of literary game first makes us victims of a deception and then lets us in on the joke, the purpose being to teach us that choices which seem to be moral are actually inventions that resolve ambiguities arbitrarily, rather than ideal distinctions deriving from the perception of absolutes. The paradox underlying the humor is that the existence of fraud makes faith necessary for salvation, while faith makes a believer vulnerable to fraud. The humor is sustained by Melville's deployment of the satirist's wisdom: it is possible to have thesis and antithesis without synthesis. Every unmasking reveals another mask; beneath appearances lie not realities but further appearances. All interpretations of the Confidence-Man's identity can be supported and all can be refuted, but none can be proved because Melville has deliberately confounded our usual modes of interpreting. The character is a red herring. We are to chase him until our capacity for perplexity is exhausted and we begin to realize that something else is happening.

It is instructive to reflect upon the conditions under which Melville wrote the book. He was not well; his vision was deteriorating. He was bitterly disappointed by the critics' reception of *Pierre* and the indifference of his readership at large—hard blows to a career which had begun with warm acceptance by the public. His critics complained that his characters had become too "metaphysical." Readers understood Ahab and Pierre as portraits of Byronic despair, and they associated these characters with Melville himself. Doubtless, Melville was told constantly that he should stop writing about the labyrinthine mysteries of the soul and start introducing some nice folks into his fiction. Melville's reaction to such sentimental simplism was to deflect the advice back to his advisers in the form of the Confidence-Man's series of good fellows. The masquerade refutes the complaint by demonstrating to every reader his own propensity for suspicion. If he really were to encounter a nice person in a fiction, he would not acknowledge the value of charity but would instead judge the character too good to be true. So it is that critics have jumped to the conclusion that the Confidence-Man must be the devil.

To see the Confidence-Man exclusively as the devil is to fail to see that his is the strategy of the devil's advocate. Each appearance of the Confidence-Man is a device for generating satire: he initiates and manipulates every dialogue so as to bring out his marks' beliefs. His masquerade challenges the favorite pseudosciences of the age by forcing characters who believe in them to speak for themselves until their logic is reduced to absurdity. A good example of this catalytic process can be seen whenever the Confidence-Man pretends to believe in phrenology or physiognomy, which are ways to read a person's character from the shape of his head or the appearance of his face; and his marks, taking him seriously, debate him on the grounds of phrenological and physiognomical assumptions. In the rite of canonization, the devil's advocate is a scholar who is assigned the task of tearing down the arguments presented by other church officials who are trying to prove that the candidate is a saint. The rite does not create a saint but is a method of testing the evidence of his saintliness. Like the devil's advocate in the rite, the Confidence-Man works to expose his mark's true character; unlike the scholar, he does not attack claims of saintliness with overt skepticism but instead directs veiled skepticism towards any claim of moral self-knowledge. A more general idea of the devil's advocate is that of someone who champions an unpopular cause for the sake of argument: the Confidence-Man uses Socratic irony, pretending to be ignorant of evil and promoting the idea that everyone is a saint. Usually his simple call for charity provokes an immediate revelation of mistrust. If the mark pretends to be charitable while withholding confidence, the Confidence-Man works him until he expresses his doubt; if the mark is stubbornly skeptical, the Confidence-Man torments him until he understands at least that he has shown a perverse kind of confidence, trust in mistrust. A very few marks *do* seem to have charity in their hearts. At least one, Pitch, is driven back through multiple layers of suspicion until he expresses at last his innermost desire for that which is too good to be true: he would like to have faith in things as they seem to be. This comprehensive and incisive satirical pattern is the reason the book serves so well as a window to the age.

One of the crucial tactics in the devil's advocate's strategy is to avoid closing any of his own arguments. This allows the satire of the Confidence-Man's masquerade to cut in several directions. Mistrust is shown to be destructive of charity, while nonjudgmental confidence in man and the universe—the kind of faith urged upon his marks by the Confidence-Man—is shown to be foolish unless it is an emblem of saintliness, an untestable condition. What we are watching is a challenge—"I believe in goodness; do you?"—the responses to which define the true complexities of human nature. Sometimes we believe and sometimes we don't. We want to believe and can't. Usually we're skeptical of all assertions of trust. By challenging skeptics, the Confidence-Man forces the logic of skepticism until it shows itself to be a self-annihilating system of belief—belief in nonbelief. When, as the cosmopolitan, he confronts Charlie Noble, Mark Winsome, and Egbert, and later when he confirms his hope that the Bible contains no warning against confidence, the Confidence-Man mocks his own pretense and demonstrates the limits of the gesture of faith. We cannot see beneath the surface of his confidence. All we can conclude is that simple faith is best because the authenticity of its motive is not subject to proof. The unassuming faith which is the Confidence-Man's mask seems an absolute expression of charity, but since it could as easily be the guise of deceit, we can affirm its value only if we also take up the attendant burden of extreme irony. This devil's advocate teaches us that faith is by definition absurd.

The opening scene of the book displays the pattern of unresolved dialectic which governs the whole. Ambiguity permeates the first sentence, disallowing from the start any exclusive determination of the Confidence-Man's underlying identity. "At sunrise on a first of April, there appeared, suddenly as Manco Capac at the lake Titicaca, a man in cream-colors, at the water-side in the city of St. Louis." He is not said to be Manco Capac; he simply appears as suddenly as did the god, arriving with the light which illuminates a day of tricks. Subsequently, he is called "Odd fish," "stranger," and "lamb-like figure," so he is also compared indirectly to Vishnu, Lucifer, and Christ. He does not speak and does not seem to hear, afflictions which prevent doubletalk and dialectic. Catching the passengers' attention, he holds up, or upholds, a slate upon which he writes the simple lessons in charity from I Corinthians 13. "Charity thinketh no evil." "Charity suffereth long, and is kind." "Charity endureth all things." "Charity believeth all things." "Charity never faileth." He has given the world a sign. The reasoning behind his message is humorous, since it is perfectly circular and absolutely indisputable: that which fails is obviously not true charity. The barber, William Cream, steps out of his shop and hangs up his sign, "No Trust." A handbill posted nearby describes a mysterious imposter from the East—a warning against the Confidence-Man. These two signs and the aphorisms on the slate represent the terms of the book's unresolved dialectic, and the crowd is caught between them. Everyone naturally applauds "No Trust" and rejects "Charity never faileth," since to live according to I Corinthians 13 is to become the easy target of fraud. There are among the crowd numerous sharpers and pickpockets, as well as hunters of all sorts—hunters after gold, happiness, or truth, "and still keener hunters after all these hunters" (ch. 2). The latter are the foxes, who increase in number when the wolves, or frontier marauders, have decreased. The crowd represents a world of mundane dishonesty and suspicion in which a simple show of innocent faith is taken to be an intrusion or even a crime. If a savior were to appear among us, we would flatten his hat, as an on-looker does the lamb-like man's. Wearing the thorny crown of their rebuke, he withdraws and collapses at the foot of the ladder to the captain's cabin. The world re-jects the simplest message of faith because everyone be-lieves that any claim to charity is a deception and that "No Trust" is the only safe course. Whether he is Christ or the devil, the lamb-like man has set up the crowd as potential marks. From here on, all messages from the light-bringer will be mockeries of their failure to have faith. Unable to extend confidence towards a simple call for charity, the citizens of the world are caught up in the con game. We have been set up, too: from here on, the continuity of the Confidence-Man's masquerade is entirely dependent upon our willingness to have confidence that Melville's title means what it says.

After showing how everyone rebukes the lamb-like man, Melville does a curious thing. He again describes the rich mixture of character types in the crowd, compar-ing them to Chaucer's pilgrims and "those oriental ones crossing the Red Sea towards Mecca." They are about to depart from St. Louis, the heart of the country and the gateway to the West, for a water journey upon the na-tion's lifeline. The reader is thus prepared for an image of America as the place where the world's footloose travel-ers and exiles are gathered in the spirit of *e pluribus unum.* But this expectation is abruptly contradicted as the crowd begins "in all parts to break up from a concourse into various clusters or squads, which in some cases disintegrated again into quartettes, trios, and couples, or even solitaires; involuntarily submitting to that natural law which ordains dissolution equally to the mass, as in time to the member." Chapter 2 ends with the storyteller's ironic observation that this natural law governs "the dashing and all-fusing spirit of the West, whose type is the Mississippi itself, which, uniting the streams of the most distant and opposite zones, pours them along, helter-skelter, in one cosmopolitan and confident tide." As if in consequence of the people's dismissal of the lamb-like man, the scene ends in dissolution rather than resolution. The *Fidèle*'s microcosmic world is now a helter-skelter clustering of folks whose confidence in their communal purposes can only be an illusion and whose common direction is towards disintegration. The proper setting for the Confidence-Man's games is a scene of universal disorder.

The Confidence-Man next appears in the role of Black Guinea. Good evidence of Melville's deliberation in intercepting the connections between any two of the Confidence-Man's disguises is the extraordinary physical difficulty of this role. How could anyone with normal legs achieve Black Guinea's quite literal deformity? The Confidence-Man's identity is always that of the character he plays, and since he is a character playing characters, he always has at least two identities. Here, he is the allegorical character named in the book's title playing an allegorical character in a morality play. Black Guinea represents mankind's common weakness, our crippling fallibility or moral darkness. That he is a black adds an extra dimension to the ironies of the human condition: he is a freed Negro who is still a slave to the system which crippled him and the race which despises him. His infirmity is in turn an emblem of every man's need for charity. This is true whether or not his role is played by a fraud, because the meaning of his act lies with the allegorical character, not with the actor's identity. He is rebuked by another cripple, a "limping, gimlet-eyed, sour-faced person," and defended by "the noble Methodist," a militant preacher who waxes hateful in his criticism of the uncharitable on-lookers. The storyteller addresses the reader with a straightforward interpretation of the gimlet-eyed man's scorn and its effect among the crowd: "That cripples, above all men should be companionable, or, at least, re-frain from picking a fellow-limper to pieces, in short, should have a little sympathy in common misfortune, seemed not to occur to the company." The crowd mocks Black Guinea by throwing pennies towards his open, grinning mouth. He catches a few in his teeth; some crack him on the head. Several missiles turn out to be buttons. Melville calls this grotesque exchange a "game of charity." One passenger, a wealthy man who is called the good merchant, intervenes and extends pity towards Black Guinea, apparently without giving thought to the real effect of his words of comfort or the true destination of his proferred half-dollar (ch. 3).

The good merchant's expression of charity is one of a small number of rare events in the book which indicate that it is possible the Confidence-Man's challenges bring to light three saints. This merchant is one, and the others are the widow in chapter 8, who gives twenty dollars to the philanthropist, and Pitch, who for a little while seems at bottom still to believe that faith should transcend evi-dence. The possible saintliness of each is revealed but not proved by a collision with the Confidence-Man, and of course their good nature does not protect their money. When the merchant accidentally drops his business card, Black Guinea quickly covers it with his stump, and sure enough, the Confidence-Man in his next disguise, as John Ringman, is able to address the merchant by name. "'How do you do, Mr. Roberts?'" Mr. Roberts is ruffled, does not understand how this stranger could know his name, denies knowing him. John Ringman grasps the good merchant's hand and asks, "'If I remember, you are a mason, Mr. Roberts?'" (ch. 4). At that moment, Mr.

Roberts's resistance crumbles. The secret handshake is the proof of Masonic brotherhood, an absolutely irrefutable signal that the applicant for aid is what he says he is. A Mason is bound by oath to help. It is perfectly possible that Mr. Roberts is being bilked; we will never know for sure. What is certain is that Mr. Roberts has much more to lose if he gives up his Christian charity and his Masonic loyalty than if he drops a bit of cash.

The widow in chapter 8, "A Charitable Lady," is confused for a moment by the polite approach of the philanthropist, but as soon as she hears that he solicits funds for widows and orphans, she opens her purse and gives him twenty dollars. Has she been cheated? Out of her twenty dollars, perhaps, but not out of her heart's stock of charity. Writing in his notebook, the philanthropist says, "'Though I here but register the amount, there is another register, where is set down the motive. Good-bye; you have confidence.'" We can hardly argue with the Con-. fidence-Man's assertion that true motives are not recorded in this world's register. The charitable lady has been reading I Corinthians 13, and she is "just breaking the chrysalis of her mourning." Whether her metamorphosis to sainthood is verified by this exposure to the devil's advocate is a puzzle not to be solved. But this much is true: she expresses charity, and the Confidence-Man never approaches her again.

Pitch, the canny backwoods farmer from the Show-Me State, understands the game perfectly. "'I have confidence in distrust,'" he says to the herb-doctor. Later, in response to the PIO man, Pitch recalls all his experiences with untrustworthy mankind. He has used up no fewer than thirty-five bad boys, each hired as a helper and each proved a thief. "'St. Augustine on Original Sin is my text book,'" says wise Pitch. Quite right. But the PIO man is right, too. "'Confidence is the indispensable basis of all sorts of business transactions'" (chs. 21–22). In the interval between the aphorisms upon distrust and confidence, the Confidence-Man, in different disguises, has cajoled Pitch with circular reasoning, false analogies, and bad puns. Yet Pitch finally agrees to try one more boy. Why? Because to refuse forever to believe that at least one boy may yet prove honest is to let the world's evil outweigh his good nature. Whether or not Pitch's investment ever comes home, he has demonstrated that he still holds one slim hope for man's future.

The title of chapter 5, like many of the chapter titles, is a joke drawing upon the book's dialectic. "The Man with the Weed Makes It an Even Question Whether He Be a Great Sage or a Great Simpleton." The question applies to all saints, light-bringers, mysterious strangers, lamb-like figures, children, and satirists whose primary tactic is to let erroneous modes of hunting the truth speak for themselves. It also applies literally to the mark who is featured in the chapter, a wise fool, the sophomore. In this scene, John Ringman warns the student not to read Tacitus. "'But Tacitus—I hate Tacitus; not, though, I trust, with the hate that sins, but a righteous hate. Without confidence himself, Tacitus destroys it in all his readers.'" Doubletalk. The sophomore is embarrassed and parries the thrust. He does not know that he has already been set up by the Confidence-Man in an earlier disguise and is being further set up for other games to come. Later, the sophomore will buy stock from Mr. Truman, convinced that he has inside information, which was actually let out for him to hear while he was eavesdropping upon the conversation between Mr. Roberts and Mr. Ringman in chapter 4. The dialectic in chapter 5 expands academically as the sophomore's Tacitus is opposed to a book that Ringman carries, Mark Akenside's *The Pleasures of Imagination* (1744), a treatise which equates Goodness, Beauty, and Truth and declares the universe to be benevolent. Is there a certain sagacity in simplicity? Whenever the story examines a claim that an attitude of earnestness, sincerity, skepticism, or misanthropy is a final solution, the supporting argument is alternately confirmed and contradicted until every one-sided point of view disintegrates before our eyes. The humorous wisdom of such a chapter lies in its rhetorical balancing act, a continual keeping in suspension of the two kinds of simplism represented by Tacitus and Akenside.

Disguised as the herb-doctor, the Confidence-Man states diagnoses that complement the prescriptive aphorisms of I Corinthians 13. "'A sick philosopher is incurable,'" he tells the sick man, "'Because he has no confidence.'" Shortly, he adds, "'I know this, that never did a right confidence come to naught.'" These are as circular or indisputable as the biblical verses: that which comes to naught is not a right confidence, and a philosopher who has confidence would not be sick. He says further, in reference to his medicine bottles, "'Prove all the vials; trust those which are true.'"

From Elizabeth Foster we learn that the parodied biblical verse "was a sort of motto of the New England Transcendentalists" (n. 93.34). The original, I Thessalonians 5:21, reads, "Prove all things; hold fast that which is good." The sick man almost catches the herb-doctor out by asking if "Prove all the vials" does not imply distrust. "'But to doubt, to suspect, to prove—to have all this wearing work to be doing continually—how opposed to confidence. It is evil!'" The herb-doctor replies, "'From evil comes good. Distrust is a stage to confidence'" (ch. 16). Absurd reasoning indeed, but of exactly the kind promoted by the transcendentalists.

Finally, however, the herb-doctor has articulated at least one half of a sound argument for the connection between mental and physical health. While it is not necessarily true that a physically sick person can be well merely by thinking he is, it is probably true that a person who thinks he is sick when he is physically well is in fact sick. In one respect, the dialogue between the herb-doctor and the sick man is a satire upon widely held ideas which would lead by 1875 to the founding of Christian Science. On the other hand, the herb-doctor, in the manner of a Christian Scientist, has encouraged the sick man to renew a healthier hope for himself. We will never know whether his medicinal herbs do the patient any good, but quite literally, the sick man has no hope when the herb-doctor approaches him and does have hope when the herb-doctor leaves him.

As the Confidence-Man acts the simpleton-sage, his marks, in response, undergo rapid changes revealing the simplism in their sagacity. The most common pattern is for a mark to resist, engage in dialogue, drop his guard, extend confidence, and then either conclude that he is satisfied or, upon reflection, regret his gesture. The miser, for example, is one who is immediately wracked by second thoughts. He gives in initially because he is essentially greedy, then changes his mind, pressing Mr. Truman hard in an attempt to find out what will happen to his investment and complaining to the herb-doctor that he needs a guardian. The miser is thus confirmed in his miserliness. The wooden-legged, gimlet-eyed man, who claims to see through Black Guinea's disguise, never advances past resistance and violent argument; he is locked in his crippled, one-dimensional cynicism. He tells the philanthropist and the noble Methodist that Black Guinea, who has of course moved offstage by this time, is a white masquerading as a black. The philanthropist asks, "'Tell me, sir, do you really think that a white could look the negro so? For one, I should call it pretty good acting.'" The gimlet-eyed man responds, "'Not much better than any other man acts.'" The philanthropist mocks the gimlet-eyed man's correct perception by asking, "'How? Does all the world act? Am *I*, for instance, an actor? Is my reverend friend here, too, a performer?'" Scoring again, the gimlet-eyed man says, "'Yes, don't you both perform acts? To do, is to act; so all doers are actors.'" Shakespeare's words upon the subject are recalled much later in the day, at the end of chapter 41, by Egbert, who, watching the cosmopolitan's exit, finds himself "at a loss to determine where exactly the fictitious character had been dropped, and the real one, if any, resumed." The humor of the interposed "if any" is immeasurable.

In the present scene, the philanthropist continues, "'The sham is evident, then?'" "'To the discerning eye,'" returns the other, "with a horrible screw of his gimlet one." The gimlet-eyed man probably does comprehend the facts of the matter, and his interpretation of the philanthropist's hidden identity is literalistic: "'Money, you think, is the sole motive to pains and hazard, deception and deviltry, in this world. How much money did the devil make by gulling Eve?'" (ch. 6). But the ironies of this scene fall upon the gimlet-eyed man, not the philanthropist. What the gimlet-eyed man needs most of all is the fellow-feeling which has been displaced by the realistic view to which he clings. If all the world's a stage, the refusal to suspend disbelief is nothing less than a failure of the imagination. Only a misanthrope insists that we are all actors without at the same time acknowledging the need that lies beneath the mask. Opposing the cynic is the noble Methodist, whose enthusiasm for promoting charity is but a form of misanthropy: he swears he will force love and brotherhood down the gimlet-eyed man's throat. In the middle of all this stands the Confidence-Man, calmly countering cynicism and evangelicism with his simple demonstration of the universal need for charity. The quotation from *As You Like It* ends, "And one man in his time plays many parts." Every player needs to elicit his audience's confidence before his act can begin to work.

An exchange between the good merchant and the Black Rapids stock salesman tells why charity cannot survive a single-minded insistence upon the cold truth — truth as perceived by the cynic's gimlet eye or as revealed by Pitch's bad experience, considered separately from his good nature. Mr. Roberts has just told Mr. Truman the story of Goneril, a sad tale of a wife's betrayal and a subsequent perversion of justice. The story, which Mr. Roberts says was told him by John Ringman, supposedly accounts for the weed in John Ringman's hat: he is mourning the loss of his daughter, who was taken from him by a deluded court, and of his estranged wife, who has died since deceiving him so grievously. Naturally, Mr. Truman already knows the story, having told it as

John Ringman, but he pretends otherwise. While they discuss the story, the two drink champagne and congratulate themselves upon their charity. Suddenly, however, the merchant pushes his glass away and says, "'Ah, wine is good, and confidence is good; but can wine or confidence percolate down through all the stony strata of hard considerations, and drop warmly and ruddily into the cold cave of truth? Truth will *not* be comforted. Led by dear charity, lured by sweet hope, fond fancy essays this feat; but in vain; mere dreams and ideals, they explode in your hand, leaving naught but the scorching behind!'" This serious consideration of the nihilism which can follow understanding is deflated by the awful pun at the end and refuted by Mr. Truman, who scolds the merchant for his moment of weakness and withdraws the champagne, which he says has betrayed the motto, *in vino veritas.* "'That wine, good wine, should do it! Upon my soul,' half seriously, half humorously, securing the bottle, 'you shall drink no more of it. Wine was meant to gladden the heart, not grieve it; to heighten confidence, not depress it'" (ch. 13). Half seriously, half humorously, the Confidence-Man confirms that the function of fellowship—the wine of life—is to keep the spirit from dwelling in the abyss. The cold cave of truth is reality; the act of communion is an appearance. The Confidence-Man speaks in favor of imagining the act redemptive while leaving unspoken the irony—our knowledge that the ritual is an illusion.

II

The first half of the book culminates in the dialogues with Pitch, who is challenged by the Confidence-Man in three different disguises. In these exchanges, the transcendentalists' favorite modes of confidence are reviewed: faith in nature, man, youth, analogical thinking, and, above all, in the correspondence between the world's emblems and universal Spirit. Many of the other games played in the first half show that certain broad areas of social endeavor—economics, medicine, philanthropy, religion, business, law—are themselves games, institutions built not upon God's design as discovered in natural law but upon tenuous contracts invented and maintained by sheer imaginative energy and intellectual machination. Opening the second half, the Confidence-Man appears as the cosmopolitan and confronts Pitch for the third time. Both Pitch and the cosmopolitan argue ironically. What, then, are we to make of the cosmopolitan's refutation of the ironic mode? Read it ironically, of course. "'Ah, now,'" says he, "'irony is so unjust; never could abide irony; something Satanic about irony. God defend me from Irony, and Satire, his bosom friend.'" As the devil's advocate, he is saying that irony and satire are his best weapons. This time, his remarks elicit irony and satire from Pitch in return, but Pitch loses control of his tone when he tries to expose the cosmopolitan directly: "'You are . . . Diogenes masquerading as a cosmopolitan.'" The Confidence-Man retains command of the irony and wins the skirmish with "'For God's sake . . . get you confidence'" (ch. 24). The PIO man uncovered Pitch's good-heartedness in the exchange that leads to the hiring of a new boy, but now the cosmopolitan sadly verifies that Pitch's usual style of battle is nonetheless skepticism. What a practical man must do every day may very well contrast sharply with what he would like in his heart to believe.

Beginning with Pitch, the cosmopolitan leads all his marks into dialogues which are wholly moral and epistemological. They must now try to secure their prejudices rather than their wallets. Indeed, the Confidence-Man no longer seems interested in making money at all. His only score in the second half of the book is a free shave, and to win that, he has to expend a terrific amount of energy conning William Cream into a contract which requires the barber to give credit without showing mistrust. Of course, the barber breaks the contract right away, when the cosmopolitan walks off without paying. As it builds towards the conclusion, in which the cosmopolitan will critique his own confidence act, the second half shows him most active in displaying his message of charity so that his marks may try to destroy it if they think they can. As he once held it up on a slate, he now sets it up as a target for skeptics. This surprising pattern, which is also an expansion of the game of irony he played with Pitch, is brought to the surface in a very funny exchange between the cosmopolitan and Charlie Noble. For the sake of their game upon games, the cosmopolitan assumes the name of Frank Goodman. The joke underlying all the other jokes in this scene is that Frank may be the true Confidence-Man and Charlie a false confidence man; that is, it seems, one of them believes in pretending to believe in his work and the other only pretends to believe in his work.

The exchange between Frank Goodman and Charlie Noble is an illustration of how the seemingly digressive stories told by various characters throughout the novel contribute to Melville's ironic critique of the belief that understanding always leads to synthesis and faith. Every story confirms the moral ambivalence of the heart by both supporting and contradicting its teller's own one-sided opinion, while each teller, except the Confidence-Man, believes only that his story supports his idea without realizing that it also contradicts it. Charlie Noble shows that he is the lesser confidence man by telling two stories which, he says, reveal the motives for Indian-hating, a quality of character coexisting in backwoodsmen with good heartedness. His first story features a chief named Mocmohoc, who promised five white settlers living in his territory that he would leave them in peace unless they were to gather in one place, in which case he would be obliged to kill them. As time went by, however, his congenial behavior seemed to suggest that he had changed his mind. Finally, he invited the five to his lodge for a feast. They accepted what they took to be a gesture of good will, and he carried out his prior threat. Accused of treachery, Mocmohoc claimed that the fault lay with the whites, who broke the original contract by gathering in one place. The second story poses Colonel Moredock as a man well known to have a loving heart but who became a fierce Indian-hater after Indians killed his family.

Charlie Noble tells these stories with the intention of proving that the evil in the character of Indians is a verifiable reality, justifying the righteous enmity of backwoodsmen. He argues that experience can dictate actions which may appear to be misanthropic, but a right interpretation will prove that charity lies beneath the appearance. In his example, Indian-hating is supposed to be the appropriate response of a good man to the fact of evil. Frank Goodman pretends to be shocked at the suggestion that love can be a motive for hatred, especially in a man famous for his charity. Charity, he repeats, appears only in the form of perfect confidence and has nothing to do with an appearance of ruthless misanthropy. Such unthinkable combinations can only have been discovered by an uncharitable interpretation. "'Charity, charity!' exclaimed the cosmopolitan, 'never a sound judgment without charity. When man judges man, charity is less a bounty from our mercy than just allowance for the insensible lee-way of human fallibility'" (ch. 28). The cosmopolitan's ironic disquisition upon the true emblem of charity neatly sets aside the whole question of true virtue and innate depravity, which is the theme of moral ambivalence illustrated by Charlie's stories without Charlie's knowing it.

In evaluating the cosmopolitan's pragmatic refusal to probe beneath the appearances of confidence and misanthropy, it is useful to recall that a few of Melville's earlier major characterizations, especially those of Ahab and Pierre, did reveal soul-deep moral ambivalence. In the Frank–Charlie dialogues, Melville is showing that a congenial man can remain congenial only as long as he confines his observations upon mankind to the superficially congenial behavior of other good fellows. The irony, however, goes deeper than this, into the very nature of charity. The Confidence-Man's position, argued Socratically in the manner of devil's advocate, is that any investigation of the soul must lead finally to loss of confidence in the notion that unalloyed charity can ever be a quality of character. The cosmopolitan's act shows that charity can be understood only as behavior. Frank expands his debate with Charlie by telling the story of Charlemont, a tale which suggests the reasons for defining charity as a display, without reference to the sincerity of hidden motives. Charlemont was a young merchant who suffered some sudden reversal of fortune and in one day "'turned from affable to morose.'" He cut his friends, his business went to ruin, he sank into despair and disappeared. Years later he returned, apparently having rebuilt some of his resources. His friends welcomed him back, and everyone seemed to understand that they ought not pursue the question of what had happened to him. Late one evening, however, after a good dinner and enough wine, an old friend broached the subject. Charlemont sank into melancholy and "in a choked voice" said, "'No, no! when by art, and care, and time, flowers are made to bloom over a grave, who would seek to dig all up again only to know the mystery?—The wine'" (ch. 34). The cosmopolitan's story opposes Charlie's story about the easy comprehensibility of Indian-hating and refutes in general all claims that a person's true heart can be known. His story may also hint at his own reason for being an actor, but this we can only infer. The meaning of the act is clear, however; it warns against that cold intellect which, as in Hawthorne's tales, violates the heart. With this, we have a clue to Melville's mysterious inscription for the novel, "Dedicated to victims of Auto da Fe." The victims of the oppressive rituals of the Inquisition were forced to confess the true condition of their faith. Any honest person expressing doubt was judged guilty; true believers who looked hesitant or uncertain were punished, too. Only good actors, whether hypocrites or believers, could survive the test.

Charlie Noble meets the fate of all the marks who are skeptics: his basic trust of mistrust is exposed. When the cosmopolitan speaks to the efficacy of humor, Charlie agrees and then laughs at a child—a small, pale pauper—on the deck below. The cosmopolitan in turn sarcastically says that Charlie's brand of joking certainly does show him to be a humorous fellow, and then he comments upon the paradoxical interdependence of seriousness and humor (ch. 29). We understand that laughter at the expense of helpless victims is nothing but a cruel lie, but the cosmopolitan's ironies are entirely lost on Charlie. When the cosmopolitan abruptly asks Charlie for a loan, Charlie is outraged. The cosmopolitan then demonstrates once and for all the superiority of his credentials by spreading ten half-eagles in a circle around the embarrassed false con man. Through a process of ironic mimicry, the Confidence-Man repeatedly exposes the dangers of the theory that a penetrating examination of the heart will reveal reasons for faith. In the face of abundant evidence that detached or skeptical scrutiny can reveal only universal moral ambivalence, our man instead says he believes in the simple, self-fulfilling formula: confidence leads to charity and charity leads to confidence. This pretense is a creative act, in both senses: an act of invention and a theatrical act.

Mark Winsome and Egbert, the cosmopolitan's next marks, have been extensively critiqued as caricatures of Emerson and Thoreau. Actually, Winsome's position represents only one side of Emersonian philosophy, the side which emphasizes the roles of scrutiny and doubt in the processes leading to cognition. Egbert's skepticism reflects the pragmatic side of Thoreau's view of man. Both Emerson and Thoreau believed that every man has the potential to become the idealist, to share God's wisdom, to achieve a synthesis of goodness, beauty, and truth through a systematic expansion of the imagination, but both were sure that only a very few would actually achieve such a level of comprehension. The cosmopolitan articulates the optimistic side of their belief. He responds to the skepticism of Winsome and Egbert with arguments resembling Emerson's airy sermons upon ideal perception: a man will see the higher law in nature when his eye is governed by the higher law in his soul. The Confidence-Man is most distinctly the devil's advocate in these scenes. He brings up the question about whether a rattlesnake is in essence benign; Winsome follows with a ridiculous declaration of the beauty of the snake's amorality. Winsome says that if a man is bitten, it is his own fault, for if he were truly perceptive he would see that nature has clearly labeled the snake poisonous by marking it with diamonds and attaching a rattle to its tail! In response to this astonishing theory of correspondences, the cosmopolitan weaves like a snake and hypnotically leads Winsome into an epistemological maze.

Likewise seduced, Egbert tells the story of China Aster, with the intention of proving that no one should offer or accept a loan. Orchis's insistence upon lending money to China Aster led to the poor candlemaker's downfall, which came after Orchis, in violation of the original agreement, recalled the loan. Although Egbert does not realize it, the story also shows that things go better when all parties keep confidence. Throughout the Winsome-Egbert sequences, the cosmopolitan blithely contends that charity overrules the appearances of evil —a simplistic Emersonian principle which is irrefutable in the way I Corinthians 13 is irrefutable. The juxtaposition of Winsome's assertion that our moral perceptions cannot encompass nature's indifference and the cosmopolitan's echo of the Emersonian solution to the problem of evil exposes the contradiction in Emersonian idealism. The cosmopolitan's manipulations have led Winsome and Egbert into unintentional demonstrations of the principle underlying his own games, which is a radical departure from Emersonian optimism: even if one's perceptions were inspired, the facts would never support a divine idea; on the contrary, one's divine idea, invented rather than inspired, and arbitrarily maintained, is all that saves him from the facts. When one perceives nature's indifference as mindlessness, "Compensation" will be seen as an absurd creation of the human imagination rather than the definition of a higher law.

III

Three essays on the nature of fiction punctuate the narrative. They are not digressions. They display the same ironic, tongue-in-cheek tone as the Confidence-Man's instructive doubletalk and are addressed to the reader in a manner analogous to his satirical asides. With these, Melville, as the trickster-novelist, humorously cons the reader into understanding the incongruous features of the narrative art, and during the course of the game we see that the essays contribute to and reduplicate his whole satire. Throughout, the Confidence-Man's farcical scenes reveal that our institutions and customs are fictions which pass as realities because everyone has unwittingly agreed to regard them as such. The essays say much the same thing about the narrative art: fiction is a fiction, and a story can achieve an illusion of truth even though it is not literally true because the audience and the author enter an implied contract to suspend disbelief. This tacit agreement recognizes the limitations and liberates the potentials of the form. As a credible and witty theory of fiction, these essays illuminate the strategy of the Confidence-Man's masquerade. The mind organizes past and present events and projects future possibilities by reconstructing experience into a continuously evolving history, or mental recapitulation. This means that a story produced by one person's imagination can seem to the consciousness of another more coherent than unordered perceptions, especially when the fiction lends shape to the various abstract and indefinite, or unthinkable, realities which the mind ordinarily finds incomprehensible. Seriously forcing the question "Is this real?" violates the confidence shared by reader and writer, actor and audience.

Melville begins his satire upon the demand for absolute verisimilitude in fiction by applying the critical criteria for realism to reality itself. Such an approach to nature leads, of course, straight to the discovery that life is unreal.

If reason be judge, no writer has produced such inconsistent characters as nature herself has. It must call for no small sagacity in a reader unerringly to discriminate in a novel between the inconsistencies of conception and those of life as elsewhere. Experience is the only guide here; but as no one man can be coextensive with *what is,* it may be unwise in every case to rest upon it. When the duck-billed beaver of Australia was first brought stuffed to England, the naturalists, appealing to their classifications, maintained that there was, in reality, no such creature; the bill in the specimen must needs be, in some way, artifically stuck on.

The naturalists' hilarious error is a matter of historical record. Besides this, the paragraph is funny because it is done in the style of the most elegant variant of the con, the reverse con: having established a context in which deception is expected, the trickster directly states a simple and humorous truth. While studying Melville's revisions in the few surviving manuscript fragments, Elizabeth Foster noted a certain crucial sentence originally included in this paragraph between the first and second sentences and preserved through four revisions. Melville deleted it just before publication, perhaps in "fear of wounding religious sensibilities." It reads: "So that the worst that can be said of any author in this particular, is that he shares a fault, if fault it be, with the author of authors" ("Appendix," pp. 375, 387). This sentence reinforces and expands Melville's fine joke: when it comes to displaying reality, the author's risks are the same as God's.

From the incongruities of nature, Melville moves to the incongruities of human nature, and the chapter becomes a satire upon "certain psychological novelists" and the notion, apparently a favorite of Melville's critics, that fiction ought to clarify the motives of behavior rather than portray ambiguously the mysteries of the spirit. Melville categorizes psychology as a pseudoscience, along with palmistry, physiognomy, and phrenology, and concludes the essay with a warning. "But as, in spite of seeming discouragement, some mathematicians are yet in hopes of hitting upon an exact method of determining the longitude, the more earnest psychologists may, in the face of previous failures, still cherish expectations with regard to some mode of infallibly discovering the heart of man" (ch. 14). The chances of resolving the incongruities of human nature are the same as the chances of finding the line at which East meets West.

The second essay, chapter 33, begins with the passage which indirectly instructs us to think of the Confidence-Man as Harlequin. Continuing his satire upon untenable claims for realism and extending his definition of the implied contract between audience and artist, Melville pretends to be appalled that anyone should demand of a fiction "severe fidelity to real life" when it should be obvious that a reader sets aside real life to "turn, for a time, to something different." He says, half seriously, half humorously, that he sides with "another class," those "who sit down to a work of amusement tolerantly as they sit at a play, and with much the same expectations and feelings." A play or novel, when artful, presents characters and events in styles appropriate to the form. "It is with fiction as with religion: it should present another world, and yet one to which we feel the tie." The satirical content of the analogy between art and religion is amplified when we recall that many church groups in Melville's New England were busily proving their special revelations by evidence they rather freely called scientific. Melville's commentary also expresses a principle which an artist must wholly understand before he can hope to master the complex processes of characterization: neither the actor nor the writer merely imitates behavior; each succeeds only when he has achieved a convincing illusion of character.

In chapter 44, Melville poses the question "Where does any novelist pick up any character?" The answer is "For the most part, in town, to be sure. Every great town is a kind of man-show." As for a truly original character, no novelist is likely to invent more than one. In the nineteenth century, "quite an original" was a catchphrase referring to a nonconformist, especially a wag or trickster. As for the Confidence-Man and *The Confidence-Man,*

Melville hints, "But for new, singular, striking, odd, eccentric, and all sorts of entertaining and instructive characters, a good fiction may be full of them. To produce
such characters, an author, beside other things, must have
seen much, and seen through much: to produce but one
original character, he must have had much luck." The
ironic tone invites us to understand both Melville's novel
and the Confidence-Man's masquerade as "a good fiction"
full of "all sorts of entertaining and instructive characters."

The last chapter is titled "The Cosmopolitan Increases in Seriousness." If we have read the book's didactic ironies correctly, we understand that the cosmopolitan
also increases in humor. This is confirmed as we discover
that there will be no resolution of the dialectic upon
whether confidence expresses charity or fraud. Rather,
this chapter's humor can be readily associated with the
title of chapter 41, in which the cosmopolitan's debate
with Egbert was concluded, "Ending with a Rupture of
the Hypothesis." The last chapter ruptures all hypotheses.
It is close to midnight of this April Fools' Day; the scene
is the gentleman's cabin, lit by a solar lamp whose
ground-glass shade bears the image of a horned altar.
Some of the helter-skelter crowd of passengers are here
reassembled outside the circle of light, racked in their
bunks for sleep. The definition of entropy would serve
nicely as an interpretation of Melville's image of the dis-
integrating mass which has moved inexorably towards a
static pool of darkness. A "clean, comely, old man,"
whose head is "encircled by a halo," sits at a table under
the lamp, reading the cabin's Bible. The cosmopolitan
enters, sits down, and looks at him with "a kind of waiting expression." The old man says, "'Sir . . . one would
think . . . I had a newspaper here with great news. . . you
sit there looking at me so eager.'" The cosmopolitan replies, "'And so you *have* good news there, sir—the very
best of good news.'" Out of the darkness from one of the
bunks comes a voice, "'Too good to be true.'"

Half seriously, half humorously, the cosmopolitan
searches the Bible and quizzes the old man, as if seeking

to confirm the validity of his arbitrary assertions of confidence. He is not about to reveal his true identity, except, as usual, to reveal that he is truly the Confidence-Man. He illuminates the irony of his having to invent confidence by seeming sincere about his inquiry. His role as the congenial man who is too good to be true is fulfilled in one of his best jokes. This happens when the old man, who is a Christian pilgrim trying to protect himself against the world's fraud, looks around for a life preserver to take with him to his state-room when he retires for the night. The cosmopolitan picks up one of the little brown stools in the cabin, turns it over, and shows him that it has a curved tin compartment underneath. The cosmopolitan says, "'yes, this, I think, is a life-preserver, sir; and a very good one, I should say, though I don't pretend to know much about such things, never using them myself.'" This disquisition upon the life-preserving capacity of a commode is delivered with a straight face, we presume; it's a deadpan mockery of the reader's literal expectations in regard to the behavior of devils and gods and a devastating joke upon the idea that a thoughtful person could have faith without irony. He is so pure in heart he knows nothing of either death or defecation.

Earlier, when the ragged boy enters to con the old man, a humorous sequence begins which has as its ostensible subject the true nature of money. The sequence is an allegory reinforcing the message of the Confidence-Man's masquerade. The old man buys a lock and a money belt and, as a bonus, the ragged boy gives him a copy of the *Counterfeit Detector* (an actual periodical of the time), which describes tests for discovering whether a banknote is genuine or counterfeit. The old man takes out a three dollar bill, drawn on the Vicksburgh Trust and Insurance Banking Company. The *Detector* tells him to look for a tiny figure of a goose in one corner of the bill. He cannot see it, but the cosmopolitan can. "'A perfect goose; beautiful goose . . . don't you see what a wild-goose chase it has led you? The bill is good. Throw the Detector away.'" The cosmopolitan says the old man simply ought to have confidence in the words "Trust" and "Insurance."

Actually, all this proof-testing has nothing whatever to do with the banknote's value, for every Mississippi state bank has failed. But this isn't the only joke; counterfeiters commonly issued counterfeit *Counterfeit Detectors* to match their bogus money. Where will the old man buy a counterfeit *Counterfeit Detector* detector? No one in the scene seems aware of these jokes, so they are clearly for the reader's benefit. (Melville's contemporaries would have understood them, and they are open to us because of the detective work of scholars.) The larger lesson of this scene is that currency is precisely as good as its users believe it to be. Even gold, which currency then represented, has no intrinsic value beyond its usefulness to the jeweler or dentist. Suppose everyone lost confidence in gold? Since gold cannot be eaten, lived in, or burned for fuel, the genuine content of coins or the actuality of a reserve in a bank has nothing to do with money as a computer of the value of goods and services exchanged. Marked pieces of paper would serve if all parties agreed upon their value, which would imply, of course, that all parties had agreed upon a system of control which would limit the number of counters in some ratio to the actual value of goods and services. To assign its own symbolic value to money is to confuse wealth with the tokens by which we count wealth. The ideal would be a direct barter system, but on board the *Fidèle*—the complex and transitory everyday world, with its fluid community of endlessly changing faces—money is the only method of computation which everyone will honor. But confidence and control continually evade all users, and the cosmopolitan is quite right: we might as well believe in Trust and Insurance.

Likewise, no one can proof-test the connection between charity and its visible token, confidence. Though barter could, theoretically, replace the fiction called money, charity could never be exchanged without confidence, since charity is by definition a quality of the heart and is apparent only when expressed as behavior. We, the marks of this world, cannot separate counterfeit confidence from genuine confidence because the true value of an appearance of confidence lies with its irretrievable motive, which can be either authentic charity or a hypocritical intent to deceive. Sometimes even the actor cannot retrieve his true motive. In any matter of money, literature, or belief, a contract is no better than the parties who enter upon it. A signed piece of paper does not guarantee honest workmanship. This recognition does not wholly negate the necessity of investigation; rather, the point is that investigation does not necessarily reveal trustworthy facts—appearances hide further appearances. In this sense, the satire does not imply a norm, since it denies the finality of any supposed reality. Instead, the satire implies that having confidence in appearances may be the best we can do. The book laments the impossibility of verifying the authenticity of charity while demonstrating that, in every human interchange, confidence must begin somewhere.

When the cosmopolitan thumbs through the Bible to see if it ever speaks against confidence, he is dismayed to find that it does. But the passage he is looking at turns out to be Apocryphal—not proof-tested, genuine, divinely inspired text. Having detected the counterfeit, he seems satisfied. Of course, he is joshing our desire to prove that which cannot be proved. When the Confidence-Man puts out the light at the end of the book, he is saying we are all in the dark. If a person could proof-test charity, he would not need confidence; if a person could proof-test divinity or goodness, truth, and beauty, he would not need faith. The Confidence-Man's masquerade reduplicates this lesson perfectly. We are left with no way to prove our suspicion that beneath his disguises there is a real self or to disprove his claim that beneath his confidence act there is authentic charity.

Emerson believed that the absolute law of Spirit would make itself known to the man who could disencumber himself of the limitations of separate facts, contextual impressions, and immediate influences. The transcendentalist's goal was a comprehension like God's. Once his soul governed his intellect and his perceptions, he could build his own universe, if not in actuality, then in his understanding. The humor of the Confidence-Man and *The Confidence-Man* teaches us, instead, that understanding reveals the absolute ambiguity underlying all phenomena, including understanding itself. Faith, as Melville succinctly illustrated in "The Lightning-Rod Man" (1854), as well as in the life preserver-commode sequence, is purely an arbitrary assertion: the only way to transcend death and pain is to declare, if it is God's universe, I cannot be hurt; if it is not God's universe, it does not matter if I am hurt. The formula is circular, self-fulfilling, and dependent entirely upon its *if*s.

Emerson said that we will know the whole truth when our selves become coextensive with nature and spirit. The trickster-novelist says "no one man can be coextensive with *what is*." It is Melville who tells the truth in this matter. Any truth, including this one, is an illusion towards which the mind has finally made its conclusive leap. Melville understood very well that the human brain is a model maker, its center of consciousness set well behind the eyes and at a distance from the other centers of sensory reception, where it coordinates perceptions and memories into an anticipatory, flexible, and continuous recapitulation of experience. The self is a story, always once removed from *what is*. A person thinks his world view is universal when he convinces himself that he has extrapolated enough information from experience to imagine a whole. A sense of wholeness can be thought of as a fiction invented by a powerful imagination, which may or may not be divinely inspired. Whereas Emerson thought that understanding would lead to faith by proving the divinity in all things, Melville saw that understanding, if not preceded by faith, leads to disillusionment. If there is a progression, it is from confidence to cognition, not from cognition to confidence.

The moral of both the masquerade and the book is that charity cannot arise from experience and must therefore be continually invented in an act of confidence, in spite of the horrendous risk of being defrauded or being thought a fraud. The unresolved dialectic leaves the mark or the reader with a choice. If charity is an expression of belief in the goodness of man and the universe, then those who express belief in the good have charity. If misanthropes and atheists believe in the malignancy of man and the indifference of the universe, then they are lost from the communities of man and nature. Community is a fiction which continues until the contract of confidence is broken. If this seems to resemble Emerson's opinion, it is well to remember that Emerson took faith to be essential, innate, and natural—a given quality of the soul, waiting to be discovered. The Confidence-Man, on the contrary, acts out his charitable and ironic fiction without once revealing what lies beneath the surface of his deep wellspring of confidence. Something further may follow of this Masquerade if we choose to attend.

NOTES

1. New York: Hendricks House, 1954—the text for all quotations. For a thorough investigation of the relationship between the processes of composition and the problems of interpreting the novel, see Watson G. Branch, "The Genesis, Composition, and Structure of *The Confidence-Man*," *Nineteenth-Century Fiction*, 27 (1973), 424–448.

2. *The Wake of the Gods* (Stanford, Calif.: Stanford University Press, 1963) and the introduction to the Bobbs-Merrill edition of the novel (New York, 1967). Three interesting essays illustrating the extreme variations of the basic mythic interpretation are Elizabeth Keyser, "'Quite an Original': The Cosmopolitan in *The Confidence-Man*," *Texas Studies in Literature and Language*, 15 (1973), 279–300; R. W. B. Lewis, Afterword to *The Confidence-Man* (New York: Signet, 1964), pp. 261–276; and John R. May, in *Toward a New Earth: Apocalypse in the American Novel* (Notre Dame: University of Notre Dame Press, 1972), pp. 61–74.

3. *PMLA*, 82 (1967), 14–27.

4. *Studies in the Novel*, 1 (1969), 421–435.

5. *Texas Studies in Literature and Language*, 16 (1974), 147–193.

6. Princeton, N.J.: Princeton University Press, 1975.

7. Chapel Hill: University of North Carolina Press, 1973; the title is from a description of the herb-doctor (ch. 18). In a very perceptive analysis of the author-reader relationship as it is evoked in this novel, Charles Watson argues that Melville's "final disillusionment . . . concerns not only the capacity of his art to *tell* the truth but also the capacity of his audience to *receive* the truth when it is told"; "Melville and the Theme of Timonism: *Pierre* to *The Confidence-Man*," *American Literature*, 44 (1972), 398–413.

8. Bloomington: Indiana University Press, 1971.

Poe's Unnecessary Angel:
"ISRAFEL" RECONSIDERED

Barton Levi St. Armand

Poe's poem "Israfel" has traditionally been seen as an idealized portrait of the artist, as a bold aesthetic manifesto, or as a failed exercise in romantic agony. T. O. Mabbott states that "It has been customary to identify Poe with his angel,"[1] Edward Davidson calls "Israfel" "a poem on the theory and practice of poetry,"[2] and Hyatt Waggoner, contrasting it with Emerson's vigorous "Merlin," writes that although both poems point toward the Platonic, "Poe's figure implies self-pity, while Emerson's figure implies only the poet's transcendence of ordinary logic and mundane rationality."[3] "The final effect of 'Israfel' is that of pathos," Waggoner concludes, and he adds insult to injury by remarking parenthetically that "a man is not likely to think of himself as an angel unless he secretly thinks of himself as less than a man."

The automatic association of Poe and angels is understandable since these supernatural beings figure so prominently in his work, ranging from the ridiculous boor of "The Angel of the Odd" to the sublime seraphim

283

whose footfalls "tinkle" on the tufted floor in "The Raven." Gustave Doré's famous illustrations and Allen Tate's masterful essay on Poe's "Angelic Imagination" make this connection familiar and convincing. But while Poe's "Israfel" has been read out of his supposed impotence and out of his assumed egomania, no one, to my knowledge, has attempted a close study of the poem in the context of Poe's art and the overall shape of the metaphysic which informs that art. This I now attempt to do, for "Israfel" is such a well-made poem that its deeper meanings are in danger of being explained away, rather than understood in, by, and for Poe's terms. To appropriate Darrel Abel's words about "The Fall of the House of Usher" in his landmark essay on that tale, "Israfel," considered only as a New Critical artifact, is "too successful: readers take it to be all shell, and, although it irresistibly makes its intended impression, its method is so concealed that the too casual reader may take the impression to be meretricious."[4]

One of the few readers who has not done this is David Halliburton, who, in his phenomenological study of Poe, compared the original version of 1831 with the final revision of 1845. Discerning an eight-part structure in the poem—four stanzas of objective narration, three stanzas of objectivity and direct address, and a concluding stanza of first-person expostulation—Halliburton maintains that "the aim of this 4-3-1 pattern . . . is to hold Israfel before the reader while allowing the speaker gradually to establish his own identity and presence. Little by little we see that the speaker and Israfel have moved toward a kind of subdued confrontation that will allow the former to challenge—or to be more precise, to talk about challenging—the angel's power."[5] What Halliburton establishes, then, is that the poem is not merely didactic but dramatic—a subtle and shifting monologue that anticipates Robert Browning's revelatory confessionals. Indeed, it is odd that critics like Floyd Stovall have insisted on the didactic nature of "Israfel,"[6] when we have Poe's explicit warnings against such bald truth-telling in his "The Poetic Principle," the essay that has been most often cited as an extended explication of the ethereal, ephemeral, and negligible "philosophy" behind the poem.

While happy to see that what he calls "the epic mania" or intolerable prolixity in verse has, "by dint of its own absurdity," been dying out of late, Poe discovers an even more potent nemesis. "We find it succeeded," he writes,

> by a heresy too palpably false to be long tolerated, but one which, in the brief period it has already endured, may be said to have accomplished more in the corruption of our Poetical Literature than all its other energies combined. I allude to the heresy of *The Didactic*. It has been assumed, tacitly and avowedly, directly and indirectly, that the ultimate object of all Poetry is Truth. Every poem it is said, should inculcate a moral and by this moral is the poetical merit of the work to be judged. We Americans especially have patronized this happy idea; and we Bostonians, very especially, have developed it in full. We have taken it into our heads that to write a poem simply for the poem's sake, and to acknowledge such to have been our design, would be to confess ourselves radically wanting in the true Poetic dignity and force:—but the simple fact is, that, would we but permit ourselves to look into our own souls, we should immediately there discover that under the sun there neither exists nor *can* exist any work more thoroughly dignified—more supremely noble than this very poem—this poem *per se*—this poem which is a poem and nothing more—this poem written solely for the poem's sake.[7]

By his mention of Boston, Poe indicates that he is taking particular aim at one of his favorite strawmen, the New England transcendentalists. Poe despises the gnomic, truth-telling, epigrammatic "wisdom poetry" practiced by Emerson and his ilk; in his view, the truth-telling mode and the poetic mode are literally worlds apart. The poetic mode is lyrical and elevating, concerned only with the "Rhythmical Creation of Beauty" and subject only to the dictates of taste; the truth-telling mode is "simple, precise, terse," and entirely under the dominion of the moral sense. Thus "Israfel," though it was originally published five years before Emerson's "Nature," could stand in its final form as a refutation of everything that transcendentalism implied. Because it is a poem that shuns truth-telling and opens itself to a different kind of "knowing" or "seeing," "Israfel" can be compared with a poem by Emerson that is remarkably similar in general conception though radically different in effect.

This poem is not "Merlin" but "Uriel," a brief epic, which, as Stephen Whicher notes, is also an "ironic allegory" where the Sage of Concord "made clear his unrepentant delight in the consternation his 'treason' had caused,"[8] that treason being his notorious "Divinity School Address" of 1838. As the hero of his poem, Emerson chooses an unorthodox but respectable angel, Uriel, who appears in the apocryphal Book of Enoch as one of the four messengers of God and who was appropriated by Milton for his *Paradise Lost*. In this latter work, Uriel is the ruler of the sun, who, in spite of his association with luminosity, is deceived by Satan (disguised as a lesser angel) and cajoled into giving that evil spirit directions which allow him to penetrate the sacred precincts of the Garden of Eden.

Uriel was popular with Emerson's contemporaries (the American painter Washington Allston titled one of his grandiose canvases "Uriel in the Sun"), and with Emerson he seems to take on some of the romantic rebelliousness of his original Miltonic adversary, being of the devil's party and delighting in it. The poem "Uriel" is set in an archaic prehistory, antedating the creation of man, and therefore partakes of the legendary "Once upon a time," which is actually no time at all:

> It fell in the ancient periods
> Which the brooding soul surveys,
> Or ever the wild Time coined itself
> Into calendar months and days.

The poem details "the lapse of Uriel," the fall of an angel, but Emerson's picture of heaven is obviously a celestial version of what was to be the Saturday Club. His paradise is an elysium of thought, an eclectic pantheon that contains "young gods" and minor deities, "stern old war gods," cherubs, seraphs, and all manner of "celestial kind." Interestingly enough, it omits mention of a supreme God *per se*. Emerson's heaven seems to be both evolutionary and Oedipal, more pagan than Christian, where baby gods grow up to take the places of tyrannical parents. Uriel's "lapse" is an outburst of adolescent freethinking, asserting the relativity of all things:

> One, with low tones that decide,
> And doubt and reverend use defied
> With a look that solved the sphere,
> And stirred the devils everywhere,
> Gave his sentiment divine
> Against the being of a line.
> "Line in nature is not found;
> Unit and universe are round;
> In vain produced, all rays return;
> Evil will bless, and ice will burn."

As Whicher writes, "Uriel is the deadly child in the house who does not know better than to speak the truth in company."[9] Less a bloody revenge on the father (like Zeus's castration of Saturn) than a breach of social decorum, Uriel's rebellion causes much tittering and shaking of celestial heads, as the "holy festival" is disrupted and Hades lets loose its horde of mythological ne'er-do-wells. Emerson's revenge-comedy obviously applauds the demise of an original, static perfection, but the price that Uriel pays for his bold truth-telling seems hardly commensurate with the awesome effects it precipitates ("The balance-beam of Fate was bent"). His beauty suffers a sad and "withering" self-knowledge, foreshadowing the conscious shame of Adam and Eve, and like an obstreperous pupil banished to the cloakroom: "In heaven once eminent, the god / Withdrew, that hour, into his cloud." Uriel's other compeers agree to forget his outburst, as if it never happened, but the natural law the young god has spoken is now an integral part of the universe (there is an interesting correspondence here with the idea behind Poe's 1845 sketch, "The Power of Words") and so its evidences pop up again, uncomfortably and unexpectedly nibbling away at the *status quo* upheld by the older, Whiggish gods. Yet the consequences of their cover-up, continually hinted at by Uriel's "voice of cherub scorn," seem at best no more than the celestial equivalent of aging shock: "And the gods shook, they knew not why."

I have summarized Emerson's poem in this irreverent manner because I believe that Emerson intended the irony as much as he did the allegory; it is difficult to imagine a heaven where seraphs "frown from their myrtle beds," unless that heaven is a purely intellectual one, a tongue-in-cheek paradise, constructed of bits and pieces of various pantheons, where the tinsel furnishings are less important than the thought that is being expressed. Again, Emerson's heaven is a cosmic debating society where the main offense is breaking the rules of decorum. As he wrote in his journal on 13 June 1838:

> The unbelief of the age is attested by the loud condemnation of trifles. Look at our silly religious papers. Let a minister wear a cane, or a white hat, go to a theatre, or avoid a Sunday School, let a school-book with a Calvinistic sentence or a Sunday School book without one be heard of, and instantly all the old grannies squeak and gibber and do what they call 'sounding an alarm,' from Bangor to Mobile. Alike nice and squeamish is its ear. You must on no account say "stink" or "Damn." [10]

"Uriel" is as much a poem of social satire as an expression of transcendental freethinking. It is a nineteenth-century *Dunciad;* hence its troops of heroic couplets, mindful of Pope's example, for Emerson's angels are only those clerical grannies and Scottish Commonsense School fuddy-duddies who banished him from the lecture halls of Harvard for preaching what Andrews Norton called "The Latest Form of Infidelity." The true spiritual descendants of "Uriel" as an American poem are T. S. Eliot's "Mr. Appollinax," E. E. Cummings's "Cambridge ladies who live in furnished souls," and Allen Ginsberg's "Howl." But while "Uriel" may be heretical in its relation to a corpse-cold Unitarianism, it perfectly expresses that poetic intellectualism which Poe had labeled the *Heresy of the Didactic.*

Uriel may speak with force, but he speaks not from the soul but from the conscience, the intellect, and the moral sense. Emerson's angel consciously puts himself in the romantic posture of Luciferian rebellion by throwing on the mantle of the prophet and talking down to his fellow deities. Yet what he says is a rhymed cosmology rather than a lyrical ballad, a truth-telling closer to Erasmus Darwin's *Loves of the Plants* than Shelley's visionary *Prometheus Unbound*. Although nature follows his example, none of his associates do; so in one main respect Uriel is quite literally "all talk." Uriel might be an angelic doctor but he is really no poet; and Emerson's poem, according to Poe's aesthetics, is not poetical at all, precisely because it remains versified philosophy.

It may seem at this point, as I prepare to make a detailed analysis of "Israfel," that I have painted myself into a critical corner. That is, how can I presume to discuss the meaning of Poe's poem when the poet seems to indicate that meaning itself is of no essence, merely the production of an elevating effect, the "rhythmical creation of beauty"? This dilemma is easily solved by maintaining that Poe's poetry produces a different kind of meaning through a different kind of irony or paradox. In Emerson's "Uriel," the irony results from the implication that paradise is just as stuffy and hidebound as earth; the drawing-room manners of the gods lead to Biedermeier thoughts, which are in turn challenged by rash, petulant, egotistical, but ultimately "truth-telling" juvenile delinquents. Such is Emerson's version of the fall of the angels, a social fall, while his "moral" might be parodied as "out of the mouths of babes...." Emerson's paradise is whimsical, his tone a mixture of romantic hauteur, righteous indignation, and chuckling bemusement.

There are also two worlds in Poe's "Israfel," a heaven and an earth, but unlike Emerson's amalgam there is no coincidence of spheres, no mingling of elements. Where Emerson speaks through and for "Uriel," Poe speaks of, back, and up to "Israfel." Painfully aware of his own mortality, Poe does not so much want to regain the paradise he pictures as to undermine it, displace it, or annihilate it. If Emerson's parodic stance can be related to the waspish satire of Pope, Poe's can be matched by the avenging fury of Swift. While Emerson's philosophy dominates his poetry, Poe so fuses his meaning with his metrics that his philosophy becomes his poetry. Emerson claimed that a meter-making argument creates poetry; Poe's only argument for poetry is the creation of beauty. Since beauty has nothing to do with logical argument or rationality, only with taste, the content of a poem by Poe is in stark contrast to the iron meters and symmetrical form that usually govern its structure. In "Israfel," that content is deliberately skewed, distended, oxymoronic; the images fall to pieces when we attempt to make logical sense of them, save that apocalyptic sense which is dictated by Poe's hatred for a limited, stratified, hierarchical universe. It is profound despair, not the desire to preach or to teach, which ultimately creates the terrible beauty of "Israfel."

Whereas Emerson's Uriel is a petulant Byronic rebel, banished from the lecture halls of the gods, Poe's Israfel is the poet-laureate of paradise, predestined to fill that role by the remarkable character of his unique anatomy:

> In Heaven a spirit doth dwell
>   "Whose heart-strings are a lute;"
> None sing so wildly well
> As the angel Israfel,
> And the giddy stars (so legends tell)
> Ceasing their hymns, attend the spell
>   Of his voice, all mute.

Israfel emerges as a nineteenth-century avatar of that familiar twentieth-century phenomenon, the popular crooner or rock star, complete with his groupies. But rather than shatter the peace of heaven or disturb the natural laws of the universe, the effect of Israfel's performance is not frenzy but stasis—a stupid, deadening cessation of activity. Poe makes this stasis deliberately ambiguous by scrambling his adjectives, so that we are unsure whether the stars were "giddy" to begin with or are merely driven to vertigo by Israfel's song, while he makes "mute" seem to modify "voice" as much as it does "stars."

One might explain this placement by claiming that Poe was trying to climb for his rhyme, but I believe his device introduces a deliberate, uneasy confusion which accelerates as the ballad progresses, since, in the original 1831 draft of his poem, Poe wrote unequivocally "And the giddy stars are mute." As for the meaning of the kind of silence, stoppage, hypnosis, and bondage created by Israfel's song, it is best defined by David Ketterer:

> Fundamental to Poe's philosophical framework is the rationale that man lives in a condition of total deception as a consequence of the imprisoning co-ordinates of time, space and self. . . . By means of the blurring perspective of the "half-closed eye" (Poe's image initially for the imagination and later for the imagination plus reason, or intuition), he aims, primarily in the poems and arabesque tales, at dissolving the various barriers which constitute the material state—including the line which divides the living from the dead—and revealing fluid arabesque reality.[11]

Rather than accelerate the vertiginous arabesque music of the spheres, Israfel's song has the effect of palsying and slowing the cosmic dance:

> Tottering above
> In her highest noon,
> The enamoured moon
> Blushes with love,
> While, to listen, the red levin
> (With the rapid Pleiads, even,
> Which were seven,)
> Pauses in Heaven.

Israfel stops even Jove's lightning in its tracks, while the moon, goddess of love, is captivated and made a faltering, "love-sick" prisoner. Israfel is as much the jailor of heaven as its chief minstrel, while in the next stanza (which Poe begins with the undercutting phrase, "And they say," deepening the hearsay quality of Israfel's character), his power is equated with "fire" and his coronary lute suddenly becomes a "lyre," equipped (like a barred window) with "trembling" wires and "unusual" strings. If Israfel is heaven's official poet, we must ask—as with Emerson's "Uriel"—what kind of heaven Poe envisions. A clue is given by his earlier celestial extravaganza "Al Aaraaf" (1829), where spirits must do the bidding of a tyrant-god whose "eternal voice" is announced by "the red winds. . . withering in the sky." As in so many of Poe's works, both fiction and poetry, "red" is a danger signal, a sign that the narrator is approaching the threshold of a potentially destructive experience.[12] In "Al Aaraaf," this tyrant-god, like Blake's Urizen, demands absolute obedience to his unyielding laws, while he mocks the earth where

> . . . all my love is folly and the crowd
> Still think my terrors but the thunder cloud,
> The storm, the earthquake, and the ocean-wrath—

Poe's God is pure will and pure intellect, and what makes Al Aaraaf a paradise for Poe is that it is a wandering star, not one of the fixed crystalline realms of Ptolemaic cosmology. Its fallen angels are blessed beings precisely because they remain half-formed, evolving, ignorant spirits, untouched by a withering knowledge of Platonic truths:

> Spirits in wing, and angels to the view,
> A thousand seraphs burst th' Empyrean thro',
> Young dreams still hovering on their drowsy flight—
> Seraphs in all but "Knowledge," the keen light
> That fell, refracted, thro' thy bounds, afar
> O Death! from eye of God upon that star:
> Sweet was that error—sweeter still that death—
> Sweet was that error—ev'n with *us* the breath
> Of Science dims the mirror of our joy—
> To them 'twere the Simoon, and would destroy—
> For what (to them) availeth it to know
> That Truth is Falsehood—or that Bliss is Woe?

Israfel's "fire," then, is only a reflection of the burning eye of a supreme God, whose intolerable heaven is ironically described in stanza four of Poe's lyrical ballad:

But the skies that angel trod,
  Where deep thoughts are a duty—
Where Love's a grown-up God—
  Where the Houri glances are
Imbued with all the beauty
  Which we worship in a star.

In contrast to the Wordsworthian vision of childhood, depicted in such poems as "Annabel Lee," "Romance," and "Tamerlane," where love is perfect because it is prepubescent and not grown-up, Cupid here is fully an adult. Eros has become Priapus. As in Emerson's "Uriel," "deep thoughts are a duty," for we realize that the angel Israfel is only another avatar of that greater rapist, science, who in "Sonnet—to Science" brutally "dragged Diana from her car" and whose hot breath ever pants for ultimate "knowledge." Since Israfel has caused the moon to "totter" and her virginally white cheek to "blush," obviously the song he sings must be one of experience rather than innocence. In this too solid Garden of Delights, the Houris are characteristically whorish and even the Pleiads are "rapid."[13] That "distant fire" which Poe admired in his poem "Evening Star" (1827), because it was so loftily "proud" and full of "glory," is now uncomfortably close, cloying, and fleshly. "Stay! turn thine eyes afar!" is the injunction Poe inserts in his 1831 version of "Israfel," a warning which is implicit in his mocking revision. The "Simoon" of knowledge has transformed an arabesque paradise of free sensations into the fixed, promiscuous, seething wasteland of desire.

Israfel is the mouthpiece of this heavenly Hades, the main articulator of its commanding deity's wrathful voice. Poe's "praise" of him is correspondingly equivocal, for Poe's ideal of the poet is not the primitive tribal bard, celebrated by Collins or Gray and epitomized by Emerson's "Merlin," but a careful, discriminating craftsman who eschews both cold intellectuality and unrestrained emotion. As Poe wrote of Amelia Welby's poetry:

True passion is prosaic—homely. Any strong mental emotion stimulates *all* the mental faculties; thus grief the imagination:—but in proportion as the effect is strengthened, the cause surceases. The excited fancy triumphs—the grief is subdued—chastened,—is no longer grief. In this mood we are poetic, and it is clear that a poem now written will be poetic in the exact ratio of its dispassion. A passionate poem is a contradiction in terms. [*Works,* XVI, 56]

The fifth stanza of Poe's "Israfel" is thus a direct address to the angel, whose spontaneous outbursts leave no room for recollection in tranquility or careful, dispassionate composition:

> Therefore, thou are not wrong,
>   Israfeli, who despisest
> An unimpassioned song;
> To thee the laurels belong,
>   Best bard, because the wisest!
> Merrily live, and long!

Israfel rules through sheer emotional power, like the blustering God whom he obeys; since he is by nature immortal, Poe's wish for his long life is consciously absurd—more a taunt than a toast. We remember Montresor's means of heightening his revenge on Fortunato in "The Cask of Amontillado": "I replied to the yells of him who clamoured," Poe writes. "I re-echoed, I aided, I surpassed them in volume and in strength. I did this, and the clamourer grew still." Israfel is the duplicitous Fortunato of heaven, who is biologically determined ("fated") to be the aristocratic poet-hero ("the fortunate one") of creation. Poe trivializes this privileged angel's accomplishments by reducing them to mindless, hollow merriment and hypocritical academic honors, while he dares to make an audacious equation with the personal voice now speaking in his own poem. T. O. Mabbott notes, for example, that "'Israfeli' means grammatically 'my Israfel,' but Dr. John L. Mish tells me the usage is almost unknown, and Poe's note, which suggests that he thought Israfeli a variant nominative makes one feel that here Poe builded better than he knew." But Poe's note, citing the Koran as the source for the name, is also a red herring, which draws the reader's attention from the fact that "Israfeli" is compounded of "Israfel" and "I," a construction boldly equating the remote imperiousness of the angel with the immediate living presence of Poe himself. It is this latter "I," like the suppressed side of a schizophrenic personality, who now begins to take over the poem and clamor against its supposed hero, but in ironic tones that maintain a shrewd, surly composure that contrasts markedly with the counterfeit wisdom of "the bard":

> The ecstacies above
> With thy burning measures suit—
> Thy grief, thy joy, thy hate, thy love,
> With the fervour of thy lute—
> Well may the stars be mute!

It is interesting to see that Israfel is no alabaster figurine but fully capable of grief and hatred, and so he emerges as a fitting rival in this contest of *Meistersingers* which the poem has now become. Indeed, it would not be extreme to claim that "Israfel" is only "Uriel" in another guise, since, according to Gustav Davidson's *Dictionary of Angels,* the name Uriel means (literally) "fire of God," and in the noncanonical literature in which he appears he is a "presider over Tartarus" and the angel who watches over fire and thunder.[14] "Israfel," in turn, is "in Arabic folklore, 'the burning one,' the angel of resurrection and song, who will blow the trumpet on Judgment Day." Significantly, too, Israfel "is one of the same four angels to be destroyed in the universal conflagration at the end of the world, of which the Koran speaks and which will occur at the sounding of the third and final blast" (p. 152). In a separate article, Davidson argues that Poe could not have derived his knowledge of the Arabic Israfel from the Koran, since this angel is nowhere mentioned by name in that sacred book, and that he probably resorted to a note appended to Thomas Moore's enormously popular poem, *Lallah Rookh* (1817).[15] Mabbott confirms this suspicion in his authoritative text of Poe's poem, but both scholars gloss over the fact that Moore's note would have led directly back to the passage in George Sale's *Preliminary Discourse* to his 1734 translation of the Koran, where Israfel (Israfil) is mentioned in connection with the Mohammedan idea of paradise:

> Lest any of the senses should want their proper delight, we are told the ear will there be entertained, not only with the ravishing songs of the Angel Israfil, who has the most melodious voice of all God's creatures, and of the daughters of Paradise; but even the trees themselves will celebrate the divine praises with a harmony exceeding whatever mortals have heard; to which will be joined the sound of bells hanging on the trees, which will be put in motion by the wind proceeding from the throne of God, so often as the blessed wish for music.[16]

In the 1845 version the full text of Poe's note to the title (which Mabbott prints as a motto but which Davidson insists should remain a subscript) reads: "And the angel Israfel, whose heart-strings are a lute, and who has the sweetest voice of all God's creatures—KORAN." Variants of this note, as Mabbott points out, name the angel "Israfel" or "Israfeli," and ascribe the information not simply to the Koran in general but to Sale's Koran in particular. What is important here is the fact that Sale connects the music of the angel with the wind generated by God: obviously, the lyre or lute, which is an adjunct of Poe's description of his angelic anatomy, is thus but another version of the popular romantic motif of the Aeolian harp. All angels are in some sense manifestations of God, but Israfel is especially maddening to Poe because his singing is purely mechanical; Israfel simply "sits and sings" as the celestial winds (the "withering Simoon" of thought and intellect) play over the passive instrument of his talent.

In like manner, when God so wills, Israfel will blow the trumpet of doom and destroy the earth with as much felicity and nonchalance as now he croons the cosmic love songs of heaven. It is this aloof, rational heaven that Poe willingly cedes to the angel:

> Yes, Heaven is thine; but this
>   Is a world of sweets and sours;
>   Our flowers are merely—flowers,
> And the shadow of thy perfect bliss
>   Is the sunshine of ours.

Israfel is, once again, ideal, perfect, wise, pure, and passionate—but he is also a "born poet," a native bard, a medium with a message and not a creator of supernal beauty in and of himself. Rather than whine over his own, human condition, Poe uses the contrast of sunshine and shadow to highlight the ironic—and totally unmerited—exaltedness of Israfel's position. Earthly poets are not pale imitations of Israfel, nor should they attempt to be, for this would be to follow the Emersonian ladder of Platonic ascent from discordant multiplicity to an approximation of "the flying perfect." Poe's way is never onward and upward but always down and out. The only escape is through rebellion, destruction, catastrophe: the startling *bouleversement* afforded by whirlwind or whirlpool. For Poe there is no theory of correspondences linking earthly flowers with heavenly thoughts; Israfel's heaven is so far from the realities of our existence that its very negatives are our positives. Rather, in this world we dwell in a totally alien state, in the Valley of the Shadow. Natural facts are *not* signs of spiritual facts; Poe is more a Gnostic or a Manichaean than a neo-Platonist or a Monist, and Hans Jonas's abstract of Gnostic doctrines defines the threatening cosmology which rules the background of "Israfel," as well as that of "Al Aaraaf" and *Eureka:*

> The cardinal feature of gnostic thought is the radical dualism that governs the relation of God and world, and correspondingly of man and world. The deity is absolutely transmundane, its nature alien to that of the universe, which it neither created nor governs, and to which it is the complete antithesis: to the divine realm of light, self-contained and remote, the cosmos is opposed as the realm of darkness. The world is the work of lowly powers which though they may be mediately descended from Him do not know the true God and obstruct the knowledge of Him in the cosmos over which they rule. The genesis of these lower powers, the Archons (rulers), and in general that of all the orders of being outside God, including the world itself, is a main theme of gnostic speculation. . . . The transcendent God Himself is hidden from all creatures and is unknowable by natural concepts. Knowledge of Him requires supernatural revelation and illumination and even then can hardly be expressed otherwise than in negative terms.[17]

The angel Israfel is but another one of these ignorant Archons, who are themselves at the complete service of the tyrant-god of a prison-house universe. In traditional Gnostic thought, there are seven Archons, ruling seven separate spheres, which in turn are bars or barriers to a knowledge of the Hidden God, the God of Gnosis—true (intuitive) knowledge as opposed to false (rational) knowledge. As Jonas writes, "The Archons collectively rule over the world, and each individually in his sphere is a warder of the cosmic prison. Their tyrannical world-rule is called *heimarmene,* universal Fate, a concept taken over from astrology but now tinged with the Gnostic anti-cosmic spirit" (p. 43). And now we see that Poe's stress in the second stanza of his poem on the contrived rhymes "levin—even—seven—Heaven" makes appropriate metaphysical sense, especially his mention of the enchained Pleiades, those seven stars in the constellation Taurus, a fixed, earth-bound sign which bodies forth the stifling materialism and unendurable fixity of the Gnostic universe. In such a universe, passion (appealing to the heart) and thought (appealing to the intellect) can only get the human poet more deeply entangled in the coils of the Archons. Israfel despises an "unimpassioned song," but it is just this kind of song that Poe privately equates with the highest kind of poetry, which is a true *gnosis,* appealing to the soul alone. As Poe wrote in his Drake-Halleck review of 1836:

> The Faculty of Ideality . . . is the sentiment of Poesy. This sentiment is the sense of the beautiful, of the sublime, and of the mystical. Thence spring immediately admiration of the fair flowers, the fairer forests, the bright valleys and rivers and mountains of the Earth—and love of the gleaming stars and other burning glories of Heaven—and, mingled up inextricably with this love and this admiration of Heaven and Earth, the unconquerable desire—*to know.* Poesy is the sentiment of Intellectual Happiness here, and the Hope of a higher intellectual Happiness hereafter. Imagination is its soul. With the *passions* of mankind—although it may modify them greatly—although it may exalt, or inflame, or purify, or control them—it would require little ingenuity to prove that it has no inevitable, and indeed no necessary co-existence. [*Works,* VIII, 282–283]

We are now in a position, I believe, to understand the restrained but cataclysmic meanings implicit in the last stanza of Poe's poem:

> If I could dwell
> Where Israfel
>   Hath dwelt, and he where I,
> He might not sing so wildly well
>   A mortal melody,
> While a bolder note than this might swell
>   From my lyre within the sky.

What manner of "bolder note" would Poe sing out if he were in Israfel's position? We remember that Israfel is associated with the Mohammedan apocalypse, and is the angel designated to blow the last trumpet on the Day of Judgment. Yet Israfel, too, will eventually be destroyed by the tyrant-god who holds both men and angels in his grip. Against the power of this demiurge and his false wisdom (a wisdom celebrated by Israfel, his Archon, or henchman), there is only the thrust of *gnosis,* a personal kind of apocalypse which destroys the neat, fixed universe of the Archons and shatters their seven imprisoning spheres. The symbolic language of Gnosticism characterizes this act of *gnosis* as "the call from without." As Jonas writes, quoting from various Gnostic texts:

> The transmundane penetrates the enclosure of the world and makes itself heard therein as a call. It is the one and identical call of the other-worldly: "One call comes and instructs about all calls"; it is the "call of Life" or "of the great Life," which is equivalent to the breaking of light into the darkness: "They [the Uthras] shall make heard the call of Life and illumine the mortal house." It is directed into the world: "I sent a call out into the world"; in its din it is discernible as something "profoundly different"; "He called with heavenly voice into the turmoil of the worlds."
>
> Finally, the call can also be the apocalyptic call announcing the end of the world:
>
> A call rang out over the whole world, the splendor departed from every city. Manda d'Hayye revealed himself to all the children of men and redeemed them from the darkness into the light. [pp. 74–75]

Jonas adds in a footnote that "'Caller of the Call' is the title of the Manichaean missionary," and it is just such a redeemer-missionary that Poe dreams of becoming in "Israfel" and *does* become in *Eureka*. He, too, would be Uthra, a divine being comparable to the angels but radically different from the *mal'ach* of the Old Testament, for as Jonas writes of this Semitic word for angel, "where the older term occurs in Mandaean writings it denotes genii of sorcery or evil spirits" (p. 99). Ultimately, Poe's poem is fully consistent with his metaphysic, for it appeals neither to the passions nor to the intellect but as an anti-cosmic criticism reflects his transmundane "Hope of a higher intellectual Happiness hereafter." Throughout, it damns with faint praise, by the deliberate use of such shallow adjectives as "giddy" and "unusual," or mocks an unthinking adulation by the use of such empty superlatives as "best" and "wisest." At the same time, Poe accomplishes a transvaluation of values which goes far beyond the timid philosophizing of Emerson's "Uriel." Not only does he subvert the message of his unnecessary angel, he calls for a true *gnosis,* a poetry of power, which would annihilate the alien ramparts of heaven and wreak a revenge on the stifling demiurge who staffed them with the likes of Israfel in the first place.

NOTES

1. T. O. Mabbott, *Collected Works of Edgar Allan Poe,* vol. I: *Poems* (Cambridge, Mass.: Harvard University Press, 1969), p. 173. The text of "Israfel" that I utilize is the 1845 version, from the J. Lorimer Graham copy of *The Raven and Other Poems,* designated by Mabbott as "G" and printed by him (pp. 175–177).

2. Edward H. Davidson, *Poe: A Critical Study* (Cambridge, Mass.: Harvard University Press, 1966), p. 36.

3. Hyatt H. Waggoner, *American Poets* (Boston: Houghton Mifflin, 1968), p. 142.

4. Darrel Abel, "A Key to the House of Usher," in *Twentieth Century Interpretations of "The Fall of the House of Usher,"* ed. Thomas Woodson (Englewood Cliffs, N. J.: Prentice-Hall, 1969), p. 55.

5. David Halliburton, *Edgar Allan Poe: A Phenomenological View* (Princeton: Princeton University Press, 1973), p. 84.

6. See Floyd Stovall, *Edgar Poe the Poet,* (Charlottesville: University Press of Virginia, 1969), pp. 211–212.

7. *The Complete Works of Edgar Allan Poe,* ed. James A. Harrison (New York: Thomas Y. Crowell, 1902), XIV, 271–272. Hereafter, all references to Poe's critical writings will cite this edition, with volume and page number parenthetically included in the text.

8. Stephen E. Whicher, *Selections from Ralph Waldo Emerson* (Boston: Houghton Mifflin, 1960), p. 98. I follow the 1846 text of Emerson's "Uriel," reprinted by Whicher (pp. 426–428).

9. Stephen E. Whicher, *Freedom and Fate* (New York: A. S. Barnes and Co., 1961), p. 75.

10. Emerson, *Selected Prose and Poetry,* ed. Reginald L. Cook (New York: Holt, Rinehart and Winston, 1969), p. 535.

11. David Ketterer, "Devious Voyage: The Singular *Narrative of A. Gordon Pym,*" *American Transcendental Quarterly,* 37 (Winter 1978), 21–22.

12. In "The Masque of the Red Death," the spectre confronts Prince Prospero in the black velvet chamber, which is illuminated by blood-red windows; in "MS. Found in a Bottle," the narrator notes "the dusky red appearance of the moon" before the storm, which spirits him to a confrontation with the Flying Dutchman; in "The Fall of the House of Usher," Roderick's "distempered ideality threw a sulphureous lustre over all"; in "Metzengerstein," Baron Frederick meditates over the figure of "a gigantic and fiery-coloured horse" that suddenly becomes frighteningly real; etc. I follow the "K" text of Poe's "Al Aaraaf," reprinted by Mabbott in *Poems* (pp. 99–115).

13. I am grateful to Gregory Small for this insight into the adult nature of Israfel's heaven. Poe mentions the houris, so called for their large black eyes (*Hûr al Oyûn:* the pure-eyed ones) also in "Ligeia." In his *Preliminary Discourse* to the Koran, George Sale, speaking of the Mohammedan paradise, writes: "But all these glories will be eclipsed by [these] resplendent and ravishing girls . . . the enjoyment of whose company will be a principal felicity of the faithful." Poe compares Ligeia's eyes to "the beauty of the fabulous Houri of the Turk," and says that "they were even fuller than the fullest of the gazelle eyes of the tribes of the valley of Nourjahad." As T. O. Mabbott notes, Poe here refers to Mrs. Frances Sheridan's eighteenth-century romance, *The History of Nourjahad,* but he does not make it clear that the title character stocks his seraglio with the most beautiful female slaves in order to disguise himself as the prophet Mohammed and so create a counterfeit Aidenn with imitation houris. And Ligeia, we remember, was "most violently a prey to the tumultuous vultures of stern passion." In Poe, the idea of the houri always seems to be linked with an unseemly, earthly, or illusory satisfaction. See T. O. Mabbott, *Collected Works,* II, 332, notes 8, 9.

14. Gustav Davidson, *A Dictionary of Angels* (New York: The Free Press, 1967), p. 152.

15. Gustav Davidson, "Poe's 'Israfel,'" *Literary Review,* 12 (1968), 86–91.

16. George Sale, *Preliminary Discourse, The Koran* (Philadelphia: J. W. Moore, 1853), p. 71.

17. Hans Jonas, *The Gnostic Religion* (Boston: Beacon Press, 1963), pp. 41–43. For other discussions of the relation of Poe's work to Gnostic thought, see my article, "Usher Unveiled: Poe and the Metaphysic of Gnosticism," *Poe Studies,* 5 (1972), 1–8, and Richard Wilbur, "Introduction," *The Narrative of Arthur Gordon Pym* (Boston: David R. Godine, 1973), pp. vii–xxv. For a detailed analysis of *Eureka* as "the blueprint of a Gnostic cosmos," see Joseph M. Auer, "Angels and Beasts: Gnosticism in American Literature" (unpublished dissertation, University of North Carolina [Chapel Hill]), pp. 73–100.

A Misreading of Poe's "The Fall of the House of Usher"

Patrick F. Quinn

DH. Lawrence advised readers of fiction to trust the book and not the author, but he neglected to say what or who should be trusted when the book consists of a story told by a narrator who is unreliable. Presumably one then looks for guidance from that convenient abstraction, the critic, who, along with his other duties, attempts to clarify the author's intention and to unmask narrators with bogus claims to credibility. In *Poe's Fiction: Romantic Irony in the Gothic Tales* (Madison: University of Wisconsin Press, 1973), G. R. Thompson argues that it was part of Poe's intention as an ironical author to make the most of the unreliable narrator device, and that he did so in a good many of his most famous tales, including "MS. Found in a Bottle," "Ligeia," and "The Fall of the House of Usher."

Having long believed that Poe wanted his readers to give credence to, indeed to the identify with, the visitor to Usher's house, and finding myself unpersuaded by the opposite proposals in Thompson's book, I should like to review the matter in some detail. Taking up four points that are worth more or less discussion: the appearance of the house, the narrator's experience, the ending of the story, and its theme, I shall try to show that in this case it may be the critic of the story rather than its narrator whose reliability is more open to question.

The Appearance of the House

"It is curious," Thompson writes, "that no one has ever seen fit to remark that when the narrator rides up to the house of Usher he is immediately confronted with a death's head looming up out of the dead landscape. Poe obviously intended the image of the skull-like face of the house to dominate as the central image of the tale, for he returns to it again and again, placing the most extended descriptions of it at symmetrically located places in the narrative."

There can be no objection to describing as "dead" the landscape in which the house is sited, but two other assertions are made here which are not so self-evident. To take the house first: what does it look like? Very few architectural specifications are given, but it is obvious that the house is very old and very large. It dates back to feudal times and, though no doubt remodeled since then, remains what it originally was, a castle. Poe's misuse of the recherché words *donjon* and *donjon-keep* does not inspire one with confidence in his expertise about castles, but he conveys, nonetheless, a sufficiently graphic picture: the house of Usher is a castellated mansion of medieval origin. And of considerable size. "Vast" is the narrator's word for it, when, in the final paragraph, he records his last look at the front of the house. Approximately *how* vast may be inferred from the dimensions of Usher's "studio," the windows of which are at "so vast a distance from the black oaken floor as to be altogether inaccessible from within." If this is only the studio, imagine the scale of the great hall! But the question is whether a vast, castellated mansion, seen from in front, where the entrance is, can have a plausible resemblance to a death's head. I would say no. The proportions of the building, its generally rectilinear structure, its turrets, and above all its dimensions make this resemblance extremely difficult to visualize. And so I, for one, do not find it curious that the alleged house-skull resemblance has, prior to Thompson, gone unremarked.

Nor can I go along with Thompson's other contention, that the image of the skull-like facade of the house dominates the tale, with Poe returning to it again and again to give it more extensive treatment. The disagreement here may be reduced to a matter of statistics. "The Fall of the House of Usher" has 41 paragraphs. Counting "The Haunted Palace" as part of paragraph 18, and scrutinizing the text for evidence Thompson would use to support his view, I come up with only paragraphs 1, 4, 5, 18, possibly 19, and 41. In these paragraphs I do not find "extended descriptions," nor do I find them, as Thompson does, "at symmetrically located places in the narrative."

The Experience of the Narrator

It is of importance to Thompson's case that a close link be discerned between the narrator and his host, since the essence of the case is that the two are psychological doubles and hence the initial uneasiness felt by the narrator develops into a "frenzy of terror, engendered by and parallel to Usher's terrors." As evidence of such a link, Thompson adduces the three-way relationship he sees between the face of the narrator, the facade of the house, and the face of Usher. He pairs the first two this way: "The narrator's first impression of the house is that it is like a human face, especially with its two vacant eyelike windows. Then he looks down into the pool, but sees only the reflection of the 'face' of the house. What is equally likely, of course, is that he should see imaged there his own reflected features, since Poe is careful to point out that the narrator wheels his horse up to 'the precipitous brink' of the tarn and thus gazes straight down."

So far there is no mention of a *three*-way connection, but two passages on a later page deal with this emphatically: "Usher's 'arabesque' face and the face of the house are the same, and when the narrator gazes into the pool the reflected 'arabesque' face is merged with his own— symbolically is his own . . . [plus] the image of the house as skull or death's head and the merging of the narrator's face with the face of the house which is also Usher's face in the pool."

In my opinion, the evidence offered for a three-way tie-up is unconvincing, for these reasons:

1. The narrator's first impression of the house is that it is "melancholy," and to such a degree that he feels overcome by a "sense of insufferable gloom." Neither in the first scene nor elsewhere does he allude, even distantly, to a resemblance between the house and a human face, much less a skull. To be sure, there would be some basis for imputing to the narrator the impression of such a resemblance if the text read, per Thompson's paraphrase, "two vacant eyelike windows." In fact, the numeral *two* is not used by the narrator. (It is probable that Thompson borrowed it from the third stanza of "The Haunted Palace," but Usher's poem is hardly relevant evidence about the narrator's first impression of the house.)

2. When the narrator gazed at the tarn, could he have seen his face reflected, overlaid, as it were, on the reflected image of the house? It seems to me that, given his initial position, across the water from the house, he could have seen one or the other, but not both. Only after crossing over the causeway, standing with his back to the house, and *then* looking down could he have seen his reflection, within the frame of the reflected facade of the house. But since he does not cross the causeway until after his visual experiment is made, the laws of geometric optics would seem to rule out the possibility of the double-reflection phenomenon.

3. Another reason for questioning the face-facade theory may be worth mentioning. When the narrator enters the house and meets his host, his attention, Thompson says, "is focused on the odd appearance of Usher's face," which recalls to the reader "the facelike structure of the house." In a very general way this deduction is correct, for a basic *donnée* of the story is that some kind of occult connection, necessarily imprecise, exists between the house and its owner. But by giving such minute attention to Usher's face—its luminous eyes, its curved lips, its delicately shaped nose (distinguished, moreover, by an unusual "breadth of nostril")—the description negates Thompson's earlier suggestion that, *de rigueur,* an association is to be made between the house and a skull or death's head.

A more important contention in Thompson's argument is that the story is essentially about the mental collapse of the narrator, and that the stages of the collapse are given careful documentation: "Poe meticulously . . . details the development of the narrator's initial uneasiness into a frenzy of terror," etc. The word *uneasiness* is perhaps not sufficiently strong to do justice to the state of mind of the narrator when he has a *mauvais quart d'heure* in the opening scene. But once he is inside the house does this uneasiness augment by differentiated stages and eventually partake of the terrors that afflicted Usher? This is not shown.

Between paragraphs 6 and 24 the narrator's account does not reflect any progressive deterioration of mind or feeling. How could it? For his account is concerned almost entirely with Usher, his appearance, behavior, and obsessions with several varieties of fear. And rather than respond to and interiorize these obsessions, the narrator attempts to distract Usher from them. For several days after his arrival, he says, "I was busied in earnest endeavors to alleviate the melancholy of my friend." Following the interment of Madeline, "some days of bitter grief having elapsed," Usher's condition takes a serious turn for the worse. As he reads the symptoms, the narrator is unsure whether to diagnose their cause as "extreme terror" or "the more inexplicable vagaries of madness." Either way, Usher's condition has become terrifying, and it is *now*, after perhaps a week of residence in the house, that the narrator begins to feel real distress. Up to this point there has been no meticulous recording of a developing uneasiness. The development starts now, but it does not approach the intensity ("frenzy of madness") of Thompson's estimate.

Thompson's version of what takes place at this crucial juncture (paragraphs 24, 25, 26) adds some details to the text and, inexplicably, ignores others. The text reads: "There were times, indeed, when I thought his [Usher's] unceasingly agitated mind was laboring with some oppressive secret, to divulge which he struggled for the necessary courage." In Thompson's version of this statement the emotional ante is raised considerably: ". . . the narrator feels growing in himself a vague fear that Usher has some horrible 'oppressive secret' to divulge." Recognizing that Usher's terror is becoming contagious, the narrator says: "I felt creeping upon me, by slow yet certain degrees, the wild influence of his own fantastic yet impressive superstitions." Thompson renders this as "slow yet uncertain degrees"; but whether certain or uncertain, the degrees by which the infection spreads are not itemized. Instead, Poe at once sets his final scene, which is enacted a week or so after Madeline's burial.

The scene begins with the narrator's account of experiencing "the full power of such feelings"—that is, those induced by Usher's condition. He is, to quote Thompson again, "unable to sleep, especially since, as with the reflected image of the house in the tarn, he is aware of his increased terror: 'an irrepressible tremor gradually pervaded my frame; and, at length, there sat upon my very heart an incubus [of] utterly causeless alarm.'" What the resumé as quoted does not reflect are two sentences in the text which describe the narrator's efforts to deal with, to dispel, his feelings of terror. The

resumé continues: "'Overpowered by an intense sentiment of horror,' the narrator begins pacing nervously;
suddenly he is startled by a light footstep outside his
door. But it is only Usher. Usher's intensely agitated
condition is the more unnerving, especially when he
suggests that a supernatural and luminous vapor has surrounded the house in spite of the rising wind without."

Here also is an omission of some consequence. The
narrator does not pace to and fro *because,* as Thompson
seems to imply, he feels "overpowered by an intense
sentiment of horror." Rather, he resorts to this action as a
means of fighting back, "to arouse myself," as he puts it,
"from the pitiable condition into which I had fallen." He
is not "startled" (nor could he be) by Usher's light
footstep; the sound merely "arrested [his] attention." He
does not find Usher's distraught appearance "the more
unnerving." What he says is quite simply and credibly
this: "His air appalled me—but anything was preferable
to the solitude which I had so long endured, and I even
welcomed his presence as a relief."

Usher does not "suggest that a supernatural and
luminous vapor" has surrounded the house; all he does,
without comment, is open a casement window. The narrator sees for himself an "unnatural" light glowing about
the house. It seems, then, that one of Usher's specific
fears—that the house would become increasingly sentient, with increasingly ominous implications for
himself—is in fact borne out. But instead of succumbing
to this fear the narrator tries to explain away both it and
the apparent basis for it. The phenomenon, he tells
Usher, is only hallucinatory. "You must not—you shall
not behold this!" he exclaims, and further to deflect
Usher's attention he begins reading aloud from the "Mad
Trist." As things turn out, the reading proves less than
therapeutic, but the intention behind it was certainly
sane.

At this point the action of the story is within a few
moments of its close. Surely by now, if Thompson is
right, the narrator, despite himself, would reveal how he

is being victimized by a "frenzy of terror" on a par with Usher's. He is not so victimized. Usher is the one who succumbs, "a victim to the terrors he had anticipated." The narrator, on the other hand, "unnerved" and "aghast" as he understandably is, retains sufficient *sang-froid* to get out of the house in time and witness what happened to it.

What Happened to the House?

The question is not as frivolous as it looks, for it involves one of the major theses of Thompson's book. The thesis is that Poe, as an ironical writer in the romantic mode of irony, characteristically provides in his tales one kind of meaning for the average, untutored reader, and plants, or "insinuates," another meaning, which, in Poe's words, "only minds congenial with that of the author will perceive." In the present instance, the thesis applies in this way: The reader of average gullibility will not think of questioning the veracity of Usher's visitor, and his account of what took place will be appreciated for the uncanny kind of excitement the tale gives rise to; whereas an inner circle of readers, aware that Poe's technique is one of "deceptive, ironic, psychological realism," will read the story for its clues (Thompson's word), just as a detective does in a mystery story. Therefore we either accept the narrator's word about what happened to the house, or, following Thompson's lead, we "clue in" to a different hypothesis.

According to the narrator, the house of Usher, almost immediately after his exit from it, split into two great sections and sank into the tarn. Since Thompson's opinion is that the man is revealed as "completely untrustworthy," he sees no reason why this professedly eyewitness report should be accepted as definitive. He offers an alternative explanation. The copper-floored vault in which Madeline was interred, he points out, was once a storage place for powder or some other highly combustible substance. This is textually exact. And so, Thompson continues, "if the house cracks open and crumbles, rather than a necessarily supernatural occurrence, as it seems to the hysterical narrator, it is explainable as the combustion generated when the lightning of the storm crackles near the previously airless crypt—the inrushing electricity being conducted along the copper floor and igniting the remnants of powder." This is an ingenious explanation, but it depends on too many improbabilities.

It seems improbable, for instance, that there was enough residual gunpowder in what is described as a small and damp vault to cause (when ignited) an explosion adequate to blow up the house; for the house, it can be assumed, is "vast." I have no idea what critical mass of gunpowder would be required to blow up a castle of even average size, but what Thompson refers to as "remnants of powder" would not seem to be nearly enough, for the phrase suggests only a few scattered, unswept grains. (The text, incidentally, makes no mention of such "remnants." It was apparently the copper sheathing that led the narrator to infer that the place had once been a powder magazine.)

If we assume that there was gunpowder in sufficient quantity to cause, when ignited, the blowing up of the house, a question arises as to the agency that might have caused the ignition. Thompson's theory is that a lightning bolt, finding access to and then conducted along the copper flooring, provided the spark. What is not explained is how such a bolt could have found access to the burial vault. Located "at great depth" underground, and therefore windowless, and of course damp, it would seem as lightning proof as any interior chamber could imaginably be.

There is the further (or rather preliminary) question as to whether the storm produced lightning. Rain is not mentioned, or thunder, and as for lightning, all that is said on this score is: "nor was there any flashing forth of the lightning." Thompson would certainly have a better case if the statement were less negative. I think it is possible that one reason why the tempestuous final night of the story is described as "wildly singular" is that all the makings of a thunderstorm were present—but, singularly, there was neither rain, nor thunder, nor lightning. Since, however, the text is not absolutely negative on this point, the possibility may be entertained that there was lightning that night. It was not seen as "flashing forth" because, presumably, it was concealed by the cloud cover, which was very dense and hung low enough to "press upon the turrets of the house." Such lightning as there may have been, therefore, was of the cloud-to-cloud variety, for flashes from cloud to ground, given the unnatural visibility of the occasion, would have been seen. So perhaps a bolt or two may have struck one of the turrets. But an explanation is still in order as to the route and the conducting material by which an electric charge traversed the anfractuous distance between turret level and the vault, sequestered well below ground level. The text offers no basis for such an explanation.

The Theme of the Story

In "The Fall of the House of Usher," as Thompson interprets it, Poe, through the narrator's account of his experience, ironically mocks "the ability of the human mind ever to know anything with certainty, whether about the external reality of the world or the internal reality of the mind." I find it impossible to reconcile this definition of the story's theme with the contention, variously phrased, that the narrator of the story is mentally unstable, disturbed, prone to hysteria and hallucination —that he is, in fine, "completely untrustworthy." Surely it was as obvious to Poe as it is to us that a deranged mind, mired in its own subjectivity, is unable successfully to perceive objective reality, much less cope with it. There would be no point, ironical or otherwise, in mocking such inability. Therefore, only if the narrator's mental credentials are in good order, and the story he tells is accepted as reliable, can there be any possibility that the thematic drift of the story is as Thompson describes it.

Poe and the Paradox of Terror:

STRUCTURES OF HEIGHTENED CONSCIOUSNESS IN "THE FALL OF THE HOUSE OF USHER"

*There can be no doubt that the consciousness
of the rapid increase of my superstition. . .
served mainly to accelerate the increase itself.
Such, I have long known, is the paradoxical law
of all sentiments having terror as a basis.*

G. R. Thompson

As Patrick Quinn recognizes, my reading of "The Fall of the House of Usher" is central to my whole approach to Poe's fiction. It was, in fact, with this awareness that I placed the analyses of "Ligeia" and "Usher" together in the middle of *Poe's Fiction* to argue that "Usher" modifies and extends the first-person narrative technique of "Ligeia."[1] Although the observing narrator of "Usher" seems to provide objective corroboration of the preternatural events that take place, Poe subtly reveals the increasing subjectivity of this "objective" narrator so as to allow the reader simultaneously to perceive both the terror that Roderick Usher and the narrator feel and the dramatic irony, which is, I believe, the most impressive feature of the tale.

In this approach, I am not especially original. It is the logical extension of the brilliant analysis of the tale as a symbolic conflict between a complex of opposed forces by Darrel Abel in "A Key to the House of Usher."[2] I should observe, however, that by emphasizing one aspect of Abel's complicated argument I somewhat misrepresent his main concern, which is to show how various tensions (life vs. death, reason vs. madness, or more intricately life-reason vs. death-madness) are symbolized in a totally integrated pattern by the landscape, the house, the narrator, and Roderick Usher. But it seems to me that one of the major implications of Abel's observations on the progression of the narrator's state of mind, to the point where he desperately tries to cling to "rational explanations," is that the very intensity of his efforts reveals his increasing subjective involvement in what he thinks he sees. This pattern, I maintain, is clearly delineated not only in the plot line of the tale but also in the structures of various sets of images, especially sounds, sight, the human face, and architecture.

Mr. Quinn is not the first traditionalist critic to object to my suggestion that the house of Usher presents to the narrator the image of a face as he rides up at the beginning of the tale. Quinn, it is clear, understands both my general thesis about Poe and my critical strategy for dealing with this specific work; yet he shares with others a puzzling reluctance to see the carefully emphasized centrality of the consistent image system of the human face and facelike structures in "Usher." While focusing on this particular problem, I shall take up each of the major points Quinn raises in the order in which he presents them. At the end, I shall offer an observation on the broader significance of my reading of "Usher."

The Appearance of the House

It is, I think, still a workable axiom of analytic criticism that a successful artistic work, whatever its complexity, is ideally to be regarded as a single fabric, tightly woven together, that loose ends are flaws, and that the various strands of the work cannot be separated without altering the texture and design of the whole. "The Haunted Palace" is an integral part of the tale; it has an imagistic, symbolic, thematic, and structural function, and these functions cannot be separated without damage to the story's overall meaning. The poem, placed exactly in the middle of the narrative, is the central focus of the central of three episodes; it acts as an emblem of the entire narrative, and, symmetrically, divides the tale in two.

Perhaps I erred in taking for granted the allegorical meaning of the poem. Yet "The Haunted Palace" is a transparent allegory with a single conceit, carefully and simply worked out in terms of two major images, the castellated palace and the human head, and a subsidiary metaphor of sound with two aspects: music and voice, harmony and discord. All these are elaborated in the prose text. In the first half of the poem, the architecture of a castellated palace, where the "monarch Thought" resides, takes on the aspects of a human face. The palace "reared its head" in the monarch Thought's dominion. It has "yellow" and "golden" banners on its roof, corresponding to light-color hair. In happier times, the monarch Thought was attended by "spirits moving musically" to a "well-tunéd law."

This orderliness and harmony is perceived by an observer through "two luminous windows," which correspond to eyes. If the allegory of building/face is consistent, we should, as we descend from the roof downward, come to some other salient feature of a human face, such as a mouth. And indeed the palace door is "all with pearl and ruby glowing," through which "Echoes" sing the "wit and wisdom" of the monarch Thought—the mouth and the human voice, in other words.

But in the second half, "evil things" assail the palace of Thought. The two windows become "red-litten" (bloodshot; cf. "encrimsoned" in par. 7 of the prose text); the formerly sweet melody of reason becomes "discordant," and the echoes of Thought become a "hideous throng," rushing out in a stream of incessant, insane laughter. The "smile" of sweet, harmonious reason is no more.

At least to me, this seems transparent allegory. But if we need external evidence, it can be found in a letter

from Poe to R. W. Griswold on 29 May 1841, in which
Poe wrote that by the palace he meant "to imply a mind
haunted by phantoms—a disordered brain."[3] T. O. Mabbott, in his edition of Poe's *Poems,* observes: "This simple
explanation can escape few readers, but J. L. O'Sullivan,
editor of the *United States Magazine and Democratic Review,* is said to have refused the poem because he did not
understand it."[4] Mabbott makes a further point. Since
Poe told Griswold specifically that he had published the
poem first and then "afterwards" had "embodied the
poem in a tale called 'The House of Usher,'" the poem
"had something to do with the genesis of the story" (p.
312).

In any event, we have a poem about a disordered
mind, haunted by the phantoms of madness, placed at the
center of a tale about a man, the poem's fictive author,
who fears he may be going mad. In his use of the two
major metaphors—an architectural structure and a
human face—the "author" of this poem employs a poetic
setting that generally is parallel to the dramatic setting in
which he is a fictional character, namely, a castellated
structure. There is thus a three-way connection. In the
poem, the allegorical castle/head is topped with "float-
[ing]" and "flow[ing]" light-colored banners/hair and has
two "luminous" windows/eyes. In the tale, Usher, the
writer of the poem, has a "luminous" eye and "silken,"
"gossamer" hair that "float[s]" about his head in a "web-
like" fashion. The house he lives in is topped with a
"web-work" of gray fungi and has "eye-like" windows. It
seems to me a short critical step to extend the palace/
head equation of the poem to the castellated house of
Usher and its mentally precarious owner. Even the sec-
ondary metaphor of music/sound has its echo, from
Roderick Usher's hypersensitivity to sound to his sickly,
smiling "gibbering" at the end. The dominant images of
the poem are also dominant in the tale. Images radiate
out, as it were, from this center.

Quinn's main objection to seeing the house of Usher
as facelike is that the number of windows is not specified.

There might, he suggests, be more than two. But the association of the windows of a house and the human eye has long been recognized by architects, and the word "window" itself derives from "wind-eye" (before the introduction of glass). In a charming publication, *Remodeling Old Houses without Destroying Their Character,* George Stephen remarks: "It is not surprising . . . that the windows establish the basic character of many buildings in much the same way as the eyes do in a human face"; moreover, "if the windows can be considered the eyes of a building, entrances—particularly the main one—can be likened to the mouth."[5] More to the point, then, is the general evocativeness of the opening description and the contrastive precision with which Poe gives us the narrator's subjective responses. Eyes normally occur in pairs in nature, and at the structural and symbolic center of the tale, the poem, the number of windows in the haunted palace *is* specified—two. But even if we grant that there might be more than two windows in the prose narrative, the text does not specify that all of them were eyelike, or even that all the windows were the same size and shape.

I have always imagined the house of Usher in what I think are very conventional terms, with two large fronting and trellised windows on either side of a causeway leading into the central opening of the mansion—as in the pictures of castellated houses, encircled by water, representing the mouth of hell in the paintings of Bruegel and others. These facelike architectural structures have a long tradition, allied with that of the *memento mori,* and I believe Poe was consciously working within it in his verbal painting of the house of Usher. How many other windows of smaller dimension there might be, placed elsewhere, does not matter. What matters is the dominant impression that such large fronting windows give—that very impression of a face that gives rise to Usher's poem. Usher is obsessed with the possibility that his house is somehow alive, and as the author of "The Haunted Palace" he structures his poem around a building that looks like a human face. When the narrator steps into the Gothic structure, he enters the mouth of an internal human hell, a nightmare world of Gothic terror, where, paradoxically, Usher has taken narcissistic refuge from what he fears is some malign, providential wrath — the family curse of madness and death.

More important than any precise architectural details, then, is the general, impressionistic correspondence between the house in the tale, Usher's face, the palace in the poem, the reflecting surface of the tarn, and the twin motif, twice emphasized in the tale, as these matters impinge upon the conscious and subconscious awareness of Usher and the narrator.

Quinn disagrees with my contention that the architecture/face motif dominates the tale, with Poe returning to it at symmetrically located places in the narrative. Precise statistical division in an ongoing narrative requires counting words, or at least pages, rather than paragraphs. Counting as Quinn does, however, I too get 41 paragraphs. By this count, with the poem as the concluding part of paragraph 18, we find that the "Haunted Palace" paragraph comprises more than two full pages in the standard Harrison edition;[6] thus it is nearly twice as long as the longest prose paragraph (the first) by virtue of typography. This fact, along with its medial position in the tale, suggests considerable emphasis. By pages, the first half of the tale consists of $11\frac{2}{3}$ pages (followed by the poem, which takes $1\frac{2}{3}$ pages), while the second half of the tale consists of $11\frac{1}{2}$ pages. Such a division is noticeably arithmetical and is characteristic of Poe; it is but the largest structure of doubling in a tale about self-divided characters that doubles itself as in a mirror. (Another compatible and equally arithmetical way of analyzing narrative segments is also possible, which I shall discuss momentarily.)

In the first half of the tale, the human face is implied, referred to, or described at four major points. Similarly, in the second half, though there is increasing emphasis on rising sounds, the human face is referred to or described at four major points:

1. In the opening scene (the narrator's confrontation with the facelike exterior of the house), the "eyelike" windows are mentioned twice in the first paragraph, setting up subsequent references to eyes in paragraphs 4 and 5.
2. In paragraph 6, as the narrator is conducted into the house, the peculiar "countenance" of the physician on the staircase arrests the narrator's attention.
3. In paragraph 8, when the narrator confronts Usher for the first time, Usher's face is described at length and in such a way as to recall the descriptions of the exterior of the house.
4. In paragraph 13, Madeline passes by, and the narrator's "glance sought instinctively and eagerly the countenance of the brother," who has "buried his face in his hands."

In the first printing of the tale, the emphasis on the face in paragraph 13 was greater; the narrator notices the striking resemblance between Roderick and Madeline: "Her figure, her air, her features—all, in their very minutest development were those—were identically (I can use no other sufficient term) were identically those of the Roderick Usher who sat beside me." This resemblance was made more specifically facial in the second half of the tale.

Concomitant with these references to the face are several other symmetrically developed motifs, such as the repetition of references to the increasingly oppressive atmosphere, as though the house were breathing, and the sense of a suffocating dream, along with the rising intensity of discordant noise and the recurrent imagery of ascent and descent. But the motifs that are most important for our purposes here have to do with Usher's hypersensitivity, especially his hearing and vision, with emphasis on eyes. The eyes of the house are mentioned twice in paragraph 1, along with the narrator's conscious act of "gaz[ing] down" into the tarn at the image of the house with the eyelike windows. The narrator's eyes are mentioned in paragraph 3 in the same connection. The "eye" of a scrutinizing observer" might see, we are told in paragraph 5, the "barely perceptible" fissure extending from the top to the bottom of the house and becoming lost in the mirroring waters of the tarn. In paragraph 7, "the eye" struggles to discern the interior features of the house. In paragraph 8, one of the salient features of Usher (like his house) is his "eye," twice mentioned here, and repeatedly described as having a "lustre" or as "luminous"—the very word applied to the windows of the haunted palace. In paragraph 10, Usher's "eyes were tortured by even a faint light." In paragraph 12, Usher refers to the gray walls and turrets of the house as "look-[ing] down" into the tarn, as though the house, like the narrator in paragraph 1, were gazing down at its own reflection. In paragraph 13, the narrator's "eyes followed [Madeline's] retreating steps." And so it goes.

In the second half of the tale, the facial motifs of the first half are duplicated. Again, there are four major references:

1. In paragraph 21, the narrator vividly recalls the "sinister countenance" of the physician, first mentioned in paragraph 6.

2. In paragraph 23, Usher and the narrator look down at Madeline's face as she lies in the coffin, and again the narrator remarks on the "striking similitude between the brother and sister."

3. In paragraphs 24 through 26, the narrator describes his increased agitation and sleeplessness and that of Usher; he remarks on the increased "pallor of [Usher's] countenance" and the dimming of the "luminousness of his eye" in paragraph 24, and in 26 he notes again that Usher's "countenance was, as usual, cadaverously wan" and that "there was a species of mad hilarity in his eyes."

4. In paragraphs 36 and 38, after the reading of the "Mad Trist," Usher sits with "his face to the door of the chamber," so that the narrator can "but partially perceive his features." Although Usher's "head had

dropped upon his breast," the narrator "knew that he was not asleep, from the wide and rigid opening of the eye." Momentarily, the narrator observes that Usher's "eyes were bent fixedly before him" and that throughout his "countenance" there "reigned" (cf. the ruler of "The Haunted Palace") a "stony" rigidity (cf. the house).

References to the human face and to eyes in the second part of the story duplicate those in the first part, with a poem, employing a building/face metaphor at the exact center, dividing the tale in half: in itself, and by the events just before and after the singing of the poem, the sequence comprises the central of three episodes. Moreover, paralleling them, the tale moves in the first part from a "soundless" day to Usher's hypersensitivity to sound and to his taste in music. Proceeding from silence, music and sound in the prose text become a complementary image pattern for the same set in "The Haunted Palace," where the harmony of reason gives way to a discordant melody and a "hideous throng" of laughing echoes, and where Usher's "wild" words and music fuse together.

In the second half of the prose narrative, the self-fulfilling prophecy of the poem is borne out, as the noise of the storm, the noises of the interpolated tale of the "Mad Trist," the noises in the house, and the noises of Usher's "gibbering murmur" and hysterical "shriek[ing]" culminate in the "tumultuous shouting sound" of the house, engulfed by the waters of the tarn, which close over it "silently." Surely such a pattern is "symmetrical."

The Experience of the Narrator

The more speculative part of my argument is the contention that the imagery of the human face and its duplication in the architecture and in the tarn symbolically suggest that the narrator becomes the psychological double of Usher. I contend that all the carefully worked out images provide a reenforcing symbolic texture to what is less speculative (for it is clearly detailed in the narrative), the steadily increasing anxiety and subjectivity of the narrator. Quinn makes three specific objections to the "face-facade theory" and one general objection concerning the progressive collapse of the narrator's mind. I shall take them up in Quinn's order—but cannot resist remarking that our English word "facade" comes from the French *façade* through the Italian *facciata* and *faccia*, presumably from the vulgar Latin *facia*, meaning face.

1.   Quinn says that "neither in the first scene nor elsewhere does [the narrator] allude, even distantly, to a resemblance between the house and a human face, much less to a skull." But if the narrator is incompletely aware of the influences acting upon him, how should we expect *him* to make the explicit connections that the dramatic irony of the tale requires its readers to make? Quinn, to be sure, concedes that "there would seem to be some basis for *imputing to the narrator* the *impression* of such a resemblance if the text did read . . . 'two vacant eyelike windows'" (my italics). What Quinn does not remark is that Usher makes this connection, later reads the result (his poem) to the narrator, and even suggests to the narrator that his house may be alive, intimating, however vaguely, that it may also be the instrument of some occult wrath. Nor does Quinn note that immediately after the reading of "The Haunted Palace" there is an extended scene in which the narrator's references to faces multiply rapidly (pars. 21, 23, 24, 26), accompanied, as mentioned, with references to eyes. Although these references are to be superseded momentarily by references to sound, such an increase of reference to the face and eyes at this point is the natural, immediate consequence of Usher's reading the architecture/face poem to the narrator, who already is dimly aware of such resemblances in Usher's domain.

2.   Quinn objects to seeing a symbolic merging of the narrator's reflected face in the tarn and the reflected features of the house, since the two "faces" would not merge perfectly but would be upside down to one an-

other. This objection calls for a too rigidly literal reading of a highly evocative, imagistic scene. The connection is suggested by a series of verbal associations in concert with the narrator's angle of vision. The house, as Quinn notes, is apparently of some height, so that its reflection could easily be contiguous with any reflection of the narrator's face in the pool. Quinn does not object to my point about the "precipitous brink" on which the narrator stands, so that his angle of vision is steeply vertical, thereby facilitating the confluence of the two facelike images in the black water, upside down or not. Quinn writes that for the symbolic merging of the narrator's (implied) face in the water and the "facelike" facade of the house to be effective, the narrator would have to cross the causeway, turn his back to the house, and *then* look down into the tarn, but that in fact he crosses the causeway only "after his visual experiment is made." This "visual experiment," however, comprises paragraphs 1 through 5 and the opening sentence of 6, with paragraphs 2 and 3 setting the background of Usher's summons and his family history, which are in the forefront of the narrator's mind as he looks down into the pool.

These background passages include the long segment about the correspondences between the house and the character of the family, marked by "undeviating transmission, from sire to son, of the patrimony with the name." The country folk had "so identified the two" as to "merge" in their minds the physical estate and the family in the single name "house of Usher." Thinking of this "merging" of the house with its tenants, the narrator contemplates the nature of fear, observing that consciousness of one's own fear, rather than alleviating it by rational confrontation, serves merely to increase it. With this paradoxical thought, he endeavors to explain away the impact that the reflected image of the house, with its eyelike windows, has had on him. These speculations merely serve, however, to lead him to lift his "eyes" from the tarn to the house itself (par. 4), which he examines from top to bottom, while his "eye" traces a faint zigzag fissure, until he is again looking at the house, reflected in the "sullen waters of the tarn" (par. 5). Our examination of the house, through the narrator's eyes, follows the same pattern of descent (from top to bottom) as Usher's description of "The Haunted Palace."

The paragraph ends here, and Quinn asserts that it is then (in par. 6) that the narrator rides over the causeway. But this is not textually precise, for the narrator says, "Noticing these things, I rode over a short causeway to the house." In other words, the passage in which the narrator shifts his attention between the physical house and its reflection in the tarn allows for the entire sequence of his riding up to the house, pausing to consider his perplexing nervousness at its aspect, and, finally, looking down into the tarn, up to the house, and down again into the tarn—while noticing a number of details that later are echoed in Usher's facial appearance—*as* he rides over the causeway. A camera eye would see the faces in the pool turn, so that they do indeed "merge." But the real point of all this is the subconscious impression that *any* such merging, upside down, sideways, or rightside up, would make on the admittedly nervous narrator.

3.   Quinn admits that "in a very general way" I am "correct" in my suggestion that when the narrator enters the house and meets his host, his attention is focused on the odd appearance of Usher's face, so that the encounter recalls to the reader the facelike structure of the house. A "basic *donnée* of the story," Quinn notes, "is that some kind of occult connection, necessarily imprecise, exists between the house and its owner." Nevertheless, Quinn goes on to argue that the "minute attention" to the details of Usher's face negates any precise association of Usher's house, Usher's face, and a death's head.

As a matter of textual fact, the narrator emphasizes that Usher looks like a walking corpse when they first meet. His extreme pallor, his "cadaverousness" of complexion, his large eyes, his extreme emaciation, and, later, his resemblance to the "corpse" of Lady Madeline, as she lies in her coffin, are insisted upon. The house resembles

Usher and may have some occult relation with his destiny as the instrument of a curse, some seemingly supernatural wrath which Usher both seeks and flees. In its exterior appearance, it foreshadows the events of the narrative as the line and the house of Usher die. The narrator's entrance into the house is tantamount to entering the mouth of hell and proceeding to the realm of the dead, an archetypal journey that is underscored by the death's head motif.

4. Quinn's most extended rebuttal is his denial that several stages of mental collapse in the narrator are carefully documented by Poe. Yet this is the most *literal* of all the structures I delineate in the tale.

The stages of the narrative form a symmetrical pattern. The tale divides into three major episodes, compatible with the imagistic development detailed earlier. The first episode (pars. 1–14) has two scenes; the medial episode (pars. 15–23) has three scenes; the third episode (pars. 24–41) has two scenes. The initial narrative episode details, first, the narrator's encounter with the facade of the house and its reflection in the black tarn, and, second, the narrator's encounter with the appearance and condition of Roderick Usher. The second narrative episode, signaled (par. 15) by the lapse of "several days," details, first, the narrator's more intimate experiences with Usher; second, the key experience of hearing Usher read his poem about the decay of reason; and third, the narrator's experience of hearing what he later (par. 24) calls Usher's "fantastic yet impressive superstitions" about his house, himself, and his family—the implications of which seem borne out by Madeline's wasting away and mysterious "death." The third narrative episode, also signaled by the lapse of "some days" (par. 24), details, first, the narrator's most intimate experience with Usher's fears and, second, the narrator's experience of trying to calm Usher by reading to him. This final scene, of course, encompasses an apparent occult correspondence between the "fictional" narrative that the narrator reads (the "Mad Trist") and the "actual" situation,

structurally paralleling the correspondence of the opening description and the poem, so that at the end he seems
to witness Madeline's return from the grave and the preternatural collapse of the house of Usher into the black
tarn. The impressive symmetry of this structure is
obscured, however, by a paragraph method of reckoning;
by bulk of words, the first episode consists of some eight
pages, the middle episode about seven pages, and the
final episode some eight pages—each approximately
one-third of the entire narrative.

In such a symmetrical structure, it should be easy to
ascertain if the narrator's state of mind is documented by
stages. In the opening scene of the first narrative episode,
when he first sees the house of Usher, the narrator remarks that a "sense of insufferable gloom" prevades his
spirit. He tries to analyze his feelings in order to discover
what has "so unnerved" him, but he fails. "It was a mystery all insoluble; nor could I grapple with the shadowy
fancies that crowded upon me as I pondered." Then he
gazes down into the tarn, only to see the (more unnerving) remodeled images of the house and the dead landscape. Thus the narrator is in an agitated state even
before the action proper begins.

Paragraph 2 presents the probable cause of his agitation. He has received a letter from Usher of a "wildly
importunate nature," in which Usher has spoken not only
of bodily illness but also of a "mental disorder which oppressed him." Thus early is the pervading sense of mental
"oppression" introduced—perhaps the most repeated
idea and, certainly, one of the most frequently repeated
words in the tale. In the next paragraph, the narrator recalls his early association with Usher and what had been
said about the possible influence of the house and the
family line each on the other. This is followed by one of
the most significant remarks of the entire tale (par. 4): the
narrator observes that his action of looking into the tarn
had deepened his first impression because "the consciousness of the rapid increase of my superstition . . .
served mainly to accelerate the increase itself." Such, he

says, "is the paradoxical law of all sentiments having terror as a basis"—a concise thematic statement for the entire story.

When the narrator lifts his eyes to the house, he is aware that, growing in his mind, is a "strange fancy." "I had *so worked upon my imagination,*" he says (my italics), "as really to believe" that a pestilent and mystic vapor hung about the house and the grounds. In the conventional Gothic tale, his apparent rationality would contrast with the supernatural events that are about to reform the hero's skepticism. But by the terms upon which Poe's story is predicated, if the narrator becomes aware that he has "worked upon [his] imagination," the enunciated paradoxical law of consciousness of terror will accelerate these workings of the imagination. Such is the process that enmires both the narrator and Usher, more and more intensely, from this point on.

The first scene of "Usher" concludes with the narrator's further attempt to shake from his spirit "what *must* have been a dream" and to scan more minutely the "real aspect" of the building. Of course, this attempt cannot work either, and the description in the rest of paragraph 5 proceeds downward, from the top of the house, until the observer's eye is again lost in "the sullen waters of the tarn." The rest of the episode (pars. 6–14) pictures the narrator entering the dark passages of the house, encountering Usher, and learning more about his malady and about his sister, Madeline, who is said to be wasting away. In paragraph 6, as the narrator enters the house, he comments that the structure and its contents served "I know not how, to *heighten* the vague sentiments" of superstition and terror he had felt outside (my italics). Once again, he confesses a vague awareness of what is happening to his feelings, but again concludes that his mere understanding cannot comprehend it.

For nearly three paragraphs, he describes the darkness, the ebony floor, the dark draperies, and the like, which have this effect of heightening his nervousness. Moreover, he twice comments on his *awareness* of his subjective apprehensiveness. In paragraph 6 he observes: "I still wondered to find how unfamiliar were the fancies which ordinary images were stirring up"—yet another instance of the rational part of his mind attempting to dispel fear, and failing. At the end of paragraph 7 he comments: "I felt that I breathed an atmosphere of sorrow." Thus the first seven-and-a-half paragraphs, comprising (by bulk) nearly one-fifth of the story, are not as Quinn implies, solely about Usher, but equally about the responses of the narrator.

The narrator now records his first encounter with Usher, who is physically described in the rest of paragraph 7 and whose mental state is described in paragraph 9 as "excessive nervous agitation," marked by "an habitual trepidancy." These are but exaggerations of the incipient nervous agitation and fearfulness we have already seen in the narrator. Moreover, although our primary attention in this second scene of the first episode is on Usher's strange condition, the narrator is revealed by his responses to the Ushers. In paragraph 10, Usher tells the narrator that the nature of his malady is a "mere nervous affection," resulting in "morbid acuteness of the senses." The narrator, however, sees Usher (par. 11) as a "bounden slave" to "an anomalous species of terror." Being terrorized by the thought of terror itself is, of course, another expression of the paradoxical law of terror that the narrator articulates in the opening scene. Thus Usher's parallel awareness of his terror will only accelerate it. As Usher says: "In this unnerved—in this pitiable condition—I feel that the period will sooner or later arrive when I must abandon life and reason together, in some struggle with the grim phantasm, FEAR!"

In paragraph 12, Usher communicates what the narrator calls his "superstitious impressions in regard to the dwelling which he tenanted." We learn more precisely what these superstitions are in the second half of the tale (see par. 19), namely, that the building has become sentient and is exercising a malignant influence upon Usher and his sister. These superstitions also have great influence on the narrator, as we shall see. In paragraph

13, when Madeline passes slowly through a remote portion of the apartment, the narrator remarks: "I regarded her with an utter astonishment *not unmingled with dread* . . ." (my italics). Once again, he tries rationally to explain his feelings and once again fails: ". . . and yet I found it impossible to account for such feelings." The narrator next observes that a "sensation of stupor oppressed me, as my eyes followed her steps." Usher, in the next paragraph, explains the partially cataleptical character of her gradual wasting away. If the narrator has regarded Madeline with "astonishment" and even "dread" before, this turn of events must considerably raise what Quinn calls the "emotional ante."

As mentioned, the second narrative episode is signaled by the lapse of several days. Paragraph 15 describes this passage of time, during which the narrator comes to a "closer and still closer intimacy" with the "recesses of [Usher's] spirit." As this intimacy grows, the narrator becomes convinced of the futility of trying to cheer Usher's dark mind, though he continues to try. In paragraphs 15, 16, and 17, the narrator responds to Usher's painting and music, at times listening to Usher's guitar "as if in a dream." His reactions tell us something about Usher's state of mind, to be sure, but they also tell us about the complex conscious and unconscious awareness of the narrator. In response to the "vaguenesses," the abstraction, of Usher's paintings, the narrator says: ". . . I shuddered the more thrillingly, because I shuddered not knowing why. . . ." Here we not only have the intense physical response of "shudder" but another failure of the rational mind to comprehend fully. "For me at least," the narrator continues, calling attention to himself, Usher's paintings carried a strange "intensity of intolerable awe." Contrary to Quinn's claims, then, Poe, step by step, has depicted the growing emotional intensity and agitation of his narrator, long before the "Mad Trist" scene.

We come now to the pivotal section of the story, paragraph 18, with the six stanzas of "The Haunted Palace." This is the middle scene of the middle narrative episode. The introduction of the poem by the narrator is especially significant; he says he recalls this particular poem, one of many such "rhapsodies," because "in the under or mystic current of its meaning, I fancied that I perceived, and for the first time, a full consciousness on the part of Usher, of the tottering of his lofty reason upon her throne." If so, then, by the paradoxical law of terror presented in the opening scene of the story, Usher's terror of impending madness will rapidly accelerate, as will the narrator's more generalized terror, if the latter becomes more conscious of his own fear of Usher's terror. Which is precisely what happens.

Immediately after this reading, Usher specifies (paragraph 19) his fears that the house and its surroundings have over the long years become sentient and exhale a "gradual yet certain condensation of an atmosphere of their own." At this, the narrator "start[s]," having already had (as noted) some "shadowy fancies" of his own (par. 1) and a "strange fancy" (par. 4) on the matter in the first episode of the tale. The narrator resists, but again his rational control is limited, and in the next two paragraphs, in the burial vault of Madeline Usher, neither the narrator nor Usher can look upon her face "unawed," for her disease has given her face and bosom "the mockery of a faint blush," as well as a "suspiciously lingering smile" which the narrator finds "terrible."

The third and final narrative sequence is signaled by the lapse of "some days of bitter grief." The narrator remarks "an observable change" in the "mental disorder" of Usher; he has become even more pale of face, the luster of his eye has dulled, and a "tremulous quaver, as if of *extreme terror,* habitually characterized his utterance" (par. 24; my italics). The emotional ante has been raised again, and the phrase "extreme terror" is momentarily to be applied to the narrator himself. At this point, however, the narrator remarks that "there were times . . . when I thought his unceasingly agitated mind was laboring with some oppressive secret," though at other times "I was obliged to resolve it all into the mere inexplicable vagaries of madness." Here is the familiar pattern once again: a mysterious circumstance (Usher's oppressive secret) is explained away (as madness).

But how consoling or successful an explanation is the possibility that one's only companion may be mad? "It was no wonder," the narrator says, "that his condition *terrified*—that it *infected* me. I felt creeping upon me, by slow yet certain degrees, the wild influences of his own fantastic yet impressive superstitions" (my italics). And what is the paradoxical law of consciousness of one's own superstitious terror? To increase it.

Quinn is right to point out that I erred in my original argument by misquoting Poe's phrase as "by slow yet uncertain degrees." Yet Poe's actual words, "certain degrees," in fact underscore the dramatic action of the narrator's slowly becoming not only terrified by Usher's condition but also infected by it. And it is appropriate to observe the epigraph from De Béranger (heading the story) provides a precise synecdoche, in musical images (cf. the "lute" in "The Haunted Palace"), for this relationship. Although the epigraph seems to (and in fact does) describe Usher's extreme sensitivity, it also describes the narrator, whose taut nerves respond to Usher's touch.

Quinn believes that only *now,* in paragraph 25, the narrator's terror begins to develop. But clearly, his increased terror is the product of previous fears, working by the circular mechanism of terror that Poe articulated as early as paragraph 4. The terror, in Usher and in the narrator, continues, with the narrator as before "struggl[ing] to reason off the nervousness" which has "dominion" over him. As in each prior instance, the effort to "reason off" the irrational has failed. Now (par. 25), the narrator begins to experience what he calls "the *full power* of such feelings" (my italics) as those induced by Usher's condition. "Full power" indicates that their feelings have been building and thus are not new emotions. Then, as in many another Poe story, hours of sleeplessness are added to the narrator's nervous agitation, along with the "bewildering influence" of his gloomy surroundings.

How objective can our nervous narrator be under such conditions? "An *irrespressible tremor* gradually pervaded my frame," he tells us (my italics); yet it must be, he reasons, merely "an incubus of utterly causeless alarm," which he shakes off—but only "with a gasp and a struggle"—so that, paradoxically, he finds himself listening intently for certain "low and indefinite sounds" that seem to come through the noise of a rising tempest. Psychologically, this sequence duplicates his experience with the exterior of the house in the opening scene, and once again the focus is directly on the condition of the narrator.

Quinn writes that this scene does not have the emotional intensity that I claim for it; and yet the narrator reveals that he feels "overpowered" by an "intense" sense of "horror." He begins to pace to and fro "rapidly," in an effort to fight off this feeling of horror, which is, as before, "unaccountable"—but now it is also "unendurable." The ultimate failure of efforts to control terror by confronting it finds natural expression in this frenetic pacing. In paragraph 26, the attention of our rapidly pacing narrator, who in spite of himself has been listening for sounds in the night, is "arrested" by a "light step."

I had read this as sudden cessation of movement and as fixed concentration on the sound outside the door, though I concede that my word "startled" may not have been exact. The narrator's response to Usher's appearance, however, is surely higher on the rapidly ascending scale of emotional intensity. He mentions Usher's "cadaverously wan" face, the "mad hilarity" of his eyes (paralleling the poem once again), and an "evidently restrained *hysteria*" (Poe's italics) in Usher's whole demeanor. Usher's very air, he says, "appalled me." How, then, does all this argue for a *lessening* of emotional intensity—especially when, as some relief from the self-engendered terrors of the solitude he has just endured, he *even* (Poe's word) welcomes the *appalling* presence of the nearly hysterical Usher? It seems to me to indicate the reverse—namely, the high intensity of his nervous state. Meanwhile, the agitation of the physical elements outside the trembling house has increased, in symbolic parallel to the psychological agitation of the two characters inside.

Quinn denies that Usher suggests to the narrator that a supernatural and luminous vapor has surrounded the house: "All he does, without comment, is open a casement window." Surely Quinn's remark is an inadvertent oversight, for Usher addresses the narrator rapidly (should I say "breathlessly"?) three or four times before opening the window. "'And have you not seen it?' he said abruptly, after having stared about him for some moments in silence—'You have not then seen it?—but, stay! you shall.' Thus speaking . . . [he] hurried to one of the casements, and threw it freely open to the storm" (par. 27). In paragraph 19, Usher had vaguely intimated that the vapor around the house and grounds was evidence of supernatural sentience. Since the narrator knows full well (in par. 27) the nature of Usher's fears about the vapor, he says to him (par. 29): "You must not—you shall not behold this!"

Quinn notes that "further to deflect [Usher's] attention he begins reading aloud from 'The Mad Trist.' As things turn out, the reading proves less than therapeutic." Quite so. Like every preceding rational effort, the attempt serves merely to heighten superstitious fancies— both of Usher and of the narrator, who pauses abruptly several times with a "feeling of wild amazement" at what his own "excited fancy" distinguishes among the "commingled noises of the still increasing storm." At one point (par. 36), he characterizes his state of mind as "a thousand conflicting sensations, in which wonder and *extreme terror* were predominant" (my italics). The emotional ante for the narrator is now that "extreme terror" earlier attributed to Usher.

Momentarily, Usher calls the narrator a "madman" and says that they have put Madeline in the tomb alive, that she has broken out, and *"now stands without the door"* (par. 39; Poe's italics). As before, with the "supernatural" vapor, Usher leads the narrator ("I *tell you* that she now stands without the door" [my italics]), so that, in what he now calls his "*completely* unnerved" (my italics) state, the narrator finally sees her too: ". . . without those doors there *did* stand the lofty and enshrouded figure of the lady Madeline of Usher" (par. 40; Poe's italics).

The theme of the terrible terror of terror itself— that paradoxical law of terror set forth in the opening scene of the tale—is what Poe returns to in the narrator's final view of Usher. In seeking refuge from rising subconscious awareness in a concept of an exterior occult wrath, Usher has actually turned further inward. He falls to the floor a corpse and "a victim of the *terrors* he had *anticipated*" (my italics). Then the frenzied narrator flees from that chamber and from that mansion, "aghast."

What Happened to the House?

I am concerned here only with the *possibility* that a rational explanation is built into the tale, a point I shall return to when we consider the theme of the story. Quinn argues that "a few scattered, unswept grains" of gunpowder seem hardly enough to blow up a "vast" castle. The text is not specific as to the quantity of gunpowder, nor the size of the house, though we know (par. 5) that the house is in a condition of "extensive decay," that the individual stones are in a "crumbling condition," reminiscent of "rotted" woodwork. We learn in paragraph 22 that "in later days" the crypt under the house had been used "as a place of deposit for powder, or some other *highly combustible* substance, as a portion of its floor, and the *whole interior of a long archway* through which we reached it, were *carefully sheathed with copper*" (par. 22; my italics). Moreover, the door is of "massive iron," which grates on its hinges.

Why such emphasis on the traditional damp vault of supernaturalist Gothic fiction as a storage place, not only for powder but for some "highly combustible" substance?

Why the emphasis on a floor, sheathed with a highly conductive metal, which also sheathes "the whole interior" of a "long archway," leading to a door of "massive iron"? Momentarily, an electrical storm is introduced (par. 28–29), and the "coppered archway of the vault" is mentioned a second time (par. 39).

Although Quinn (somewhat hedgingly) contends there is probably no lightning, there is in fact an electrical storm, within a whirlwind configuration. Paragraph 28 describes its "impetuous fury." The "exceeding density of the clouds (which hung so low as to press upon the turrets of the house) did not prevent our perceiving the lifelike velocity with which they flew careering from all points against each other, without passing away into the distance." Quinn quotes the next sentence as reading "Nor was there any flashing forth of the lightning," but he fails to quote enough for us to see the overall structure of the passage. He omits the full grammatical structure of that sentence and the parallel structure of the just-quoted sentence, which precedes it—structures which radically alter the sentences' combined meaning.

The narrator writes: "I say that even their exceeding density did not prevent our perceiving this [the whirling of the clouds]—yet we had no glimpse of the moon or stars—nor was there any flashing forth of the lightning." The sentence does not *deny* the presence of lightning, any more than it denies the existence of the moon or stars beyond the cloud mass. In fact, it *evokes* the idea of (the) lightning in the reader's mind. The ambiguity in evoking, yet concealing, the lightning is typical of Poe's irony. But the text is even more explicit as the scene develops. The narrator observes that objects on the ground, under these clouds, were "glowing" in the "unnatural light" of a faintly "luminous and distinctly visible" gaseous mass. These "appearances," he observes, are *"electrical phenomena not uncommon"* to the region (par. 29; my italics)— adding, as if to placate Usher's disbelief, the *possibility* of electrical phenomena arising simultaneously from the tarn.

So we have electrical phenomena of a "not uncommon" variety in a cloud cover that not only swirls around the house of Usher but also presses down upon its very eaves and apparently mingles with the miasma from the tarn. Quinn sees no way for the lightning to get from the roof to the crypt. But the house of Usher has a "zigzag" fissure extending from its top to beneath the ground, obviously symbolic of the cracked edifice of reason, but an actual fissure nevertheless. Reaching upwards from beneath the ground is the long, carefully copper-sheathed archway, the interior of which leads to the iron-doored vault. Could not the lightning-shaped fissure—itself possibly the product of other lightning strikes—provide access to that coppered archway leading to a vault recently used for storing gunpowder or some other "highly combustible substance"?

The Theme of the Story

If we require that all the details of a work be tied together in a meaningful pattern, we must object that Quinn's reading of "The Fall of the House of Usher" leaves too many loose ends. Why, for example, are there so many references to the narrator's terror and his consciousness of its steady increase? Why the thematic insistence on the paradoxical law of terror? Why the structure of resemblances between the haunted palace, the house of Usher, the face of Roderick Usher, the face of Madeline Usher—and why the singular emphasis in the opening scene on both the narrator and the house "looking" down into the mirroring waters of the tarn? Why the peculiar details about gunpowder, copper, iron, electricity? Further, how does a solely supernatural reading square with Poe's pride in never "overstepping the limits of the real"?

On this matter of insinuated rational explanation, there has been some confusion. I do not mean to argue that the house is *necessarily* split apart by lightning, just as I do not argue that one should read the story *only* as a tale of dual hallucination. My position is that the text *allows* for such explanation, and does so without dissolving the characters' sense of occult mystery and, therefore, to some degree, the reader's. Simultaneity of contrasting meanings is at the heart of Poe's romantic irony, and to accept any one reading to the exclusion of others is to lessen an integral part of the tale and to misapprehend the ironic tension of the total system of structures.

Although in *Poe's Fiction* I may have emphasized the rational and psychological patterns underlying the preternatural texture of the tales, my real concern was to show that Poe carefully allows for a rational explanation in conjunction with the weird, so that the supernatural and the natural are played off against each other. As in a Hawthorne story, we get multiple explanations, held in tension. Here I have argued that the core structure of the tale involves gradual, heightened awareness of irrational terror and that the central paradox of this heightened awareness of the irrational—the generation of further irrational terror—is further heightened by the "rational" elements of the tale. The possibility that the narrator has been subtly terrorized, to the point of hallucinating at the end of the tale, is just as strong and carefully structured an element in the tale as its apparent supernaturalism. But a sense of incomprehensible mystery, whether of outside occult forces or the inner workings of the mind, remains.

This debate strikes to the heart of our understanding of Poe. On one hand, we have the traditional version, which sees Poe as capable of a limited number of striking Gothic effects, including direct presentation of psychological states and early perfection of narrative emblems and symbols. On the other hand, we have a more complex version of Poe, involving intricate manipulation of narrative points of view and narrative frames to achieve ironic balance—a view that adds levels of meaning to Poe's works rather than restricting them to the simpler Gothic formulae. Poe, Hawthorne, and Melville are thus much closer in world view and literary technique than is generally acknowledged. Indeed, I would argue that the dominant mode of romantic fiction in America is the "ambiguous" Gothic tale. As such, it is an American version of European romantic irony, the complicated theory of which it was (in part) the purpose of *Poe's Fiction* to explain.

The theme of the horrible possibility (rather than certainty) of void both within the mind and without in the external world, pervades Poe's fiction—generating a despair simultaneously held in check, confronted, and even indulged by intricate structures of philosophical and dramatic irony. Although in the ambiguous Gothic tale the occult element is undercut by insinuated natural and psychological explanations, the events often cannot be taken as either actual or mental but must be seen as an ambivalent combination of both. This ambivalence of meaning in the tales is a structural parallel to Poe's themes of the growing awareness of the paradox of human existence, so that Poe's ironic vision has, as its philosophical basis, the "question" of epistemology: the ambiguity of human experience suggests a meaningless or absurd universe, but this apprehension is itself ambiguous. This paradox is parallel to, and part of, the paradoxical law of terror set forth in the opening scene of "Usher" and other stories.

What emerges from the complexity of "Usher" as its overriding subject is the paradoxical structure of the mind. As Darrel Abel has shown, the narrator constantly fights with his rationality the forces of irrationality. But it is a battle he cannot completely win, and the meaning of his descent into the maelstrom of the unconscious is uncertain. Indeed, the seeming double conquest of life and reason by death and madness may be the central myth of all Poe's fiction. In this regard, I originally argued that the pervasive image of the psychically split face of the house of Usher reflects the internal landscape of both Usher and the narrator, so that at the end, when the house sinks into the pool, the internal spiraling of the complete subjectivity of consciousness is symbolized. The sinking of the house into its own image in the pool symbolizes the final collapse into that void which is both the self and the universe simultaneously. I would extend this interpretation to suggest that when the narrator flees "aghast," he seems merely on a literal level to have escaped the wrath of the house of Usher by fleeing into the wrath of the storm; but the nightmare vision remains. Writing in retrospect (par. 16), he carries the apocalyptic vision within, for how does one flee an internal hell?

The real terror of the tale comes from the uncertain dynamics of the dual struggle within the mind of Usher and that of the narrator. The haunting mystery of Poe's vision is its ambiguity, wherein we are given the limited knowledge of the entrapped characters and the larger knowledge that proceeds from the artistic structuring of the events. Our response is to both. In terms of the aesthetics of reader response, such a conception of Gothic mystery in the ambiguous mode parallels the formulation by the structuralist critic Tzvetan Todorov of the key element in what he calls "fantastic" literature.[7] He formulates a principle of "reader hesitation" between the acceptance of events in a narrative as the "marvelous" (supernatural) or the "uncanny" (capable of eventual natural explanation). He locates the "fantastic" at the moment of hesitation, where the responsive reader is unable to decide one way or the other and is left momentarily in a terrible limbo. This is the point where ambiguous mystery engulfs the reader's response in perception of epistemological uncertainty dramatically embedded in the fictive world of the work.

Depending on the reader's willing suspension of disbelief (is not this part of the purpose of the "rational" elements of the story?), the inward-spiraling consciousness of the narrator of "Usher" is paralleled to some extent by the reader immersed in the text. At the same time, the reader is detached from the subjective vision of the narrator as he becomes aware of the carefully structured dramatic irony enfolding the narrator's heightened

consciousness of terror. The reader's heightened awareness is the romantic ironic vision. More than the
possibility of occult malevolence or the insanity of
Roderick Usher, it is this heightened double consciousness, combined with tantalizing, ambiguous suggestions
of those still deeper psychological impulses explored by
Freudian and Jungian critics, that is so profoundly disturbing, so paradoxically satisfying. At the dark heart of
the tale is this essential ambiguity. The central, enduring
paradox is: what really happens in "The Fall of the House
of Usher"?

NOTES

1. *Poe's Fiction: Romantic Irony in the Gothic Tales* (Madison:
University of Wisconsin Press, 1973), pp. 68–104.

2. *University of Toronto Quarterly,* 18 (1949), 176–185.

3. *Letters of Edgar Allan Poe,* ed. John Ward Ostrom, reprint
with supplement (New York: Gordian Press, 1966), I, 161.

4. *Collected Works of Edgar Allan Poe,* ed. Thomas Ollive Mabbott (Cambridge, Mass.: Belknap Press of Harvard University Press,
1969), I, 312.

5. George Stephen, *Remodeling Old Homes without Destroying
Their Character* (New York: Knopf, 1973), pp. 87, 97.

6. *The Complete Works of Edgar Allan Poe,* ed. James A. Harrison, reprint (New York: AMS Press, 1965).

7. *The Fantastic: A Structural Approach to a Literary Genre,*
trans. Richard Howard (Cleveland: The Press of Case Western Reserve University, 1973).

"Usher" Again:
TRUST THE TELLER!

Patrick F. Quinn

Both G. R. Thompson and I see "The Fall of the House of Usher" as central to and probably the best example of Poe's work in fiction, and yet we are at odds as to how the story should read. Since it is in the nature of imaginative/symbolist writing to lend itself to diverse interpretations, our disagreement is perhaps simply a matter of course (though the extent to which we differ seems unusual). Not only do we read Poe's story in quite different ways, we part company in the way we read a classic essay about that story, an essay for which Thompson and I have the highest regard.

At the start of his discussion of "Usher" in his book *Poe's Fiction,* and again at the outset of his new discussion, "The Paradox of Terror," Thompson refers to Darrel Abel's "A Key to the House of Usher" as a "brilliant analysis." He also, in both places, speaks as if he considers his own explication not simply consonant and continuous with Abel's but as indebted to it, and in this vein he writes: "In my approach I am not especially original." Although I go along with Thompson in his admiration of Abel's essay, I must disagree with him on this second point. The originality of Thompson's proposals can best be shown by juxtaposing them against those of Abel in an essay which, though published thirty years ago, seems to me persuasively corrective of what Thompson says about "Usher." And so, in this response to "The Paradox of Terror," I should like to start with the Abel essay and attempt to show the basic respects in which I find its views more convincing than Thompson's.

Abel vs. Thompson

The dramatic irony which Thompson perceives in "Usher" is there, according to him, because of Poe's use of the convention of the unreliable narrator. If the visitor to the house had written a reliably objective report on what he experienced, there would be no ironical dimension for readers to become aware of. Thompson therefore must, and does, in his examination of "Usher," see the observer, the teller of the tale, as the central figure in it and makes what he terms "the increasing subjectivity" of the man's experience its central interest. The opposite contention, by Abel, is that the story is "the tragedy of Roderick Usher," that though "five persons figure in the tale . . . the interest centres exclusively on one—Roderick Usher," and that "the central action and symbolism of the tale dramatize [a] contest between Life and Death for the possession of Roderick Usher." In brief, for Abel it is Usher's story; for Thompson, it is not. For Thompson, the story is primarily about the narrator, whose unwitting revelations of his emotional instability are mainly responsible for producing the ironical effect which Thompson considers the story's most impressive feature.

Abel's remarks about the narrator, his role in the story, and in effect his reliability as its teller add up to a judgment that is incompatible with Thompson's. The visitor-narrator, Abel writes, is "uncharacterized, undescribed, even unnamed," and hence is not a matter of interest but utility. That is, he is "a mere point of view for the reader to occupy." For convenience, Abel assigns him the name "Anthropos," a name implying, presumably, that he is an average and sane Everyman, our old friend *l'homme moyen sensuel.* His credentials, as Abel sees them, are in good order:

> He . . . lends the reader some acute, though not individualizing faculties: five keen senses which shrewdly perceive actual physical circumstances; a sixth sense of vague and undescribable realities behind the physical and apparent; and finally a sceptical and matter-of-fact propensity to mistrust apparitional appearances and to seek natural and rational explanations. In short, he is an habitual naturalist resisting urgent convictions of the supernatural.

This seems to me to give the observer-narrator an unqualifiedly clean bill of health—and on the basis of his behavior *throughout* the story. To quote Abel again: "Throughout the tale he scrupulously tries to find rational explanations for the horrors which agitate him." Thus, early in his stay at the house, he concludes that Usher must be laboring under "certain superstitious impressions"—which way of expressing himself shows what Abel calls his "sceptical judgment." Later, describing one of the unusual phenomena witnessed during the story's final episode, he speaks with almost phlegmatic precision about "the unnatural light of a faintly luminous and distinctly visible gaseous exhalation." Here, once again, Abel observes, is "our matter-of-fact Anthropos." These notations and others like them, one has to remind oneself, pertain to the same character for whom Thompson's typical adjectives are *suggestible, subjective, hysterical, frenzied, deranged.*

Abel describes the narrator's experience as one that occurred to a man "presumably sane," a "determined doubter," who despite his positivistic presuppositions fled from the house of Usher "with a sense of supernatural fatality accomplished." In section V of his essay, Abel reviews the impressions of Anthropos and the way he dealt with them on the ten or so occasions (or moments) when he felt that things were more or less Not Right. Each time, he reverts to his conviction that there must exist a naturalistic, cause-and-effect explanation for the bizarre phenomena he encounters. In his resumé of these occasions, Abel mentions no symptoms of "progressive" derangement; no accumulating desperation or mounting frenzy is remarked on; and the word "hallucination" is brought up only to be ruled out. The narrator remains to the end—and here Abel, as his last word on the subject, repeats his earlier description—"our matter-of-fact Anthropos."

A third matter that is seen differently by Thompson and Abel concerns the last lines of the story, its very last scene, the fall of the house—if it did fall. In *Poe's Fiction* it is suggested that "we do not know for sure that the house splits apart and sinks into the tarn in a lurid blaze [sic], for the narrator has by now been revealed to be completely untrustworthy." Even if we give the narrator the benefit of the doubt, and accept his word that the house collapsed, we should not, Thompson claims, accept the "hysterical" narrator's inference that this was "a necessarily supernatural occurence," since there is an alternative, naturalistic explanation available (that is, a lightning bolt blew up the house).

Abel, on the contrary, does not see the narrator as susceptible to hysteria, much less overcome by it. But for even so "determined" a doubter as he, the collapse of the house proves to be a bit too much: *that* event he is unable to account for naturalistically. And so *no comment at all is made on it.* Abel remarks that we, as readers, could, "if we wish . . . attribute the stupendously shattering collapse . . . to merely physical and natural causes—the violent thrust of the storm itself against its frail fabric and dilapidated structure." A realistic theory, which this is, can be devised; but should we wish to have one? Abel implies we should not. He concludes: "Significantly, our matter-of-fact Anthropos does not suggest any natural explanations; he merely flees 'aghast.'" With his matter-of-fact bent, he characteristically could not opt for a supernatural explanation. Because no alternative hypothesis occurs to him, he simply reports what he saw and infers nothing.

The Appearance of the House

In discussing this in "The Paradox of Terror," Thompson unquestionably demonstrates the pervasive presence in the story of a face-motif. But the question I brought up concerned his statement that when the visitor arrived and first viewed the house, he was "immediately confronted with a death's head looming up out of the dead landscape," and the subsequent claim that "Poe obviously intended the image of the skull-like face of the house to dominate as the central image of the tale" (*Poe's Fiction*, p. 89). I took these phrases to mean that not simply "face" but "skull-like face of the house" were pointed out as the central image, the one which recurs "again and again." Apparently I misread, for Thompson, in his reply confines himself pretty much to an inventory of references to "face," "countenance," and "features."

At one point, however, he invokes the man/house analogy—an analogy certainly basic in the story—to suggest that if Usher had a skull-like face, then his house also must have looked that way. The point is made this way: "As a matter of textual fact, the narrator emphasizes that Usher looks like a walking corpse when they first meet. His extreme pallor, the 'cadaverousness' of his complexion, his large eyes, his extreme emaciation . . . are all insisted upon." It is Thompson, rather, who insists, and only on selected details.[1] Here is a fuller version of the passage in question: "A cadaverousness of complexion; an eye large, liquid, and luminous beyond comparison; lips somewhat thin and very pallid, but of a surprisingly beautiful curve; a nose of a delicate Hebrew model but with a breadth of nostril unusual in similar formations; a finely moulded chin . . . hair of a more than web-like softness." If Thompson associates this portrait with the skull-like face of a death's head, he cannot have examined any real skulls lately.[2]

The Experience of the Narrator

Should Thompson be right in his main contention, that "the steadily increasing anxiety and subjectivity of the narrator [is] clearly revealed in the narrative," the most revelatory scene should be the one in which the man's cumulative duress would be reaching its peak. Granted that, let us examine what takes place in what both Thompson and I identify as the final episode of the story.

A few days after his sister's burial, Usher's mental disorder manifests itself in new symptoms, which the narrator describes and attempts to account for. Does his friend's condition result from a feeling of guilt about some "oppressive secret"? Or should it be diagnosed simply as "vagaries of madness" and, hence, inexplicable? He wavers between these two hypotheses. But whatever the cause of Usher's condition, one of its effects is to alarm his friend, who begins to recognize that Usher's fears are proving contagious. The contagion reaches crisis stage during the night of the seventh or eighth day after Madeline's burial. The feelings which Usher's presence and behavior have induced in him reach "full power." Now, the relevant question is: does he succumb? At this juncture, Thompson's reading of the episode and mine diverge. I would say, on the evidence, that he does not succumb; although severely battered emotionally, he manages not to cave in. His rational powers survive.

The crucial experience is detailed in paragraph 25, and three stages are involved. Alone in his room and sleepless, the narrator feels profoundly disturbed—but also, be it noted, he is profoundly reluctant to be victimized, as Usher has evidently let himself be, by fear and superstition. And so, he says, while agitated by the full power of those feelings, "I struggled to reason off the nervousness which had dominion over me. I endeavored to believe that much if not all of what I felt was due to the bewildering influence of the gloomy furniture of the room—of the dark and tattered draperies [etc.]. . . ." He is seeking, need I say, to find plausibly objective causes for the nervousness he feels. But his effort to account for the feeling, and so explain it away, fails: "My efforts were fruitless." End of first stage.

He now begins to feel physically as well as mentally distraught. An "irrepressible tremor" shakes his body, while an "incubus" (code word for nightmare) sits on his heart. That incubus, however, he knows to be one of "utterly causeless alarm" and therefore unreal, and so it *can* be shaken off. "Shaking this off with a gasp and a struggle, I uplifted myself upon the pillows. . . ." So ends the second stage. But his *mauvais quart d'heure* is not over yet.

The third trial is more severe, because seemingly more real than the other two. It involves sound. He "hearkened . . . to certain low and indefinite sounds which came, through pauses of the storm, at long intervals. . . ." Since this auditory experience cannot be shaken off, he feels momentarily trapped, or, as he puts it, "overpowered by an intense sentiment of horror, unaccountable and unendurable." Because it is unendurable, he refuses to endure it, and so he gets out of bed and gets dressed, explaining (in a gem of understatement) "I felt that I should sleep no more that night," and begins rapidly to pace the floor. Why? Thompson interprets this as "an effort to fight off [the] feeling of horror." But this emphatic diction does not reflect the laconic dryness of the text: "to arouse myself from the pitiable condition into which I had fallen."

To summarize: In the three stages of the crisis experience, the narrator's sanity and *savoir-faire* are three times tested and three times they survive. The ordeal, clearly, increases in intensity, but he keeps his wits. (He writes indeed as if he felt somewhat embarrassed in having to describe the "pitiable condition" he let himself get into.) Now having survived his solitary ordeal, he is able to handle the demands put upon him by the strange developments that follow.

One of these developments, not mentioned by Thompson, is particularly worth attention, and I shall attend to it in a moment, but first I must mention that, in his commentary on paragraph 25, Thompson rhetorically asks: "How objective can our nervous narrator be under such conditions?" The kind of answer that Thompson would give may be deduced from the way the "nervous narrator" very soon becomes, in Thompson's description, "frenzied" (or, as in *Poe's Fiction,* "completely deranged").

Let us now go back to the text of the story and see how Madeline's reappearance is described. Usher shrieks: "Madman! I tell you that she now stands without the door!" The narration now enters its second-last paragraph: "As if in the superhuman energy of his utterance, there had been found the potency of a spell, the huge antique panels . . . threw slowly back, upon the instant, their ponderous and ebony jaws. *It was the work of the rising gust. . . .*" (My italics). This hardly calls for comment; a question will suffice. Would Thompson insist that we read this commonsense explanation of an apparently occult event as evidence that the narrator's mind, in this final episode, should be characterized as hallucinated, frenzied, deranged?

Since our controversy is fundamentally about how much and when, if at all, the teller of the tale may be trusted, I should like to pursue the matter a bit further. My case so far has been that he should be trusted, should be the reader's surrogate, mainly because, under very trying conditions, his sanity proves to be inextinguishable. Thompson, of course, takes the opposite line. I will now try to put my case in another way: to suggest that this opposite line is one that Thompson does not consistently follow. To me, his case seems vitiated by the way, perhaps necessarily, it contradicts itself.

Here are two instances. (1) Among the questions I originally brought up was why the narrator—in Thompson's opinion subjective, nervous, and impressionable—did not, when he first saw the house, associate it with a death's head. Thompson's reply: The narrator should be seen as "a character incompletely aware of the influences acting upon him." But while describing the scene in which he first observes the house, the narrator provides a specimen of his ability in psychological self-analysis. The analysis is precisely about how the scene before him works to influence his feelings. This analysis is embraced by Thompson as if it were the definitive statement of "the paradoxical law of terror," and he brings the statement forward as the epigraph to, hence the keynote of, his new essay on "Usher." (2) A parallel inconsistency occurs when Thompson, apparently forgetting how increasingly subjective he considers the narrator's statements to be, quotes what the latter tells Usher about electrical phenomena of a "not uncommon variety." On this basis, Thompson believes that the reality of an "electrical storm" can be established and so give plausibility to his theory that a lightning bolt brought down the house of Usher.

One therefore concludes that the narrator's testimony is to be taken as factual when it suits a detail in Thompson's case. When it runs counter to that case or is irrelevant to it, the testimony is disparaged as less than objective. This comes dangerously close to "heads-I-win, tails-you-lose".

What Happened to the House?

In *Poe's Fiction* we are told that the collapse of the house was construed by the narrator as a "necessarily supernatural occurrence." Perhaps it was, but there is no basis in the text for saying so. I lean to Abel's opinion, that the narrator abstained from forming any explanation of the event.

As for the specific, nonsupernatural explanation proposed in *Poe's Fiction* —that a lightning-caused explosion blew up the house—this strains my credulity to the breaking point.[3] I infer from Thompson's more recent remarks that he is now less keen about this hypothesis, for he writes: "I do not mean to argue that the house is *necessarily* split apart by lightning. . . . My position is that the text allows for such explanation." Further on, he says that his "real concern [is] to show that Poe carefully allows for a rational explanation in conjunction with the weird, so that the supernatural and the natural are played off against each other."

As we have seen, Poe, through his narrator, certainly allows for a rational explanation of what caused the ponderous doors to open and reveal Madeline at the threshold. The wind did it. Why does Thompson not just downplay his improbable explosion theory but discard it altogether, in favor of this same rational explanation? If he were to do this, he would be lining himself up with the narrator, whereas the essence of Thompson's case is that the man, at this stage of the story, has lost almost all contact with reality.

The Theme of the Story

When he takes up this topic, Thompson implies that if his reading is not accepted, too many loose ends would be left. To make this point, he raises a number of questions. I shall deal briefly with three.

"Why," he asks, "are there so many references to the narrator's terror and his consciousness of its steady increase?" Surely, on the first point, because he *was* repeatedly terrified. But I cannot see it all as one integrated and cumulative terrifying experience. The disturbing stimuli came and went, evoking, on each occasion, the narrator's ability to respond successfully.

"Why the thematic insistence on the paradoxical law of terror itself?" I cannot see that this "law" is insisted on. The narrator formulates it only once, in the context of the story's opening scene, and never recalls it. And it applies, I would say, to his traversal of each separate experience of terror. To put it bluntly, the "law" is simply a sophisticated restatement of the "here we go again" phenomenon. In any event, it is the narrator who expresses the "law." By having him do so, Poe insinuates a positive opinion of his reliability, for his formulation implies that he has had alarming experiences before and has analyzed their nature. Therefore, as the story begins, the narrator is knowledgeable, psychologically astute, and self-critical, rather than naively impressionable.

So too with the details about gunpowder, copper, iron, and (later) electricity. The man has a penchant for facts and whatever plausible inferences can be drawn from facts. Even on so gruesome an errand as that in which he aided in Madeline's interment, he takes careful note of *what is there*. He notices, for example, that the floor of the burial vault was only partially covered with copper, while the entire archway, leading to the vault, was copperlined. In brief, there are no narrative loose ends here.[4]

The last pages of "The Paradox of Terror" are written as if my various demurs had been properly disposed of and the time had come to move to a higher, more speculative level, relatively free from any need for further textual back-up. For instance, "Although in the ambiguous Gothic tale the occult element is undercut by insinuated natural and psychological explanations, the events often cannot be taken as either actual or mental but must [*must?*] be seen as an ambivalent combination of both."

This is a very large proposition indeed. How does it apply to the story we are discussing? In that story, which are the "insinuated" explanations, as distinguished from any that are openly stated by the narrator? Which events in the story can or must be seen—and how is this done?—as neither actual nor mental but both? And which events are not to be so taken? No guidance is offered as to what the proposition specifically means. I find other passages, toward the end of the essay, similarly opaque.

Conclusion

In emphasizing my disagreement with Thompson's paper I do not want to give the impression that nothing but fault can be found with it. Its basic thesis is what I dispute. Marginal to that thesis, certainly, are some original and perceptive observations, the most striking of which, I would say, concerns the silence-music-noise pattern in "Usher."

In our exchange of views, the crucial question, first and last, is: what do we make of the narrator? Thompson and I look at the same evidence and interpret it differently. Although in his essay he tones down the harsh judgments in his book, Thompson is steadfast in his conviction that the visitor, while in the house, succumbed to "forces of irrationality" and that his narrative therefore reflects his "limited," his "purely subjective" vision.

Thompson's large generalizations about the art of the story—his account of "its multiple explanations, held in tension"; the way it presents an "intricate manipulation of narrative points of view and narrative frames"; and so on—all presume that the narrator's unreliability has been demonstrated. Because I do not believe it has, either in *Poe's Fiction* or in Thompson's restatement of his case, the various superstructures that make a "more complex" version of Poe that Thompson advocates, seem to me deficiently underpinned.

NOTES

1. I made the same objection to the skull-face-facade theory in my first critique, but apparently with insufficient emphasis (for Thompson does not take it up); hence this restatement.

2. Thompson seems unsound on the subject of skulls. His treatment of Ligeia is another instance. Among the details used to describe her are "a delicately outlined nose, a short upper lip and a voluptuously curved underlip, and, above all, profoundly expressive eyes" (*Works,* Harrison edition, II, 250–251). Nonetheless, Thompson sees her portrait as that of a "death's head," a "grinning skull" (*Poe's Fiction,* p. 87).

3. It is odd that Thompson is so willing to accept the narrator's veracity in his report on what must have been a very disturbing experience. He accepts as fact not only what the man says he saw but also the inference he draws from what he saw. Thompson then goes *beyond* that point to assert his belief in "remnants of powder" in the vault. I will not repeat the reasons I originally gave for my skep-

ticism about the lightning, but it is increased by Thompson's new suggestion: the lightning bolt struck at the same spot where the house had been hit by previous bolts, and it followed the zigzag fissure which (perhaps) they had caused.

4. One might guess that the reason *copper* is mentioned is that Poe quite idiosyncratically associated that metal, and especially its color, with what is (a) ominous and (b) down under. The doomed first ship in "MS. Found in a Bottle" was "copper-fastened." In "A Descent into the Maelström," the appearance of "a singular copper-colored cloud" presaged disaster. In the first of Pym's adventures, the ship that ran over the *Ariel*, and nearly killed Pym in doing so, was "coppered and copper-fastened."

Playful "Germanism" in "The Fall of the House of Usher":
THE STORYTELLER'S ART

Benjamin Franklin Fisher IV

During the past thirty years, few approaches to Poe's great tale have failed to pay respects to Darrel Abel's "A Key to the House of Usher," first published in 1949 and several times reprinted, wherein he analyzes the centrality of symbolism embodying the conflict between life-reason and death-madness.[1] In no way will I challenge this or other readings that argue for serious import inherent in "Usher," although I wish to examine a facet of Poe's technique not charted by Abel, nor by many others who use his justly famous essay as a foundation for their theories. My aim is to illuminate Poe's comic impulses, as I discern them, in this tale. Comedy and burlesque, to be sure, have been noticed, but not extensively treated, by James M. Cox, G. R. Thompson, and, implicitly, Daniel Hoffman.[2] External and internal evidence support a comic perspective within "Usher," as I will show. Although my "key" may unlock only the back door of the house of Usher, I trust that it will nevertheless afford entrance to yet another area of Poe's artistic imagination.

I

What is the "text" of "Usher"? Recent critical theory suggests that "textuality" is also a matter of "contextuality." External evidence places "Usher" inescapably within the realms of Gothic tradition. Indeed, Abel's critique begins with the "exquisitely artificial manipulation of Gothic claptrap and décor," but careful reading reveals admirable and clever method in Poe's handling of materials generally regarded as mere decoration. Recent critics have paid attention to the "otherness,"— if I may so term the artistry that surpasses the mere horrific, as the Gothicism in "Usher" does—while noting the abundant clichés from the tradition. Clark Griffith mentions Poe's drawing upon older Gothicists, like Radcliffe and Walpole, as well as upon the *Blackwood's* variety of his day, although he emphasizes the former. An equally certain influence was the vastly popular novelist of contemporaneous fame, G. P. R. James, whose numerous "solitary horsemen" stand as literary brethren to the narrator, who reins in before the house of Usher to survey the scene and begins to register fears for his readers, eager for the anticipated thrills in terror literature.[3] If we admit that Poe embraced the entirety of Gothicism, we might, in the light of recent studies, perceive "Usher" as parodic of not just the Gothic in general but, like some of his other tales, a hit at some of his own characteristic tendencies as a fictionist. If we also admit that "Usher" betrays its creator's ambivalent attitudes toward his art, as Roppolo suggests, we might see the tale as one of many examples of American romantic writing that simultaneously uses and attacks the Gothic legacy from European literature.

An important aspect of the European impact on American literature, by way of its British parent, is "Germanism," or Gothicism, that oft mentioned term of disapprobation in critical circles. In the autumn of 1839, the time in which "Usher" appeared in the September issue of *Burton's,* Poe had good reason to think of "Germanism," and think of it he did, as is attested in the repeatedly cited (and perhaps as often misunderstood) preface to his collected fiction, *Tales of the Grotesque and Arabesque.*[4] Poe's assertion that "terror is not of Germany, but of the soul" may imply (whatever else it indicates) that the "soul," given his current frame of mind, is that of a humorist, so far as one level of "Usher" (and perhaps other tales) is concerned—a connotation that does not exclude possibilities of equal sobriety in any given piece. Furthermore, if "Metzengerstein" or "Von Jung" comes more readily to mind as the "single exception" to Poe's disclaimers of "that species of pseudo-horror which we are taught to call Germanic," we must remember that he called no attention to them in the critical extracts he included in volume II. "Usher," however, was highlighted, more than any other tale, with five notices that called attention to it and, moreover, emphasized its stern, somber, and terrible elements. One commentator states that it "would have been considered a *chèf d'oeuvre* if it had appeared in the pages of *Blackwood.*" Reasonably, we may wonder whether Poe presented all these encomiums for clues to alert readers as to what lay under the *Blackwood* article surface of "Usher."

The charge of "Germanism" was hurled at Poe from the time he began to publish fiction in the *Southern Literary Messenger.* He quickly had to apologize to editor White for the horrors in "Berenice," his first tale for the journal, though he justified his creation by pointing out how common (and remunerative) such Gothicism was in the literary marketplace. With the appearance of "Morella" in the next number came adverse criticism of Poe's ventures into "the German school," which recurred over the next several years.[5]

Such hostility toward German Gothicism had a long history by the time Poe got around to countering it, and for examples (surprising ones, no less), let us look to the beginning of the nineteenth century. In the preface to *The Bravo of Venice,* Monk Lewis stated that the original German might be "too harsh for the taste of English readers"; consequently, he altered passages to soften them. But his bowdlerization failed to deter critical stricture: "The writers of the German school have introduced a new class [of novel], which may be called the electric. Each chapter contains a shock; the reader not only stares, but starts, at the close of every paragraph."[6] Apologetics like Lewis's continued; apparently, no respectable British writer wished to be bracketed with German excesses. Maturin, for instance, remarked in his first novel, *The Fatal Revenge; or, The Family of Montorio* (1807): "Whatever literary articles have been imported in the *plague ship* of German letters, I heartily wish were pronounced contraband by competent inspectors."[7] Turning the pages of this lurid novel, we must conclude that Maturin's practice and preaching diverged. He continues, though, in phraseology anticipating Poe's notions of "Germany": "I question whether there be a source of emotion in the whole mental frame, so powerful or universal as *the fear arising from objects of invisible terror.*" Thirty-three years later, Poe said much the same thing: "I maintain that terror is not of Germany, but of the soul,—that I have deduced this terror only from its legitimate sources, and urged it only to its legitimate results."[8] The rub may be in determining the precise nature of those sources and results.

Another circumstance that is relevant to Poe's sensitivity about "Germanism" is his practice of alternating serious with comic Gothic tales. We know that such tales as "Ligeia," "How to Write a Blackwood Article," and "A Predicament," published prior to "Usher," provide clues to his divided aims in writing terror fiction. So do later tales, such as "The Premature Burial," "Tarr and Fether," and "The Sphinx." Why not, then contemplate possibilities for perceiving a mixed mode in "Usher"?

I believe that in "Usher" we find an allegorical (dare I say it?) presentation of the baneful effects of taking the sensational aspects of "Germanism" too seriously. As in "Silence—A Fable," we are spectators as a man (the narrator) looks at another man (Roderick) whose story is his own. In "Usher," too, what happens to the second man symbolizes what happens within the first. In meeting again his childhood friend who is named, interestingly enough, for the last of the Goths (in Poe's sly manner of wordplay) and whose all too "Gothic" adventures amidst all too "Gothic" surroundings quite literally enchant him, our narrator resembles earlier Gothic personages who were duped because of their credulity, such as Catherine Moreland or Cherry Wilkinson. That Poe's two characters were previously acquainted might be apprehended as a revelation by the narrator (carefully manipulated by Poe) of his immature reading tastes. Although he has become a man, he has not put away childish things, and in remaining too near his Gothic background, as exemplified in "Usher," he has paved the way for yielding to the effects of irrationality. Like the heroes in "The Man Who Was Used Up" and "Tarr and Fether," this narrator is used up in the course of events—not so much as to preclude his telling his tale again but enough to indicate to readers the hazards in subscribing wholeheartedly to "Germanism." Sensing that it is going askew, he can do nothing to break the spell, so to speak, and, like Coleridge's wedding guest, he cannot choose but to participate in the drama (the tragedy) of collapse.

II

With these matters in mind, let us scrutinize the text of "Usher." Some of the exaggerations and repetitions, the veritable gallery of Gothic horrors, may make better sense if we consider their comic potential. I mentioned above the solitary horseman; other elements are equally recognizable as primary features of Gothicism: the supersensitized narrator-protagonist; the persecuted, frail maiden; the diabolic villain, modified in Roderick (à la Byron and Bulwer) into a latter-day hero-villain; the minor characters; the hyberbolic language; the eerie setting; the weird art and music; and the "supernatural." All are constituents of a fine "German" tale, and I suggest that Poe worked his materials for as much comic, ironic value as for any Gothic impact.

First, the teller of the tale could not be more appropriate. By means of this figure, Poe burlesques the quenchless sensibility of those virtuous, high-minded, sexless, arty types in Gothicism, whose curiosity always outruns their rationality in prompting them to actions and emotions altogether rash, daring, or ridiculous in the face of what readers readily size up as horrors for out-Heroding Herod (to use one of Poe's favorite phrases). The narrator approaches the house of Usher through a foreboding countryside (to understate its negative implications), surely passing beyond the natural scenery of a Radcliffe or Maturin and into the spooky *qua* spooky. Those "few rank sedges . . . and . . . few white trunks of decayed trees" partake of the "desolate and terrible," not because they convey "half-pleasurable" sensations of the well-known "Sublime" but because they do not. Their sole inspiration is "insufferable gloom" for our narrator, who, as the tale runs its course, proves unable to suffer (in the biblical sense) any terrors, present or future. Later, he is moved to tell his story, after the manner of Poe's other confessional narrators, because he is actuated by the worst features in his chronicle. And if the overt aim of Gothic fiction is to arouse a sense of gloom, this tale fulfills, and overshoots, that aim.[9]

We also sense that, gloomy or not, the narrator relishes the substance of his tale. Like other Gothic protagonists, he unceasingly conveys sensations of uneasiness, but his repetition of such stock "Germanisms" as "singular," "gloom," "melancholy," and "ghastly" causes us to wonder whether his reiteration is not more than "half-pleasurable." Also, it may be no accident that several times he tells us he "found" himself confronting menacing phenomena, as Gothic protagonists always do. He is ripe, we quickly discover, for his first "view of the melancholy House of Usher" (a haunted castle that out-Gothicizes many of its species), which to him appears to be human (or inhumanely human)—a fine touch in a tale wherein the characters look like their haunted house and vice versa. The narrator's function, first and foremost, is to tell a story, which he does with gusto, festooning his tale with rhetoric that passes beyond the edge of credibility, in comparison with most terror tales. For example, the visual persuaders commence "within view" of the Usher mansion and intensify with such phraseology as "first glimpse," "I looked upon the scene before me," "I reflected," "gazed down." These and other like passages urge that we realize Poe is manipulating the narrator, in such fashion that this character seems almost an avid reader of a terror tale, who, like the central figure within, is only too willing to register trauma. Maybe Poe intends another turn of the comic Gothic screw, in that he creates a figure who resembles an ordinary reader, eager for thrills, as well as (simultaneously) epitomizing all that is worst in Gothic protagonists.

Significantly, the narrator states that "in this mansion of gloom I now proposed to myself a sojourn of some weeks" and that the "proprietor, Roderick Usher, had been one of my boon companions in boyhood." Twice, he emphasizes the "personal" nature of their friendship, adding: "As boys, we had been even intimate associates." Can such rhetoric be Poe's subtle dropping of clues, implying immaturity among fans of "Germanism," who he knows cannot subdue their propensities for the horrific? That is, we behold in the narrator a being who is long familiar with thrillers and who nonetheless enters the house of Gothic fiction, as symbolized in the Usher mansion, only to become enmeshed in its toils. The bond between the narrator and comic Gothicism is strengthened when we remember that Roderick is modeled upon a doomed hero, well known to Poe and his audience through contemporary literary sources.

Elsewhere, the narrator unwittingly reveals his intent preoccupation with sensationalism. For example, in language that echoes a more overtly burlesque Poe character, the Signora Psyche Zenobia, he remarks, after yet another glance at the mansion: "There grew in my mind a strange fancy—a fancy so ridiculous, indeed, that I but mention it to show the vivid force of the sensations which oppressed me. I had so worked upon my imagination. . . ." Those devilish terms, "fancy," "sensations," "imagination," all obviously hallmarks of overstrained sensibility, add bold relief to the personality through whom "Usher" is sketched for us. He suggests, on one hand, his uneasiness with the environment that we (and doubtless he himself) understand as Gothic, or "German," and, on the other, he undercuts his reasons for such agitation in betraying the subjectivity with which he creates this atmosphere. Perhaps his penchant is enjoyment of grim Gothic mansions.

By now, we should be ready to conclude that we are dealing with a "sick" narrator, whose malady stems from overindulgence in the "pseudo-horrors of Germanism." In this light, the journey into the self, perceived by numerous readers of "Usher," may be viewed as a journey by someone akin to the stock types travestied by Jane Austen, E. S. Barrett, or T. L. Peacock. Poe's Mr. Lackobreath also comes to mind as one of their literary descendants. Such questers encounter comic Gothic situations (to us, if not them), and may embody salient traditional traits, combinations that heighten the fun for readers who can laugh at the ludicrous, ever lurking near the fringes of terror tales. The "Usher" narrator falls into these ranks. He is irresistibly drawn to the house of Usher, earmarked for extremes with Gothic appurtenances or by what he ingenuously accepts as such.

His relish for the Gothic or "Germanic" is more evident after he enters the house. His familiarity with the environs of foreboding and decay becomes apparent when he informs us: "The carvings of the ceilings, the sombre tapestries of the walls, the ebon blackness of the floors, and the phantasmagoric armorial trophies which rattled as I strode, were but matters to which, or to such as which, I had been accustomed from my infancy." In tandem with his boyhood ties to Roderick, this exposition hints of another facet of our narrator, steeped in matters "Germanic" and smacking of the apartments in "Metzengerstein." Furthermore, he is so "practiced" upon (in the Elizabethan sense) that, by the end of the tale, he can no longer function, except as a participant in the spirit of Gothicism, which Poe presents at its most exaggerated. Our narrator articulates a welter of hyperboles as he reads the "Mad Trist," certainly a farrago of Gothic nonsense and a parody of the same in "Usher." The "Mad Trist" resembles "The Haunted Palace," but contains none of the serious undercurrent in the poem. The narrator continues to purvey sensationalism in "seeing" Madeline's return from the tomb, in witnessing the "fall" of the mansion into the tarn, and in going through it all again in telling "the fall of the house of Usher."

These experiences result from his enchantment by the Gothic tradition, so to speak, and, implicitly, a similar fate awaits others (characters within tales as well as the unwitting, who are eager to read about them) who succumb to the witchery of overdone Gothicism. As the narrator flees the scene of Madeline's overpowering of Roderick, amid a barrage of Gothic props, he "finds" himself again, this time in crossing the causeway; in other words, he realizes that he was attempting to escape the mansion of gloom. But he has taken flight too late; the Gothic spell has undone him. His brain reels, and his last, emphatic impression is of "fragments of the *'House of Usher'*" — or what he designates as such (as Poe indicates in the punctuation). Like the too curious, sensation-oriented visitor to the madhouse in "Tarr and Fether," whose perceptions are battered by the close of the tale, the narrator of "Usher" is spiritually drubbed because of his febrile submission to "Germanism."

Two more anomalies attest the narrator's unreliability, implying that his sensations are prone to irrationality.

First, one may ask where he learns that "House of Usher" is "a quaint and equivocal appellation . . . in the minds of the peasantry who used it." Had he perchance lingered to gossip with such persons as he journeyed toward the mansion, or does this inconsistency align him with Melville's Ishmael (who cannot be present in certain situations he details as if he were on the scene) as a first-person narrator whose authority many readers would not dispute? This discrepancy in "Usher" is functional, if Poe intends the character's recountings of this circumstance to appear valid to readers who revel uncritically in the supernatural.

Second, what are we to make of the narrator's statement that "many years had elapsed" since his last meeting with Roderick and, shortly afterward, continuing: "Surely, man had never before so terribly altered in so brief a period as had Roderick Usher!" A lapse may not be apparent, were we to discern in Usher's malady a submerged commentary upon the decadence of Gothicism. If he represents the last stages of the tradition, then, so far as the span of the tradition goes, his rapid decline is plausible because of the mode's sudden decline from favor. Poe's censors believed that "Germanism" was passé and wished he would heed their criticism.

We may ask, then, what initially drew the narrator into this "Germanic" atmosphere. A letter, of course (which often substitutes for the "mouldering ms."), and a strange one. It is "wildly importunate," revealing "nervous agitation . . . acute bodily illness" and, as Poe originally phrased it, "pitiable mental idiosyncrasy."[10] A good Gothic come-on—and unable to resist, the narrator responds with a "personal reply" by journeying to visit Roderick. The consequence of this personal involvement is the narrator's growing awareness of his increasing superstition, which multiplies because of his "infection" from the "wild influences of [Roderick's] fantastic yet impressive superstitions." These terrors wax noticeably after his assistance with the premature burial of Madeline, as if participation in another bit of shopworn Gothic horror topples his rational faculties and prepares for his direct attendance in the uproar of her "return." Maybe the repeated use of "wild" and compounds incorporating it is another device by which Poe calculated to insinuate comedy relevant to the crazy developments in the chronicle of the Ushers and their guest.

Having drawn the narrator through a landscape "horrid" enough to titillate Catherine Moreland and into the frights within the Usher mansion, Poe involves him with characters who are hackneyed personages of Gothicism. At the same time, Poe contrives to lead his narrator farther and farther from the mundane world outside of romance. The narrator meets the other *dramatis personae* in a series of encounters that are staged with Poe's subtlest artistry.

At the entrance to the house, his horse is taken by "a servant in waiting," who does not enter the mansion. His presence may symbolize normal humanity. Then, as if Poe wished to sketch lightly with the brush of suspense, our narrator is led by a "valet of stealthy step" (why "stealthy," if not to indicate that this opinion is the narrator's subjectivity?) to the master of the strange house. Along the way, they meet the family physician, whose "countenance, *I thought* [italics mine], wore a mingled expression of low cunning and perplexity," who "accosted me with trepidation and passed on." This storyteller's imagination grows irrational and untrustworthy because of his eagerness "to think Gothically," as it were.

Next, the narrator is greeted by Roderick, whose physique and emotions epitomize the decadence of Gothic hero-villains as a type, engendering in his friend that "species of pseudo-horror, which we are taught to call Germanic." Indeed, the description of Roderick is a visual aid to such instruction. With Poe arranging these meetings in ascending order of importance for their terrifying effects upon the narrator and those who enjoy his tale, our quester attains a high "Germanic" peak when, finally, he watches Madeline glide through a distant section of her brother's apartment and sees her as Roderick's feminine counterpart. Of course, the narrator stands upon the "German" summit, in terms of his emotional responses to the terrors that surround him, when (later) he "sees" Madeline come back from the tomb.

III

We must now attend to Roderick Usher and his sister. Years ago, Mabbott emphasized the significance of his name, which derives from the last great ruler of the Visigoths. As the last master of his weird, tottering house, where the commonplace traits of hero and villain of Gothic romance are confusedly intermingled, Poe's Roderick may be intended to exemplify the last "Goth" of another decadent tribe, the timeworn literary populace of terror tales. Lest my reading be considered "ingenious," we must not overlook the implications in Usher's premature burial of his twin sister. Siblings and premature burials were linked phenomena, with parricides or near parricides (only slightly less sensational) occurring frequently among the cast of Gothic figures from the days of Walpole. Twins seemed especially fated to come to early and awful ends, and Madeline's "illness" triggers Roderick's downfall. Just so, the grim atmosphere in the opening scenes may symbolize more "sickness"—not only of the twins, whose contagion affects the narrator, but of the tale and, through it, Gothicism in general.[11]

To detect a travesty of Gothic hero-villains in Roderick is no absurdity. Like the narrator, whose makeup as a Gothic hero he shares, he is sensitive to art, music, poetry, romance (if we may so designate the "Mad Trist"), and architecture—in this case the overdone Gothic variety, his house. Because he epitomizes his type at the end of its tether, Roderick allows his "home" to dominate him (haunted castles often assume dimensions of characters), until he can no longer resist its evil charms. The approaching dissolution of the mansion is evident in the fissure in its facade and its crumbling stones. Like the one-hoss shay, this house, undeniably a Gothic castle, has endured, but its time draws nigh. Like the narrator, Roderick also is "practiced" upon and, more readily, acknowledges the baneful influence of his house and the sensations it engenders: "I *must* perish in this deplorable folly . . . I must inevitably abandon life and reason together, in my struggles with some fatal demon of fear."[12]

Like many another Gothic character, Roderick encounters a "fatal demon," and his characteristics from this point become more and more those of the villain, with his deliberate burial of Madeline deepening his fears, until he becomes a madman, though sufficiently forceful to persuade his companion, the narrator, that the vision of vengeful Madeline is genuine. Roderick portrays the necromancer or magician, common in terror tales. If we have difficulty accepting that Madeline can not only survive the airlessness of her tomb but manage her incredible escape, we might perceive her as a genuine supernatural being (as she is in the narrator's mind), drawn from her grave by the fears of her brother, which effect the "spell" that can summon spirits. These fears, in turn, are symbolized in the great storm. That they ought to be viewed by readers as rationally explainable is clear in the narrator's words to Roderick: "'These appearances, which bewilder you, are merely electrical phenomena not uncommon,'" and miasma from the tarn may account for the terrifying atmosphere. Once more the narrator unwittingly reveals the truth. A debilitated hero-villain, from a decayed tradition, however, will have none of such explanations. Roderick persists in "Germanically" interpreting the "Mad Trist" of multiple meanings and, consequently, falls prey to its suggestions of his own situation, with disastrous results.

It is proper now to turn our attention to the lady Madeline, because all interpreters of "Usher" see Roderick's fate inextricably linked to hers. Her name, so redolent of Maddalenas and Rosalinas in earlier Gothic works, bears special import here, because it derives from "Mary Magdalen" and means "a tower" and "a lady of house."[13] Madeline, as lady of the house of Usher, unfolds additional ironies. Initially, she brings qualities of passivity together, typifying Gothic heroines with features of the dying consumptive, another stock figure. Of course, her baffling malady recalls the catalepsy that afflicts Berenice and Ligeia, as well as their innumerable sisters in literature of the age. Perhaps this fated maiden is Poe's ironic bow to still another hackneyed aspect of "Germanism," particularly in the terms that describe her appearance in the tomb, with "the mockery of a faint blush upon the bosom and the face, and that suspiciously lingering smile upon the lip which is so terrible in death." To alert readers, the mockery and the smile might intimate a "hoaxical" aspect in this seemingly ordinary Gothic heroine.

Remembering that Mary Magdalen was among those at the Crucifixion, should we conclude that Poe, ever alert to scriptural themes, added another irony in naming Roderick's sister for one who was present at a colossal sacrifice? Madeline's reappearance as a terrible "ghost," which frightens Roderick to death and the narrator *nearly* to death, is couched in terms that suggest hallucination (in Roderick or the narrator, as the case might be). In the ornate, hysterical language, detailing a perfect medley of "sensations," we may discern Poe's wily hand pulling all stops for a crescendo conclusion. Literally and figuratively, this crescendo brings down the house.

Well it might, considering the probable exacerbation of Poe's imagination after several years' charges of "Germanism" had rung in his ears. His imagination could set forth literary Gothicism in well-appointed forms yet, simultaneously, jeer at its excesses. Such is the tenor of the preface to *Tales of the Grotesque and Arabesque.* Nor need we wonder, as we perceive his conscious manipulation of the "Usher" narrator's sensibilities, undone by overexposure to Gothic castles, abbeys, and mansions and peopled by such haunting types as Roderick, Madeline, the valet, and the doctor. Poe's artistry leads the narrator, himself a cliché figure of Gothicism, a kinsman of the Cherry Wilkinsons and Catherine Morelands, to pull the house down around his ears.[14] With it falls (figuratively) the accumulated nonsense of overdone Gothicism, a lineage, to be sure, as time-honored as the Usher family itself. Perhaps Poe insinuated another sly bit of wordplay in "Usher," with its connotation of "bringing in" a new era of fiction after the demise of a debilitated stock. As the protagonist-narrator of "Tarr and Fether" concludes his chronicle on an ironically rueful note, the narrator in "Usher" closes his: with the implied moral that outrageous "Germanism" is indeed treacherous.

IV

That the narrator senses the weaknesses inherent in typical Gothicism, in terror for terror's sake, is by no means assured at the end of his tale. Like many of his Gothic relatives, he seems compelled by the onslaught of terrors he endured to retell them to others. Unlike Catherine Moreland, he has no Jane Austen to chasten his discernible *Blackwood's raison d'être*. He remains a creature of feeling, or, in Poe's descriptive phrase, "all soul"—a proper consort for the ridiculous Signora Psyche Zenobia.[15] She, in turn, serves to lampoon Poe's more serious portraits of Psyche and, with the "Usher" narrator, repeatedly reminds us how thin is the line differentiating the serious from the ludicrous.

If our "Usher" narrator possessed a broader outlook, he would not view his situation so Gothically. Doubtless from his "childhood" (read "immaturity"), acquaintance with the fantastic—that is, steeping himself in Gothic romance—has unbalanced his vision. Thus he enters and is overwhelmed by the "world" controlled by Roderick's wizardry. Although this storyteller senses that something is amiss within the world of his tale (it's too Gothic), he cannot comprehend the nature of its defects. This subservience to the witchery of the *roman noir* is highlighted in the reading of the "Mad Trist," an evident (to perceptive readers of Poe's tale) distillation of all the hokey "medieval" ingredients of the Gothic. Mad it is, and mad

its readers grow, if they are not already halfway there—
so that they "see" the specter of the lady Madeline.

Again, we must examine some of Poe's phraseology.
Dubbing the "Mad Trist" a favorite romance of Roderick,
the narrator seems to derive greater pleasure in its
perusal than does his companion. What Usher detects,
and much more quickly than his impercipient friend, is
his own death knell, sounding in this overdone tale. How
ironic that a Gothic romance signals the end of Gothic
romance! And as with many others of its ilk, this Gothic
tale evinces "uncouth and unimaginative prolixity," which
had been under fire from the days of Mrs. Radcliffe.
Scott's review of Maturin's *The Fatal Revenge; or, The
Family of Montorio* censured its length, and Poe was later
to lament "the devil in 'Melmoth,' who plots and coun-
terplots through three octavo volumes for the entrap-
ment of one or two souls, while any common devil would
have demolished one or two thousand."[16]

In such light we return to our too-Gothic narrator,
exhorting his too-Gothic friend: "I will read, and you
shall listen;—and so *we will pass away* this terrible night
together" (italics mine). Recalling that the physician,
whose brief appearance is colored by the narrator's subjectivity, had also "passed on," we may read this passage
as covert, sly mockery of dying Gothicism. Such wordplay keeps good company if we also remember that, earlier, the valet "threw open a door and *ushered* me into the
presence of his master," or that, previously, the narrator
had "entered the *Gothic* archway of the hall." With final
italicizing for my emphasis, I note that Roderick's favorite reading was "an exceedingly rare and curious book in
quarto *Gothic*," perhaps not uncoincidentally the *Vigils
for the Dead* of an old German church. Other books that
are listed among Roderick's delights may also hint at
comic undertones, one a burlesque that features a comic
parrot.

It may not be amiss to comment that Roderick's
painting of nothingness is deemed worthy of emphasis by

the narrator and that the "last Waltz of Von Weber" is recalled as a sample of his performances. The painting ought to alert us to absurdity, because it depicts glaring light where no light can shine. The music was composed just prior to its supposed creator's death; as such it is a swan song for Usher and all that he represents of faded Gothicism. Poe had elsewhere engaged in such innuendoes, and I think we should not discount their importance in "Usher."[17] Indeed, all these things, every one redolent of "Germanism," will pass away.

From the foregoing, it should be evident that Poe's comic impulse was active in "Usher." Although in his famous preface to *Tales of the Grotesque and Arabesque* he apparently eschewed the "Germanic," we cannot pretend that he never served it up liberally in some of his tales (witness "Metzengerstein," "Berenice," and the Mesmeric tales). Given the brief time between conception and publication of "Usher," and then between the *Burton's* and *Tales of the Grotesque and Arabesque,* we cannot ignore implications in this tale of covert lampooning of the Gothic tradition, tied to Poe's commentary on "Germanism," like a pudding richly studded with Gothic clichés.[18] Not the first, or last, attempt by Poe to mock the very sort of fiction that earned him a (meager) living, "Usher" accomplishes far more subtle humor at the expense of Gothicism than, say, "Loss of Breath" or "The Premature Burial."

Disenchanted with the terror tale that was so much in demand but unwilling to lay down the reins with which he could so ably steer its course, Poe satisfied two audiences in "Usher." For one, he provided the horrors they expected and enjoyed. For the other, he created a work that embodies (among much else) a moral about succumbing to the extravagances of the Gothic. Thus, to paraphrase Abel, "Usher" is a matchless example of "Poe's . . . art which conceals art."[19] Although he composed other tales that mingle tragic with comic substance, nowhere else was he so artistic.

NOTES

1. *University of Toronto Quarterly,* 18 (1949), 176–185. It appears, with other influential studies, in Thomas Woodson, ed. *Twentieth-Century Interpretations of "The Fall of the House of Usher"* (Englewood Cliffs, N.J.: Prentice-Hall, 1969), pp. 43–55, and Eric W. Carlson, ed. *Edgar Allan Poe: "The Fall of the House of Usher"* (Columbus, O.: Charles E. Merrill, 1971), pp. 32–42. Clark Griffith also attests the importance of Abel's work in "Poe and the Gothic," *Papers on Poe: Essays in Honor of John Ward Ostrom,* ed. Richard P. Veler (Wittenburg, O.: Chantry Music Press, 1972), pp. 24–25. Another significant reading is Joseph Patrick Roppolo's "Undercurrents in Poe's 'The Fall of the House of Usher,'" *Tulane Studies in English,* 23 (1978), 1–16.

2. Respectively, their works are "Edgar Poe: Style as Pose," *Virginia Quarterly Review,* 44 (1969), 67–89; *Poe's Fiction: Romantic Irony in the Gothic Tales* (Madison: University of Wisconsin Press, 1973), pp. 87–97; and *Poe Poe Poe Poe Poe Poe Poe* (Garden City, N.Y.: Doubleday, 1972), ch. XI.

3. Not so typical as is commonly supposed, James's gambit with the lone horseman, which ceased after Thackeray's parody in "Barbazure" (1847), prompted S. M. Ellis to title his biography *The Solitary Horseman, or the Life and Adventures of G. P. R. James.* See also Thomas O. Mabbott, ed. *Collected Works of Edgar Allan Poe* (Cambridge, Mass.: Belknap Press of Harvard University Press, 1978), II, 417. The solitary horseman reappears in Poe's "Tarr and Fether," parodically, no doubt—as I note in "Poe's 'Tarr and Fether': Hoaxing in the Blackwood Mode," *Topic,* 17 (1977), 32–33. Roppolo (p. 15) also detects reminiscence of *Udolpho* in "Usher," although, unlike Griffith, he does not mention *Otranto* as another literary ancestor.

4. Dated 1840 but available by December 1839. Few students admit to comic effects in either the preface or "Usher." See, for example, Richard H. Hart, *The Supernatural in Edgar Allan Poe* (Baltimore: Enoch Pratt Free Library, 1936), p. 7; Arthur H. Quinn, *Edgar Allan Poe: A Critical Biography* (New York: Appleton-Century-Crofts, 1941), p. 289; Ian Walker, "The 'Legitimate Sources' of Terror in 'The Fall of the House of Usher,'" *Modern Language Review,* 6 (1966), 585–592; Joseph J. Moldenhauer, "Murder as a Fine Art: Basic Connections between Poe's Aesthetics, Psychology, and Moral Vision," *PMLA,* 83 (1968), 284–297; Paul A. Newlin, "Scott's Influence on Poe's Grotesque and Arabesque Tales," *American Transcendental Quarterly,* 2 (1969), 9–12; and Robert D. Jacobs, *Poe: Journalist and Critic* (Baton Rouge: Louisiana State University Press, 1969), pp. 164–166, 324, where he states categorically that humor is absent from "Usher." Cf. the spirited reading by Charles Thomas Samuels, "Usher's Fall: Poe's Rise," *Georgia Review* 18 (1964), 208–216.

5. To defend Poe, one might note that his remarks concerning his "Germanism" had been anticipated by an anonymous re-

viewer of Körner's *Rosamunda:* "There have been half-witted critics, not few in number, who have imputed to the *German School,* as they sagaciously term it, (as if there were but *one* school in Germany, where there are hardly two authors that resemble each other), the invariable attributes of mysticism,—improbability,—fatalism, —demonology,—and a special delight in dwelling on every instance of the most horrible crimes" *(Blackwood's,* 8 *[1820],* 47). That attitudes toward the subject were inconsistent, to say the least, is revealed in another discussion of Gothic fiction, in which the writer states that denigrators of the terror tale would inevitably brand such fiction "a vile German idea" ("The Devil's Elixir," *Blackwood's,* 16 [1824], 55).

6. London: J. F. Hughes, 1805, pp. v–vi. This book is a free adaptation of J. H. D. Zschokke's *Abaellino, der grosse Bandit.* See also *Critical Review,* 3d. ser., 5 (1805), 252.

7. I cite the reprint, introduction by Maurice Lévy (New York: ARNO Press, 1974), I, 111.

8. *Tales of the Grotesque and Arabesque* (Gloucester, Mass.: Peter Smith, 1965), p. 8.

9. Charles Thomas Samuels, (p. 210) actually berates Poe's words about the desolate or terrible as an inferior pastiche of Burke on the Sublime. Might this bad Sublimity be travesty? I quote from the Mabbott Edition, cited in n. 3 above (pp. 397–417), noting, where pertinent, Poe's alterations in texts.

10. *Collected Works,* II, 398. Poe revised this phrase to "mental disorder."

11. "Poe's Vaults," *Notes and Queries,* 198 (1953), 542–543; William Bysshe Stein, "The Twin Motif in 'The Fall of the House of Usher,'" *Modern Language Notes,* 75 (1960), 109–111.

12. Poe ultimately altered this reading to "some struggle with the grim phantasm, FEAR," thus eliminating suggestions of Madeline as demon and making her, upon her reappearance from the depths, far less tangible. The change puts "Usher" in its final form—more squarely within psychological, symbolic fiction—at a time when Poe was perhaps less intent than he was in 1839 on its substance as a spoof on Gothicism.

13. "Poe's Vaults," p. 543.

14. Coral Ann Howells comments on the obsessionalism of Cherry, the heroine in E. S. Barrett's travesty of Gothic tradition, *The Heroine* (1813)—known, and maybe reviewed, by Poe in the *Southern Literary Messenger* for 1835—as contrasted to the return from fanciful Gothicizing by Catherine Moreland, in *Northanger Abbey; see Love, Mystery and Misery: Feeling in Gothic Fiction* (London: Athlone Press, 1978; Atlantic Highlands, N.J.: Humanities Press, 1978), pp. 120–121.

15. Howells (p. 58) proclaims "feeling as the distinctive attribute of Gothic," precisely what Mr. Blackwood means when he informs Psyche Zenobia: "Sensations are the great things after all." His words are a paradigm for the situations in Poe's terror tales in which "things" and "sensations" often become indistinguishable. That the

setting for "Usher" is the house so much like a skull, with resemblances to the faces of Roderick and the narrator himself (whose reflection faces him as he gazes into the tarn), all registering gloom and terror, reinforces the simultaneous serious and comic pulses coursing through the tale.

16. The review first appeared in the *Quarterly Review,* 3 (1810), 339–347. It is conveniently reprinted in *Sir Walter Scott on Novelists and Fiction,* ed. Ioan Williams (London: Routledge & Kegan Paul, 1968; New York: Barnes and Noble, 1968), pp. 204–213. Because of several close resemblances, one might suspect that Poe had this review in mind, with its quotation from Maturin's preface (cited in n. 7 above), as well as other remarks by Scott concerning terror, when he wrote "Usher" and the preface to *Tales of the Grotesque and Arabesque.* Poe's strictures on *Melmoth the Wanderer* appear in his 1842 review of Henry Cockton's *Stanley Thorn,* accessible in *The Complete Works of Edgar Allan Poe,* ed. James A. Harrison (New York: Thomas Y. Crowell, 1902; reprint ed., New York: AMS Press, 1965), XI, 13. He had previously commented in like manner in "Letter to B—."

17. Thomas Thornburg, "Poe's 'Letter to B—': A Query," *Poe Studies,* 9 (1976), 54, questions whether Poe puns on the nature of German Gothicism in the "Letter," to which, I believe, we must say yes. See also *Collected Works,* II, 419–421.

18. Mabbott, "Poe's Vaults" (p. 543), argues that "An Opinion on Dreams," by "William Landor" (H. B. Wallace), in the August number of *Burton's,* directly inspired Poe's writing of "Usher."

19. "A Key," p. 185. The reviewer of Poe's *Tales,* who several years later commented "'The Black Cat' would have been a proper inmate for the 'Castle of Otranto,'" might better have used "Usher" for an example. (see *New-York Mirror,* Dec. 6, 1846, p. 131). He continues: "Mr. Poe's tales are out of place. They are things of the past, but the past has retired from them." How true in the case of "Usher." Compare, within this context, a review written some years later: "Washington Irving undoubtedly did some mischief to our literature when he introduced the style of grave yet facetious grotesque, mingling as it often did an under-current of reality with obvious burlesque." This remark, so applicable to "Usher," appears in an unsigned review of George Meredith's *Farina, A Legend of Cologne,* in the 22 August 1857 issue of *Spectator.*

I acknowledge my gratitude to Miss Kathleen Reilly, of Hahnemann Medical College and Hospital, for her assistance in the preparation of this essay.

Contributors

Nina Baym is professor of English and director of the School of Humanities at the University of Illinois, Urbana. She is author of numerous articles on nineteenth- and twentieth-century American writers and of *The Shape of Hawthorne's Career* and *Woman's Fiction: A Guide to Novels by and about Women in America, 1820–1870*. She has been a contributor to *American Literary Scholarship: An Annual* (1970–1974).

Chester E. Eisinger, professor of English at Purdue University and director of the Program in American Studies, has written articles on nineteenth- and twentieth-century American writers and on the history of ideas in seventeenth- and eighteenth- century America. He is author of *Fiction of the Forties* and editor of *The 1940's: Profile of a Nation in Crisis.*

Benjamin Franklin Fisher IV, associate professor of English at the University of Mississippi, has written many articles on nineteenth-century British and American writers. He is coeditor of *Sensation Fiction in a Minor Key: The Ordeal of Richard Feveral in Nineteenth-Century Literary Perspectives,* editor of *Poe at Work: Seven Textual Studies* and other symposia, and editor of *Mississippi Studies in English.*

Richard Harter Fogle, a fellow student of Darrel Abel at the University of Michigan, is University Distinguished Professor of English at the University of North Carolina at Chapel Hill. His principal writings include *The Imagery of Keats and Shelley, Hawthorne's Fiction: The Light and the Dark, Melville's Shorter Tales, The Idea of Coleridge's Criticism, Romantic Poets and Prose Writers, Hawthorne's Imagery,* and *The Permanent Pleasure: Essays in Classics of Romanticism.*

Seymour L. Gross, Burke O'Neill professor of American Literature at the University of Detroit, has edited or coedited three of Hawthorne's novels for the Norton Critical Edition series and is the author of over eighty articles on English and American literature.

Richard Boyd Hauck, professor of English at the University of West Florida, is author of *A Cheerful Nihilism: Confidence and the Absurd in American Humorous Fiction* and of articles on humorous fiction.

Brian Higgins, associate professor of English at the University of Illinois, Chicago Circle, is the compiler of *Herman Melville: An Annotated Bibliography* and author of articles on textual problems in American literature, frequently in collaboration with Hershel Parker.

Buford Jones, associate professor of English at Duke University, is author of articles on nineteenth-century American literature, compiler of the annotated bibliography of Hawthorne criticism, and editor of *Hawthorne's Maturity: A Symposium on the Romances.*

Virgil L. Lokke is professor of English at Purdue University. On Fulbright appointments, he has taught at major universities in Norway and Finland, where he received awards for excellence in teaching. He is coeditor of *Frontiers of American Culture* and author of articles on Utopian literature.

Roy R. Male, Boyd professor of English at the University of Oklahoma, is coeditor of *American Literary Masters,* editor of *Types of the Short Story,* and author of *Hawthorne's Tragic Vision* and *Enter, Mysterious Stranger: American Cloistral Fiction.* He has been a contributor to *American Literary Scholarship: An Annual* (1968–1969).

Robert Milder, associate professor of English at Washington University, is author of articles and review-essays on Melville and other American writers.

Hershel Parker, H. Fletcher Brown Professor of Romanticism at the University of Delaware, is author of numerous articles on nineteenth-century American writers and the editing of texts. He is editor of *The Recognition of Herman Melville* and the Norton Critical Edition of *The Confidence-Man.* He is coeditor of the Norton Critical Edition of *Moby-Dick* and *Moby-Dick as Doubloon,* and coeditor of the Northwestern-Newberry Edition of the *Works of Herman Melville.* He has been a contributor to *American Literary Scholarship: An Annual* since 1972.

Patrick F. Quinn, professor of English at Wellesley College, has written numerous articles on nineteenth-century American literature and is author of *The French Face of Edgar Poe.* He has been a contributor to *American Literary Scholarship: An Annual* (1968–1971).

Donald A. Ringe is professor of English at the University of Kentucky. He has written numerous articles on nineteenth-century American literature and is author of three books on American writers: *James Fenimore Cooper, Charles Brockden Brown,* and *The Pictorial Mode: Space and Time in the Art of Bryant, Irving, and Cooper.*

Barton Levi St. Armand, professor of English at Brown University, has written a wide variety of essays on nineteenth-century and early twentieth-century American literature and is author of *The Roots of Horror in the Fiction of H. P. Lovecraft.*

William H. Shurr, professor of English at Washington State University, has written articles on nineteenth- and twentieth-century British and American literature, is editor of *Prose and Poetry of England,* and is author of *The Mystery of Iniquity: Melville as Poet* and *Rappaccini's Children: Calvinism in American Literature.*

G. R. Thompson, professor of English at Purdue University, is author of *Poe's Fiction: Romantic Irony in the Gothic Tales.* He is editor of volumes of critical essays on the Gothic, of Gothic tales from the romantic period, of the writings of Poe, and of other works. He has been editor of two journals, *Poe Studies* and the *Emerson Society Quarterly,* and contributor to *American Literary Scholarship: An Annual* (1969–1974).

Selected Bibliography of the Writings of Darrel Abel

1942

"The Significance of the 'Letter to the Abbé Raynal' in the Progress of Thomas Paine's Thought." *Pennsylvania Magazine of History and Biography* (April), pp. 176–190.

1943

"Intellectual Criticism." *American Scholar,* 12 (Autumn), 414–428.

1944

"Our New Gongorists." *Crescendo,* 3 (Autumn), 4–7.
"On 'The New Criticism.'"*American Scholar,* 13 (Autumn), 500–502.
"A Biography of Gerard Manley Hopkins." *South Atlantic Quarterly,* 52 (October), 415–417. Review.

1949

"A Key to the House of Usher." *University of Toronto Quarterly,* 18 (January), 176–185.
"Strangers in Nature—Arnold and Emerson." *University of Kansas City Review,* 15 (Spring), 205–214.
"Edgar Poe: A Centennial Estimate." *University of Kansas City Review,* 16 (Winter), 77–96.
"Housman's 'The True Lover.'" *Explicator,* 8 (December), item no. 23.

1951

"The Theme of Isolation in Hawthorne, Part I." *Personalist,* 32 (January), 42–49.
"Hawthorne's Pearl: Symbol and Character." *ELH,* 18 (March), 50–66.
"The Theme of Isolation in Hawthorne, Part II." *Personalist,* 32 (April), 182–190.

1952

"Hawthorne's Hester." *College English,* 13 (March), 303–309.

1953

"R. L. S. and 'Prufrock.'" *Notes & Queries,* 198 (January), 37–38.
"Modes of Ethical Sensibility in Hawthorne." *Modern Language Notes,* 68 (February), 80–86.
"Hawthorne's Skepticism about Social Reform: With Especial Reference to *The Blithedale Romance.*" *University of Kansas City Review,* 19 (Spring), 181–193.
"Le Sage's Limping Devil and 'Mrs. Bullfrog.'" *Notes & Queries,* 198 (April), 165.
"The Devil in Boston." *Philological Quarterly,* 32 (October), 366–381.
"A Masque of Love and Death." *University of Toronto Quarterly,* 23 (October), 9–25.
"Hawthorne's House of Tradition." *South Atlantic Quarterly,* 52 (October), 561–578.

1955

"Coleridge's 'Life-in-Death' and Poe's 'Death-in-Life.'" *Notes & Queries,* 2 (May), 218–220.

1956

"Immortality versus Mortality in Septimus Felton: Some Possible Sources." *American Literature,* 27 (January), 566–570.
"Who Wrote Hawthorne's Autobiography?" *American Literature,* 28 (March), 73–77.
"Hawthorne's Dimmesdale: Fugitive from Wrath." *Nineteenth-Century Fiction,* 2 (September), 81–105.

1957

"Frozen Movement in *Light in August.*" *Boston University Studies in English,* 3 (Spring), 32–44.
"'Howells or James?'—An Essay by Henry Blake Fuller." *Modern Fiction Studies,* 3 (Summer), 159–164.

1959
"A Key to the House of Usher." Edited reprinting from *University of Toronto Quarterly,* 18 (1949), in *Interpretations of American Literature,* edited by Charles Feidelson, Jr., and Paul Brodtkorb. New York: Oxford University Press.

1960
"'Laurel Twined with Thorn': The Theme of Melville's *Timoleon."* *Personalist,* 41 (Summer), 330–340.

"Hester the Romantic." Edited reprinting from "Hawthorne's Hester," *College English,* 13 (1952), in *A Scarlet Letter Handbook,* edited by Seymour L. Gross. San Francisco: Wadsworth.

"Dimmesdale: Fugitive from Wrath." Edited reprinting from "Hawthorne's Dimmesdale: Fugitive From Wrath," *Nineteenth-Century Fiction* (1956), in *A Scarlet Letter Handbook.*

"Chillingworth as Miltonic Satan." Edited reprinting from "The Devil in Boston," *Philological Quarterly* (1953), in *A Scarlet Letter Handbook.*

"Pearl as Regenerative Symbol." Edited reprinting from "Hawthorne's Pearl: Symbol and Character," *ELH,* 18 (1951), in *A Scarlet Letter Handbook.*

1962
"'Howells or James?'—an Essay by Henry Blake Fuller." Reprinted in *Howells: A Century of Criticism,* edited by Kenneth E. Eble. Dallas: Southern Methodist University Press.

1963
American Literature. 3 vols. Great Neck, New York: Barron's.
Vol. I. *Colonial and Early National Writing.*
Vol. II. *Literature of the Atlantic Culture.*
Vol. III. *Masterworks of American Realism.*

1964
A Simplified Approach to Henry James. Great Neck, New York: Barron's.

A Simplified Approach to Herman Melville. Great Neck, New York: Barron's.

A Simplified Approach to Mark Twain. Great Neck, New York: Barron's.

A Simplified Approach to Walt Whitman. Great Neck, New York: Barron's.

1965
Barron's Simplified Approach to Moby-Dick. Woodbury, New York.

1966
"C. H. Foster, *Beyond Concord: Selected Writings of David Atwood Wasson.*" *New England Quarterly,* 39 (June), 266–268. Review.
"The American Renaissance and the Civil War: Concentric Circles." *Emerson Society Quarterly,* no. 44 (Third Quarter), pp. 89–91.

1969
Critical Theory in the American Renaissance. Hartford, Connecticut: Transcendental Books. Edited symposium; simultaneously published in *American Transcendental Quarterly.*
"Brooks, Van Wyck." *Encyclopedia Americana.*
"Bryant, William Cullen." *Encyclopedia Americana.*
"Burroughs, John." *Encyclopedia Americana.*
"'A More Imaginative Pleasure': Hawthorne on the Play of Imagination." *Emerson Society Quarterly,* no. 55 (Second Quarter), pp. 63–71.
"Black Glove and Pink Ribbon: Hawthorne's Metonymic Symbols." *New England Quarterly,* 42 (June), 163–180.
"'This Troublesome Mortality': Hawthorne's Marbles and Bubbles." *Studies in Romanticism,* 8 (Summer), 193–197.
"Giving Lustre to Gray Shadows: Hawthorne's Potent Art." *American Literature,* 41 (November), 373–388.
"Frozen Movement in *Light in August.*" Reprinted from *Boston University Studies in English,* 3 (1957), in *Twentieth-Century Interpretations of Light in August,* edited by David L. Minter. Englewood Cliffs, New Jersey: Prentice-Hall.
"A Key to The House of Usher." Reprinted in *Twentieth-Century Interpretations of the Fall of the House,* edited by Thomas Woodson. Englewood, Cliffs, New Jersey: Prentice-Hall.
"A Key to The House of Usher." Reprinted in *Configuration Critique de Edgar Allan Poe,* translated by Claude Richard. Paris: Minard.

1970
"Expatriation and Realism in American Fiction in the 1880's: Henry Blake Fuller." *American Literary Realism,* 3 (Summer), 245–257.
"'A Vast Deal of Human Sympathy': Idea and Device in Hawthorne's 'The Snow-Image.'" *Criticism,* 12 (Fall), 316–332.

1971
"Hawthorne's *Scarlet Letter.*" *Explicator,* 29 (April), item no. 62.
"Charles J. Woodbury, *Talks with Emerson.*" *New England Quarterly,* 44 (December), 679–681. Review.
"A Key to the House of Usher." Edited reprinting in *"The Fall of The House of Usher,"* edited by Eric Carlson. Columbus, Ohio: Charles E. Merrill.

1972

"Hawthorne on 'The Strong Division-Lines of Nature.'" *American Transcendental Quarterly,* no. 14 (Spring), pp. 23–31.

1974

"Hawthorne, Ghostland, and the Jurisdiction of Veracity." *American Transcendental Quarterly,* no. 24 (Fall), pp. 30–38.
"Who Keeps Here His Quiet State?" *Melville Society Extracts,* 20 (November), 6.

1975

"I Look, You Look, He Looks: Three Critics of Melville's Poetry." *Emerson Society Quarterly,* 21 (Second Quarter), 116–123.

1978

"Emerson's 'Apparition of God' and Frost's 'Apparition of the Mind.'" *University of Toronto Quarterly,* 48 (Fall), 41–52.
"Robert Frost's 'True Make-Believe.'" *Texas Studies in Literature and Language,* 20 (Winter), 552–578.

1979

"Two Philosophical Poets: Frost, Emerson, and Pragmatism." *Emerson Society Quarterly,* 25 (Second Quarter), 119–136.
"Robert Frost's 'Flirting with the Entelechies." *Renascence,* 32 (Autumn), 33–44.

1980

"Robert Frost's 'Second-Highest Heaven.'" *Colby Library Quarterly,* 16 (June), 78–90.
"The Instinct of a Bard: Robert Frost on Science, Logic, and Poetic Truth." *Essays in Arts and Sciences,* 9 (May), 59–75.